Numerical Analysis and Optimization

Numerical Analysis and Optimization

Guest Editors

Milena J. Petrović
Predrag S. Stanimirović
Gradimir V. Milovanović

MDPI • Basel • Beijing • Wuhan • Barcelona • Belgrade • Novi Sad • Cluj • Manchester

Guest Editors

Milena J. Petrović
Faculty of Sciences and Mathematics
University of Pristina in Kosovska Mitrovica
Kosovska Mitrovica
Serbia

Predrag S. Stanimirović
Faculty of Sciences and Mathematics
University of Niš, Višegradska
Niš
Serbia

Gradimir V. Milovanović
Mathematical Institute
Serbian Academy of Sciences and Arts
Belgrade
Serbia

Editorial Office

MDPI AG
Grosspeteranlage 5
4052 Basel, Switzerland

This is a reprint of the Special Issue, published open access by the journal *Axioms* (ISSN 2075-1680), freely accessible at: https://www.mdpi.com/journal/axioms/special_issues/0454E7HGRH.

For citation purposes, cite each article independently as indicated on the article page online and as indicated below:

Lastname, A.A.; Lastname, B.B. Article Title. *Journal Name* **Year**, *Volume Number*, Page Range.

ISBN 978-3-7258-4171-4 (Hbk)
ISBN 978-3-7258-4172-1 (PDF)
https://doi.org/10.3390/books978-3-7258-4172-1

Contents

About the Editors

Milena J. Petrović

Milena J. Petrović has been a full professor at the Faculty of Sciences and Mathematics, University of Pristina in Kosovska Mitrovica since 2024. She received a B.Sc. in Mathematics from the Faculty of Mathematics, Department of Numerical Mathematics and Optimization, University of Belgrade; an MSc. in Numerical Analysis from the Center for Mathematical Sciences, Lund University, Sweden; and a PhD in Mathematics from the Faculty of Science and Mathematics, University of Niš. Her research interests include numerical analysis, nonlinear optimization, operational research, and computational and applied mathematics. She has published over 60 publications, among which are twenty-five conference papers, four books, one technical solution, and one editorial. She has been the project leader of several internal junior projects and the director of the Center of Scientific studies and Projects at the Faculty of Sciences and Mathematics, University of Pristina in Kosovska Mitrovica since 2021. She is a reviewer for Mathematical Reviews (American mathematical society), *Optimization, Optimization Letters, Numerical Algorithms, Filomat, Mathematical Problems in Engineering, Mathematics, Symmetry, Axioms, Fractal Fractional,* and *Algorithms.*

Predrag S. Stanimirović

Predrag S. Stanimirović earned his Ph.D.in Computer Science at the University of Nis, Serbia. He is a full professor at the University of Nis, Faculty of Sciences and Mathematics, Departments of Computer Science, Nis, Serbia. He has acquired thirty-six years of experience in scientific research in diverse fields of mathematics and computer science, which span multiple branches of numerical linear algebra, recurrent neural networks, linear algebra, nonlinear optimization, symbolic computation, and others. His main research topics include numerical linear algebra, operations research, recurrent neural networks, and symbolic computation. He has published over 350 publications in scientific journals, including seven research monographs, six textbooks, and over eighty peer-reviewed research articles published in conference proceedings and book chapters. He is an Editorial Board Member of more than 20 scientific journals, five of which belong to the Journal Citation Report (JCR) list. Currently, he is the Section Editor of the scientific journals *Electronic Research Archive* (ERA), *Filomat, Journal of Mathematics, Contemporary Mathematics* (CM), *Facta Universitatis, Series: Mathematics and Informatics*, and several other journals. He was an author in the World Rank List of 2% best authors in 2021, 2022, and 2023.

Gradimir V. Milovanovic

Gradimir V. Milovanovic received his B.Sc. degree in electrical engineering and computer sciences and his M.Sc. and Ph.D. degrees in mathematics from the University of Nis in 1971, 1974, and 1976, respectively. He is currently a professor of Numerical Analysis and Approximation Theory and a full member of the Serbian Academy of Sciences and Arts (SASA). He was with the Faculty of Electronic Engineering and the Department of Mathematics, University of Nis, and promoted to professor in 1986. He was the Dean of the Faculty of Electronic Engineering from 2002 to 2004, a Rector of the University of Nis (2004–2006), and the Dean of the Faculty of Computer Sciences, Megatrend University, Belgrade (2008–2011). In 2011, he joined the Mathematical Institute of the SASA, Belgrade. He was the President of the National Council for Scientific and Technological Development, Serbia (2006–2010). He has co-authored three monographs, namely Topics in Polynomials: Extremal Problems, Inequalities, Zeros (World Scientific, 1994), Interpolation Processes Basic Theory and Applications

(Springer, 2008), and Extremal Problems and Inequalities of Markov-Bernstein Type for Algebraic Polynomials, Elsevier/Academic Press, London, 2022. His research interests are in applied and computational mathematics (theory of orthogonality, interpolation, quadrature processes) and its applications in several areas. He is currently serving as an Editor-In-Chief and an Associate Editor for several journals.

axioms

MDPI

Editorial

Numerical Analysis and Optimization

Milena J. Petrović [1,*], Predrag S. Stanimirović [2] and Gradimir V. Milovanović [3]

1 Faculty of Sciences and Mathematics, University of Priština in Kosovska Mitrovica, Lole Ribara 29, 38220 Kosovska Mitrovica, Serbia
2 Serbia Faculty of Sciences and Mathematics, University of Niš, Višegradska 33, 18108 Niš, Serbia; pecko@pmf.ni.ac.rs
3 Serbian Academy of Sciences and Arts, Kneza Mihaila 35, 11000 Belgrade, Serbia; gvm@mi.sanu.ac.rs
* Correspondence: milena.petrovic@pr.ac.rs; Tel.: +381-28-425-396

1. Introduction

This Editorial introduces this Special Issue of *Axioms*, which collates 10 articles showcasing the latest research related to problems in the two major scientific fields named in its title: "Numerical Analysis and Optimization". The presented scholarly papers address various topics, primarily relating to generating appropriate numerical methods designed to solve the problems posed by the authors, which concern, for example, inclusion problems, gradient neural network models, differential evolution methods, conjugate gradient methods including the projection technique, multi-product and multi-criteria supply–demand network equilibrium models, and ZNN dynamical systems. This Special Issue's principal aim is to disseminate the proposed algorithms and their applications in finding optimal solutions to the presented problems to researchers from related fields, thereby directly contributing to the further advancement of these two significant mathematical areas.

2. An Overview of the Published Papers

Regarding adequate conditions, in contribution 1, the strong convergence of a parameterized variable metric three-operator algorithm is established. In order to accelerate the operation of the algorithm, which is used for solving the monotone inclusion problem, the authors propose a multi-step inertial process. Through numerical investigations, the efficiency of the method is illustrated.

In contribution 2, the author introduces several definitions of generalized affine functions, including affinelikeness, preaffinelikeness, subaffinelikeness, and presubaffinelikeness. Through chosen examples, the author confirms that all the proposed definitions differ from each other. In this contribution, necessary and sufficient conditions for weakly solutions of vector optimization problems in real linear topological spaces are established, and practical generalizations of a number of previously published results are obtained. Additionally, the author details various optimality conditions and proves a strong duality theorem.

Using the gradient of the Frobenius norm of the traditional error function as a basis of a gradient neural network (GNN), the authors of contribution 3 propose the GGNN model for solving the general matrix equation $AXB = D$. From a theoretical perspective, the authors establish that for an arbitrary initial state matrix, $V(0)$, the neural state matrix $V(t)$ of the defined GGNN(A,B,D) model asymptotically converges to the solution of the matrix equation and coincides with the general solution of the linear matrix equation. Practically, several applications of the given method are demonstrated, and their global convergence is proved; further, its implementation in calculating various classes of generalized inverses is

 https://doi.org/10.3390/axioms14040305

presented. Extensive numerical examples confirm the effectiveness of the GGNN model compared to the GNN algorithm.

In contribution 4, the authors use a hyper-heuristic approach to design parameter adaptation methods for the scaling factor parameter in differential evolution (DE), which constitutes a black-box numerical optimization method. To define the adaptation of the scaling factor F, the authors use two Taylor expansions to obtain the mean of the random distribution for sampling F and its standard deviation. This process is compared with the L-NTADE algorithm, and the superiority of the designed model is confirmed using two sets of benchmark problems. Furthermore, the results of the numerical experiments demonstrate that the efficiency of the novel method increases at higher dimensions.

The primary achievement of contribution 5 is its combination of the subspace minimization conjugate gradient method with the projection technique for solving nonlinear monotone equations with convex constraints. The presented model is well defined and globally convergent under the posed assumptions. Numerical test results and obtained performance metrics confirm the effectiveness of the generated conjugate gradient scheme.

Using a logarithmic approach, in combination with several new approximate functions, in contribution 6, the author presents a penalty method for solving nonlinear optimization problems. Instead of utilizing line search techniques, the author focuses on a specific algorithm for calculating the displacement step according to the direction. The vector direction of the proposed model is determined on the basis of Newton's method, and numerical simulations illustrate various characteristics of the algorithm.

In contribution 7, the authors introduce a multi-product, multi-criteria supply–demand network equilibrium model with capacity constraints and uncertain demands, which are assumed to be in a closed interval. As the optimal performance of the network is obtained, in this contribution, the reader may find a significant theoretical framework for solving this type of optimization problem.

Solving a nonlinear optimization problem regarding the packing of different spheres, without mutual overlapping, into a container of a minimal height, bounded by a parabolic surface, is detailed in contribution 8. To solve this problem, the authors use a feasible direction approach combined with the hot-start technique, and containment constraints are described using Φ-function features. Included numerical experiments, provided for various relevant parameters, confirm the effectiveness of the proposed nonlinear programming model.

In contribution 9, the authors solve the equivalence and partial k-equivalence problems between WFAs. They provide an answer to whether two WFAs generate word functions that are the same or coincide for all input words whose lengths are less then a positive integer value, k. By utilizing two scientific approaches, ZNN neuro-dynamical systems and the existence of approximate heterotypic bisimulations between WFAs over $\mathbb{R}$, the authors present the ZNNL-hbfb and ZNNL-hfbb models. These two dynamical systems are implemented for solving matrix–vector equations involved in the considered heterotypic bisimulations, and extensive numerical simulations including various initial states are presented. The developed models are compared with the Matlab linear programming solver linprog and the pseudoinverse solution generated by the standard function pinv; the superiority of the presented ZNN models is confirmed.

Using the XOR and XNOR operations, the authors in contribution 10 explain the existence of solutions for a generalized Cayley variational inclusion problem. Through a fixed-point approach, they present effective methods for solving the posed problems. Numerical experiments demonstrate the features' fast convergence and efficient performance in obtaining optimal solutions.

Acknowledgments: Milena J. Petrović would like to dedicate this Editorial to students and teachers who stood against corruption and the collapse of the educational system in Serbia during the 2024–2025 academic year. This Guest Editor would also like to thank all the taxpayers in Serbia for supporting scientific and educational advancement. A fraction of tax revenue was distributed to us by the Ministry of Science and Technological Development and Innovation of the Republic of Serbia (project no. 451-03-137/2025-03/200123). Predrag S. Stanimirović acknowledges support from a project promoted by the Ministry of Science and Technological Development and Innovation of the Republic of Serbia (project no. 451-03-137/2025-03/200124).

Conflicts of Interest: The authors declare no conflicts of interest.

List of Contributions:

1. Guo, Y.; Yan, Y. Convergence of Parameterized Variable Metric Three-Operator Splitting with Deviations for Solving Monotone Inclusions. *Axioms* **2023**, *12*, 508. https://doi.org/10.3390/axioms12060508.
2. Zeng, R. Constraint Qualifications for Vector Optimization Problems in Real Topological Spaces. *Axioms* **2023**, *12*, 783. https://doi.org/10.3390/axioms12080783.
3. Stanimirović, P.S.; Tešić, N.; Gerontitis, D.; Milovanović, G.V.; Petrović, M.J.; Kazakovtsev, V.L.; Stasiuk, V. Application of Gradient Optimization Methods in Defining Neural Dynamics. *Axioms* **2024**, *13*, 49. https://doi.org/10.3390/axioms13010049.
4. Stanovov, V.; Kazakovtsev, L.; Semenkin, E. Hyper-Heuristic Approach for Tuning Parameter Adaptation in Differential Evolution. *Axioms* **2024**, *13*, 59. https://doi.org/10.3390/axioms13010059.
5. Song, T.; Liu, Z. An Efficient Subspace Minimization Conjugate Gradient Method for Solving Nonlinear Monotone Equations with Convex Constraints. *Axioms* **2024**, *13*, 170. https://doi.org/10.3390/axioms13030170.
6. Leulmi, A. An Efficient Penalty Method without a Line Search for Nonlinear Optimization. *Axioms* **2024**, *13*, 176. https://doi.org/10.3390/axioms13030176.
7. Li, R.; Yu, G. Strict Vector Equilibrium Problems of Multi-Product Supply–Demand Networks with Capacity Constraints and Uncertain Demands. *Axioms* **2024**, *13*, 263. https://doi.org/10.3390/axioms13040263.
8. Stoyan, Y.; Yaskov, G.; Romanova, T.; Litvinchev, I.; Velarde Cantú, J.M.; Acosta, M.L. Packing Spheres into a Minimum-Height Parabolic Container. *Axioms* **2024**, *13*, 396. https://doi.org/10.3390/axioms13060396.
9. Stanimirović, P.S.; Ćirić, M.; Mourtas, S.D.; Milovanović, G.V.; Petrović, M.J. Simultaneous Method for Solving Certain Systems of Matrix Equations with Two Unknowns. *Axioms* **2024**, *13*, 838. https://doi.org/10.3390/axioms13120838.
10. Arifuzzaman, Irfan, S.S.; Ahmad, I. Convergence Analysis for Cayley Variational Inclusion Problem Involving XOR and XNOR Operations. *Axioms* **2025**, *14*, 149. https://doi.org/10.3390/axioms14030149.

axioms MDPI

Article

Convergence of Parameterized Variable Metric Three-Operator Splitting with Deviations for Solving Monotone Inclusions

Yanni Guo * and Yinan Yan

College of Science, Civil Aviation University of China, Tianjin 300300, China; 2020061029@cauc.edu.cn
* Correspondence: ynguo@amss.ac.cn

Abstract: In this paper, we propose a parameterized variable metric three-operator algorithm for finding a zero of the sum of three monotone operators in a real Hilbert space. Under some appropriate conditions, we prove the strong convergence of the proposed algorithm. Furthermore, we propose a parameterized variable metric three-operator algorithm with a multi-step inertial term and prove its strong convergence. Finally, we illustrate the effectiveness of the proposed algorithm with numerical examples.

Keywords: variable metric; monotone inclusion; three-operator algorithm; multi-step inertial algorithm

MSC: 47H07; 49J45; 65J22; 90C25

1. Introduction

Let H be a real Hilbert space with inner product $\langle \cdot, \cdot \rangle$ and the induced norm $\| \cdot \|$. We consider the following monotone inclusion problem of the sum of three operators: find $x \in H$ such that

$$0 \in Ax + Bx + Cx, \tag{1}$$

where $A, B : H \to 2^H$ are maximally monotone operators and $C : H \to H$ is a β-cocoercive operator, $\beta > 0$. There have been numerous algorithms for solving the problem (1) when $B = 0$ because of the wide applications of this problem in compressed sensing, image recovery, sparse optimization, machine learning, etc.; see [1–7], to name a few. Although in theory these algorithms can be used to solve the problem (1) by bundling $A + B + C$ as $T + C$ with $T = A + B$, $(\mathrm{Id} + T)^{-1}$ is hard to compute in practice. For the past few years, problem (1) has received a lot of attention, and several algorithms have been constructed for solving it.

In 2017, Davis and Yin [8] proposed the following three-operator algorithm:

$$\begin{cases} z_k = J_{\gamma A}(x_k), \\ y_k = J_{\gamma B}(2z_k - x_k - \gamma C z_k), \\ x_{k+1} = x_k + \lambda_k (y_k - z_k). \end{cases} \tag{2}$$

Here $J_{\gamma A} = (\mathrm{Id} + \gamma A)^{-1}$, $J_{\gamma B} = (\mathrm{Id} + \gamma B)^{-1}$, $\gamma \in (0, 2\beta)$, $\lambda_k \in (0, \frac{4\beta - \gamma}{2\beta})$. Expression (2) also has the form

$$x_{k+1} = (1 - \lambda_k) x_k + \lambda_k T x_k, \tag{3}$$

where the averaged operator T is defined by

$$T = J_{\gamma B}(2J_{\gamma A} - \mathrm{Id} - \gamma C \circ J_{\gamma A}) + \mathrm{Id} - J_{\gamma A}. \tag{4}$$

Then [8] proved that the sequence $\{x_k\}$ generated by (2) converges weakly to a fixed point x^* of T under some suitable conditions by utilizing the averageness of T. In turn, $J_{\gamma A}(x^*)$ solves problem (1).

Soon after, Cui, Tang and Yang [9] put forward the inertial version of the algorithm (2):

$$\begin{cases} w_k = x_k + \theta_k(x_k - x_{k-1}), \\ z_k = J_{\gamma A}(w_k), \\ y_k = J_{\gamma B}(2z_k - w_k - \gamma C z_k), \\ x_{k+1} = w_k + \lambda_k(y_k - z_k), \end{cases} \tag{5}$$

to improve the convergence speed of the algorithm (2). For the problem (1) in which $C = 0$, B is monotone and L-Lipschitz continuous, Malitsky and Tam [10] proposed the forward-reflected-backward algorithm to solve problem (1), which consists of iterating

$$x_{k+1} = J_{\gamma A}(x_k - 2\gamma B x_k + \gamma B x_{k-1} - \gamma C x_k). \tag{6}$$

Under some appropriate conditions, they proved the convergence of (6). Furthermore, Zong et al. [11] introduced the inertial semi-forward-reflected-backward splitting algorithm to address (1):

$$x_{k+1} = J_{\gamma A}(x_k - \gamma_k B x_k + \gamma_{k-1}(B x_k - B x_{k-1}) - \alpha(x_k - x_{k-1}) - \gamma_k C x_k), \tag{7}$$

and proved the weak convergence of the algorithm. Zhang and Chen [12] proposed the parameterized three-operator splitting algorithm:

$$\begin{cases} z_k - J_{\gamma A}(x_k), \\ y_k = J_{\gamma B}([2 - \gamma(2 - \alpha)]z_k - x_k - \gamma C z_k), \\ x_{k+1} = x_k + \lambda_k(y_k - z_k), \end{cases} \tag{8}$$

which generalizes the parameterized Douglas–Rachford algorithm [13]. They proved that the sequence generated by the regularization of (8) converges to the least-norm solution of problem (1). Other algorithms for solving (1) have also been investigated in recent years; see [14–16].

In order to speed up the convergence of iterative algorithms, scholars often use acceleration techniques. The inertial extrapolation technique and variable metric technique are two popular acceleration methods. The inertial extrapolation technique, or heavy ball method [17], has been widely studied in past decades; please see [18–23] and the references therein. The variable metric technique is a method to improve the convergence speed of the corresponding algorithm by changing the step size in each iteration. This method has been widely used in various optimization problems in the past decades. To solve the monotone inclusion problem of the sum of two operators, Rockafeller [24] first combined the variable metric strategy with the forward-backward algorithm in 1997. For solving the monotone inclusion of the sum of two operators, Combettes [25] proposed the following variable metric forward-backward splitting algorithm

$$\begin{cases} y_k = x_k - \gamma_k U_k(B_k x_k + b_k), \\ x_{k+1} = x_k + \lambda_k(J_{\gamma_k U_k A}(y_k) + a_k - x_k), \end{cases} \tag{9}$$

where $\{a_k\}$ and $\{b_k\}$ are absolutely summable sequences in H, $\{U_k\}$ is a linear bounded self-adjoint positive operator sequence defined on H, and proved its strong convergence. Bonettini [26] proposed an inexact inertial variable metric proximity gradient algorithm. In [27], the author studied the variable metric forward-backward splitting algorithm for convex minimization problems without the Lipschitz continuity assumption of the gradient and proved the weak convergence of the iteration. Further, in [28], Audrey and Yves proposed a variable metric forward-backward-based algorithm for solving problems of the sum of two nonconvex functions. In [29], the authors addressed the weak convergence of a nonlinearly preconditioned forward-backward splitting method for the sum of a maximally hypermonotone operator A and a hypercocoercive operator B. For other applications of variable metric techniques, see [30–32] and the references therein.

Inspired by the above work, we propose a parameterized variable metric three-operator algorithm and a multi-step inertial parameterized variable metric three-operator algorithm. Furthermore, instead of requiring the averageness or nonexpansiveness of the operator, we directly analyze the convergence of the proposed iterative algorithm.

The rest of this paper is organized as follows. In Section 2, we recall some basic definitions and important lemmas. In Section 3, we propose the parameterized variable metric three-operator algorithm and prove its strong convergence. Then we introduce a multi-step inertial parameterized variable metric three-operator algorithm and prove a strong convergence result of it. In Section 4, we show the performance of the proposed iterative algorithm under different parameters and illustrate the feasibility of the algorithm with numerical examples.

2. Preliminaries

In this section, we list the necessary symbols, notations, definitions and lemmas and certify some results used in this paper. Let $B(H)$ be the space of bounded linear operators from H to H. Set $S(H) = \{L \in B(H) | L = L^*\}$, where L^* denotes the adjoint of L, and $P_\alpha(H) = \{L \in S(H) | \langle Lx, x\rangle \geq \alpha\langle x, x\rangle\}$, $\alpha > 0$. Given $M \in P_\alpha(H)$, define the M-inner product $\langle \cdot, \cdot \rangle_M$ on H by $\langle x, y\rangle_M = \langle Mx, y\rangle$ for all $x, y \in H$. So the corresponding M-norm on H is defined as $\|x\|_M = \sqrt{\langle Mx, x\rangle}$ for all $x \in H$. The strong convergence of a sequence $\{z_n\}$ is denoted by $\rightarrow$ and the symbol $\rightharpoonup$ means weak convergence. Id means the identity operator. $\ell^1_+(\mathbb{N})$ denotes the set of sequences $\{\eta_n\}$ in $[0, +\infty)$ such that $\sum_{n\in\mathbb{N}} \eta_n < +\infty$. Let $T : H \rightarrow H$ be an operator. We denote the fixed point set of T by $\mathrm{Fix}(T)$, that is, $\mathrm{Fix}(T) = \{x \in H | Tx = x\}$. Let $A : H \rightarrow 2^H$ be a set-valued operator. We denote its graph and domain by $\mathrm{gra}A = \{(x, u) \in H \times H | u \in Ax\}$ and $\mathrm{dom}A = \{x \in H | Ax \neq \varnothing\}$, respectively. In this paper, let S be the solution set of problem (1) and we always assume that $S \neq \varnothing$.

Definition 1. *Let $T : H \rightarrow H$ be an operator. T is said to be*

(i) ([33]) τ-cocoercive, $\tau > 0$ if

$$\langle Tx - Ty, x - y\rangle \geq \tau\|Tx - Ty\|^2, \quad \forall x, y \in H;$$

(ii) ([34]) demiregular at $x \in H$ if $\forall\{x_n\} \subset H$ with $x_n \rightharpoonup x$ and $Tx_n \rightarrow Tx$ as $n \rightarrow \infty$, it follows that $x_n \rightarrow x$ as $n \rightarrow \infty$.

Definition 2 ([33]). *Let $A : H \rightarrow 2^H$ be an operator. A is said to be*

(i) monotone if

$$\langle x - y, u - v\rangle \geq 0, \quad \forall(x, u) \in \mathrm{gra}A, \forall(y, v) \in \mathrm{gra}A.$$

(ii) strictly monotone if

$$x \neq y \Rightarrow \langle x - y, u - v\rangle > 0, \quad \forall(x, u) \in \mathrm{gra}A, \forall(y, v) \in \mathrm{gra}A.$$

(iii) β-strongly monotone if

$$\langle x - y, u - v\rangle \geq \beta\|x - y\|^2, \quad \forall(x, u) \in \mathrm{gra}A, \ \forall(y, v) \in \mathrm{gra}A.$$

(iv) maximally monotone if $\forall(x, u) \in H \times H$

$$(x, u) \in \mathrm{gra}A \Leftrightarrow \langle x - y, u - v\rangle \geq 0, \quad \forall(y, v) \in \mathrm{gra}A.$$

(v) uniformly monotone with modulus $\phi : \mathbb{R}_+ \rightarrow [0, +\infty]$ if ϕ is increasing and vanishes only at 0 and

$$\langle x - y, u - v\rangle \geq \phi(\|x - y\|), \quad \forall(x, u) \in \mathrm{gra}A, \ \forall(y, v) \in \mathrm{gra}A.$$

Definition 3 ([33]). *Let D be a nonempty subset of H. Let $\{x_n\}$ be a sequence in H. $\{x_n\}$ is called Fejér monotone with respect to D if*

$$\|x_{n+1} - \hat{x}\| \leq \|x_n - \hat{x}\|, \quad \forall \hat{x} \in D, \forall n \geq 0.$$

Lemma 1 ([33]). *Let $A : H \to 2^H$ be a maximally monotone operator and let $M : H \to H$ be a linear bounded self-adjoint and strongly monotone operator. Then*

(i) $M^{-1}A$ is maximally monotone operator.

(ii) $\forall \lambda > 0$, $J_{\lambda M^{-1}A} = (\mathrm{Id} + \lambda M^{-1}A)^{-1}$ is firmly nonexpansive with respect to M-norm, that is,

$$\langle J_{\lambda M^{-1}A}x - J_{\lambda M^{-1}A}y, x - y\rangle_M \geq \|J_{\lambda M^{-1}A}x - J_{\lambda M^{-1}A}y\|_M^2, \forall x, y \in H.$$

(iii) $J_{M^{-1}A} = (M + A)^{-1}M$.

Lemma 2 ([35]). *Let $x \in H$, $y \in H$, $z \in H$, we have*

$$2\langle x - y, x - z\rangle = \|x - y\|^2 + \|x - z\|^2 - \|y - z\|^2.$$

Lemma 3 ([33]). *Let Ω be a nonempty subset of H. Let $\{x_n\}$ be a sequence in H. If the following conditions hold:*

(i) $\forall x \in \Omega$, $\lim_{n\to\infty} \|x_n - x\|$ exists;

(ii) every weak sequential cluster point of $\{x_n\}$ is in Ω.

Then the sequence $\{x_n\}$ converges weakly to a point in Ω.

Lemma 4 ([36]). *Let $\{\alpha_n\}$ be a sequence in $[0, +\infty)$, $\{\eta_n\} \in \ell_+^1(\mathbb{N})$, $\{\delta_n\} \in \ell_+^1(\mathbb{N})$ such that*

$$\alpha_{n+1} \leq (1 + \eta_n)\alpha_n + \delta_n, \forall n \in \mathbb{N}.$$

Then $\{\alpha_n\}$ converges.

3. Iterative Algorithms and Convergence Analyses

In this section, we propose the parameterized variable metric three-operator algorithm and multi-step inertial parameterized variable metric three-operator algorithm to solve the approximate solution of the problem (1). The weak and strong convergence results are obtained. Both algorithms require the following assumptions:

Assumption 1. *$A, B : H \to 2^H$ are maximally monotone operators, $C : H \to H$ is a β-cocoercive operator, $\beta > 0$.*

Assumption 2. *$D \in B(H)$ and the solution set of $\mathrm{zer}(A + B + C + (2\mathrm{Id} - D))$ is nonempty.*

The following Proposition is mainly used to prove the convergence of the proposed algorithm.

Proposition 1. *Let $A, B : H \to 2^H$ be maximally monotone operators, $C : H \to H$ be a β-cocoercive operator and $\beta > 0$. Let $D \in B(H)$, $M \in P_\alpha(H)$ and $\gamma > 0$. Denote by*

$$J_{\gamma A}^M = (M + \gamma A)^{-1},$$
$$K_M = \{z \in H | J_{\gamma A}^M z = J_{\gamma B}^M (2MJ_{\gamma A}^M z - z - \gamma CJ_{\gamma A}^M z - \gamma(2\mathrm{Id} - D)J_{\gamma A}^M z)\}.$$

Then $\mathrm{zer}(A + B + C + (2\mathrm{Id} - D)) = J_{\gamma A}^M(K_M)$ and $K_M = \mathrm{Fix}(T)$, where $T = \mathrm{Id} - J_{\gamma A}^M + J_{\gamma B}^M(2MJ_{\gamma A}^M - \mathrm{Id} - \gamma CJ_{\gamma A}^M - \gamma(2\mathrm{Id} - D)J_{\gamma A}^M)$. Moreover,

$$\mathrm{Fix}(T) = \{Mx + \gamma a | x \in \mathrm{zer}(A + B + C + (2\mathrm{Id} - D)),\ a \in Ax \cap (-Bx - Cx - (2\mathrm{Id} - D)x)\}. \quad (10)$$

Proof of Proposition 1. Let $x \in \text{zer}(A+B+C+(2\text{Id}-D))$. We have

$$\begin{aligned}
&0 \in (A+B+C+(2\text{Id}-D))x \\
&\Leftrightarrow 0 \in \gamma(A+B+C+(2\text{Id}-D))x \\
&\Leftrightarrow \exists z \in H \text{ with } z - Mx \in \gamma Ax \text{ such that } Mx - z \in \gamma Bx + \gamma Cx + \gamma(2\text{Id}-D)x \\
&\Rightarrow x = J_{\gamma A}^{M} z \text{ and } 2Mx - z - \gamma Cx - \gamma(2\text{Id}-D)x \in Mx + \gamma Bx \\
&\Leftrightarrow x = J_{\gamma A}^{M} z \text{ and } x = J_{\gamma B}^{M}(2Mx - z - \gamma Cx - \gamma(2\text{Id}-D)x) \\
&\Leftrightarrow z \in K_M \text{ and } x \in J_{\gamma A}^{M}(K_M).
\end{aligned}$$

In turn, if $x \in J_{\gamma A}^{M}(K_M)$, there exists $z \in K_M$ such that $x = J_{\gamma A}^{M} z$. Each of the above steps can be worked backward. It follows that $\text{zer}(A+B+C+(2\text{Id}-D)) = J_{\gamma A}^{M}(K_M)$.

That $K_M = \text{Fix}(T)$ is a trivial result.

Next, we show that (10) holds.

$$\begin{aligned}
&z \in K_M \\
&\Leftrightarrow \exists x \in \text{zer}(A+B+C+(2\text{Id}-D)),\ x = J_{\gamma A}^{M} z,\ x = J_{\gamma B}^{M}(2Mx - z - \gamma Cx - \gamma(2\text{Id}-D)x) \\
&\Leftrightarrow z - Mx \in \gamma Ax,\ Mx - z \in \gamma Bx + \gamma Cx + \gamma(2\text{Id}-D)x \\
&\Leftrightarrow \exists a \in Ax \cap (-Bx - Cx - (2\text{Id}-D)x), z = Mx + \gamma a \\
&\Leftrightarrow z \in \text{Fix}(T).
\end{aligned}$$

The proof is completed. □

Proposition 2. *Let $A, B : H \to 2^H$ be maximally monotone operators, $C : H \to H$ be an operator. Let $\alpha > 0$, $\gamma > 0$, $M_1, M_2 \in P_\alpha(H)$. Given z, $\hat{z} \in H$, denote by*

$$\begin{aligned}
x &= J_{\gamma A}^{M_1} z, \quad y = J_{\gamma B}^{M_1}(2M_1 x - z - \gamma Cx - \gamma(2\text{Id}-D)x), \\
\hat{x} &= J_{\gamma A}^{M_2} \hat{z}, \quad \hat{y} = J_{\gamma B}^{M_2}(2M_2 \hat{x} - \hat{z} - \gamma C\hat{x} - \gamma(2\text{Id}-D)\hat{x}).
\end{aligned} \tag{11}$$

Then we have

$$\begin{aligned}
0 \leq &\langle z - \hat{z}, (x-y) - (\hat{x} - \hat{y})\rangle - \alpha\|(x-y) - (\hat{x}-\hat{y})\|^2 \\
&+ \gamma\langle y - \hat{y}, (2\text{Id}-D)\hat{x} - (2\text{Id}-D)x\rangle - \gamma\langle y - \hat{y}, Cx - C\hat{x}\rangle \\
&+ \langle y - \hat{y}, (M_2 - M_1)(\hat{y} - \hat{x})\rangle + \langle (M_2 - M_1)\hat{x}, (x-y) - (\hat{x} - \hat{y})\rangle.
\end{aligned} \tag{12}$$

Further, if A or B is uniformly monotone with modulus ϕ, then the above inequality holds with 0 on the left replaced by $\gamma\phi(\|x - \hat{x}\|)$ or $\gamma\phi(\|y - \hat{y}\|)$.

Proof of Proposition 2. According to (11), we have

$$\begin{aligned}
z - M_1 x \in \gamma Ax, &\quad 2M_1 x - z - \gamma Cx - \gamma(2\text{Id}-D)x - M_1 y \in \gamma By, \\
\hat{z} - M_2\hat{x} \in \gamma A\hat{x}, &\quad 2M_2\hat{x} - \hat{z} - \gamma C\hat{x} - \gamma(2\text{Id}-D)\hat{x} - M_2\hat{y} \in \gamma B\hat{y}.
\end{aligned}$$

By the monotonicity of A, B we obtain

$$0 \leq \langle x - \hat{x}, z - M_1 x - (\hat{z} - M_2\hat{x})\rangle,$$

$$\begin{aligned}
0 \leq &\langle y - \hat{y}, 2M_1 x - z - \gamma Cx - \gamma(2\text{Id}-D)x - M_1 y \\
&- (2M_2\hat{x} - \hat{z} - \gamma C\hat{x} - \gamma(2\text{Id}-D)\hat{x} - M_2\hat{y})\rangle \\
= &-\langle y - \hat{y}, z - M_1 x - (\hat{z} - M_2\hat{x})\rangle - \gamma\langle y - \hat{y}, Cx - C\hat{x}\rangle \\
&+ \langle y - \hat{y}, M_2\hat{y} - M_2\hat{x} + \gamma(2\text{Id}-D)\hat{x} - (M_1 y - M_1 x + \gamma(2\text{Id}-D)x)\rangle.
\end{aligned}$$

Adding the above two inequalities, we obtain

$$\begin{aligned}0 &\leq \langle z - M_1x - (\hat{z} - M_2\hat{x}), (x-y) - (\hat{x}-\hat{y})\rangle - \gamma\langle y-\hat{y}, Cx - C\hat{x}\rangle \\ &\quad + \langle y-\hat{y}, M_2\hat{y} - M_2\hat{x} + \gamma(2\mathrm{Id}-D)\hat{x} - (M_1y - M_1x + \gamma(2\mathrm{Id}-D)x)\rangle \\ &= \langle z-\hat{z}, (x-y)-(\hat{x}-\hat{y})\rangle - \langle M_1x - M_2\hat{x}, (x-y)-(\hat{x}-\hat{y})\rangle - \gamma\langle y-\hat{y}, Cx - C\hat{x}\rangle \\ &\quad + \langle y-\hat{y}, M_2\hat{y} - M_2\hat{x} - (M_1y - M_1x)\rangle + \gamma\langle y-\hat{y}, (2\mathrm{Id}-D)(\hat{x}-x)\rangle.\end{aligned}$$

Notice that

$$\begin{aligned}&-\langle M_1x - M_2\hat{x}, (x-y)-(\hat{x}-\hat{y})\rangle \\ &= -\langle M_1x - M_1\hat{x}, (x-y)-(\hat{x}-\hat{y})\rangle - \langle M_1\hat{x} - M_2\hat{x}, (x-y)-(\hat{x}-\hat{y})\rangle \\ &= -\langle x-\hat{x}, (x-y)-(\hat{x}-\hat{y})\rangle_{M_1} - \langle M_1\hat{x} - M_2\hat{x}, (x-y)-(\hat{x}-\hat{y})\rangle\end{aligned}$$

and that

$$\begin{aligned}&\langle y-\hat{y}, M_2\hat{y} - M_2\hat{x} - (M_1y - M_1x)\rangle \\ &= \langle y-\hat{y}, M_1\hat{y} - M_1\hat{x} - (M_1y - M_1x)\rangle + \langle y-\hat{y}, M_2\hat{y} - M_1\hat{y} - (M_2\hat{x} - M_1\hat{x})\rangle \\ &= \langle y-\hat{y}, (x-y)-(\hat{x}-\hat{y})\rangle_{M_1} + \langle y-\hat{y}, (M_2-M_1)(\hat{y}-\hat{x})\rangle.\end{aligned}$$

By $M_1 \in P_\alpha(H)$, we have,

$$\begin{aligned}0 &\leq \langle z-\hat{z}, (x-y)-(\hat{x}-\hat{y})\rangle - \|(x-y)-(\hat{x}-\hat{y})\|_{M_1}^2 \\ &\quad + \gamma\langle y-\hat{y}, (2\mathrm{Id}-D)\hat{x} - (2\mathrm{Id}-D)x\rangle - \gamma\langle y-\hat{y}, Cx - C\hat{x}\rangle \\ &\quad + \langle y-\hat{y}, (M_2-M_1)(\hat{y}-\hat{x})\rangle + \langle (M_2-M_1)\hat{x}, (x-y)-(\hat{x}-\hat{y})\rangle \\ &\leq \langle z-\hat{z}, (x-y)-(\hat{x}-\hat{y})\rangle - \alpha\|(x-y)-(\hat{x}-\hat{y})\|^2 \\ &\quad + \gamma\langle y-\hat{y}, (2\mathrm{Id}-D)\hat{x} - (2\mathrm{Id}-D)x\rangle - \gamma\langle y-\hat{y}, Cx - C\hat{x}\rangle \\ &\quad + \langle y-\hat{y}, (M_2-M_1)(\hat{y}-\hat{x})\rangle + \langle (M_2-M_1)\hat{x}, (x-y)-(\hat{x}-\hat{y})\rangle.\end{aligned}$$

Further, if A or B is uniformly monotone, we just need to replace 0 with $\gamma\phi(\|x-\hat{x}\|)$ or $\gamma\phi(\|y-\hat{y}\|)$ from (12). □

3.1. Parameterized Variable Metric Three-Operator Algorithm

In this subsection, we study the following parameterized variable metric three-operator algorithm and its convergence.

Pick any $z_0 \in H$,

$$\begin{cases} x_n = J_{\gamma A}^{M_n} z_n, \\ y_n = J_{\gamma B}^{M_n}(2M_nx_n - z_n - \gamma Cx_n - \gamma(2\mathrm{Id}-D)x_n), \\ z_{n+1} = z_n + \mu_n(y_n - x_n),\ n \geq 0, \end{cases} \tag{13}$$

where $J_{\gamma A}^{M_n} = (M_n + \gamma A)^{-1}$, $M_n \in P_\alpha(H)$, $\forall n \in \mathbb{N}$, $\alpha > 0$. $\gamma > 0$.

Theorem 1. *Let $\{z_n\}$ be generated by Algorithm* (13)*. Suppose that the following conditions hold:*

(C1) $\|D\| \in [0,2)$, $\gamma \in (0, \frac{4\alpha\beta(2-\|D\|)}{2-\|D\|+\beta\|2\mathrm{Id}-D\|^2})$;

(C2) $\sum_{n=0}^{\infty} \mu_n = +\infty$, $0 < \mu_n \leq \limsup_{n\to\infty} \mu_n = \overline{\mu} \leq 2\alpha - \gamma(\frac{1}{2\beta} + \frac{\|2\mathrm{Id}-D\|^2}{2(2-\|D\|)})$;

(C3) $M \in P_\alpha(H)$, $\sum_{n=0}^{\infty} \frac{1}{\mu_n}\|M - M_n\| < +\infty$.

Then we have

1. *$\{z_n\}$ is bounded;*
2. *$y_n - x_n \to 0$, $z_n \rightharpoonup z^* \in K_M$, $x_n \rightharpoonup x^*$, $y_n \rightharpoonup x^*$, $Cx_n \to Cx^*$, where $x^* = J_{\gamma A}^{M} z^* \in$ $\mathrm{zer}(A+B+C+(2\mathrm{Id}-D))$, K_M is defined as Proposition 1;*

3. *Suppose that one of the following holds:*
   (a) *A is uniformly monotone on every nonempty bounded subset of* $\mathrm{dom}A$*;*
   (b) *B is uniformly monotone on every nonempty bounded subset of* $\mathrm{dom}B$*;*
   (c) $\forall x \in \mathrm{zer}(A+B+C+(2\mathrm{Id}-D))$*, C is demiregular at x,*

then $x_n, y_n \to x^*$.

Proof of Theorem 1. 1. Set $w_n = y_n - x_n$. By (13), we have

$$\begin{aligned}&(x_n, z_n - M_n x_n) \in \mathrm{gra}\gamma A,\\&(y_n, 2M_n x_n - z_n - \gamma C x_n - \gamma(2\mathrm{Id}-D)x_n - M_n y_n) \in \mathrm{gra}\gamma B.\end{aligned} \tag{14}$$

Let $x \in \mathrm{zer}(A+B+C+(2\mathrm{Id}-D))$. Then there exist $p \in K_M$ and $p_n \in K_{M_n}$, respectively, such that $x = J_{\gamma A}^{M}(p)$ and $x = J_{\gamma A}^{M_n}(p_n)$ in view of Proposition 1, where $K_{M_n} = \{p_n \in H | J_{\gamma A}^{M_n} p_n = J_{\gamma B}^{M_n}(2M_n J_{\gamma A}^{M_n} p_n - p_n - \gamma C J_{\gamma A}^{M_n} p_n - \gamma(2\mathrm{Id}-D) J_{\gamma A}^{M_n} p_n)\}$. By taking $z = p_n$, $\hat{z} = z_n$, $M_1 = M_2 = M_n$ and noting that $\hat{x} = x_n$, $\hat{y} = y_n$, $x = y$ in Proposition 2, we obtain

$$\begin{aligned}0 &\le \langle p_n - z_n, w_n\rangle - \alpha\|w_n\|^2 - \gamma\langle x - y_n, Cx - Cx_n\rangle\\&\quad + \gamma\langle x - y_n, (2\mathrm{Id}-D)x_n - (2\mathrm{Id}-D)x\rangle.\end{aligned} \tag{15}$$

Multiplying the first two terms on the right of (15) by $2\mu_n$, we obtain

$$\begin{aligned}&2\mu_n(\langle p_n - z_n, w_n\rangle - \alpha\|w_n\|^2)\\&= 2\langle p_n - z_n, z_{n+1} - z_n\rangle - 2\alpha\mu_n\|w_n\|^2\\&= \|z_n - p_n\|^2 - \|z_{n+1} - p_n\|^2 + \mu_n(\mu_n - 2\alpha)\|w_n\|^2.\end{aligned} \tag{16}$$

Since C is a β-cocoercive operator, it follows from Young's inequality that

$$\begin{aligned}&-\gamma\langle x - y_n, Cx - Cx_n\rangle\\&= -\gamma\langle x - x_n, Cx - Cx_n\rangle + \gamma\langle w_n, Cx - Cx_n\rangle\\&\le -\beta\gamma\|Cx - Cx_n\|^2 + \gamma\langle w_n, Cx - Cx_n\rangle\\&\le -\beta\gamma\|Cx - Cx_n\|^2 + \beta\gamma\|Cx - Cx_n\|^2 + \frac{\gamma}{4\beta}\|w_n\|^2\\&= \frac{\gamma}{4\beta}\|w_n\|^2.\end{aligned} \tag{17}$$

Furthermore, the last term of (15) can be expressed by utilizing Young's inequality again as

$$\begin{aligned}&\gamma\langle x - y_n, (2\mathrm{Id}-D)x_n - (2\mathrm{Id}-D)x\rangle\\&= -\gamma\langle y_n - x_n, (2\mathrm{Id}-D)x_n - (2\mathrm{Id}-D)x\rangle - \gamma\langle x_n - x, (2\mathrm{Id}-D)x_n - (2\mathrm{Id}-D)x\rangle\\&\le \gamma\langle w_n, (2\mathrm{Id}-D)x - (2\mathrm{Id}-D)x_n\rangle - 2\gamma\|x_n - x\|^2 + \gamma\|D\|\|x_n - x\|^2\\&\le \gamma(\frac{\epsilon}{2}\|w_n\|^2 + \frac{1}{2\epsilon}\|2\mathrm{Id}-D\|^2\|x - x_n\|^2) + (\gamma\|D\| - 2\gamma)\|x_n - x\|^2\\&= \gamma[\|D\| - 2 + \frac{1}{2\epsilon}\|2\mathrm{Id}-D\|^2]\|x_n - x\|^2 + \frac{\gamma\epsilon}{2}\|w_n\|^2\\&\le \frac{\gamma\epsilon}{2}\|w_n\|^2,\end{aligned} \tag{18}$$

where the positive constant ϵ satisfies

$$\frac{\|2\mathrm{Id}-D\|^2}{2(2-\|D\|)} \le \epsilon \le \frac{4\alpha\beta - \gamma - 2\beta\mu_n}{2\beta\gamma}, \tag{19}$$

which implies that $\|D\| - 2 + \frac{1}{2\epsilon}\|2\mathrm{Id}-D\|^2 \le 0$.

Now, substituting (16)–(18) into (15), we derive

$$0 \le \|z_n - p_n\|^2 - \|z_{n+1} - p_n\|^2 + \mu_n(\mu_n - 2\alpha + \frac{\gamma}{2\beta})\|w_n\|^2 + \gamma\epsilon\mu_n\|w_n\|^2.$$

Thereby,

$$\|z_{n+1} - p_n\|^2 + \mu_n(2\alpha - \frac{\gamma}{2\beta} - \mu_n - \gamma\epsilon)\|w_n\|^2 \le \|z_n - p_n\|^2. \tag{20}$$

It yields

$$\|z_{n+1} - p_n\| \le \|z_n - p_n\|$$

since $2\alpha - \frac{\gamma}{2\beta} - \mu_n - \gamma\epsilon > 0$ by (19). Hence, we obtain from $x = J_{\gamma A}^{M}(p) = J_{\gamma A}^{M_n}(p_n)$ and Proposition 1 that $p_n - p = (M_n - M)x$ and

$$\begin{aligned}\|z_{n+1} - p\| &\le \|z_{n+1} - p_n\| + \|p_n - p\| \\ &\le \|z_n - p\| + 2\|p_n - p\| \\ &\le \|z_n - p\| + 2\|M_n - M\|\|x\|.\end{aligned}$$

Note that $\sum_{n=0}^{\infty} \|M - M_n\| < +\infty$ because $\sum_{n=0}^{\infty} \frac{1}{\mu}\|M - M_n\| \le \sum_{n=0}^{\infty} \frac{1}{\mu_n}\|M - M_n\| < +\infty$. Thus we have $\lim_{n\to\infty} \|z_n - p\|$ exists by Lemma 4. As a result, $\{z_n\}$ is bounded.

In addition, we have by applying Lemma 1

$$\begin{aligned}\|x_n - x\|^2 &= \|J_{\gamma A}^{M_n} z_n - J_{\gamma A}^{M_n} p_n\|^2 \\ &\le \frac{1}{\alpha}\|J_{\gamma A}^{M_n} z_n - J_{\gamma A}^{M_n} p_n\|_{M_n}^2 \\ &= \frac{1}{\alpha}\|J_{\gamma M_n{}^{-1}A} M_n{}^{-1} z_n - J_{\gamma M_n{}^{-1}A} M_n{}^{-1} p_n\|_{M_n}^2 \\ &\le \frac{1}{\alpha}\|M_n{}^{-1} z_n - M_n{}^{-1} p_n\|_{M_n}^2 \\ &\le \frac{1}{\alpha}\|M_n{}^{-1}\|\|z_n - p_n\|^2 \\ &\le \frac{1}{\alpha^2}(\|z_n - p\| + \|p - p_n\|)^2 \\ &< \infty.\end{aligned}$$

So $\{x_n\}$ is a bounded sequence. Similarly, $\{y_n\}$ is bounded.

2. In Proposition 2, we take $z = z_{n+1}$, $\hat{z} = z_n$, $M_1 = M_{n+1}$, $M_2 = M_n$, then $x = x_{n+1}$, $y = y_{n+1}$, $\hat{x} = x_n$ and $\hat{y} = y_n$. Thus,

$$\begin{aligned}0 \le\ & \langle z_{n+1} - z_n, w_n - w_{n+1}\rangle - \alpha\|w_{n+1} - w_n\|^2 - \gamma\langle y_{n+1} - y_n, Cx_{n+1} - Cx_n\rangle \\ & + \gamma\langle y_{n+1} - y_n, (2\mathrm{Id} - D)(x_n - x_{n+1})\rangle \\ & + \langle y_{n+1} - y_n, (M_n - M_{n+1})(y_n - x_n)\rangle + \langle (M_n - M_{n+1})x_n, w_n - w_{n+1}\rangle \\ \le\ & \langle z_{n+1} - z_n, w_n - w_{n+1}\rangle - \alpha\|w_{n+1} - w_n\|^2 - \gamma\langle y_{n+1} - y_n, Cx_{n+1} - Cx_n\rangle \\ & + \|M_{n+1} - M_n\|[\|y_n - y_{n+1}\|\|w_n\| + \|x_n\|\|w_{n+1} - w_n\|] \\ & + \gamma\langle y_{n+1} - y_n, (2\mathrm{Id} - D)(x_n - x_{n+1})\rangle.\end{aligned} \tag{21}$$

Similar to (17) and (18), we obtain the following estimations of the third and the last terms of the right side in (21), respectively,

$$\begin{aligned}
&-\gamma\langle y_{n+1}-y_n, Cx_{n+1}-Cx_n\rangle \\
&= -\gamma\langle w_{n+1}-w_n, Cx_{n+1}-Cx_n\rangle - \gamma\langle x_{n+1}-x_n, Cx_{n+1}-Cx_n\rangle \\
&\leq \beta\gamma\|Cx_{n+1}-Cx_n\|^2 + \frac{\gamma}{4\beta}\|w_{n+1}-w_n\|^2 - \beta\gamma\|Cx_{n+1}-Cx_n\|^2 \\
&= \frac{\gamma}{4\beta}\|w_{n+1}-w_n\|^2
\end{aligned} \tag{22}$$

and

$$\begin{aligned}
&\gamma\langle y_{n+1}-y_n, (2\mathrm{Id}-D)(x_n-x_{n+1})\rangle \\
&= -\gamma\langle w_{n+1}-w_n, (2\mathrm{Id}-D)(x_{n+1}-x_n)\rangle - \gamma\langle x_{n+1}-x_n, (2\mathrm{Id}-D)(x_{n+1}-x_n)\rangle \\
&\leq \gamma\Big(\frac{\epsilon}{2}\|w_{n+1}-w_n\|^2 + \frac{1}{2\epsilon}\|2\mathrm{Id}-D\|^2\|x_{n+1}-x_n\|^2\Big) \\
&\quad - 2\gamma\|x_{n+1}-x_n\|^2 + \gamma\|D\|\|x_{n+1}-x_n\|^2 \\
&= \gamma\Big(\frac{1}{2\epsilon}\|2\mathrm{Id}-D\|^2 + \|D\| - 2\Big)\|x_{n+1}-x_n\|^2 + \frac{\gamma\epsilon}{2}\|w_{n+1}-w_n\|^2 \\
&\leq \frac{\gamma\epsilon}{2}\|w_{n+1}-w_n\|^2,
\end{aligned} \tag{23}$$

where ϵ is given by (19).

Multiplying (21) by 2 and substituting (22) and (23) into (21), we conclude that

$$\begin{aligned}
0 &\leq 2\langle z_{n+1}-z_n, w_n-w_{n+1}\rangle - 2\alpha\|w_{n+1}-w_n\|^2 \\
&\quad + \frac{\gamma}{2\beta}\|w_{n+1}-w_n\|^2 + \gamma\epsilon\|w_{n+1}-w_n\|^2 \\
&\quad + 2\|M_{n+1}-M_n\|[\|y_n-y_{n+1}\|\|w_n\| + \|x_n\|\|w_{n+1}-w_n\|] \\
&= 2\mu_n\langle w_n, w_n-w_{n+1}\rangle + \Big(\frac{\gamma}{2\beta}+\gamma\epsilon-2\alpha\Big)\|w_{n+1}-w_n\|^2 \\
&\quad + 2\|M_{n+1}-M_n\|[\|y_n-y_{n+1}\|\|w_n\| + \|x_n\|\|w_{n+1}-w_n\|] \\
&= \mu_n\|w_n\|^2 - \mu_n\|w_{n+1}\|^2 + \Big(\frac{\gamma}{2\beta}+\gamma\epsilon-2\alpha+\mu_n\Big)\|w_{n+1}-w_n\|^2 \\
&\quad + 2\|M_{n+1}-M_n\|[\|y_n-y_{n+1}\|\|w_n\| + \|x_n\|\|w_{n+1}-w_n\|].
\end{aligned}$$

From $\mu_n > 0$, we have

$$\begin{aligned}
\|w_{n+1}\|^2 &\leq \|w_n\|^2 - \frac{1}{\mu_n}\Big(2\alpha - \frac{\gamma}{2\beta} - \gamma\epsilon - \mu_n\Big)\|w_{n+1}-w_n\|^2 \\
&\quad + \frac{2}{\mu_n}\|M_{n+1}-M_n\|[\|y_n-y_{n+1}\|\|w_n\| + \|x_n\|\|w_{n+1}-w_n\|] \\
&\leq \|w_n\|^2 + \frac{2}{\mu_n}\|M_{n+1}-M_n\|[\|y_n-y_{n+1}\|\|w_n\| + \|x_n\|\|w_{n+1}-w_n\|]
\end{aligned}$$

since $2\alpha - \frac{\gamma}{2\beta} - \gamma\epsilon - \mu_n \geq 0$ by (19). Let

$$\delta_n = \frac{2}{\mu_n}\|M_{n+1}-M_n\|[\|y_n-y_{n+1}\|\|w_n\| + \|x_n\|\|w_{n+1}-w_n\|].$$

We have $\sum_{n=0}^{\infty}\delta_n < +\infty$ by virtue of the fact that $\sum_{n=0}^{\infty}\frac{1}{\mu_n}\|M_{n+1}-M_n\| < +\infty$ and $\{x_n\}$, $\{y_n\}$, $\{w_n\}$ are bounded sequences. Therefore, $\{\|w_n\|\}$ converges from Lemma 4.

Next, we show that $w_n = y_n - x_n$ converges to 0 as n goes to infinity.

Rearranging terms in (20), we have

$$
\begin{aligned}
&\mu_n(2\alpha - \frac{\gamma}{2\beta} - \mu_n - \gamma\epsilon)\|w_n\|^2 \\
&\leq \|z_n - p_n\|^2 - \|z_{n+1} - p_n\|^2 \\
&\leq \|z_n - p_n\|^2 - \|z_{n+1} - p_{n+1}\|^2 - \|p_n - p_{n+1}\|^2 + 2\|z_{n+1} - p_{n+1}\|\|p_n - p_{n+1}\| \\
&\leq \|z_n - p_n\|^2 - \|z_{n+1} - p_{n+1}\|^2 - \|(M_n - M_{n+1})x\|^2 \\
&\quad + 2[\|z_{n+1} - p\| + \|p - p_{n+1}\|]\|(M_n - M_{n+1})x\| \\
&= \|z_n - p_n\|^2 - \|z_{n+1} - p_{n+1}\|^2 - \|(M_n - M_{n+1})x\|^2 \\
&\quad + 2[\|z_{n+1} - p\| + \|(M - M_{n+1})x\|]\|(M_n - M_{n+1})x\| \\
&\leq \|z_n - p_n\|^2 - \|z_{n+1} - p_{n+1}\|^2 + \Omega\|(M_n - M_{n+1})x\|,
\end{aligned} \tag{24}
$$

where $\Omega = \sup_n\{2[\|z_{n+1} - p\| + \|(M - M_{n+1})x\|] - \|(M_n - M_{n+1})x\|\} < \infty$ due to the boundedness of $\{z_n\}$ and *(C2)*, *(C3)*.

Summing on both sides of (24) from 0 to k, we obtain as k goes to infinity

$$
\begin{aligned}
\sum_{n=0}^{\infty} \mu_n(2\alpha - \frac{\gamma}{2\beta} - \mu_n - \gamma\epsilon)\|w_n\|^2 &\leq \|z_0 - p_0\|^2 + \Omega \sum_{n=0}^{\infty} \|(M_n - M_{n+1})x\| \\
&< \infty.
\end{aligned} \tag{25}
$$

By $\sum_{n=0}^{\infty} \mu_n = +\infty$ and (19), it has $\sum_{n=0}^{\infty} \mu_n(2\alpha - \frac{\gamma}{2\beta} - \mu_n - \gamma\epsilon) = +\infty$. Thus, $\liminf_{n\to\infty} \|w_n\| = 0$ in view of (25). Hence, $\lim_{n\to\infty} \|w_n\| = 0$, that is $y_n - x_n \to 0$ as $n \to \infty$.

For simplicity, denote by $v_n = \gamma C(x_n)$. From 1., $\{z_n\}$, $\{x_n\}$, and $\{v_n\}$ are bounded sequences. Assume that (z^*, x^*, v^*) is a weak limit point of the sequence $\{(z_n, x_n, v_n)\}$. Then there exists its subsequence $\{(z_{n_k}, x_{n_k}, v_{n_k})\}$ such that $(z_{n_k}, x_{n_k}, v_{n_k}) \rightharpoonup (z^*, x^*, v^*)$.

Define $F : H^3 \to 2^{H^3}$ by

$$
F = \begin{pmatrix} (\gamma A)^{-1} \\ (\gamma C)^{-1} \\ \gamma B + \gamma(2\mathrm{Id} - D) \end{pmatrix} + \begin{pmatrix} 0 & 0 & -\mathrm{Id} \\ 0 & 0 & -\mathrm{Id} \\ \mathrm{Id} & \mathrm{Id} & 0 \end{pmatrix}.
$$

Then F is a maximally monotone operator (see [33] (Example 20.35, Corollary 25.5(i))). From (14), we obtain

$$
\begin{pmatrix} x_{n_k} - y_{n_k} \\ x_{n_k} - y_{n_k} \\ M_{n_k}(x_{n_k} - y_{n_k}) + \gamma(2\mathrm{Id} - D)(y_{n_k} - x_{n_k}) \end{pmatrix} \in F \begin{pmatrix} z_{n_k} - M_{n_k} x_{n_k} \\ v_{n_k} \\ y_{n_k} \end{pmatrix}.
$$

Noting that $z_{n_k} - M_{n_k} x_{n_k} \rightharpoonup z^* - Mx^*$, $v_{n_k} \rightharpoonup v^*$, $y_{n_k} \rightharpoonup x^*$ by $w_{n_k} \to 0$, and that $\mathrm{gra}F$ is sequentially closed in $H^{weak} \times H^{strong}$, we deduce

$$
\begin{pmatrix} 0 \\ 0 \\ 0 \end{pmatrix} \in \left(\begin{pmatrix} (\gamma A)^{-1} \\ (\gamma C)^{-1} \\ \gamma B + \gamma(2\mathrm{Id} - D) \end{pmatrix} + \begin{pmatrix} 0 & 0 & -\mathrm{Id} \\ 0 & 0 & -\mathrm{Id} \\ \mathrm{Id} & \mathrm{Id} & 0 \end{pmatrix} \right) \begin{pmatrix} z^* - Mx^* \\ v^* \\ x^* \end{pmatrix}.
$$

In other words,

$$
x^* = J_{\gamma A}^M z^*,\ v^* = \gamma C x^*,\ x^* = J_{\gamma B}^M (2Mx^* - z^* - \gamma C x^* - \gamma(2\mathrm{Id} - D)x^*).
$$

Thus $z^* \in K_M$. This gives $z_n \rightharpoonup z^* \in K_M$ according to Lemma 3. Furthermore, $x^* = J_{\gamma A}^M z^* \in \mathrm{zer}(A + B + C + (2\mathrm{Id} - D))$ by Proposition 1. Since z^* is the unique weak limit point of $\{z_n\}$, $x^* = J^M_{\gamma A}z^*$ and $v^* = \gamma Cx^*$ are the unique weak limit points of $\{x_n\}$, $\{v_n\}$, respectively. So, $x_n \rightharpoonup x^*$, $v_n \rightharpoonup v^*$. By $w_n \to 0$, we have $y_n \rightharpoonup x^*$.

Taking $z = z^*$, $\hat{z} = z_n$, $M_1 = M$ and $M_2 = M_n$ in Proposition 2 and applying (17) and (18), we have

$$\begin{aligned}0 \le &\langle z^* - z_n, w_n\rangle - \alpha\|w_n\|^2 + \frac{\gamma\epsilon}{2}\|w_n\|^2 - \beta\gamma\|Cx^* - Cx_n\|^2\\&+ \gamma\langle w_n, Cx^* - Cx_n\rangle + \langle x^* - y_n, (M_n - M)w_n\rangle + \langle (M_n - M)x_n, w_n\rangle.\end{aligned}$$

Then,

$$\begin{aligned}\beta\gamma\|Cx^* - Cx_n\|^2 \le &\langle z^* - z_n, w_n\rangle + (\frac{\gamma\epsilon}{2} - \alpha)\|w_n\|^2 + \gamma\langle w_n, Cx^* - Cx_n\rangle\\&+ \langle x^* - y_n, (M_n - M)w_n\rangle + \langle (M_n - M)x_n, w_n\rangle\\&\to 0, \quad \text{as } n \to \infty.\end{aligned}$$

That is, $Cx_n \to Cx^*$ as $n \to \infty$.

3. As seen in 2., there exists $x^* \in \text{zer}(A + B + C + (2\text{Id} - D))$ such that $x_n \rightharpoonup x^*$ as $n \to \infty$.

(a) Set $O = \{x^*\} \cup \{x_n\}$. Obviously, O is a bounded subset of dom$A$. Since A is uniformly monotone on O, which means that there exists an increasing function $\phi_A : \mathbb{R}_+ \to [0, +\infty]$ satisfying that $\phi_A(x) = 0$ if and only if $x = 0$, which allows us to write the result of Proposition 2 as if we set $z = z^*$, $\hat{z} = z_n$, $M_1 = M$, $M_2 = M_n$

$$\begin{aligned}\gamma\phi_A(\|x^* - x_n\|) \le &\langle z^* - z_n, w_n\rangle - \alpha\|w_n\|^2 - \gamma\langle x^* - y_n, Cx^* - Cx_n\rangle\\&+ \gamma\langle x^* - y_n, (2\text{Id} - D)(x_n - x^*)\rangle\\&+ \langle x^* - y_n, (M_n - M)w_n\rangle + \langle (M_n - M)x_n, w_n\rangle.\end{aligned}$$

Hence, we have by using (18) and the results of 2.

$$\begin{aligned}0 &\le \gamma\phi_A(\|x^* - x_n\|)\\&\le \langle z^* - z_n, w_n\rangle - \alpha\|w_n\|^2 - \gamma\langle x^* - y_n, Cx^* - Cx_n\rangle + \frac{\gamma\epsilon}{2}\|w_n\|^2\\&\quad + \langle x^* - y_n, (M_n - M)w_n\rangle + \langle (M_n - M)x_n, w_n\rangle\\&\to 0, \quad \text{as } n \to \infty,\end{aligned}$$

where ϵ is a positive constant satisfying (19). $\lim_{n\to\infty} \|x_n - x^*\| = 0$ follows from $\lim_{n\to\infty} \|\phi_A(\|x^* - x_n\|)\| = 0$ and the definition of ϕ_A. Moreover, $\{y_n\}$ converges strongly to x^* holds due to $\lim_{n\to\infty} \|y_n - x_n\| = 0$.

(b) The proof is the same as (a).

(c) From 2., we have $x_n \rightharpoonup x^* \in \text{zer}(A + B + C + (2\text{Id} - D))$ and $Cx_n \to Cx^*$. The demiregularity of C at x^* guarantees $x_n \to x^*$ as $n \to \infty$. □

Remark 1. *(i) The operator T defined in Proposition 1 is similar in form to the operators that appeared in [8] (Proposition 2.1) and [12] (Lemma 3.4), but it is no longer an averaged operator. We prove the weak and strong convergence results of the proposed algorithm in this more general case.*

(ii) Algorithm (13) *can be seen as a generalization of (8). In fact, if we choose* $M_n = \text{Id}$ *and* $D = \alpha$, $\alpha \in (0, 2)$, *Algorithm* (13) *becomes (8).*

3.2. Multi-Step Inertial Parameterized Variable Metric Three-Operator Algorithm

In this subsection, we present the multi-step inertial parameterized variable metric three-operator algorithm, which combines Algorithm (13) and the multi-step inertial technique. Meanwhile, we show the convergence of the proposed algorithm.

Let $s \in \mathbb{N}_+$ and $U = \{0, \cdots, s-1\}$. Let $\{\theta_{i,n}\}_{i\in U} \in (-1,1)^s$. Choose $z_0 \in H$, $z_{-i-1} = z_0$, $i \in U$ and set

$$\begin{cases} v_n = z_n + \sum\limits_{i\in U} \theta_{i,n}(z_{n-i} - z_{n-i-1}), \\ x_n = J_{\gamma A}^{M_n} v_n, \\ y_n = J_{\gamma B}^{M_n}(2M_n x_n - v_n - \gamma C x_n - \gamma(2\mathrm{Id} - D)x_n), \\ z_{n+1} = v_n + \mu_n(y_n - x_n),\ n \geq 0, \end{cases} \tag{26}$$

where $J_{\gamma A}^{M_n} = (M_n + \gamma A)^{-1}$, $M_n \in P_\alpha(H)$.

Theorem 2. *Let $\{z_n\}$ be defined by Algorithm (26), K_M be defined as Proposition 1. Set $\|D\| \in [0,2)$, $\gamma \in (0, \frac{4\alpha\beta(2-\|D\|)}{2-\|D\|+\beta\|2\mathrm{Id}-D\|^2})$ and provided the following conditions hold:*

(C3) $\sum\limits_{n=0}^{\infty} \mu_n = +\infty, 0 < \underline{\mu} \leq \mu_n \leq 2\alpha - \frac{\gamma}{2\beta}(1 + \frac{\beta\|2\mathrm{Id}-D\|^2}{2-\|D\|})$;

(C4) $M_n \in P_\alpha(H)$ such that $\sum\limits_{n=0}^{\infty} \|M - M_n\| < +\infty$;

(C5) $\overline{\theta_i} = sup_{n\in\mathbb{N}}|\theta_{i,n}|$, $\sum\limits_{i\in U} \overline{\theta_i} < 1$, $\lim\limits_{n\to\infty} \theta_{i,n} \neq 0$ and

$$\sum_{n=1}^{+\infty} \max_{i\in U} |\theta_{i,n}| \sum_{i\in U} \|z_{n-i} - z_{n-i-1}\| < +\infty, \tag{27}$$

Then the following assertions hold:

1. *For every $q \in K_M$, $\lim\limits_{n\to\infty} \|z_n - q\|$ exists;*
2. *$\{z_n\}$, $\{v_n\}$ converge weakly to the same point of K_M, $\{x_n\}$, $\{y_n\}$ converge weakly to the same point of* $\mathrm{zer}(A + B + C + (2\mathrm{Id} - D))$;
3. *Suppose that one of the following holds:*
   - (a) *A is uniformly monotone on every nonempty bounded subset of* $\mathrm{dom}A$;
   - (b) *B is uniformly monotone on every nonempty bounded subset of* $\mathrm{dom}B$;
   - (c) *$\forall x \in \mathrm{zer}(A + B + C + (2\mathrm{Id} - D))$, C is demiregular at x,*

then $\{x_n\}$, $\{y_n\}$ converge strongly to the same point of $\mathrm{zer}(A + B + C + (2\mathrm{Id} - D))$.

Proof of Theorem 2. 1. Given $q \in K_M$, arbitrarily, there exists $\overline{x} \in \mathrm{zer}(A + B + C + (2\mathrm{Id} - D))$ such that $\overline{x} = J_{\gamma A}^{M}(q)$, and for this $\overline{x}$, there exists $q_n \in K_{M_n}$ such that $\overline{x} = J_{\gamma A}^{M_n}(q_n)$ according to Proposition 1. We choose $z = q_n$, $\hat{z} = v_n$, $M_1 = M_2 = M_n$ in Proposition 2. Then we have $x = y = \overline{x}$, $\hat{x} = x_n$, $\hat{y} = y_n$, and

$$\begin{aligned} 0 \leq\ & \langle q_n - v_n, y_n - x_n\rangle - \alpha\|y_n - x_n\|^2 - \gamma\langle \overline{x} - y_n, C\overline{x} - Cx_n\rangle \\ & + \gamma\langle \overline{x} - y_n, (2\mathrm{Id} - D)x_n - (2\mathrm{Id} - D)\overline{x}\rangle. \end{aligned} \tag{28}$$

Applying Lemma 2, we have

$$\begin{aligned} & 2\mu_n(\langle q_n - v_n, y_n - x_n\rangle - \alpha\|y_n - x_n\|^2) \\ & = 2\langle q_n - v_n, z_{n+1} - v_n\rangle - 2\alpha\mu_n\|y_n - x_n\|^2 \\ & = \|v_n - q_n\|^2 - \|z_{n+1} - q_n\|^2 + \mu_n(\mu_n - 2\alpha)\|y_n - x_n\|^2. \end{aligned} \tag{29}$$

As same as (17) and (18), we obtain

$$\begin{aligned} -\gamma\langle \overline{x} - y_n, C\overline{x} - Cx_n\rangle & \leq -\beta\gamma\|C\overline{x} - Cx_n\|^2 + \gamma\langle y_n - x_n, C\overline{x} - Cx_n\rangle \\ & \leq \frac{\gamma}{4\beta}\|y_n - x_n\|^2, \end{aligned} \tag{30}$$

$$\gamma\langle \bar{x} - y_n, (2\mathrm{Id} - D)x_n - (2\mathrm{Id} - D)\bar{x}\rangle \leq \frac{\gamma\epsilon}{2}\|y_n - x_n\|^2, \tag{31}$$

where $\frac{\|2\mathrm{Id}-D\|^2}{2(2-\|D\|)} \leq \epsilon \leq \frac{4\alpha\beta-\gamma-2\beta\mu_n}{2\beta\gamma}$.

Combining (28)–(31), we have

$$0 \leq \|v_n - q_n\|^2 - \|z_{n+1} - q_n\|^2 + \mu_n(\mu_n - 2\alpha + \frac{\gamma}{2\beta} + \gamma\epsilon)\|y_n - x_n\|^2,$$

from which it follows that

$$\|z_{n+1} - q_n\|^2 + \mu_n(2\alpha - \frac{\gamma}{2\beta} - \mu_n - \gamma\epsilon)\|y_n - x_n\|^2 \leq \|v_n - q_n\|^2.$$

Since $2\alpha - \frac{\gamma}{2\beta} - \mu_n - \gamma\epsilon \geq 0$, it has

$$\|z_{n+1} - q_n\|^2 \leq \|v_n - q_n\|^2,$$

which implies

$$\begin{aligned}
\|z_{n+1} - q_n\| &\leq \|v_n - q_n\| \\
&\leq \|z_n - q_n\| + \|\sum_{i\in U}\theta_{i,n}(z_{n-i} - z_{n-i-1})\| \\
&\leq \|z_n - q\| + \|q - q_n\| + \max_{i\in U}|\theta_{i,n}|\sum_{i\in U}\|z_{n-i} - z_{n-i-1}\| \\
&\leq \|z_n - q\| + \|M - M_n\|\|\bar{x}\| + \max_{i\in U}|\theta_{i,n}|\sum_{i\in U}\|z_{n-i} - z_{n-i-1}\|.
\end{aligned}$$

By *(C4)*, *(C5)* and Lemma 4, we have $\lim_{n\to\infty}\|z_n - q\|$ exists and $\{z_n\}$ is bounded. Hence, $\{v_n\}, \{x_n\}$ and $\{\gamma C x_n\}$ are bounded.

2. Since $\lim_{n\to\infty}\theta_{i,n} \neq 0$ and (27) holds, for all $i \in U$, it has

$$\lim_{n\to\infty}|\theta_{i,n}|\|z_{n-i} - z_{n-i-1}\| = 0.$$

Particularly,

$$\lim_{n\to\infty}\|z_{n+1} - z_n\| = 0. \tag{32}$$

Further, we have

$$\|z_{n+1} - v_n\| \leq \|z_{n+1} - z_n\| + \sum_{i\in U}|\theta_{i,n}|\|z_{n-i} - z_{n-i-1}\| \to 0, \textit{ as } n \to \infty. \tag{33}$$

By (32) and (33), we have

$$\begin{aligned}
0 \leq \|z_n - v_n\| &= \|\sum_{i\in U}\theta_{i,n}(z_{n-i} - z_{n-i-1})\| \\
&\leq \sum_{i\in U}|\theta_{i,n}|\|z_{n-i} - z_{n-i-1}\|,
\end{aligned}$$

which indicates that $\|z_n - v_n\| \to 0$.

Since $\lim_{n\to\infty}\|y_n - x_n\| = \lim_{n\to\infty}\frac{1}{\mu_n}\|z_{n+1} - v_n\| = 0$. Then, $y_n - x_n \to 0$.

Set $u_n = \gamma C x_n$. Let $(\bar{z}, \bar{x}, \bar{u})$ be a weak limit point of the sequence $\{(z_n, x_n, u_n)\}$. Then there exists a subsequence $\{(z_{n_k}, x_{n_k}, u_{n_k})\}$ such that $(z_{n_k}, x_{n_k}, u_{n_k}) \rightharpoonup (\bar{z}, \bar{x}, \bar{u})$. Without loss of generality, we assume that $\exists\{v_{n_k}\} \subset \{v_n\}$ such that $v_{n_k} \rightharpoonup \bar{z}$. In addition, we have $M_{n_k} \to M$ as $k \to \infty$ by *(C4)*.

Define a maximally monotone operator $F : H^3 \to 2^{H^3}$ by

$$F = \begin{pmatrix} (\gamma A)^{-1} \\ (\gamma C)^{-1} \\ \gamma B + \gamma(2\mathrm{Id} - D) \end{pmatrix} + \begin{pmatrix} 0 & 0 & -\mathrm{Id} \\ 0 & 0 & -\mathrm{Id} \\ \mathrm{Id} & \mathrm{Id} & 0 \end{pmatrix}.$$

By (26), we have

$$\begin{aligned} (x_n, v_n - M_n x_n) &\in \mathrm{gra}\gamma A, \\ (y_n, 2M_n x_n - v_n - \gamma C x_n - \gamma(2\mathrm{Id} - \gamma D)x_n - M_n y_n) &\in \mathrm{gra}\gamma B. \end{aligned} \tag{34}$$

Therefore, from (34), we obtain

$$\begin{pmatrix} x_{n_k} - y_{n_k} \\ x_{n_k} - y_{n_k} \\ M_{n_k}(x_{n_k} - y_{n_k}) + \gamma(2\mathrm{Id} - D)(y_{n_k} - x_{n_k}) \end{pmatrix} \in F \begin{pmatrix} v_{n_k} - M_{n_k} x_{n_k} \\ u_{n_k} \\ y_{n_k} \end{pmatrix}.$$

Since gra$F$ is sequentially closed in $H^{weak} \times H^{strong}$,

$$\begin{pmatrix} 0 \\ 0 \\ 0 \end{pmatrix} \in \left(\begin{pmatrix} (\gamma A)^{-1} \\ (\gamma C)^{-1} \\ \gamma B + \gamma(2\mathrm{Id} - D) \end{pmatrix} + \begin{pmatrix} 0 & 0 & -\mathrm{Id} \\ 0 & 0 & -\mathrm{Id} \\ \mathrm{Id} & \mathrm{Id} & 0 \end{pmatrix} \right) \begin{pmatrix} \overline{z} - M\overline{x} \\ \overline{u} \\ \overline{x} \end{pmatrix},$$

it yields that

$$\overline{x} = J^M_{\gamma A}\overline{z},\ \overline{u} = \gamma C\overline{x},\ \overline{x} = J^M_{\gamma B}(2M\overline{x} - \overline{z} - \gamma C\overline{x} - \gamma(2\mathrm{Id} - D)\overline{x}).$$

Hence, $\overline{z} \in K_M$. Using Lemma 3, $v_n \rightharpoonup \overline{z} \in K_M$. Meanwhile, $z_n \rightharpoonup \overline{z} \in K_M$ by $\|z_n - v_n\| \to 0$. Furthermore, $\overline{x} = J^M_{\gamma A}\overline{z} \in \mathrm{zer}(A + B + C + (2\mathrm{Id} - D))$ by Proposition 1. From that $z_n \rightharpoonup \overline{z}$, $\overline{x} = J^M_{\gamma A}\overline{z}$ and $\overline{u} = \gamma C\overline{x}$, we conclude that $x_n \rightharpoonup \overline{x}$, $u_n \rightharpoonup \overline{u}$. Using $y_n - x_n \to 0$, we obtain $y_n \rightharpoonup \overline{x}$.

By (30) and (31) and Proposition 2 with $z = \overline{z}$, $\hat{z} = v_n$, $M_1 = M$, $M_2 = M_n$, we have

$$\begin{aligned} \beta\gamma\|C\overline{x} - Cx_n\|^2 \le{}& \langle \overline{z} - v_n, y_n - x_n\rangle + (\frac{\gamma\epsilon}{2} - \alpha)\|y_n - x_n\|^2 + \gamma\langle y_n - x_n, C\overline{x} - Cx_n\rangle \\ &+ \langle \overline{x} - y_n, (M_n - M)(y_n - x_n)\rangle + \langle (M_n - M)x_n, y_n - x_n\rangle. \end{aligned}$$

Hence, $Cx_n \to C\overline{x}$.

3. Taking $z = \overline{z}$, $\hat{z} = v_n$, $M_1 = M$, $M_2 = M_n$ and using similar arguments in the proof of 3. in Theorem 1, we obtain $x_n \to \overline{x}$ and $y_n \to \overline{x}$, where $\overline{x} \in \mathrm{zer}(A + B + C + (2\mathrm{Id} - D))$. □

Remark 2. *If $\theta_{i,n} \in [0,1)$, (27) reduces to*

$$\sum_{n=1}^{+\infty} \max_{i\in U} \theta_{i,n} \sum_{i\in U} \|z_{n-i} - z_{n-i-1}\| < +\infty. \tag{35}$$

(35) can be implemented by the following simple online updating rule

$$\theta_{i,n} = \min\{\theta_i, b_{i,n}\},$$

where $\theta_i \in [0,1)$, $\{b_{i,n}\}$ and $\{\max b_{i,n} \sum_{i\in U} \|z_{n-i} - z_{n-i-1}\|\}$ are summable sequences for each $i \in U$. For example, one can choose

$$b_{i,n} = \frac{b_i}{n^{1+\delta} \sum_{i\in U} \|z_{n-i} - z_{n-i-1}\|},\ b_i > 0,\ \delta > 0.$$

4. Numerical Results

We consider the following LASSO problem with a nonnegative constraint:

$$\min_{x\in\mathbb{R}^N}\{\frac{1}{2}\|Ax-b\|^2+\|x\|_1+\iota_c(x)\}, \tag{36}$$

where $A\in\mathbb{R}^{J\times N}$, $b\in\mathbb{R}^{J\times 1}$, $C=\{x\in\mathbb{R}^N|x_i\geq 0, i=1,2,\cdots,N\}$. Let $\iota_C(x)$ be the indicator function of the closed convex set C, that is,

$$\iota_C(x)=\begin{cases} 0, & x\in C,\\ +\infty, & \text{otherwise.}\end{cases}$$

Set $f_1(x)=\|x\|_1$, $f_2(x)=\iota_c(x)$ and $f_3(x)=\frac{1}{2}\|Ax-b\|^2$. Obviously, $\nabla f_3(x)=A^T(Ax-b)$, $\nabla f_3(x)$ is $\|A^TA\|$-Lipschitz continuous and the i-th component of $J^M_{\gamma_n\partial f_1}x$ is

$$\begin{aligned}(J^M_{\gamma_n\partial f_1}x)_i &= (J_{\gamma_n M^{-1}\partial f_1}M^{-1}x)_i\\ &= (prox_{\gamma_n M f_1}M^{-1}x)_i=\begin{cases}\frac{x_i}{m_i}-\frac{\gamma_n}{m_i}, & \frac{x_i}{m_i}>\frac{\gamma_n}{m_i},\\ \frac{x_i}{m_i}+\frac{\gamma_n}{m_i}, & \frac{x_i}{m_i}<\frac{\gamma_n}{m_i},\\ 0, & otherwise,\end{cases}\end{aligned}$$

where $M=diag(m_1,m_2,\cdots,m_N)$. Similarly, we have

$$J^M_{\gamma_n\partial f_2}(x)=J_{\gamma_n M^{-1}\partial f_2}(M^{-1}x)=prox_{\gamma_n M f_2}(M^{-1}x)=P_C(M^{-1}x).$$

Problem (36) is equivalent to the problem of finding $x\in\mathbb{R}^N$ such that

$$0\in\partial f_1(x)+\partial f_2(x)+\nabla f_3(x).$$

Select any initial value $z_0,z_{-1},z_{-2}\in\mathbb{R}^N$, $U=\{1,2\}$, $i\in U$, $\theta_{1,n}=\theta_{2,n}=\min\{0.1,\frac{n-1}{n+2}\}$. Set $J=N=20$, $\mathrm{E}\in\mathbb{R}^{20\times 20}$, $M_n=M=2\mathrm{E}$, $\alpha=\frac{1}{2}$, $L=\|A^TA\|$, $\zeta=\frac{4\alpha(2-\|D\|)}{L(2-\|D\|)+\|2\mathrm{E}-D\|^2}$, and take $\|z_{n+1}-z_n\|<$ eps as the stopping criteria. In the following, we denote Algorithm (13) as PVMTO and Algorithm (26) as MIPVMTO.

In Algorithms (13) and (26) take $D=k\mathrm{E}$, $k\in[0.009,1.999]$, and take $\gamma=\frac{1}{2}\zeta$, $\mu_n=0.499$, eps $=10^{-5}$. In Figures 1 and 2, we show the effect of the parameter D on the CPU time and iteration numbers of the PVMTO and the MIPVMTO. As can be seen from the figure, compared with PVMTO, MIPVMTO has a great improvement in the number of iterations and CPU. Furthermore, we list the CPU time of PVMTO and MIPVMTO at different stopping criteria and different D in Table 1.

In Algorithms (13) and (26) take $D=0.009\mathrm{E}$, $e\in[\frac{0.999}{20},\frac{19.999}{20}]$, $\mu_n=0.999-e$, $\gamma=e\zeta$ and eps $=10^{-5}$. The effect of choosing different γ on the number of iterations of the two algorithms is shown in Figure 3. It can be concluded that, when $\gamma=\frac{1}{2}\zeta$, the number of iterations of our two proposed algorithms is the least, and the number of iterations of MIPVMTO is less than that of the PVMTO.

In Algorithms (13) and (26) take $D=0.009\mathrm{E}$, $M_n=M=2\mathrm{E}$ and $\gamma=\frac{1}{2}\zeta$, $\mu_n=0.499$. In Figure 4, we compare the number of iterations of PVMTO and MIPVMTO under different stopping criteria, and it can be seen that the parameterized variable metric three-operator algorithm with inertia term has more advantages.

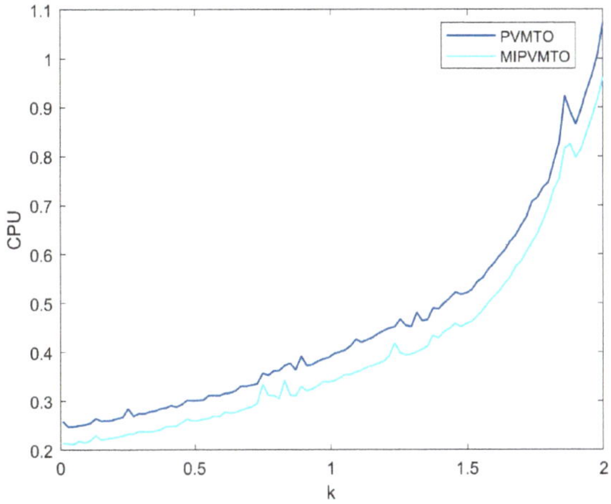

Figure 1. The effect of $D = k\mathrm{E}$ on CPU (s).

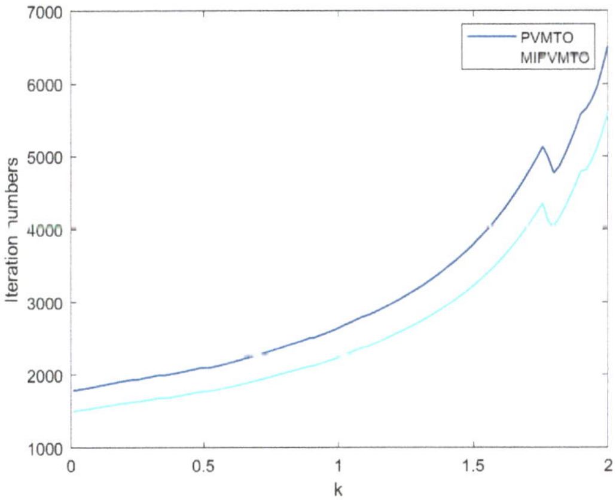

Figure 2. The effect of $D = k\mathrm{E}$ on iteration numbers.

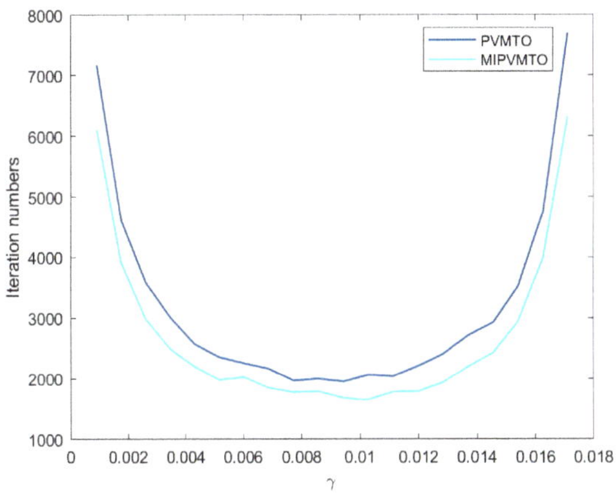

Figure 3. Different γ with $\|z_{n+1} - z_n\| < 10^{-5}$.

Table 1. Numerical results of the PVMTO (Algorithm (13)) and the MIPVMTO (Algorithm (26)).

	PVMTO				MIPVMTO			
eps	D	**Iter**	$\|\|x_n\|\|$	**CPU (s)**	D	**Iter**	$\|\|x_n\|\|$	**CPU (s)**
	0.00999E	531	0.892097	0.075116	0.00999E	473	0.896813	0.101615
	0.50659E	564	0.909472	0.079004	0.50659E	526	0.917201	0.078163
	1.00499E	624	0.932223	0.083093	1.00499E	592	0.942767	0.080023
	1.50599E	725	0.965979	0.098467	1.50599E	615	0.969368	0.088909
	1.91199E	745	0.987424	0.103177	1.91199E	668	0.994628	0.093426
10^{-3}	1.93599E	746	0.988654	0.102805	1.93599E	676	0.996532	0.095638
	1.95699E	747	0.989739	0.106307	1.95699E	685	0.998393	0.092109
	1.97899E	749	0.990939	0.097910	1.97899E	696	1.000491	0.094137
	1.98999E	750	0.991522	0.098771	1.98999E	702	1.001613	0.093303
	1.99999E	750	0.991941	0.098490	1.99999E	707	1.002606	0.094370
	2.00000E	750	0.991941	0.113851	2.00000E	750	0.991941	0.113851
	0.00999E	1114	0.869743	0.159736	0.00999E	958	0.870160	0.131419
	0.50659E	1223	0.880358	0.165580	0.50659E	1063	0.880900	0.142245
	1.00499E	1487	0.893068	0.193978	1.00499E	1314	0.893768	0.175073
	1.50599E	1878	0.909894	0.245709	1.50599E	1675	0.910860	0.224609
	1.91199E	2523	0.928138	0.328125	1.91199E	2249	0.929321	0.302159
10^{-4}	1.93599E	2538	0.929595	0.342751	1.93599E	2297	0.931024	0.324058
	1.95699E	2586	0.931119	0.350296	1.95699E	2302	0.932462	0.309686
	1.97899E	2635	0.932768	0.347120	1.97899E	2357	0.934105	0.315834
	1.98999E	2623	0.933456	0.341721	1.98999E	2388	0.934962	0.318405
	1.99999E	2652	0.934230	0.349495	1.99999E	2417	0.935759	0.321433
	2.00000E	2652	0.934231	0.314799	2.00000E	2652	0.934231	0.314799
	0.00999E	2017	0.893855	0.518356	0.00999E	1692	0.893916	0.237726
	0.50659E	2370	0.915375	0.312055	0.50659E	1990	0.915430	0.267332
	1.00499E	2998	0.939446	0.389901	1.00499E	2520	0.939509	0.340453
	1.50599E	4365	0.968586	0.563529	1.50599E	3667	0.968661	0.485276
	1.91199E	6464	0.999046	0.832374	1.91199E	5530	0.999158	0.735078
10^{-5}	1.93599E	6717	1.001373	0.864062	1.93599E	5748	1.001488	0.765171
	1.95699E	6957	1.003502	1.488362	1.95699E	5956	1.003622	2.570363
	1.97899E	7229	1.005861	3.010892	1.97899E	6190	1.005987	2.856389
	1.98999E	7374	1.007065	3.209643	1.98999E	6315	1.007196	2.881690
	1.99999E	7511	1.008205	3.351171	1.99999E	6433	1.008341	2.996621
	2.00000E	7511	1.008206	3.024831	2.00000E	7511	1.008206	3.024831

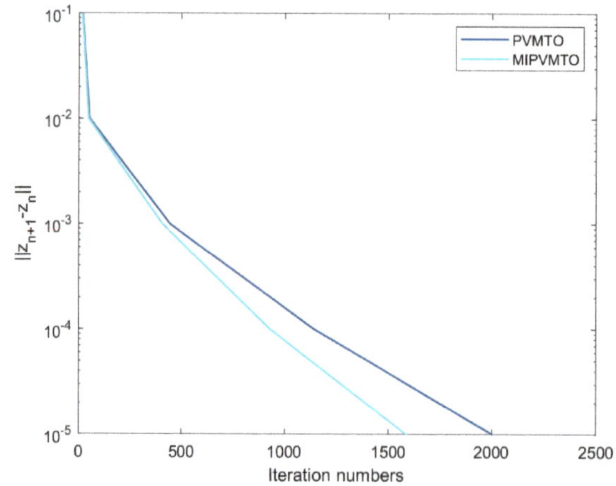

Figure 4. Numerical results with different stopping criterion.

5. Conclusions

In this paper, we propose a parameterized variable metric three-operator algorithm to solve the monotone inclusion problem involving the sum of three operators and prove the strong convergence of the algorithm under some appropriate conditions. The multi-step inertial parameterized variable metric three-operator algorithm is also proposed and its strong convergence is analyzed in order to speed up the parameterized variable metric three-operator algorithm. To a certain extent, the proposed algorithm can be seen as a generalization of the parameterized three-operator algorithm [12]. The constructed numerical examples show the efficiency of the proposed algorithms and the effects of the choices of the parameter operator D on running time. In future development, we can consider proving that the regularization of parameterized variable metric three-operator algorithm converges to the least norm solution of the sum of three maximally monotone operators as shown in [12] and show the real applications of the algorithms in practice. Another direction of consideration is to study the self-adaption version of the currently proposed algorithms.

Author Contributions: All authors contributed equally to this article. All authors have read and agreed to the published version of the manuscript.

Funding: This research was supported by the Fundamental Research Funds for the Central Universities under Grant No. 3122019185.

Data Availability Statement: The data that support the findings of this study are available from the corresponding author upon reasonable request.

Acknowledgments: The authors sincerely thank the reviewers and the editors for their valuable comments and suggestions, which will make this paper more readable.

Conflicts of Interest: The authors declare no conflict of interest.

References

1. Qin, X.; An, N.T. Smoothing algorithms for computing the projection onto a minkowski sum of convex sets. *Comput. Optim. Appl.* **2019**, *74*, 821–850. [CrossRef]
2. Combettes, P.L.; Wajs, V.R. Signal recovery by proximal forward-backward splitting. *Multiscale Model. Simul.* **2005**, *4*, 1168–1200. [CrossRef]
3. Izuchukwu, C.; Reich, S.; Shehu, Y. Strong convergence of forward–reflected–backward splitting methods for solving monotone inclusions with applications to image restoration and optimal control. *J. Sci. Comput.* **2023**, *94*, 73. [CrossRef] [CrossRef]
4. Briceño-Arias, L.M.; Combettes, P.L. Monotone operator methods for nash equilibria in non-potential games. *Comput. Anal. Math.* **2013**, *50*, 143–159. [CrossRef]
5. An, N.T.; Nam, N.M.; Qin, X. Solving k-center problems involving sets based on optimization techniques. *J. Glob. Optim.* **2020**, *76*, 189–209. [CrossRef]
6. Nemirovski, A.; Juditsky, A.B.; Lan, G.; Shapiro, A. Robust stochastic approximation approach to stochastic programming. *SIAM J. Optim.* **2009**, *19*, 1574–1609. [CrossRef]
7. Tang, Y.; Wen, M.; Zeng, T. Preconditioned three-operator splitting algorithm with applications to image restoration. *J. Sci. Comput.* **2022**, *92*, 106. [CrossRef] [CrossRef]
8. Davis, D.; Yin, W. A three-operator splitting scheme and its optimization applications. *Set-Valued Var. Anal.* **2017**, *25*, 829–858. [CrossRef]
9. Cui, F.; Tang, Y.; Yang, Y. An inertial three-operator splitting algorithm with applications to image inpainting. *arXiv* **2019**, arXiv:1904.11684.
10. Malitsky, Y.; Tam, M.K. A forward-backward splitting method for monotone inclusions without cocoercivity. *SIAM J. Optim.* **2020**, *30*, 1451–1472. [CrossRef]
11. Zong, C.; Tang, Y.; Zhang, G. An inertial semi-forward-reflected-backward splitting and its application. *Acta Math. Sin. Engl. Ser.* **2022**, *38*, 443–464. [CrossRef]
12. Zhang, C.; Chen, J. A parameterized three-operator splitting algorithm and its expansion. *J. Nonlinear Var. Anal.* **2021**, *5*, 211–226. [CrossRef]
13. Wang, D.; Wang, X. A parameterized Douglas-Rachford algorithm. *Comput. Optim. Appl.* **2021**, *164*, 263–284. [CrossRef]
14. Ryu, E.K.; Vũ, B.C. Finding the forward-Douglas–Rachford-forward method. *J. Optim. Theory Appl.* **2020**, *184*, 858–876. [CrossRef]
15. Yan, M. A primal-dual three-operator splitting scheme. *arXiv* **2016**, arXiv:1611.09805v1.

16. Briceño-Arias, L.M.; Davis, D. Forward-backward-half forward algorithm for solving monotone inclusions. *SIAM J. Optim.* **2018**, *28*, 2839–2871. [CrossRef]
17. Polyak, B.T. Some methods of speeding up the convergence of iteration methods. *USSR Comput. Math. Math. Phys.* **1964**, *4*, 1–17. [CrossRef]
18. Chen, C.; Chan, R.H.; Ma, S.; Yang, J. Inertial proximal ADMM for linearly constrained separable convex optimization. *SIAM J. Imaging Sci.* **2015**, *8*, 2239–2267. [CrossRef]
19. Combettes, P.L.; Glaudin, L.E. Quasi-nonexpansive iterations on the affine hull of orbits: From Mann's mean value algorithm to inertial methods. *SIAM J. Optim.* **2017**, *27*, 2356–2380. [CrossRef]
20. Qin, X.; Wang, L.; Yao, J.C. Inertial splitting method for maximal monotone mappings. *J. Nonlinear Convex. Anal.* **2020**, *21*, 2325–2333.
21. Dey, S. A hybrid inertial and contraction proximal point algorithm for monotone variational inclusions. *Numer. Algorithms* **2023**, *93*, 1–25. [CrossRef] [CrossRef]
22. Ochs, P.; Chen, Y.; Brox, T.; Pock, T. iPiano: Inertial proximal algorithm for nonconvex optimization. *SIAM J. Imaging Sci.* **2014**, *7*, 1388–1419. [CrossRef]
23. Dong, Q.L.; Lu, Y.Y.; Yang, J.F. The extragradient algorithm with inertial effects for solving the variational inequality. *Optimization* **2016**, *65*, 2217–2226. [CrossRef]
24. Chen, G.H.G.; Rockafellar, R.T. Convergence rates in forward-backward splitting. *SIAM J. Optim.* **1997**, *7*, 421–444. [CrossRef]
25. Combettes, P.L.; Vũ, B.C. Variable metric forward-backward splitting with applications to monotone inclusions in duality. *Optimization* **2014**, *63*, 1289–1318. [CrossRef]
26. Bonettini, S.; Porta, F.; Ruggiero, V. A variable metric forward-backward method with extrapolation. *SIAM J. Sci. Comput.* **2016**, *38*, A2558–A2584. [CrossRef]
27. Salzo, S. The variable metric forward-backward splitting algorithm under mild differentiability assumptions. *SIAM J. Optim.* **2017**, *27*, 2153–2181. [CrossRef] [CrossRef]
28. Audrey, R.; Yves, W. Variable metric forward-backward algorithm for composite minimization problems. *SIAM J. Optim.* **2021**, *31*, 1215–1241. [CrossRef]
29. Vũ, B.C.; Papadimitriou, D. A nonlinearly preconditioned forward-backward splitting method and applications. *Numer. Funct. Anal. Optim.* **2022**, *42*, 1880–1895. [CrossRef] [CrossRef]
30. Bonettini, S.; Rebegoldi, S.; Ruggiero, V. Inertial variable metric techniques for the inexact forward-backward algorithm. *SIAM J. Sci. Comput.* **2018**, *40*, A3180–A3210. [CrossRef]
31. Lorenz, D.; Pock, T. An inertial forward-backward algorithm for monotone inclusions. *J. Math. Imaging Vis.* **2015**, *51*, 311–325. [CrossRef]
32. Cui, F.; Tang, Y.; Zhu, C. Convergence analysis of a variable metric forward-backward splitting algorithm with applications. *J. Inequal. Appl.* **2019**, *141*, 1–27. [CrossRef]
33. Bauschke, H.H.; Combettes, P.L. CMS books in mathematics. In *Convex Analysis and Monotone Operator Theory in Hilbert Spaces*, 2nd ed.; Springer: Berlin/Heidelberg, Germany, 2017.
34. Aragón-Artacho, F.J.; Torregrosa-Belén, D. A Direct Proof of Convergence of Davis-Yin Splitting Algorithm Allowing Larger Stepsizes. *Set-Valued Var. Anal.* **2022**, *30*, 1011–1029. [CrossRef]
35. Marino, G.; Xu, H.K. Convergence of generalized proximal point algorithms. *Commun. Pure Appl. Anal.* **2004**, *3*, 791–808. [CrossRef]
36. Combettes, P.L.; Vũ, B.C. Variable metric quasi-Fejér monotonicity. *Nonlinear Anal.* **2012**, *78*, 17–31. [CrossRef]

axioms

MDPI

Article

Constraint Qualifications for Vector Optimization Problems in Real Topological Spaces

Renying Zeng

Mathematics Department, Saskatchewan Polytechnic, Saskatoon, SK S7L 4J7, Canada; renying.zeng@saskpolytech.ca

Abstract: In this paper, we introduce a series of definitions of generalized affine functions for vector-valued functions by use of "linear set". We prove that our generalized affine functions have some similar properties to generalized convex functions. We present examples to show that our generalized affinenesses are different from one another, and also provide an example to show that our definition of presubaffinelikeness is non-trivial; presubaffinelikeness is the weakest generalized affineness introduced in this article. We work with optimization problems that are defined and taking values in linear topological spaces. We devote to the study of constraint qualifications, and derive some optimality conditions as well as a strong duality theorem. Our optimization problems have inequality constraints, equality constraints, and abstract constraints; our inequality constraints are generalized convex functions and equality constraints are generalized affine functions.

Keywords: real linear topological spaces; affine functions; generalized affine functions; convex functions; generalized convex functions; constraint qualifications

MSC: 90C26; 90C29; 90C48

1. Introduction and Preliminary

The theory of vector optimization is at the crossroads of many subjects. The terms "minimum," "maximum," and "optimum" are in line with a mathematical tradition, while words such as "efficient" or "non-dominated" find larger use in business-related topics. Historically, linear programs were the focus in the optimization community, and initially, it was thought that the major divide was between linear and nonlinear optimization problems; later, people discovered that some nonlinear problems were much harder than others, and the "right" divide was between convex and nonconvex problems. The author has determined that affineness and generalized affinenesses are also very useful for the subject "optimization".

Suppose X, Y are real linear topological spaces [1].

A subset $B \subseteq X$ is called a linear set if B is a nonempty vector subspace of X.

A subset $B \subseteq X$ is called an affine set if the line passing through any two points of B is entirely contained in B (i.e., $\alpha x_1 + (1-\alpha)x_2 \in B$ whenever $x_1, x_2 \in B$ and $\alpha \in R$);

A subset $B \subseteq X$ is called a convex set if any segment with endpoints in B is contained in B (i.e., $\alpha x_1 + (1-\alpha)x_2 \in B$ whenever $x_1, x_2 \in B$ and $\alpha \in [0,1]$).

Each linear set is affine, and each affine set is convex. Moreover, any translation of an affine (convex, respectively) set is affine (convex, resp.). It is known that a set B is linear if and only if B is affine and contains the zero point 0_X of X; a set B is affine if and only if B is a translation of a linear set.

A subset Y_+ of Y is said to be a cone if $\lambda y \in Y_+$ for all $y \in Y_+$ and $\lambda \geq 0$. We denote by 0_Y the zero element in the topological vector space Y and simply by 0 if there is no confusion. A convex cone is one for which $\lambda_1 y_1 + \lambda_2 y_2 \in Y_+$ for all $y_1, y_2 \in Y_+$ and $\lambda_1, \lambda_2 \geq 0$. A pointed cone is one for which $Y_+ \cap (-Y_+) = \{0\}$. Let Y be a real topological vector space with pointed convex cone Y_+. We denote the partial order induced by Y_+ as follows:

$$y_1 \succ y_2 \text{iff} y_1 - y_2 \in Y_+, \text{ or, } y_1 \prec y_2 \text{iff} y_1 - y_2 \in -Y_+$$

$$y_1 \succ\succ y_2 \text{iff} y_1 - y_2 \in \text{int}Y_+, \text{ or } y_1 \prec\prec y_2 \text{iff} y_1 - y_2 \in -\text{int}Y_+$$

where intY_+ denotes the topological interior of a set Y_+.

A function f: $X \rightarrow Y$ is said to be linear if

$$f(\alpha x_1 + \beta x_2) = \alpha f(x_1) + \beta f(x_2)$$

whenever $x_1, x_2 \in X$ and $\alpha, \beta \in R$; f is said to be affine if

$$f(\alpha x_1 + (1-\alpha)x_2) = \alpha f(x_1) + (1-\alpha)f(x_2)$$

whenever $x_1, x_2 \in D, \alpha \in R$; and f is said to be convex if

$$\alpha f(x_1) + (1-\alpha)f(x_2) \prec f(\alpha x_1 + (1-\alpha)x_2)$$

whenever $x_1, x_2 \in D, \alpha \in [0,1]$.

In the next section, we generalize the definition of affine function, prove that our generalized affine functions have some similar properties with generalized convex functions, and present some examples which show that our generalized affinenesses are not equivalent to one another.

In Section 3, we recall some existing definitions of generalized convexities, which are very comparable with the definitions of generalized affinenesses introduced in this article.

Section 4 works with optimization problems that are defined and taking values in linear topological spaces, devotes to the study of constraint qualifications, and derives some optimality conditions as well as a strong duality theorem.

2. Generalized Affinenesses

A function f: $D \subseteq X \rightarrow Y$ is said to be affine on D if $\forall x_1, x_2 \in D, \forall \alpha \in R$, there holds

$$\alpha f(x_1) + (1-\alpha)f(x_2) = f(\alpha x_1 + (1-\alpha)x_2)$$

We introduce here the following definitions of generalized affine functions.

Definition 1. *A function f: $D \subseteq X \rightarrow Y$ is said to be affinelike on D if $\forall x_1, x_2 \in D, \forall \alpha \in R$, $\exists x_3 \in D$ such that*

$$\alpha f(x_1) + (1-\alpha)f(x_2) = f(x_3)$$

Definition 2. *A function f: $D \subseteq X \rightarrow Y$ is said to be preaffinelike on D if $\forall x_1, x_2 \in D, \forall \alpha \in R$, $\exists x_3 \in D$, $\exists \tau \in R \backslash \{0\}$ such that*

$$\alpha f(x_1) + (1-\alpha)f(x_2) = \tau f(x_3)$$

In the following Definitions 3 and 4, we assume that $B \subseteq Y$ is any given linear set.

Definition 3. *A function f: $D \subseteq X \rightarrow Y$ is said to be B-subaffinelike on D if $\forall x_1, x_2 \in D$, $\forall \alpha \in R$, $\exists u \in B$, $\exists x_3 \in D$ such that*

$$u + \alpha f(x_1) + (1-\alpha)f(x_2) = f(x_3)$$

Definition 4. *A function f: $D \subseteq X \to Y$ is said to be B-presubaffinelike on D if* $\forall x_1$, $x_2 \in D$, $\forall \alpha \in R$, $\exists u \in B$, $\exists x_3 \in D$, $\exists \tau \in R \backslash \{0\}$ *such that*

$$u + \alpha f(x_1) + (1-\alpha) f(x_2) = \tau f(x_3)$$

For any linear set B, since $0 \in B$, we may take $u = 0$. So, affinelikeness implies subaffinelikeness, and preaffinelikeness implies presubaffinelikeness.

It is obvious that affineness implies preaffineness, and the following Example 1 shows that the converse is not true.

Example 1. *An example of an affinelike function which is not an affine function.*

It is known that a function is an affine function if and only it is in the form of $f(x) = ax + b$; therefore

$$f(x) = x^3, x \in R$$

is not an affine function.

However, f is affinelike. $\forall x_1, x_2 \in R, \forall \alpha \in R$, taking

$$x_3 = [\alpha f(x_1) + (1-\alpha) f(x_2)]^{1/3}$$

then

$$\alpha f(x_1) + (1-\alpha) f(x_2) = f(x_3)$$

Similarly, affinelikeness implies preaffinelikeness ($\tau = 1$), and presubaffinelikeness implies subaffinelikeness. The following Example 2 shows that a preaffinelike function is not necessary to be an affinelike function.

Example 2. *An example of a preaffinelike function which is not an affinelike function.*

Consider the function $f(x) = x^2, x \in R$

Take $x_1 = 0, x_2 = 1, \alpha = 2$, then $\alpha f(x_1) + (1-\alpha) f(x_2) = -1$; but

$$\forall x_3 \in R, f(x_3) = x_3^2 \geq 0$$

therefore

$$\alpha f(x_1) + (1-\alpha) f(x_2) \neq f(x_3), \forall x_3 \in R$$

So f is not affinelike.

But f is an preaffinelike function. For $\forall x_1, x_2 \in R, \forall \alpha \in R$, taking $\tau = 1$ if $\alpha f(x_1) + (1-\alpha) f(x_2) \geq 0$, $\tau = -1$ if $\alpha f(x_1) + (1-\alpha) f(x_2) < 0$, then

$$\alpha f(x_1) + (1-\alpha) f(x_2) = \tau f(x_3)$$

where $x_3 = |\alpha f(x_1) + (1-\alpha) f(x_2)|^{1/2}$.

Example 3. *An example of a subaffinelike function which is not an affinelike function.*

Consider the function $f(x) = x^3 + 8, x \in D = [0,1]$, and the linear set $B = R$.

$\forall x_1, x_2 \in D = [0,1], \forall \alpha \in R$, taking $x_3 = 1 \in D$, $u = 8 - [\alpha f(x_1) + (1-\alpha) f(x_2)] \in B$, then

$$u + \alpha f(x_1) + (1-\alpha) f(x_2) = f(x_3)$$

therefore $f(x) = x^3 + 8, x \in [0,1]$ is B-subaffinelike on $D = [0,1]$.

$f(x) = x^3+8, x \in [0,1]$ is not affinelike on $D = [0,1]$. Actually, for $\alpha = -8 \in R$, $x_1 = 1 \in D, x_2 = 0 \in D = [0,1]$, one has $\alpha f(x_1) + (1-\alpha)f(x_2) = 0$, but

$$f(x_3) = x_3^3 + 8 \neq 0, \forall x \in [0,1]$$

hence

$$\alpha f(x_1) + (1-\alpha)f(x_2) \neq f(x_3),\ \forall x_3 \in D = [0,1]$$

Example 4. *An example of a presubaffinelike function which is not a preaffinelike function.*

Actually, the function in Example 3 is subaffinelike, therefore it is presubaffinelike on D.

However, for $\alpha = 9 \in R, x_1 = 0 \in D, x_2 = 1 \in D$, one has

$$\alpha f(x_1) + (1-\alpha)f(x_2) = 0$$

but

$$f(x_3) = x_3^3 - 8 \neq 0, \forall x \in [0,1]$$

Hence

$$\alpha f(x_1) + (1-\alpha)f(x_2) \neq \tau f(x_3),\ \forall x_3 \in D = [0,1],\ \forall \tau \neq 0$$

This shows that the function f is not preaffinelike on D.

Example 5. *An example of a presubaffinelike function which is not a subaffinelike function.*

Consider the function $f(x,y) = (x^2, y^2), x, y \in R$.
Take the 2-dimensional linear set $B = \{(x,y) : y = -x, x \in R\}$.
Take $\alpha = 3, (x_1, y_1) = (0,0), (x_2, y_2) = (1,1)$, then

$$\alpha f(x_1, y_1) + (1-\alpha)f(x_2, y_2) = (-2, -2)$$

Either $x-2$ or $-x-2$ must be negative; but $x_3^2 \geq 0, y_3^2 \geq 0,\ \forall u = (x, -x) \in B$; therefore

$$u + \alpha f(x_1, y_1) + (1-\alpha)f(x_2, y_2) = (x-2, -x-2) \neq f(x_3, y_3) = (x_3^2, y_3^2)$$

And so, $f(x,y) = (x^2, y^2)$ is not B-subaffinelike.
However, $f(x,y) = (x^2, y^2)$ is B-presubaffinelike.

$$\forall x_1, x_2 \in [0,1], \forall \alpha \in R$$

$$\alpha f(x_1, y_1) + (1-\alpha)f(x_2, y_2) = (\alpha x_1^2 + (1-\alpha)x_2^2, \alpha y_1^2 + (1-\alpha)y_2^2)$$

Case 1. If both of $\alpha x_1^2 + (1-\alpha)x_2^2$, $\alpha y_1^2 + (1-\alpha)y_2^2$ are positive, we take $u = (0,0)$, $\tau = 1$, $x_3 = |\alpha x_1^2 + (1-\alpha)x_2^2|_{1/2}$, $y_3 = |\alpha y_1^2 + (1-\alpha)y_2^2|^{1/2}$, then

$$u + \alpha f(x_1) + (1-\alpha)f(x_2) = \tau f(x_3)$$

Case 2. If both of $\alpha x_1^2 + (1-\alpha)x_2^2$, $\alpha y_1^2 + (1-\alpha)y_2^2$ are negative, we take $u = (0,0)$, $\tau = -1$, $x_3 = |\alpha x_1^2 + (1-\alpha)x_2^2|_{1/2}$, $y_3 = |\alpha y_1^2 + (1-\alpha)y_2^2|^{1/2}$, then

$$u + \alpha f(x_1) + (1-\alpha)f(x_2) = \tau f(x_3)$$

Case 3. If one of $\alpha x_1^2 + (1-\alpha)x_2^2$, $\alpha y_1^2 + (1-\alpha)y_2^2$ is negative, and the other is non-negative, we take

$$x = [(\alpha y_1^2 + (1-\alpha)y_2^2) - (\alpha x_1^2 + (1-\alpha)x_2^2)]/2, \text{ and } u = (x, -x) \in B$$

Then

$$\begin{aligned} & x + \alpha x_1^2 + (1-\alpha)x_2^2 \\ & = -x + \alpha y_1^2 + (1-\alpha)y_2^2 \\ & = [\alpha x_1^2 + (1-\alpha)x_2^2 + \alpha y_1^2 + (1-\alpha)y_2^2]/2 \end{aligned}$$

And so $x + \alpha x_1^2 + (1-\alpha)x_2^2, -x + \alpha y_1^2 + (1-\alpha)y_2^2$ are both non-negative or both negative; taking $\tau = 1$ or $\tau = -1$, respectively, one has

$$u + \alpha f(x_1) + (1-\alpha)f(x_2) = \tau f(x_3)$$

where

$$x_3 = \left|x + \alpha x_1^2 + (1-\alpha)x_2^2\right|_{1/2}, y_3 = \left|-x + \alpha y_1^2 + (1-\alpha)y_2^2\right|^{1/2}$$

Therefore, $f(x,y) = (x^2, y^2)$ is B-presubaffinelike.

Example 6. *An example of a subaffinelike function which is not a preaffinelike function.*

Consider the function $f(x,y) = (x^2, y^2), x, y \in R$.
Take the 2-dimensional linear set $B = \{(x,y) : y = x, x \in R\}$.
Take $x_1 = 0, x_2 = 1, \alpha = 2$, then

$$\begin{aligned} & \alpha f(x_1, y_1) + (1-\alpha)f(x_2, y_2) \\ & = (\alpha x_1^2 + (1-\alpha)x_2^2, \alpha y_1^2 + (1-\alpha)y_2^2) \\ & = (-2, 3) \\ & \neq \tau f(x_3, y_3) = (\tau x_3^2, \tau y_3^2). \end{aligned}$$

In the above inequality, we note that either $\tau x_3^2 \geq 0, \tau y_3^2 \geq 0$ or $\tau x_3^2 \leq 0, \tau y_3^2 \leq 0$, $\forall \tau \neq 0$.

Therefore, $f(x,y) = (x^2, y^2)$ is not preaffinelike.
However, $f(x,y) = (x^2, y^2), x, y \in R$ is B-subaffinelike.
In fact, $\forall x_1, x_2 \in R, \forall \alpha \in R$, we may choose $u = (x, x) \in B$ with x large enough such that

$$u + \alpha f(x_1, y_1) + (1-\alpha)f(x_2, y_2) = (x + \alpha x_1^2 + (1-\alpha)x_2^2, x + \alpha y_1^2 + (1-\alpha)y_2^2) \succ 0$$

Then,

$$u + \alpha f(x_1, y_1) + (1-\alpha)f(x_2, y_2) = f(x_3, y_3)$$

where

$$x_3 = (x + \alpha x_1^2 + (1-\alpha)x_2^2)^{1/2} \text{and } y_3 = (x + \alpha y_1^2 + (1-\alpha)y_2^2))^{1/2}$$

Example 7. *An example of a preaffinelike function which is not a subaffinelike function.*

Consider the function $f(x,y) = (x^2, -x^2), x, y \in R$.
Take the 2-dimensional linear set $B = \{(x,y) : y = x, x \in R\}$.
Take $x_1 = 0, x_2 = 1, \alpha = 2$, then

$$\alpha f(x_1, y_1) + (1-\alpha)f(x_2, y_2) = (\alpha x_1^2 + (1-\alpha)x_2^2, -(\alpha x_1^2 + (1-\alpha)x_2^2)) = (-1, 1)$$

So, $\forall u = (x, x) \in B$,

$$u + \alpha f(x_1, y_1) + (1-\alpha)f(x_2, y_2) == (x+1, x-1)$$

However, for $f(x_3, y_3) = (x_3^2, -x_3^2), \forall x_3 \in R$,

$$(x_3^2, -x_3^2) \neq (x-1, x+1), \forall x, x_3 \in R \tag{1}$$

Actually, if $x = 0$, it is obvious that $(x_3^2, -x_3^2) \neq (-1, 1)$; if $x \neq 0$, the right side of (1) implies that $x_3^2 + (-x_3^2) = 0$, and the left side of (1) is $(x-1) + (x+1) = 2x \neq 0$. This proves that the inequality (1) must be true. Consequently,

$$u + \alpha f(x_1, y_1) + (1-\alpha) f(x_2, y_2) \neq f(x_3, y_3), \forall \alpha \in R, \forall x_1, x_2, x_3, y_1, y_2, y_3 \in R$$

So $f(x,y) = (x^2, -x^2), x, y \in R$ is not B-subaffinelike.

On the other hand, $\forall x_1, x_2 \in R, \forall \alpha \in R$, we may take $\tau = 1$ if $\alpha x_1^2 + (1-\alpha) x_2^2 \geq 0$ or $\tau = -1$ if $\alpha x_1^2 + (1-\alpha) x_2^2 \leq 0$, then

$$\begin{aligned} &\alpha f(x_1, y_1) + (1-\alpha) f(x_2, y_2) \\ &= (\alpha x_1^2 + (1-\alpha) x_2^2, -(\alpha x_1^2 + (1-\alpha) x_2^2)) \\ &= \tau (x_3^2, -x_3^2) \\ &= \tau f(x_3, y_3) \end{aligned}$$

where $x_3 = \left|\alpha x_1^2 + (1-\alpha) x_2^2\right|^{1/2}$.

Therefore, $f(x,y) = (x^2, -x^2), x, y \in R$ is preaffinelike.

So far, we have showed the following relationships (where subaffinelikeness and presubaffinelikeness are related to "a given linear set B"):

$$\text{affineness} \underset{\textit{not true}}{\overset{\textit{true}}{\rightleftarrows}} \text{affinelikeness} \underset{\textit{not true}}{\overset{\textit{true}}{\rightleftarrows}} \text{preaffinelikeness}$$

$$\textit{nottrue} \uparrow\downarrow \textit{true} \quad \textit{nottrue} \swarrow\nearrow \textit{nottrue} \quad \textit{nottrue} \uparrow\downarrow \textit{true}$$

$$\text{subaffinelikeness} \underset{\textit{not true}}{\overset{\textit{true}}{\rightleftarrows}} \text{presubaffinelikeness}$$

The following Proposition 1 is very similar to the corresponding results for generalized convexities (see Proposition 2).

Proposition 1. *Suppose f: $D \subseteq X \to Y$ is a function, $B \subseteq Y$* a *given linear set, and t is any real scalar.*

(a) *f is affinelike on D if and only if f (D) is an affine set;*
(b) *f is preaffinelike on D if and only if $\cup_{t \in R \setminus \{0\}} t f(D)$ is an affine set;*
(c) *f is B-subaffinelike on D if and only if f (D) + B is an affine set;*
(d) *f is B-presubaffinelike on D if and only if $\cup_{t \in R \setminus \{0\}} t f(D)$+ B is an affine set.*

Proof. (a) If f is affinelike on D, $\forall f(x_1), f(x_2) \in f(D), \forall \alpha \in R, \exists x_3 \in D$ such that

$$\alpha f(x_1) + (1-\alpha) f(x_2) = f(x_3) \in f(D)$$

Therefore, f (D) is an affine set.

On the other hand, assume that f (D) is an affine set. $\forall x_1, x_2 \in D, \forall \alpha \in R$, we have

$$\alpha f(x_1) + (1-\alpha) f(x_2) \in f(D)$$

Therefore, $\exists x_3 \in D$ such that

$$\alpha f(x_1) + (1-\alpha) f(x_2) = f(x_3)$$

And hence f is affinelike on D.

(b) Assume f is a preaffinelike function.

$\forall y_1, y_2 \in \cup_{t\in R\setminus\{0\}} tf(D)$, $\forall \alpha \in R$, $\exists x_1, x_2 \in D$, $\exists t_1, t_2 \in R\setminus\{0\}$ for $\exists x_3 \in D$, $\exists t \in R\setminus\{0\}$ such that

$$\begin{aligned} &\alpha y_1 + (1-\alpha)y_2 \\ &= \alpha t_1 f(x_1) + (1-\alpha)t_2 f(x_2) \\ &= (\alpha t_1 + (1-\alpha)t_2)[\tfrac{\alpha t_1}{\alpha t_1+(1-\alpha)t_2} f(x_1) + \tfrac{(1-\alpha)t_2}{\alpha t_1+(1-\alpha)t_2} f(x_2)]. \end{aligned}$$

Since f is preaffinelike, $\exists x_3 \in D, \exists t \in R\setminus\{0\}$ such that

$$\frac{\alpha t_1}{\alpha t_1 + (1-\alpha)t_2} f(x_1) + \frac{(1-\alpha)t_2}{\alpha t_1 + (1-\alpha)t_2} f(x_2) = tf(x_3)$$

Therefore

$$\begin{aligned} &\alpha y_1 + (1-\alpha)y_2 \\ &= \alpha t_1 f(x_1) + (1-\alpha)t_2 f(x_2) \\ &= (\alpha t_1 + (1-\alpha)t_2)[\tfrac{\alpha t_1}{\alpha t_1+(1-\alpha)t_2} f(x_1) + \tfrac{(1-\alpha)t_2}{\alpha t_1+(1-\alpha)t_2} f(x_2)] \\ &= (\alpha t_1 + (1-\alpha)t_2)tf(x_3) \\ &= \tau f(x_3) \in \cup_{t\in R\setminus\{0\}} tf(D) \end{aligned}$$

where $\tau = (\alpha t_1 + (1-\alpha)t_2)t$. Consequently, $\cup_{t\in R\setminus\{0\}} tf(D)$ is an affine set.

On the other hand, suppose that $\cup_{t\in R\setminus\{0\}} tf(D)$ is an affine set. Then, $\forall x_1, x_2 \in D$, $\forall \alpha \in R$, since $f(x_1), f(x_2) \in \cup_{t\in R\setminus\{0\}} tf(D)$,

$$\alpha f(x_1) + (1-\alpha)f(x_2) \in \cup_{t\in R\setminus\{0\}} tf(D)$$

Therefore, $\exists x_3 \in D, \exists \tau \neq 0$ such that

$$\alpha f(x_1) + (1-\alpha)f(x_2) = \tau f(x_3)$$

Then, f is an affinelike function.

(c) Assume that f is B-subaffinelike.

$\forall y_1, y_2 \in f(D) + B$, $\exists x_1, x_2 \in D$, $\exists b_1, b_2 \in B$, such that $y_1 = f(x_1) + b_1$ and $y_2 = f(x_2) + b_2$. The subaffinelikeness of f implies that $\forall \alpha \in R$, $\exists x_3 \in D$, and $\exists v \in B$ such that

$$v + \alpha f(x_1) + (1-\alpha)f(x_2) = f(x_3)$$

i.e.,

$$\alpha f(x_1) + (1-\alpha)f(x_2) = f(x_3) - v$$

Therefore

$$\begin{aligned} &\alpha y_1 + (1-\alpha)y_2 \\ &= \alpha(f(x_1) + b_1) + (1-\alpha)(f(x_2) + b_2) \\ &= f(x_3) - v + \alpha b_1 + (1-\alpha)b_2 \\ &= f(x_3) + u \in f(D) + B \end{aligned}$$

where $u = -v + \alpha b_1 + (1-\alpha)b_2 \in B$

Then, $f(D) + B$ is an affine set.

On the other hand, assume that $f(D) + B$ is an affine set.

$\forall x_1, x_2 \in D, \forall \alpha \in R, \exists b_1, b_2, b_3 \in B, \exists x_3 \in D$, such that

$$\alpha(f(x_1) + b_1) + (1-\alpha)(f(x_2) + b_2) = f(x_3) + b_3$$

i.e.,

$$u + \alpha f(x_1) + (1-\alpha)f(x_2) = f(x_3)$$

where $\alpha b_1 + (1-\alpha)b_2 - b_3 \in B$. And hence f is B-subaffinelike.

(d) Suppose f is a B-presubaffinelike function.

$\forall y_1, y_2 \in \cup_{t\in R\backslash\{0\}} tf(D) + B$, similar to the proof of (b),$\forall \alpha \in R$, $\exists x_1, x_2, x_3 \in D$, $\exists b_1, b_2, b_3, u \in B$, $\exists t_1, t_2, t_3 \in R\backslash\{0\}$, for which $y_1 = t_1 f(x_1) + b_1, y_2 = t_2 f(x_2) + b_2$, and

$$\begin{aligned}
&\alpha y_1 + (1-\alpha)y_2 \\
&= \alpha t_1 f(x_1) + (1-\alpha)t_2 f(x_2) + \alpha b_1 + (1-\alpha)b_2 \\
&= (\alpha t_1 + (1-\alpha)t_2)[t_3 f(x_3) + b_3 - u] + \alpha b_1 + (1-\alpha)b_2 \\
&= (\alpha t_1 + (1-\alpha)t_2)t_3 f(x_3) + \alpha b_1 + (1-\alpha)b_2 + (\alpha t_1 + (1-\alpha)t_2)(b_3 - u) \\
&\in tf(D) + B \subseteq \cup_{t\in R\backslash\{0\}} tf(D) + B
\end{aligned}$$

where $t = (\alpha t_1 + (1-\alpha)t_2)t_3$. This proves that $\cup_{t\in R\backslash\{0\}} tf(D)+ B$ is an affine set.

On the other hand, assume that $\cup_{t\in R\backslash\{0\}} tf(D)+ B$ is an affine set.

$\forall x_1, x_2 \in D, \forall b_1, b_2 \in B, \forall \alpha \in R$, since $f(x_1) + b_1, f(x_2) + b_2 \in \cup_{t\in R\backslash\{0\}} tf(D) + B$, $\exists x_3 \in D, \exists b_3 \in B, \exists t \in R\backslash\{0\}$ such that

$$\alpha(f(x_1) + b_1) + (1-\alpha)(f(x_2) + b_2) = tf(x_3) + b_3$$

Therefore,

$$\alpha b_1 + (1-\alpha)b_2 - b_3 + \alpha f(x_1) + (1-\alpha)f(x_2) = tf(x_3)$$

i.e.,

$$u + \alpha f(x_1) + (1-\alpha)f(x_2) = tf(x_3)$$

where $u = \alpha b_1 + (1-\alpha)b_2 - b_3 \in B$. And so f is B-presubaffinelike. □

The presubaffineness is the weakest one in the series of the generalized affinenesses introduced here. The following example shows that our definition of presubaffinelikeness is not trivial.

Example 8. *An example of non-presubaffinelike function.*

Consider the function $f(x,y,z) = (x^2, y^2, z^2), x, y, z \in R$.

Take the linear set $B = \{(x, -x, 0) : x \in R\}$.

Take $\alpha = 5, (x_1, y_1, z_1) = (0,0,1), (x_2, y_2, z_2) = (1,1,0)$, then

$$\alpha f(x_1, y_1, z_1) + (1-\alpha)f(x_2, y_2, z_2) = (-4, -4, 5)$$

Either $x-4$ or $-x-4$ must be negative, but $x_3^2 \ge 0, y_3^2 \ge 0$ hold for $\forall u = (x, -x, 0) \in B$; therefore, for any scalar $\tau \neq 0$

$$u + \alpha f(x_1, y_1, z_1) + (1-\alpha)f(x_2, y_2, z_2) = (x-4, -x-4, 5) \neq \tau f(x_3, y_3, z_3) = \tau(x_3^2, y_3^2, z_3^2)$$

(Actually, $\forall \tau < 0$, one has $\tau z_3^2 \le 0 < 5$; and $\forall \tau > 0$, either $\tau(x-4) < 0$ or $\tau(-x-4) < 0$, then, either $\tau(x-4) < 0 \le \tau x_3^2$ or $\tau(-x-4) < 0 \le \tau y_3^2$).

And so, $f(x,y) = (x^2, y^2)$ is not B-presubaffinelike.

3. Generalized Convexities

In this section, we recall some existing definitions of generalized convexities, which are very comparable with the definitions of generalized affinenesses introduced in this article.

Let Y be a topological vector space, $D \subseteq X$ be a nonempty set, and Y_+ be a convex cone in Y and $\text{int}Y_+ \neq \emptyset$.

It is known that a function $f\colon D \to Y$ is said to be Y_+-convex on D if, for all $x_1, x_2 \in D$, $\alpha \in [0,1]$, there holds

$$\alpha f(x_1) + (1-\alpha)f(x_2) \prec f(\alpha x_1 + (1-\alpha)x_2)$$

The following Definition 5 was introduced in Fan [2].

Definition 5. *A function* $f\colon D \to Y$ *is said to be* Y_+*-convexlike on* D *if* $\forall$, $\forall \alpha \in [0,1]$, $\exists\, x_3 \in D$ *such that*

$$\alpha f(x_1) + (1-\alpha) f(x_2) \prec f(x_3)$$

We may define Y_+-preconvexlike functions as follows.

Definition 6. *A function* $f\colon D \to Y$ *is said to be* Y_+*-preconvexlike on* D *if* $\forall x_1, x_2 \in D$, $\forall\, \alpha \in [0,1]$, $\exists\, x_3 \in D$, $\exists \tau > 0$ *such that*

$$\alpha f(x_1) + (1-\alpha) f(x_2) \prec \tau f(x_3).$$

Definition 7 was introduced by Jeyakumar [3].

Definition 7. *A function* $f\colon D \to Y$ *is said to be* Y_+*-subconvexlike on* D *if* $\forall u \in \mathrm{int}Y_+$, $\forall x_1, x_2 \in D$, $\forall \alpha \in [0,1]$, $\exists x_3 \in D$ *such that*

$$u + \alpha f(x_1) + (1-\alpha) f(x_2) \prec f(x_3)$$

In fact, in Jeyakumar [3], the definition of subconvexlike was introduced as the following form Definition 8.

Definition 8. *A function* $f\colon D \to Y$ *is said to be* Y_+*-subconvexlike on* D *if* $\exists u \in \mathrm{int}Y_+$, $\forall \varepsilon > 0$, $\forall x_1, x_2 \in D$, $\forall \alpha \in [0,1]$, $\exists x_3 \in D$ *such that*

$$\varepsilon u + \alpha f(x_1) + (1-\alpha) f(x_2) \prec f(x_3)$$

Li and Wang ([4]) proved that: A function $f\colon D \to Y$ is Y_+-subconvexlike on D by Definition 8 if and only if $\forall u \in \mathrm{int}Y_+$, $\forall x_1, x_2 \in D$, $\forall \alpha \in [0,1]$, $\exists x_3 \in D$ such that

$$u + \alpha f(x_1) + (1-\alpha) f(x_2) \prec f(x_3)$$

From the definitions above, one may introduce the following definition of presubconvexlike functions.

Definition 9. *A function* $f\colon D \to Y$ *is said to be* Y_+*-presubconvexlike on* D *if* $\forall u \in \mathrm{int}Y_+$, $\forall\, x_1, x_2 \in D$, $\forall \alpha \in [0,1]$, $\exists x_3 \in D$, $\exists \tau > 0$ *such that*

$$u + \alpha f(x_1) + (1-\alpha) f(x_2) \prec \tau f(x_3)$$

And, similar to ([4]), one can prove that a function $f\colon D \to Y$ is Y_+-presubconvexlike on D if and only if $\exists u \in \mathrm{int}Y_+$, $\forall \varepsilon > 0$, $\forall\, x_1, x_2 \in D$, $\forall \alpha \in [0,1]$, $\exists x_3 \in D$, $\exists \tau > 0$ such that

$$\varepsilon u + \alpha f(x_1) + (1-\alpha) f(x_2) \prec \tau f(x_3)$$

Our Definitions 7 and 9 are more comparable with our definitions of generalized affineness. Similar to the proof of the above Proposition 1, we present the following Proposition 2. Some examples of generalized convexities were given in [5,6].

Proposition 2. *Let* $f\colon X \to Y$ *be function, and* $t > 0$ *be any positive scalar, then*

(a) f is Y_+*-convexlike on* D *if and only if* $f(D) + Y_+$ *is convex;*

(b) f is Y_+*-subconvexlike on* D *if and only if* $f(D) + \mathrm{int}Y_+$ *is convex;*

(c) f is Y_+*-preconvexlike on* D *if and only if* $\cup_{t>0} t f(D) + Y_+$ *is convex;*

(d) f *is* Y_+*-presubconvexlike on* D *if and only if* $\cup_{t>0} t f(D) + \mathrm{int}Y_+$ *is convex.*

4. Constraint Qualifications

Consider the following vector optimization problem:

$$(VP)\quad \begin{array}{l} Y_+ - \min f(x) \\ g_i(x) \prec 0, i = 1,2,\cdots,m; \\ h_j(x) = 0, j = 1,2,\cdots,n; \\ x \in D \end{array}$$

where $f\colon X \to Y$, $g_i : X \to Z_i$, $h_j : X \to W_j$, Y_+, Z_{i+} are closed convex cones in Y and Z_i, respectively, and D is a nonempty subset of X.

Throughout this paper, the following assumptions will be used (τ_i, t_j are real scalars).

$$(A1)\forall x_1, x_2 \in D, \forall \alpha \in [0,1], \exists u_0 \in \text{int}Y_+, \exists u_i \in \text{int}Z_{i+}(i = 1,2,\cdots,n), \exists x_3 \in D$$

$\exists \tau_i > 0(i = 0,1,2,\cdots,m), \exists t_j \neq 0(j = 1,2,\cdots,n)$ such that

$$\begin{array}{l} u_0 + \alpha f(x_1) + (1-\alpha)f(x_2) \prec \tau_0 f(x_3) \\ u_i + \alpha g_i(x_1) + (1-\alpha)g_i(x_2) \prec \tau_i g_i(x_3) \\ \alpha h_j(x_1) + (1-\alpha)h_j(x_2) = t_j h_j(x_3) \end{array}$$

$$(A2)\text{int}h_j(D) \neq \varnothing(,j = 1,2,\cdots,n)$$

$$(A3)W_j(j = 1,2,\cdots,n)\text{arefinitedimensionalspaces.}$$

Remark 1. *We note that the condition (A1) says that f and $g_i(i = 1,2,\cdots,m)$ are presubconvexlike, and h_j (j = 1, 2, . . ., n) are preaffinelike.*

Let F be the feasible set of (VP), i.e.,

$$F := \{x \in D : g_i(x) \prec 0, i = 1,2,\cdots,m; h_j(x) = 0, j = 1,2,\cdots,n\}$$

The following is the well-known definition of a weakly efficient solution.

Definition 10. *A point $\overline{x} \in F$ is said to be a weakly efficient solution of (VP) with a weakly efficient value $\overline{y} \in f(\overline{x})$ if for every $x \in F$ there exists no $y \in f(x)$ satisfying $\overline{y} \succ\succ y$.*

We first introduce the following constraint qualification which is similar to the constraint qualification in the differentiate form from nonlinear programming.

Definition 11. *Let $\overline{x} \in F$. We say that (VP) satisfies the No Nonzero Abnormal Multiplier Constraint Qualification (NNAMCQ) at $\overline{x}$ if there is no nonzero vector $(\eta, \varsigma) \in \Pi_{i=1}^m Z_i^* \times \Pi_{j=1}^n W_j^*$ satisfying the system*

$$\begin{array}{l} \min\limits_{x \in D \cap U(\overline{x})} [\sum_{i=1}^m \eta_i g_i(x) + \sum_{j=1}^n \varsigma_j h_j(x)] = 0 \\ \sum_{i=1}^m \eta_i g_i(\overline{x}) = 0 \end{array}$$

where $U(\overline{x})$ is some neighborhood of $\overline{x}$.

It is obvious that NNAMCQ holds at $\overline{x} \in F$ with $U(\overline{x})$ being the whole space X if and only if for all $(\eta, \varsigma) \in (\Pi_{i=1}^m Z_i^* \times \Pi_{j=1}^n W_j^* \backslash \{0\}$ satisfying $\min \sum_{i=1}^m \eta_i g_i(\overline{x}) = 0$, there exists $x \in D$ such that

$$\left(\sum_{i=1}^m \eta_i g_i(x) + \sum_{j=1}^n \varsigma_j h_j(x)\right) \prec\prec 0$$

Hence, NNAMCQ is weaker than ([7], (CQ1)) (in [7], CQ1 was for set-valued optimization problems) in the constraint $\min \sum_{i=1}^m \eta_i g_i(\overline{x}) = 0$, which means that only the binding constraints are considered. Under the NNAMCQ, the following KuhnTucker type necessary optimality condition holds.

Theorem 1. *Assume that the generalized convexity assumption (A1) is satisfied and either (A2) or (A3) holds. If $\overline{x} \in F$ is a weakly efficient solution of (VP) with $\overline{y} \in f(\overline{x})$, then exists a vector $(\xi, \eta, \varsigma) \in Y^* \times \Pi_{i=1}^m Z_i^* \times \Pi_{j=1}^n W_j^*$ with $\xi \neq 0$ such that*

$$\begin{aligned} &\xi(\overline{y}) = \min_{x \in D \cap U(\overline{x})} [\xi(f(x)) + \textstyle\sum_{i=1}^m \eta_i(g_i(x)) + \sum_{j=1}^n \varsigma_j(h_j(x))] \\ &\textstyle\sum_{i=1}^m \eta_i(g_i(\overline{x})) = 0 \end{aligned} \tag{2}$$

for a neighborhood $U(\overline{x})$ of $\overline{x}$.

Proof. Since $\overline{x}$ is a weakly efficient solution of (VP) with $\overline{y} \in f(\overline{x})$ there exists a nonzero vector $(\xi, \eta, \varsigma) \in Y^* \times \Pi_{i=1}^m Z_i^* \times \Pi_{j=1}^n W_j^*$ such that (2) holds. Since NNAMCQ holds at $\overline{x}$, ξ must be nonzero. Otherwise if $\xi = 0$ then (η, ς) must be a nonzero solution of

$$\begin{aligned} &0 = \min_{x \in D \cap U(\overline{x})} [\textstyle\sum_{i=1}^m \eta_i(g_i(x)) + \sum_{j=1}^n \varsigma_j(h_j(x))] \\ &\textstyle\sum_{i=1}^m \eta_i(g_i(\overline{x})) = 0 \end{aligned}$$

But this is impossible, since the NNAMCQ holds at $\overline{x}$. □

Similar to ([7], (CQ2)) which is slightly stronger than ([7], (CQ1)), we define the following constraint qualification which is stronger than the NNAMCQ.

Definition 12. *(SNNAMCQ) Let $\overline{x} \in F$. We say that (VP) satisfies the No Nonzero Abnormal Multiplier Constraint Qualification (NNAMCQ) at $\overline{x}$ provided that*

(i) $\forall \eta \in \Pi_{i=1}^m Z_i^* \backslash \{0\} satisfying \sum_{i=1}^m \eta_i(g_i(\overline{x})) = 0,$

$$\exists x \in D, \text{ s.t. } h_j(x) = 0, \eta_i(g_i(x)) \prec\prec 0$$

(ii) $\forall \varsigma \in \Pi_{j=1}^n W_j^* \backslash \{0\}, \exists x \in D, s.t.\ \varsigma_j(h_j(x)) \prec\prec 0$ *for all* $j = 1, 2, \cdots, n.$

We now quote the Slater condition introduced in ([7], (CQ3)).

Definition 13 (Slater Condition CQ). *Let $\overline{x} \in F$. We say that (VP) satisfies the Slater condition at $\overline{x}$ if the following conditions hold:*

(i) $\exists x \in D$, s.t. $h_j(x) = 0, g_i(x) \prec\prec 0;$

(ii) $0 \in int h_j(D)$ *for all* j.

Similar to ([7], Proposition 2) (again, in [7], discussions are made for set-valued optimization problems), we have the following relationship between the constraint qualifications.

Proposition 3. *The following statements are true:*

(i) Slater CQ $\Rightarrow$ SNNAMCQ $\Rightarrow$ NNAMCQ with $U(\overline{x})$ being the whole space X;

(ii) Assume that (A1) and (A2) (or (A1) and (A3)) hold and the NNAMCQ with $U(\overline{x})$ being the whole space X without the restriction of $\sum_{i=1}^m \eta_i(g_i(\overline{x})) = 0$ at $\overline{x}$. Then, the Slater condition (CQ) holds.

Proof. The proof of (i) is similar to ([7], Proposition 2). Now we prove (ii). By the assumption (A1), the following sets C_1 and C_2 are convex:

$$\begin{aligned} &C_1 = \left\{(z, w) \in \Pi_{i=1}^m Z_i^* \times \Pi_{j=1}^n W_j^* : \exists x \in D, \tau_i, t_j > 0, \text{s.t. } z_i \in \tau_i g_i(x) + \text{int} Z_{i+}, w_j \in t_j h_j(x)\right\} \\ &C_2 = \cup_{t>0} th(D) \end{aligned}$$

Suppose to the contrary that the Slater condition does not hold. Then, $0 \notin C_1$ or $0 \notin C_2$. If the former $0 \notin C_1$ holds, then by the separation theorem [1], there exists a nonzero vector $(\eta, \varsigma) \in \Pi_{i=1}^m Z_i^* \times \Pi_{j=1}^n W_j^*$ such that

$$\sum_{i=1}^m \eta_i(\tau_i z_i + z_i^0) + \sum_{j=1}^n \varsigma_j(t_j w_j) \geq 0$$

for all $x \in D, \tau_i, t_j > 0, z_i = g_i(x), z_i^0 \in \text{int}Z_{i+}, w_j = h_j(x)$. Since $\text{int}Z_{i+}$ are convex cones, consequently we have

$$\sum_{i=1}^m \eta_i(\tau_i z_i + s_i z_i^0) + \sum_{j=1}^n \varsigma_j(t_j w_j) \geq 0 \tag{3}$$

for all $x \in D, \tau_i, t_j, s_i > 0, z_i \in g_i(x), z_i^0 \in \text{int}Z_{i+}, w_j \in h_j(x)\}$ and take $s_i \to 0$ in (3), we have

$$\sum_{i=1}^m \eta_i(z_i) + \sum_{j=1}^n \varsigma_j(w_j) \geq 0,\ x \in D, z_i \in g_i(x), w_j = h_j(x)$$

which contradicts the NNAMCQ. Similarly if the latter $0 \notin \text{int}h_j(D)$ holds then there exists $\varsigma \in \Pi_{j=1}^n W_j^* \backslash \{0\}$ such that $\varsigma_j(h_j(x)) \geq 0, \forall x \in D$, which contradicts NNAMCQ. □

Definition 14 (Calmness Condition). *Let $\overline{x} \in F$. Let $Z := \sum_{i=1}^m Z_i$ and $W := \sum_{j=1}^n W_j$. We say that (VP) satisfies the calmness condition at $\overline{x}$ provided that there exist $U(\overline{x}, 0_Z, 0_W)$, a neighborhood of $(\overline{x}, 0_Z, 0_W)$, and a map $\psi(p,q) : Z \times W \to Y_+$ with $\psi(0_Z, 0_W) = 0_Y$ such that for each*

$$(x, p, q) \in U(\overline{x}, 0_Z, 0_W) \backslash \{(\overline{x}, 0_Z, 0_W)\}$$

Satisfying

$$(g_i(x) + p_i) \prec 0, q_j = h_j(x)), x \in D$$

there is no $y \in f(x))$, such that

$$\overline{y} \in y + \psi(p,q) + \text{int}Y_+$$

Theorem 2. *Assume that (A1) is satisfied and either (A2) or (A3) holds. If $\overline{x} \in F$ is a weakly efficient solution of (VP) with $\overline{y} = f(\overline{x})$, and the calmness condition holds at $\overline{x}$, then there exists $U(\overline{x})$, a neighborhood of $\overline{x}$, and a vector $(\xi, \eta, \varsigma) \in Y_+^* \times Z_+^* \times W^*$ with $\xi \neq 0$ such that*

$$\begin{aligned} &\xi(\overline{y}) = \min_{x \in D \cap U(\overline{x})} [\xi(f(x)) + \textstyle\sum_{i=1}^m \eta_i(g_i(x)) + \sum_{j=1}^n \varsigma_j(h_j(x))] \\ &\textstyle\sum_{i=1}^m \eta_i(g_i(\overline{x})) = 0 \end{aligned} \tag{4}$$

Proof. It is easy to see that under the calmness condition, $\overline{x}$ being a weakly efficient solution of (VP) implies that $(\overline{x}, 0_Z, 0_W)$ is a weakly efficient solution of the perturbed problem: *VP(p,q)*

$$VP(p,q) \quad \begin{array}{l} Y_+ - \min f(x) + \psi(p,q) \\ s.t.(g_i(x) + p_i) \prec 0, \\ q_j = h_j(x), x \in D, \\ (x, p, q) \in U(\overline{x}, 0_Z, 0_W) \end{array}$$

By assumption, the above optimization problem satisfies the generalized convexity assumption (A1). Now we prove that the NNAMCQ holds naturally at $(\overline{x}, 0_Z, 0_W)$. Suppose that $(\eta, \varsigma) \in Z_+^* \times W^*$ satisfies the system:

$$\begin{array}{l} \min\limits_{x \in D(x,p,q) \in U(\overline{x},0_Z,0_W)} [\sum_{i=1}^m \eta_i(g_i(x) + p_i) + \sum_{j=1}^n \varsigma_j(-q_j + h_j(x))] \\ \sum_{i=1}^m \eta_i(g_i(\overline{x})) = 0 \end{array} \tag{5}$$

If $\varsigma \neq 0$, then there exists $q_j \in W_j$ small enough such that $\sum_{j=1}^n \varsigma_j(-q_j) < 0$. Since $\overline{x} \in F, 0 \in h_j(\overline{x})$, and there exists $z_i^x \in g_i(x) \cap (-Z_{i+})$, which implies that $\eta(z_i^x) \leq 0$, hence

$$\sum_{i=1}^m \eta_i(z_i^x) + \sum_{j=1}^n \varsigma_j(-q_j) < 0$$

which contradicts (5). Hence, $\varsigma = 0$ and (5) becomes

$$\begin{array}{c} \min\limits_{x \in D,(x,p,q) \in U(\overline{x},0_Z,0_W)} \sum_{i=1}^m \eta_i(g_i(x) + p_i) \\ \sum_{i=1}^m \eta_i(g_i(\overline{x})) = 0 \end{array}$$

If $\eta \neq 0$, then there exists p small enough such that $\sum_{i=1}^m \eta_i(p_i) < 0$. Let $z_i^x = g_i(x)$, then

$$\sum_{i=1}^m \eta_i(z_i^x) \leq 0$$

and hence

$$\sum_{i=1}^m \eta_i(z_i^x + p_i) = \sum_{i=1}^m \eta_i(z_i^x) + \sum_{i=1}^m \eta_i(p_i) < 0$$

which is impossible. Consequently, $\eta = 0$ as well. Hence, there exists $(\xi, \eta, \varsigma) \in Y^* \times Z_+^* \times W_+^*$ with $\xi \neq 0$ such that

$$\begin{array}{l} \min\limits_{x \in D,(x,p,q) \in U(\overline{x},0_Z,0_W)} [\xi(f(x) + \psi(p,q)) + \sum_{i=1}^m \eta_i(g_i(x) + p_i) + \sum_{j=1}^n \varsigma_j(-q_j + h_j(x))] \\ \sum_{i=1}^m \eta_i(g_i(\overline{x})) = 0 \end{array} \tag{6}$$

It is obvious that (6) implies (4) and hence the proof of the theorem is complete. □

Definition 15. *Let $Z_i (i = 1, 2, \cdots, m), W_j (j = 1, 2, \cdots, n)$ be normed spaces. We say that (VP) satisfies the error bound constraint qualification at a feasible point $\overline{x}$ if there exist positive constants λ, δ, and ε such that*

$$d(\overline{x}, \Sigma(0_Z, 0_W)) \leq \lambda ||(p,q)||, \forall (p,q) \in \varepsilon B_X, x \in \Sigma(p,q) \cap U_\delta(\overline{x})$$

where B_X is the unit ball of X, and

$$\Sigma(p,q) := \{x \in D : (g_i(x) + p_i) \cap (-Z_{i+})) \neq \varnothing, q_j \in h_j(x)\}$$

Remark 2. *Note that the error bound constraint qualification is satisfied at a feasible point $\overline{x}$ if and only if the function $\Sigma(p,q)$ is pseudo upper-Lipschitz continuous around $(0_Z, 0_W, \overline{x})$ in the terminology of ([8]) (which is referred to as being calm at $\overline{x}$ in [9]). Hence, $\Sigma(p,q)$ being either pseudo-Lipschitz continuous around $(0_Z, 0_W, \overline{x})$. in the terminology of [10] or upper-Lipschitz continuous at $\overline{x}$ in the terminology of [11] implies that the error bound constraint qualification holds at $\overline{x}$. Recall that a function $F(x) : R^n \to R^m$ is called a polyhedral multifunction if its graph is a union of finitely many polyhedral convex sets. This class of function is closed under (finite) addition, scalar multiplication, and (finite) composition. By ([12], Proposition 1), a polyhedral multifunction is upper-Lipschitz. Hence, the following result provides a sufficient condition for the error bound constraint qualification.*

Proposition 4. *Let $X = R^n$ and $W = R^m$. Suppose that D is polyhedral and h is a polyhedral multifunction. Then, the error bound constraint qualification always holds at any feasible point $\overline{x} \in F := \{x \in D : 0 = h(x)\}$.*

Proof. Since D is polyhedral and h is a polyhedral multifunction, its inverse map $S(q) = \{x \in R^n : q \in h(x)\}$ is a polyhedral multifunction. That is, the graph of S is a union of polyhedral convex sets. Since

$$gph\Sigma(p,q) := \{(q,x) \in R^m \times D : q \in h(x)\} = gphS \cap (R^m \times D)$$

which is also a union of polyhedral convex sets, Σ is also a polyhedral multifunction and hence upper-Lipschitz at any point of $\overline{x} \in R^n$ by ([12], Proposition 1). Therefore, the error bound constraint qualification holds at $\overline{x}$. □

Definition 16. *Let X be a normed space, $f(x) : X \to Y$ be a function, and $\overline{x} \in X$. f is said to be Lipschitz near $\overline{x}$ if there exist $U(\overline{x})$, a neighborhood of $\overline{x}$, and a constant $L_f > 0$ such that for all $x_1, x_2 \in U(\overline{x})$,*

$$f(x_1) \subseteq f(x_2) + L_f \left|\left|x_1 - x_2\right|\right| B_Y$$

where B_Y is the unit ball of Y.

Definition 17. *Let X be a normed space, $f(x) : X \to Y$ be a function and $\overline{x} \in X$. f is said to be strongly Lipschitz on $S \subseteq X$ if there exist a constant $L_f > 0$ such that for all $x_1, x_2 \in S y_1 = f(x_1)$, $y_2 = f(x_2)$ and $e \in B_Y \cap Y_+$,*

$$y_1 \prec y_2 + L_f \left|\left|x_1 - x_2\right|\right| e$$

The following result generalizes the exact penalization [13].

Proposition 5. *Let X be a normed space, $f(x) : X \to Y$ be a function which is strongly Lipschitz of rank L_f on a set $S \subseteq X$. Let $C \subseteq X$ and suppose that $\overline{x}$ is a weakly efficient solution of*

$$Y_+ - \min_{x \in S} f(x)$$

with $\overline{y} = f(\overline{x})$. Then, for all $K \geq L_f$, $\overline{x}$ is a weakly efficient solution of the exact penalized optimization problem

$$Y_+ - \min_{x \in S} f(x) + K d_C(x) B_Y \cap Y_+$$

where $d_C(x) := \min\{|x - c|, c \in C\}$.

Proof. Let us prove the assertion by supposing the contrary. Then, there is a point $S \subseteq X$, $y = f(x)$, and $e \in B_Y \cap Y_+$ satisfying $y + K d_C(x) e \prec \overline{y}$. Let $\varepsilon > 0$ and $c \in C$ be a point such that $||x - c|| \leq d_C(x) + \varepsilon$. Then, for any $c^* \in f(c)$,

$$c^* \prec y + K||x - c||e \prec y + K(d_C(x) + \varepsilon)e \prec \overline{y} + K\varepsilon e$$

Since $\varepsilon > 0$ is arbitrary, it contradicts the fact that $\overline{x}$ is a weakly efficient solution of

$$Y_+ - \min_{x \in S} f(x)$$

□

Proposition 6. *Suppose $X \times Z \times W$ is a normed space and f is strongly Lipschitz on D. If $\overline{x}$ is a weakly efficient solution of (VP) and the error bound constraint qualification is satisfied at $\overline{x}$, then (VP) satisfies the calmness condition at $\overline{x}$.*

Proof. By the exact penalization principle in Proposition 5 $\overline{x}$ is a weakly efficient solution of the penalized problem

$$Y_+ - \min_{x \in D} f(x) + K d_{\Sigma(0,0)}(x) B_Y \cap Y_+$$

The results then follow from the definitions of the calmness and the error bound constraint qualification. □

Theorem 3. *Assume that the generalized convexity assumption (A1) is satisfied with f replaced by $f + Kd_C(x)B_Y \cap Y_+$ and either (A2) or (A3) holds. Suppose $X \times Z \times W$ is a normed space and f is strongly Lipschitz on D. If $\overline{x}$ is a weakly efficient solution of (VP) and the error bound constraint qualification is satisfied at $\overline{x}$, then there exist $U(\overline{x})$, a neighborhood of $\overline{x}$, and a vector $(\xi, \eta, \varsigma) \in Y_+^* \times Z_+^* \times W^*$ with $\xi \neq 0$ such that (4) holds.*

Using Proposition 4, Theorem 3 has the following easy corollary.

Corollary 1. *Suppose Y is a normed space, $X = R^n$, $W = R^m$ and D is polyhedral, and f is strongly Lipschitz on D. Assume that the generalized convexity assumption (A1) is satisfied with f replaced by $f + Kd_C(x)B_Y \cap Y_+$ and either (A2) or (A3) holds. If $\overline{x}$ is a weakly efficient solution of (VP) without the inequality constraint $g(x) \succ 0$, and h is a polyhedral multifunction, then there exist $U(\overline{x})$, a neighborhood of $\overline{x}$ a vector $(\xi, \varsigma) \in Y_+^* \times W^*$ with $\xi \neq 0$ such that*

$$\xi(\overline{y}) = \min_{x \in D \cap U(\overline{x})} [\xi(f(x)) + \varsigma_j(h_j(x))]$$

Our last result Theorem 4 is a strong duality theorem, which generalizes a result in Fang, Li, and Ng [14].

For two topological vector spaces Z and Y, let $B(Z;Y)$ be the set of continuous linear transformations from Z to Y and

$$B^+(Z,Y) := \{S \in B(Z,Y) : S(Z_+) \subseteq Y_+\}$$

The Lagrangian map for (VP) is the function

$$L : X \times \Pi_{i=1}^m B^+(Z_i, Y) \times \Pi_{j=1}^n B^+(W_j, Y) \to Y$$

defined by

$$L(x, S, T) := f(x) + \sum_{i=1}^m S_i(g_i(x)) + \sum_{j=1}^n T_j(h_j(x))$$

Given $(S,T) \in \Pi_{i=1}^m B^+(Z_i, Y) \times \Pi_{j=1}^n B^+(W_j, Y)$, consider the vector minimization problem induced by (VP):

$$(VPST) \quad \begin{array}{l} Y_+ - \min L(x, S, T) \\ s.t. x \in D \end{array}$$

and denote by $\Phi(S,T)$ the set of weakly efficient value of the problem (VPST). The Lagrange dual problem associated with the primal problem (VP) is

$$(VD) \quad \begin{array}{l} Y_+ - \max \Phi(S,T) \\ s.t.(S,T) \in \Pi_{(VD)\ i=1}^m B^+(Z_i, Y) + \Pi_{j=1}^n B^+(W_j, Y) \end{array}$$

The following strong duality result holds which extends the strong duality theorem in ([7], Theorem 7) (which was for set-valued optimization problems), to allow weaker convexity assumptions. We omit the proof since it is similar to [7].

Theorem 4. *Assume that (A1) is satisfied, either (A2) or (A3) is satisfied, and a constraint qualification such as NNAMCQ is satisfied. If $\overline{x}$ is a weakly efficient solution of (VP), then there exists*

$$(\overline{S},\overline{T}) \in \Pi_{i=1}^{m} B^{+}(Z_i, Y) \times \Pi_{j=1}^{n} B^{+}(W_j, Y)$$

such that

$$\Phi(\overline{S},\overline{T}) \cap f(x) \neq \varnothing$$

5. Conclusions

We introduce the following definitions of generalized affine functions: affinelikeness, preaffinelikeness, subaffinelikeness, and presubaffinelikeness. Examples 1 to 7 show that definitions of affine, affinelike, preaffinelike, subaffinelike, and presubaffinelike functions are all different. Example 8 is an example of non-presubaffinelike function; presubaffineness is the weakest one in the series. Proposition 1 demonstrates that our generalized affine functions have some similar properties with generalized convex functions.

And then, we work with vector optimization problems in real linear topological spaces, and obtain necessary conditions, sufficient conditions, or necessary and sufficient conditions for weakly efficient solutions, which generalize the corresponding classical results in [13,15] and some recent results in [7,9,16–18]. We note that the constraint qualifications in [13,17,18] are in the differentiation form. Compared with the results in [19] and ([20], p. 297) in discussions of convex constraints, we only required weakened convexities for constraint qualifications in this article. We note that [17] works with semi-definite programming. In [17], two groups of functions $g_i(x) \geq 0$, $i \in I$ and $h_j(x) = 0$, $j \in J$ can be just considered as two topological spaces (I and J do not have to be finite sets). We also note that f is supposed to be "proper convex" in [18]; and in [18], functions are required to be "quasiconvex".

Generalized affine functions and generalized convex functions can be used for other discussions of optimization problems, e.g., dualities, scalarizations, as well as saddle points, etc.

Funding: This research received no external funding.

Data Availability Statement: Not applicable.

Conflicts of Interest: The author declares no conflict of interest.

References

1. Deimling, K. *Nonlinear Functional Analysis*; Springer: Berlin/Heidelberg, Germany, 1985.
2. Fan, K. Minimax Theorems. *Proc. Natl. Acad. Sci. USA* **1953**, *39*, 42–47. [CrossRef] [PubMed]
3. Jeyakumar, V. Convexlike Alternative Theorems and Mathematical Programming. *Optimization* **1985**, *16*, 643–652. [CrossRef]
4. Li, Z.F.; Wang, S.Y. Lagrange Multipliers and Saddle Points in Multiobjective Programming. *J. Optim. Theo. Appl.* **1994**, *1*, 63–80. [CrossRef]
5. Zeng, R. Generalized Gordan Alternative Theorem with Weakened Convexity and its Applications. *Optimization* **2002**, *51*, 709–717. [CrossRef]
6. Zeng, R.; Caron, R.J. Generalized Motzkin Theorem of the Alternative and Vector Optimization Problems. *J. Optim. Theo. Appl.* **2006**, *131*, 281–299. [CrossRef]
7. Li, Z.-F.; Chen, G.-Y. Lagrangian Multipliers, Saddle Points and Duality in Vector Optimization of Set-Valued Maps. *J. Math. Anal. Appl.* **1997**, *215*, 297–315. [CrossRef]
8. Ye, J.J.; Ye, X.Y. Necessary Optimality Conditions for Optimization Problems with Variational Inequality Constriants. *Math. Oper. Res.* **1997**, *22*, 977–997. [CrossRef]
9. Rockafellar, R.T.; Wets, R.J.-B. *Variational Analysis*; Springer-Verlag: Berlin/Heidelberg, Germany, 1998.
10. Aubin, J.-P. Lipschitz Behavior of Solutions to Convex Minimization Problems. *Math. Oper. Res.* **1984**, *9*, 87–111. [CrossRef]
11. Robinson, S.M. Stability Theory for Systems of Inequalities. Part I: Linear Systems. *SIAM J. Numer. Anal.* **1975**, *12*, 754–769. [CrossRef]
12. Robinson, S.M. Some Continuity Properties of Polyhedral Multifunctions. *Math. Program. Stud.* **1981**, *14*, 206–214.
13. Clarke, F.H. *Optimization and Nonsmooth Analysis*; Wiley-Interscience: New York, NY, USA, 1983.

14. Fang, D.H.; Li, C.; Ng, K.F. Constraint Qualifications for Optimality Conditions and Total Lagrange Dualities in Convex Infinite Programming. *Nonlinear Anal.* **2010**, *73*, 1143–1159. [CrossRef]
15. Luc, D.T. *Theory of Vector Optimization*; Springer: Berlin/Heidelberg, Germany, 1989.
16. Nguyen, M.-H.; Luu, D.V. *On Constraint Qualifications with Generalized Convexity and Optimality Conditions*; Cahiers de la Maison des Sciences Economiques; Université Panthéon-Sorbonne (Paris 1): Paris, France, 2006; Volume 20.
17. Kanzi, N.; Nobakhtian, S. Nonsmooth Semi-Infinite Programming Problems with Mixed Constraints. *J. Math. Anal. Appl.* **2009**, *351*, 170–181. [CrossRef]
18. Zhao, X.P. Constraint Qualification for Quasiconvex Inequality System with Applications in Constraint Optimization. *J. Nonlinear Convex. Anal.* **2016**, *17*, 879–889.
19. Khazayel, B.; Farajzadeh, A. On the Optimality Conditions for DC Vector Optimization Problems. *Optimization* **2022**, *71*, 2033–2045. [CrossRef]
20. Ansari, Q.H.; Yao, J.-C. *Recent Developments in Vector Optimization*; Springer Link: Berlin/Heidelberg, Germany, 2012.

axioms

MDPI

Article

Application of Gradient Optimization Methods in Defining Neural Dynamics

Predrag S. Stanimirović [1,2], Nataša Tešić [3], Dimitrios Gerontitis [4], Gradimir V. Milovanović [5], Milena J. Petrović [6,*], Vladimir L. Kazakovtsev [2] and Vladislav Stasiuk [2]

1 Faculty of Sciences and Mathematics, University of Niš, 18000 Niš, Serbia; pecko@pmf.ni.ac.rs
2 Laboratory "Hybrid Methods of Modelling and Optimization in Complex Systems", Siberian Federal University, Prosp. Svobodny 79, 660041 Krasnoyarsk, Russia; vokz@bk.ru (V.L.K.); vstasyuk@sfu-kras.ru (V.S.)
3 Department of Mathematics and Informatics, Faculty of Sciences, University of Novi Sad, 21000 Novi Sad, Serbia; natasa.tesic27@gmail.com
4 Department of Information and Electronic Engineering, International Hellenic University, 57400 Thessaloniki, Greece; dimitrios_gerontitis@yahoo.gr or dimger@iee.ihu.gr
5 Mathematical Institute, Serbian Academy of Sciences and Arts, Kneza Mihaila 35, 11000 Belgrade, Serbia; gvm@mi.sanu.ac.rs
6 Faculty of Sciences and Mathematics, University of Pristina in Kosovska Mitrovica, Lole Ribara 29, 38220 Kosovska Mitrovica, Serbia
* Correspondence: milena.petrovic@pr.ac.rs; Tel.: +381-28-425-396

Abstract: Applications of gradient method for nonlinear optimization in development of Gradient Neural Network (GNN) and Zhang Neural Network (ZNN) are investigated. Particularly, the solution of the matrix equation $AXB = D$ which changes over time is studied using the novel GNN model, termed as GGNN(A, B, D). The GGNN model is developed applying GNN dynamics on the gradient of the error matrix used in the development of the GNN model. The convergence analysis shows that the neural state matrix of the GGNN(A, B, D) design converges asymptotically to the solution of the matrix equation $AXB = D$, for any initial state matrix. It is also shown that the convergence result is the least square solution which is defined depending on the selected initial matrix. A hybridization of GGNN with analogous modification GZNN of the ZNN dynamics is considered. The Simulink implementation of presented GGNN models is carried out on the set of real matrices.

Keywords: gradient neural network; generalized inverses; Moore–Penrose inverse; linear matrix equations

MSC: 68T05; 15A09; 65F20

1. Introduction and Background

Recurrent neural networks (RNNs) are an important class of algorithms for computing matrix (generalized) inverses. These algorithms are used to find the solutions of matrix equations or to minimize certain nonlinear matrix functions. RNNs are divided into two subgroups: Gradient Neural Networks (GNNs) and Zhang Neural Networks (ZNNs). The GNN design is explicit and mostly applicable to time-invariant problems, which means that the coefficients of the equations that are addressed are constant matrices. ZNN models can be implicit and are able to solve time-varying problems, where the coefficients of the equations depend on the variable $t \in \mathbb{R}, t > 0$, representing time [1–3].

The Moore–Penrose inverse of $A \in \mathrm{R}^{p\times n}$ is the unique matrix $A^{\dagger} = X \in \mathrm{R}^{n\times p}$ which is the solution to the well-known Penrose equations [4,5]:

$$A = AXA, \qquad X = XAX, \qquad AX = (AX)^{\mathrm{T}}, \qquad XA = (XA)^{\mathrm{T}},$$

where $()^{\mathrm{T}}$ denotes the transpose matrix. The rank of a matrix A, i.e., the maximum number of linearly independent columns in A, is denoted by $\mathrm{rank}(A)$.

Applications of linear algebra tools and generalized inverses can be found in important areas such as the modeling of electrical circuits [6], the estimation of DNA sequences [7] and the balancing of chemical equations [8,9], as well as in other important research domains related to robotics [10] and statistics [11]. A number of iterative methods for solving matrix equations based on gradient values have been proposed [12–15].

In the following sections, we will focus on GNN and ZNN dynamical systems based on the gradient of the objective function and their implementation. The main goal of this research is the analysis of convergence and the study of analytic solutions.

Models with GNN neural designs for computing the inverse or the Moore–Penrose inverse and linear matrix equations were proposed in [16–19]. Further, various dynamical systems aimed at approximating the pseudo-inverse of rank-deficient matrices were developed in [16]. Wei, in [20], proposed three RNN models for the approximation of the weighted Moore–Penrose inverse. Online matrix inversion in a complex matrix case was considered in [21]. A novel GNN design based on nonlinear activation functions (AFs) was proposed and analyzed in [22,23] for solving the constant Lyapunov matrix equation online. A fast convergent GNN aimed at solving a system of linear equations was proposed and numerically analyzed in [24]. Xiao, in [25], investigated the finite-time convergence of an appropriately accelerated ZNN for the online solution of the time-varying complex matrix equation $A(t)X(t) = B(t)$. A comparison with the corresponding GNN design was considered. Two improved nonlinear GNN dynamical systems for approximating the Moore–Penrose inverse of full-row or full-column rank matrices were proposed and considered in [26]. GNN-type models for solving matrix equations and computing related generalized inverses were developed in [1,3,13,16,18,20,27–29]. The acceleration of GNN dynamics to a finite-time convergence has been investigated recently. A finite-time convergent GNN for approximating online solutions of the general linear matrix equation $AX(t)B + CX(t)D = B$ was proposed in [30]. This goal was achieved using two activation functions (AFs) in the construction of the GNN. The influence of AFs on the convergence performance of a GNN design for solving the matrix equation $AXB + X = C$ was investigated in [31]. A fixed-time convergent GNN for solving the Sylvester equation was investigated in [32]. Moreover, noise-tolerant GNN models equipped with a suitable activation function (AF) able to solve convex optimization problems were developed in [33].

Our goal is to solve the equation $AXB = D$ and apply its particular cases in computing generalized inverses in real time by improving the GNN model developed in [34]. The developed dynamical system is denoted by $\mathrm{GNN}(A, B, D)$. Or motivation is to improve the GNN model denoted by $\mathrm{GNN}(A, B, D)$ and develop a novel gradient-based GGNN model, termed $\mathrm{GGNN}(A, B, D)$, utilizing a novel type of dynamical system. The proposed GGNN model is based on the standard GNN dynamics along the gradient of the standard error matrix. The convergence analysis reveals the global asymptotic convergence of $\mathrm{GGNN}(A, B, D)$ without restrictions, while the output belongs to the set of general solutions to the matrix equation $AXB = D$.

In addition, we propose gradient-based modifications of the hybrid models developed in [35] as proper combinations of GNN and ZNN models for solving the matrix equations $BX = D$ and $XC = D$ with constant coefficients. Analogous hybridizations for approximating the matrix inverse were developed in [36], while two modifications of the ZNN design for computing the Moore–Penrose inverse were proposed in [37]. Hybrid continuous-gradient–Zhang neural dynamics for solving linear time-variant equations were investigated in [38,39]. The developed hybrid GNN-ZNN models in this paper are aimed at solving the matrix equations $AX = B$ and $XC = D$, denoted by $\mathrm{HGZNN}(A, I, B)$ and $\mathrm{HGZNN}(I, C, D)$, respectively.

The implementation was performed in MATLAB Simulink, and numerical experiments were performed with simulations of the GNN, GGNN and HGZNN models.

The GNN used to solve the general linear matrix equation $AXB = D$ is defined over the error matrix $E(t) = D - AV(t)B$, where $t \in [0, +\infty)$ is time, and $V(t)$ is an unknown state-variable matrix that approximates the unknown matrix X in $AXB = D$. The goal function is $\varepsilon(t) = ||D - AV(t)B||_F^2/2$, where $\|\cdot\|_F = \sqrt{\sum_{ij} a_{ij}^2}$ denotes the Frobenius norm of a matrix. The gradient of $\varepsilon(t)$ is equal to

$$\frac{\partial \varepsilon(t)}{\partial V} = \nabla \varepsilon = \frac{1}{2}\frac{\partial ||D - AV(t)B||_F^2}{\partial V} = -A^{\mathrm{T}}(D - AV(t)B)B^{\mathrm{T}}.$$

The GNN evolutionary design is defined by the dynamic system

$$\dot{V}(t) = \frac{\mathrm{d}V(t)}{\mathrm{d}t} = -\gamma\frac{\partial \varepsilon(t)}{\partial V}, \quad V(0) = V_0, \tag{1}$$

where $\gamma > 0$ is a real parameter used to speed up the convergence, and $\dot{V}(t)$ denotes the time derivative of $V(t)$. Thus, the linear GNN aimed at solving $AXB = D$ is given by the following dynamics:

$$\dot{V}(t) = \gamma A^{\mathrm{T}}(D - AV(t)B)B^{\mathrm{T}}. \tag{2}$$

The dynamical flow (2) is denoted as $\mathrm{GNN}(A, B, D)$. The nonlinear $\mathrm{GNN}(A, B, D)$ for solving $AXB = D$ is defined by

$$\dot{V}(t) = \gamma A^{\mathrm{T}}\mathcal{F}(D - AV(t)B)B^{\mathrm{T}}. \tag{3}$$

The function array $\mathcal{F}(C) = \mathcal{F}([c_{ij}])$ is based on the appropriate odd and monotonically increasing activation function, which is applicable to the elements of a real matrix $C = (c_{ij}) \in \mathbb{R}^{m\times n}$, i.e., $\mathcal{F}(C) = [f(c_{ij})], i = 1, \ldots, m, j = 1, \ldots, n,$.

Proposition 1 restates restrictions on the solvability of $AXB = D$ and its general solution.

Proposition 1 ([4,5]). *If $A \in \mathbb{R}^{m\times n}, B \in \mathbb{R}^{p\times q}$ and $D \in \mathbb{R}^{m\times q}$, then the fulfillment of the condition*

$$AA^{\dagger}DB^{\dagger}B = D \tag{4}$$

is necessary and sufficient for the solvability of the linear matrix equation $AXB = D$. In this case, the set of all solutions is given by

$$X = \left\{A^{\dagger}DB^{\dagger} + Y - A^{\dagger}AYBB^{\dagger} \mid Y \in \mathbb{R}^{n\times p}\right\}. \tag{5}$$

The following results from [34] describe the conditions of convergence and the limit of the unknown matrix $V(t)$ from (3) as $t \to +\infty$.

Proposition 2 ([34]). *Suppose the matrices $A \in \mathbb{R}^{m\times n}, B \in \mathbb{R}^{p\times q}$ and $D \in \mathbb{R}^{m\times q}$ satisfy (4). Then, the unknown matrix $V(t)$ from (3) converges as $t \to +\infty$ with the equilibrium state*

$$V(t) \to \tilde{V} = A^{\dagger}DB^{\dagger} + V(0) - A^{\dagger}AV(0)BB^{\dagger} \tag{6}$$

for any initial state-variable matrix $V(0) \in \mathbb{R}^{n\times p}$.

The research in [40] investigated various ZNN models based on optimization methods. The goal of the current research is to develop a GNN model based on the gradient $E_G(t)$ of $||E(t)||_F^2$ instead of the original goal function $E(t)$.

The obtained results are summarized as follows:

- A novel error function $E_G(t)$ is proposed for the development of the GNN dynamical evolution.

- The GNN design based on the error function $E_G(t)$ is developed and analyzed theoretically and numerically.
- A hybridization of GNN and ZNN dynamical systems based on the error matrix E_G is proposed and investigated.

The overall organization of this paper is as follows. The motivation and derivation of the GGNN and GZNN models are presented in Section 2. Section 3 is dedicated to the convergence analysis of GGNN dynamics. A numerical comparison of GNN and GGNN dynamics is given in Section 4. Neural dynamics based on the hybridization of GGNN and GZNN models for solving matrix equations are considered in Section 6. Numerical examples of hybrid models are analyzed in Section 6. Finally, the last section presents some concluding remarks and a vision of further research.

2. Motivation and Derivation of GGNN and GZNN Models

The standard GNN design (2) solves the GLME $AXB = D$ under constraint (4). Our goal is to resolve this restriction and propose dynamic evolutions based on error functions that tend to zero without restrictions.

Our goal is to define the GNN design for solving the GLME $AXB = D$ based on the error function

$$E_G(t) := \nabla\varepsilon(t) = A^{\mathrm{T}}(D - AV(t)B)B^{\mathrm{T}} = A^{\mathrm{T}}E(t)B^{\mathrm{T}}. \tag{7}$$

According to known results from nonlinear unconstrained optimization [41], the equilibrium points of (7) satisfy

$$E_G(t) := \nabla\varepsilon(t) = 0.$$

We continue the investigation from [40]. More precisely, we develop the GNN model based on the error function $E_G(t)$ instead of the error function $E(t)$. In this way, new neural dynamics are aimed at forcing the gradient E_G to zero instead of the standard goal function $E(t)$. It is reasonable to call such an RNN model a gradient-based GNN (abbreviated GGNN).

Proposition 3 gives the conditions for the solvability of the matrix equations $E(t) = 0$ and $E_G(t) = 0$ and the general solutions to these systems.

Proposition 3 ([40]). *Consider the arbitrary matrices $A \in \mathbb{R}^{m\times n}$, $B \in \mathbb{R}^{k\times h}$ and $D \in \mathbb{R}^{m\times h}$. The following statements are true:*

(a) *The equation $E(t) = 0$ is solvable if and only if* (4) *is satisfied, and the general solution to $E(t) = 0$ is given by* (5).
(b) *The equation $E_G(t) = 0$ is always solvable, and its general solution coincides with* (5).

Proof. (a) This part of the proof follows from known results on the solvability and general solution of the matrix equation $AXB = D$ of generalized inverses [4] (p. 52, Theorem 1) and its application to the matrix equation $E(t) = 0 \Longleftrightarrow AV(t)B = D$.
(b) According to [4] (p. 52, Theorem 1), the matrix equation

$$E_G(t) = 0 \Longleftrightarrow A^{\mathrm{T}}AVBB^{\mathrm{T}} = A^{\mathrm{T}}DB^{\mathrm{T}}$$

is consistent if and only if

$$A^{\mathrm{T}}A\left(A^{\mathrm{T}}A\right)^{\dagger}A^{\mathrm{T}}DB^{\mathrm{T}}\left(BB^{\mathrm{T}}\right)^{\dagger}BB^{\mathrm{T}} = A^{\mathrm{T}}DB^{\mathrm{T}}$$

is satisfied. Indeed, applying the properties $(A^{\mathrm{T}}A)^{\dagger}A^{\mathrm{T}} = A^{\dagger}$, $B^{\mathrm{T}}(BB^{\mathrm{T}})^{\dagger} = B^{\dagger}$ and $A^{\mathrm{T}}AA^{\dagger} = A^{\mathrm{T}}$, $B^{\dagger}BB^{\mathrm{T}} = B^{\mathrm{T}}$ of the Moore–Penrose inverse [5] results in

$$A^{\mathrm{T}}A\left(A^{\mathrm{T}}A\right)^{\dagger}A^{\mathrm{T}}DB^{\mathrm{T}}\left(BB^{\mathrm{T}}\right)^{\dagger}BB^{\mathrm{T}} = A^{\mathrm{T}}AA^{\dagger}DB^{\dagger}BB^{\mathrm{T}} = A^{\mathrm{T}}DB^{\mathrm{T}}.$$

In addition, based on [4] (p. 52, Theorem 1), the general solution $V(t)$ to $E_G(t) = 0$ is

$$\begin{aligned} V &= \left(A^{\mathrm{T}}A\right)^{\dagger} A^{\mathrm{T}} D B^{\mathrm{T}} \left(BB^{\mathrm{T}}\right)^{\dagger} + Y - \left(A^{\mathrm{T}}A\right)^{\dagger} A^{\mathrm{T}} A Y B B^{\mathrm{T}} \left(BB^{\mathrm{T}}\right)^{\dagger} \\ &= A^{\dagger} D B^{\dagger} + Y - A^{\dagger} A Y B B^{\dagger}, \end{aligned} \tag{8}$$

which coincides with (5). □

In this way, the matrix equation $E(t) = 0$ is solvable under condition (4), while the equation $E_G(t) = 0$ is always consistent. In addition, the general solutions to equations $E(t) = 0$ and $E_G(t) = 0$ are identical [40].

The next step is to define the GGNN dynamics using the error matrix $E_G(t)$. Let us define the objective function $\varepsilon_G = ||E_G||_F^2/2$, whose gradient is equal to

$$\frac{\partial \varepsilon_G(V(t))}{\partial V} = \frac{\partial ||A^{\mathrm{T}}(D - AV(t)B)B^{\mathrm{T}}||_F^2}{\partial V} = -A^{\mathrm{T}}A\left(A^{\mathrm{T}}(D - AV(t)B)B^{\mathrm{T}}\right)BB^{\mathrm{T}}.$$

The dynamical system for the GGNN formula is obtained by applying the GNN evolution along the gradient of $\varepsilon_G(V(t))$ based on $E_G(t)$, as follows:

$$\begin{aligned} \dot{V}(t) &= -\gamma \frac{\partial \varepsilon_G}{\partial V} \\ &= \gamma A^{\mathrm{T}}A\left(A^{\mathrm{T}}(D - AV(t)B)B^{\mathrm{T}}\right)BB^{\mathrm{T}}. \end{aligned} \tag{9}$$

The nonlinear GGNN dynamics are defined as

$$\dot{V}(t) = \gamma A^{\mathrm{T}} A \mathcal{F}(A^{\mathrm{T}}(D - AV(t)B)B^{T})BB^{\mathrm{T}}, \tag{10}$$

in which $\mathcal{F}(C) = \mathcal{F}([c_{ij}])$ denotes the elementwise application of an odd and monotonically increasing function $f(\cdot)$, as mentioned in the previous section for the GNN model (3). Model (10) is termed GGNN(A, B, D). Three activation functions $f(\cdot)$ are used in numerical experiments:

1. Linear function
$$f_{lin}(x) = x; \tag{11}$$
2. Power-sigmoid activation function
$$f_{ps}(x, \rho, \varrho) = \begin{cases} x^{\rho} & \text{if } \ |x| \geq 1 \\ \frac{1+e^{-\varrho}}{1-e^{-\varrho}} \cdot \frac{1+e^{-\varrho x}}{1-e^{-\varrho x}} & \text{if } \ |x| < 1 \end{cases} \tag{12}$$
where $\varrho > 2$, and $\rho \geq 3$ is an odd integer;
3. Smooth power-sigmoid function
$$f_{sps}(x, \rho, \varrho) = \frac{1}{2}x^{\rho} + \frac{1+e^{-\varrho}}{1-e^{-\varrho}} \cdot \frac{1+e^{-\varrho x}}{1-e^{-\varrho x}}, \tag{13}$$
where $\varrho > 2$, and $\rho \geq 3$ is an odd integer.

Figure 1 represents the Simulink implementation of GGNN(A, B, D) dynamics (10).

On the other hand, the GZNN model, defined using the ZNN dynamics on the Zhangian matrix $E_G(t)$, is defined in [40] by the general evolutionary design

$$\dot{E}_G(t) = \frac{\mathrm{d}E_G(t)}{\mathrm{d}t} = -\gamma \mathcal{F}(E_G(t)). \tag{14}$$

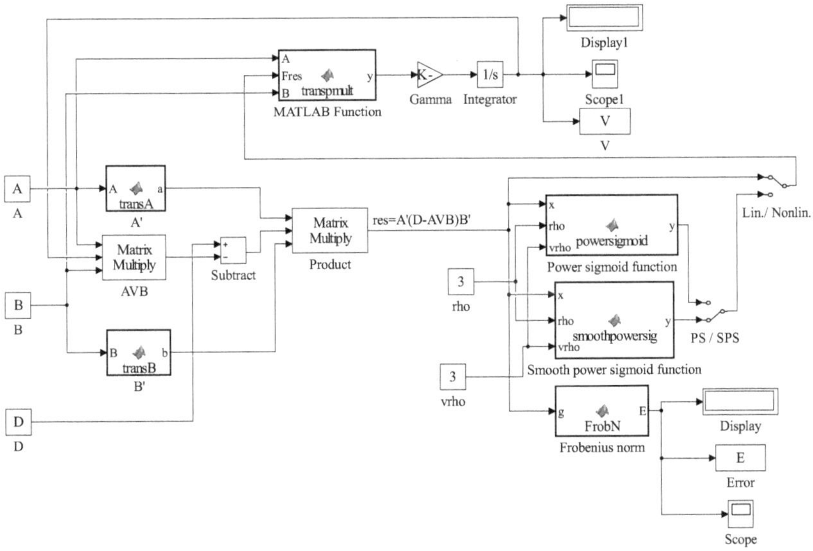

Figure 1. Simulink implementation of GGNN(A, B, D) evolution (10).

3. Convergence Analysis of GGNN Dynamics

In this section, we will analyze the convergence properties of the GGNN model given by dynamics (10).

Theorem 1. *Consider matrices $A \in \mathbb{R}^{m\times n}, B \in \mathbb{R}^{p\times q}$ and $D \in \mathbb{R}^{m\times q}$. If an odd and monotonically increasing array activation function $\mathcal{F}(\cdot)$ based on an elementwise function $f(\cdot)$ is used, then the activation state matrix $V(t) \in \mathbb{R}^{n\times p}$ of the* GGNN(A, B, D) *model* (10) *asymptotically converges to the solution of the matrix equation $AXB = D$, i.e., $A^{\mathrm{T}}AV(t)BB^{\mathrm{T}} \to A^{\mathrm{T}}DB^{\mathrm{T}}$ as $t \to +\infty$, for an arbitrary initial state matrix $V(0)$.*

Proof. From statement (b) of Proposition 3, the solvability of $A^{\mathrm{T}}AVBB^{\mathrm{T}} = A^{\mathrm{T}}DB^{\mathrm{T}}$ is ensured. The substitution $V(t) = \bar{V}(t) + A^{\dagger}DB^{\dagger}$ transforms the dynamics (10) into

$$\begin{aligned}
\frac{\mathrm{d}\bar{V}(t)}{\mathrm{d}t} = \frac{\mathrm{d}V(t)}{\mathrm{d}t} &= \gamma A^{\mathrm{T}}A\mathcal{F}\left(A^{\mathrm{T}}(D - AV(t)B)B^{\mathrm{T}}\right)BB^{\mathrm{T}} \\
&= \gamma A^{\mathrm{T}}A\mathcal{F}\left(A^{\mathrm{T}}\left(D - A\bar{V}(t)B - AA^{\dagger}DB^{\dagger}B\right)B^{\mathrm{T}}\right)BB^{\mathrm{T}} \\
&\overset{(4)}{=} \gamma A^{\mathrm{T}}A\mathcal{F}\left(A^{\mathrm{T}}(D - A\bar{V}(t)B - D)B^{\mathrm{T}}\right)BB^{\mathrm{T}} \\
&= -\gamma A^{\mathrm{T}}A\mathcal{F}\left(A^{\mathrm{T}}A\bar{V}(t)BB^{\mathrm{T}}\right)BB^{\mathrm{T}}.
\end{aligned} \tag{15}$$

The Lyapunov function candidate that measures the convergence performance is defined by

$$L(\bar{V}(t), t) = \frac{1}{2}||\bar{V}(t)||_F^2 = \frac{1}{2}\mathrm{Tr}\left(\bar{V}(t)^{\mathrm{T}}\bar{V}(t)\right). \tag{16}$$

The conclusion is $L(\bar{V}(t), t) \geq 0$. According to (16), assuming (15) and using $\mathrm{d}\,\mathrm{Tr}(X^{\mathrm{T}}X) = 2\mathrm{Tr}(X^{\mathrm{T}}\mathrm{d}X)$, in conjunction with the basic properties of the matrix trace function, one can express the time derivative of $L(\bar{V}(t), t)$ as follows:

$$\begin{aligned}\frac{\mathrm{d}L(\bar{V}(t),t)}{\mathrm{d}t} &= \frac{1}{2}\frac{\mathrm{d}\mathrm{Tr}\big(\bar{V}(t)^{\mathrm{T}}\bar{V}(t)\big)}{\mathrm{d}t} \\ &= \frac{1}{2}\cdot 2\cdot \mathrm{Tr}\left(\bar{V}(t)^{\mathrm{T}}\frac{\mathrm{d}\bar{V}(t)}{\mathrm{d}t}\right) \\ &= \mathrm{Tr}\left[\bar{V}(t)^{\mathrm{T}}\left(-\gamma A^{\mathrm{T}}A\mathcal{F}\left(A^{\mathrm{T}}A\bar{V}(t)BB^{\mathrm{T}}\right)BB^{\mathrm{T}}\right)\right] \\ &= -\gamma\mathrm{Tr}\left[\bar{V}(t)^{\mathrm{T}}A^{\mathrm{T}}A\mathcal{F}\left(A^{\mathrm{T}}A\bar{V}(t)BB^{\mathrm{T}}\right)BB^{\mathrm{T}}\right] \\ &= -\gamma\mathrm{Tr}\left[BB^{\mathrm{T}}\bar{V}(t)^{\mathrm{T}}A^{\mathrm{T}}A\mathcal{F}\left(A^{\mathrm{T}}A\bar{V}(t)BB^{\mathrm{T}}\right)\right] \\ &= -\gamma\mathrm{Tr}\left[\left(A^{\mathrm{T}}A\bar{V}(t)BB^{\mathrm{T}}\right)^{\mathrm{T}}\mathcal{F}\left(A^{\mathrm{T}}A\bar{V}(t)BB^{\mathrm{T}}\right)\right].\end{aligned} \tag{17}$$

Since the scalar-valued function $f(\cdot)$ is odd and monotonically increasing, it follows that, for $W(t) = A^{\mathrm{T}}A\bar{V}(t)BB^{\mathrm{T}}$,

$$\begin{aligned}\frac{\mathrm{d}L(\bar{V}(t),t)}{\mathrm{d}t} &= -\gamma\mathrm{Tr}\left[\left(W^{\mathrm{T}}\mathcal{F}(W)\right)\right] \\ &= -\gamma\sum_{i=1}^{m}\sum_{j=1}^{n} w_{ij}f(w_{ij})\begin{cases} <0 & \text{if} \quad W(t) := A^{\mathrm{T}}A\bar{V}(t)BB^{\mathrm{T}} \neq 0 \\ =0 & \text{if} \quad W(t) := A^{\mathrm{T}}A\bar{V}(t)BB^{\mathrm{T}} = 0,\end{cases}\end{aligned} \tag{18}$$

which implies

$$\frac{\mathrm{d}L(\bar{V}(t),t)}{\mathrm{d}t}\begin{cases} <0 & \text{if} \quad W(t) \neq 0 \\ =0 & \text{if} \quad W(t) = 0.\end{cases} \tag{19}$$

Observing the identity

$$\begin{aligned}W(t) &= A^{\mathrm{T}}A\bar{V}(t)BB^{\mathrm{T}} \\ &= A^{\mathrm{T}}A\left(V(t) - A^{\dagger}DB^{\dagger}\right)BB^{\mathrm{T}} \\ &= A^{\mathrm{T}}AV(t)BB^{\mathrm{T}} - A^{\mathrm{T}}DB^{\mathrm{T}} \\ &= A^{\mathrm{T}}(AV(t)B - D)B^{\mathrm{T}},\end{aligned}$$

and using the Lyapunov stability theory, $W(t) := A^{\mathrm{T}}(AV(t)B - D)B^{\mathrm{T}}$ globally converges to the zero matrix from an arbitrary initial value $V(0)$. □

Theorem 2. *The activation state-variable matrix $V(t)$ of the model* GGNN(A,B,D)*, defined by* (10)*, is convergent as $t \to +\infty$, and its equilibrium state is*

$$V(t) \to \tilde{V}(t) = A^{\dagger}DB^{\dagger} + V(0) - A^{\dagger}AV(0)BB^{\dagger} \tag{20}$$

for every initial state matrix $V(0) \in \mathbb{R}^{n\times p}$.

Proof. From (10), the matrix $V_1(t) = (A^{\mathrm{T}}A)^{\dagger}A^{\mathrm{T}}AV(t)BB^{\mathrm{T}}(BB^{\mathrm{T}})^{\dagger}$ satisfies

$$\begin{aligned}\frac{\mathrm{d}V_1(t)}{\mathrm{d}t} &= (A^{\mathrm{T}}A)^{\dagger}A^{\mathrm{T}}A\frac{\mathrm{d}V(t)}{\mathrm{d}t}BB^{\mathrm{T}}(BB^{\mathrm{T}})^{\dagger} \\ &= \gamma(A^{\mathrm{T}}A)^{\dagger}A^{\mathrm{T}}A\left[A^{\mathrm{T}}A\left(A^{\mathrm{T}}(D - AV(t)B)B^{\mathrm{T}}\right)BB^{\mathrm{T}}\right]BB^{\mathrm{T}}(BB^{\mathrm{T}})^{\dagger}.\end{aligned}$$

According to the basic properties of the Moore–Penrose inverse [5], it follows that

$$(BB^{\mathrm{T}})^{\mathrm{T}}BB^{\mathrm{T}}(BB^{\mathrm{T}})^{\dagger} = (BB^{\mathrm{T}})^{\mathrm{T}} = BB^{\mathrm{T}}, \qquad (A^{\mathrm{T}}A)^{\dagger}A^{\mathrm{T}}A(A^{\mathrm{T}}A)^{\mathrm{T}} = (A^{\mathrm{T}}A)^{\mathrm{T}} = A^{\mathrm{T}}A$$

which further implies

$$\frac{\mathrm{d}V_1(t)}{\mathrm{d}t} = \gamma A^{\mathrm{T}}A\Big(A^{\mathrm{T}}(D - AV(t)B)B^{\mathrm{T}}\Big)BB^{\mathrm{T}} = \frac{\mathrm{d}V(t)}{\mathrm{d}t}.$$

Consequently, $V_2(t) = V(t) - V_1(t)$ satisfies $\frac{\mathrm{d}V_2(t)}{\mathrm{d}t} = \frac{\mathrm{d}V(t)}{\mathrm{d}t} - \frac{\mathrm{d}V_1(t)}{\mathrm{d}t} = 0$, which implies

$$\begin{aligned} V_2(t) &= V_2(0) \\ &= V(0) - V_1(0) \\ &= V(0) - (A^{\mathrm{T}}A)^{\dagger}A^{\mathrm{T}}AV(0)BB^{\mathrm{T}}(BB^{\mathrm{T}})^{\dagger} \\ &= V(0) - A^{\dagger}AV(0)BB^{\dagger}, \quad t \geq 0. \end{aligned} \tag{21}$$

Furthermore, from Theorem 1, $A^{\mathrm{T}}AV(t)BB^{\mathrm{T}} \to A^{\mathrm{T}}DB^{\mathrm{T}}$, and $V_1(t)$ converges to

$$\begin{aligned} V_1(t) = (A^{\mathrm{T}}A)^{\dagger}A^{\mathrm{T}}AV(t)BB^{\mathrm{T}}(BB^{\mathrm{T}})^{\dagger} &\to (A^{\mathrm{T}}A)^{\dagger}A^{\mathrm{T}}DB^{\mathrm{T}}(BB^{\mathrm{T}})^{\dagger} \\ &= A^{\dagger}DB^{\dagger} \end{aligned}$$

as $t \to +\infty$. Therefore, $V(t) = V_1(t) + V_2(t)$ converges to the equilibrium state

$$\tilde{V}(t) = A^{\dagger}DB^{\dagger} + V_2(t) = A^{\dagger}DB^{\dagger} + V(0) - A^{\dagger}AV(0)BB^{\dagger}.$$

The proof is finished. □

4. Numerical Experiments on GNN and GGNN Dynamics

The numerical examples in this section are based on the Simulink implementation of the GGNN formula in Figure 1.

The parameter γ, initial state $V(0)$ and parameters ρ and ϱ of the nonlinear activation functions (12) and (13) are entered directly into the model, while matrices A, B and D are defined from the workspace. It is assumed that $\rho = \varrho = 3$ in all examples. The `ode15s` differential equation solver is used in the configuration parameters. In all examples, V^* denotes the theoretical solution.

The blocks *powersig*, *smoothpowersig* and *transpmult* include the codes described in [34,42].

Example 1. *Let us consider the idempotent matrix A from* [43,44]*,*

$$A = \begin{bmatrix} 1 & 0 & 1 & 1 \\ 0 & 1 & 1 & 2 \\ 0 & 0 & 0 & 0 \\ 0 & 0 & 0 & 0 \end{bmatrix}$$

of $\operatorname{rank}(A) = 2$*, and the theoretical Moore–Penrose inverse*

$$V^* = A^{\dagger} = \frac{1}{3}\begin{bmatrix} 2 & -1 & 0 & 0 \\ -1 & 1 & 0 & 0 \\ 1 & 0 & 0 & 0 \\ 0 & 1 & 0 & 0 \end{bmatrix}.$$

The matrix equation corresponding to the Moore–Penrose inverse is $A^{\mathrm{T}}AX = A^{\mathrm{T}}$ *[16], which implies the error function* $E(t) = A^{\mathrm{T}}(I - AX)$*. The corresponding GNN model is defined by* $\mathrm{GNN}(A^{\mathrm{T}}A, I_4, A^{\mathrm{T}})$*, where* I_4 *denotes the identity and zero* 4×4 *matrix. Constraint* (4) *reduces to the condition* $AA^{\dagger}A^{\mathrm{T}} = A^{\mathrm{T}}$*, which is not satisfied. The input parameters of* $\mathrm{GNN}(A^{\mathrm{T}}A, I_4, A^{\mathrm{T}})$ *are* $\gamma = 10^8$*,* $V(0) = O_4$*, where* O_4 *denotes the zero* 4×4 *matrix. The corresponding* $\mathrm{GGNN}((A^{\mathrm{T}}A)^2, I, A^{\mathrm{T}}AA^{\mathrm{T}})$ *design is based on the error matrix* $E_G(t) = A^{\mathrm{T}}AA^{\mathrm{T}}(I - AV)$*. The Simulink imple-*

mentation of GGNN(A, B, D) from Figure 1 and the Simulink implementation of GNN(A, B, D) from [34] export, in this case, the graphical results presented in Figures 2 and 3, which display the behaviors of the norms $||E_G(t)||_F = ||A^TAA^T(I - AV(t))||_F$ and $||V(t) - V^*||_F$, respectively. It is observable that the norms generated by the application of the GGNN formula vanish faster to zero than the corresponding norms in the GNN model. The graphs in the presented figures strengthen the fast convergence of the GGNN dynamical system and its important role, which can include the application of this specific model (10) to problems that require the computation of the Moore–Penrose inverse.

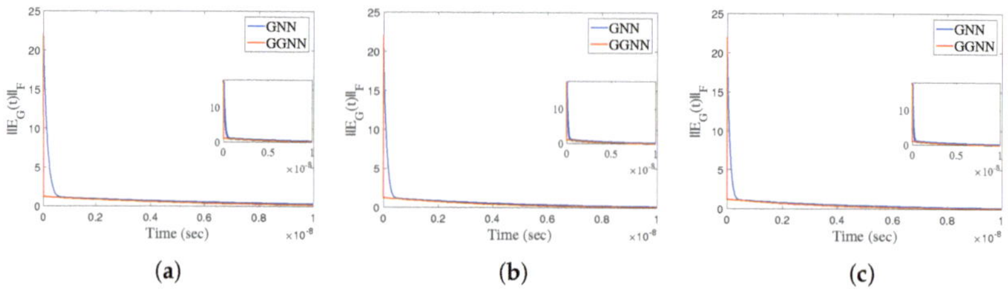

Figure 2. (**a**) Linear activation. (**b**) Power-sigmoid activation. (**c**) Smooth power–sigmoid activation. $\|E_G(t)\|_F$ in GGNN$((A^TA)^2, I, A^TAA^T)$ compared to GNN(A^TA, I_4, A^T) in Example 1.

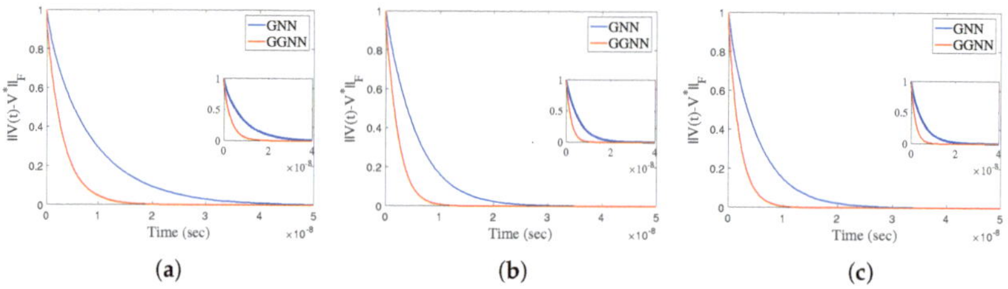

Figure 3. (**a**) Linear activation. (**b**) Power-sigmoid activation. (**c**) Smooth power–sigmoid activation. $\|V(t) - V^*\|_F$ in GGNN$((A^TA)^2, I, A^TAA^T)$ compared to GNN(A^TA, I_4, A^T) in Example 1.

Example 2. *Let us consider the matrices*

$$A = \begin{bmatrix} -8 & 8 & -4 \\ 11 & 4 & -7 \\ 1 & -4 & 3 \\ 0 & 12 & -10 \\ 6 & 12 & -12 \end{bmatrix}, \quad B = \begin{bmatrix} 1 & 0 & 0 \\ 0 & 1 & 0 \\ 0 & 0 & 1 \\ 0 & 0 & 0 \end{bmatrix}, \quad D = \begin{bmatrix} -84 & 2524 & 304 \\ -2252 & -623 & 2897 \\ 484 & -885 & -701 \\ -1894 & 2278 & 2652 \\ -2778 & 1524 & 3750 \end{bmatrix}.$$

The exact minimum-norm least-squares solution is

$$V^* = A^\dagger D B^\dagger = \begin{bmatrix} -\frac{7409}{65} & -\frac{9564}{65} & \frac{8953}{65} & 0 \\ -\frac{968}{13} & \frac{1770}{13} & \frac{1402}{13} & 0 \\ \frac{6503}{65} & -\frac{4187}{65} & -\frac{8826}{65} & 0 \end{bmatrix}.$$

The ranks of the input matrices are equal to $r = \text{rank}(A) = 2$, $\text{rank}(D) = 2$ and $\text{rank}(B) = 3$. Constraint (4) is satisfied in this case. The linear GGNN(A, B, D) formula (10) is applied to solve the matrix equation $AXB = D$. The gain parameter of the model is $\gamma = 10^9$, $V(0) = 0$, and the stopping time is $t = 0.00001$, which gives

$$X = \begin{bmatrix} -113.9846 & -147.1385 & 137.7385 & 0 \\ -74.4615 & 136.1538 & 107.8462 & 0 \\ 100.0462 & -64.4154 & -135.7846 & 0 \end{bmatrix} \approx A^\dagger D B^\dagger.$$

The elementwise trajectories of the state variables v_{ij} of the state matrix $V(t)$ are shown in Figure 4a–c with solid red lines for linear, power-sigmoid and smooth power-sigmoid activation functions, respectively. The fast convergence of elementwise trajectories to the corresponding black dashed trajectories of the theoretical solution V^* is notable. In addition, faster convergence caused by the nonlinear AFs f_{ps} and f_{sps} is noticeable in Figure 4b,c. The trajectories in the figures indicate the usual convergence behavior, so the system is globally asymptotically stable. The norms of the error matrix E_G of both models GNN and GGNN under linear and nonlinear AFs are shown in Figure 5a–c. The power-sigmoid and smooth power-sigmoid activation functions show superiority in their convergence speed compared with linear activation. On each graph in Figure 5a–c, the Frobenius norm $\|E_G(t)\|_F$ of the error matrix $E_G(t)$ in the GGNN formula vanishes faster to zero than that in the GNN model. Moreover, in each graph in Figure 6a–c, the Frobenius norm $\|E(t)\|_F$ in the GGNN formula vanishes faster to zero than that in the GNN model, which strengthens the fact that the proposed dynamical system (10) *initiates accelerated convergence compared to* (3).

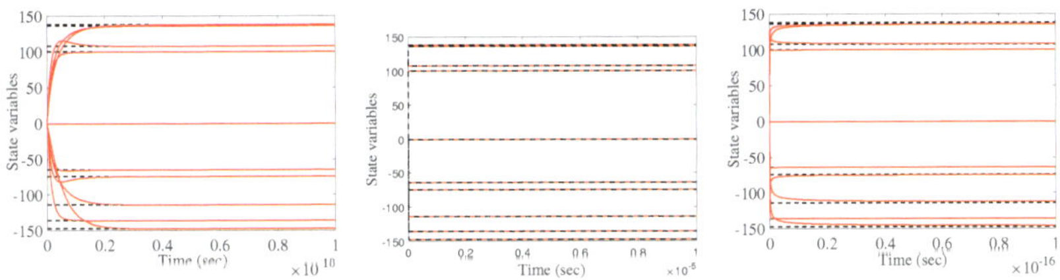

(a) (b) (c)

Figure 4. (**a**) Linear activation. (**b**) Power-sigmoid activation. (**c**) Smooth power–sigmoid activation. Elementwise convergence trajectories $v_{ij} \in V(t)$ of the GGNN(A, B, D) network in Example 2.

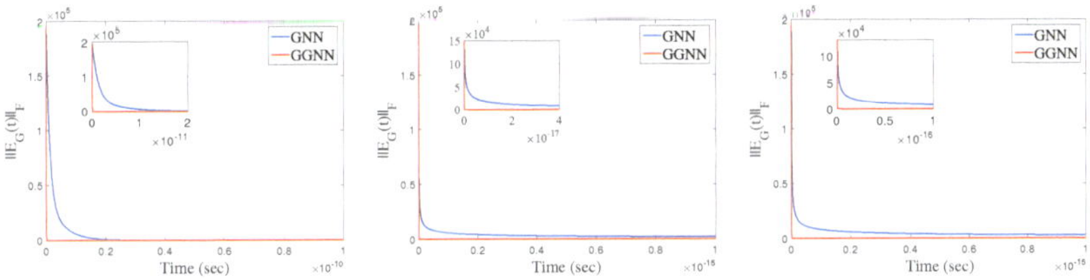

(a) (b) (c)

Figure 5. (**a**) Linear activation. (**b**) Power-sigmoid activation. (**c**) Smooth power–sigmoid activation. $\|E_G(t)\|_F$ in GGNN(A, B, D) compared to GNN(A, B, D) in Example 2.

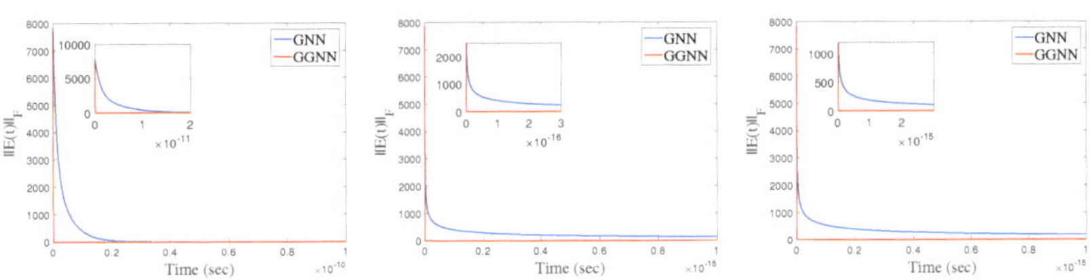

(a) (b) (c)

Figure 6. (**a**) Linear activation. (**b**) Power-sigmoid activation. (**c**) Smooth power–sigmoid activation. $\|E(t)\|_F$ in GGNN(A, B, D) compared to GNN(A, B, D) in Example 2.

All graphs shown in Figures 5 and 6 confirm the applicability of the proposed GGNN design compared to the traditional GNN design, even if constraint (4) holds.

Example 3. *Let us explore the behavior of GNN and GGNN dynamics for computing the Moore–Penrose inverse of the matrix*

$$A = \begin{bmatrix} 9 & 3 & -3 \\ -1 & 1 & 0 \\ 4 & 7 & 2 \\ 2 & 4 & -4 \\ 13 & 5 & 8 \end{bmatrix}.$$

The Moore–Penrose inverse of A is equal to

$$A^{\dagger} = \begin{bmatrix} \frac{9908}{127779} & -\frac{18037}{766674} & -\frac{6874}{127779} & -\frac{2663}{383337} & \frac{29941}{766674} \\ -\frac{5690}{127779} & \frac{14426}{383337} & \frac{16741}{127779} & \frac{25130}{383337} & -\frac{6392}{383337} \\ -\frac{3517}{42593} & \frac{1979}{255558} & \frac{1073}{42593} & -\frac{7373}{127779} & \frac{15049}{255558} \end{bmatrix}$$
$$\approx \begin{bmatrix} 0.0775 & -0.0235 & -0.0538 & -0.0069 & 0.0390 \\ -0.0445 & 0.0376 & 0.1310 & 0.0655 & -0.0167 \\ -0.0826 & 0.0077 & 0.0252 & -0.0577 & 0.0589 \end{bmatrix}.$$

The rank of the input matrix is equal to $r = \mathrm{rank}(A) = 3$. *Consequently, the matrix A is left invertible and satisfies* $A^{\dagger}A = I$. *The error matrix* $E(t) = I - VA$ *initiates the* $\mathrm{GNN}(I, A, I)$ *dynamics for computing* $A^{\dagger}$. *The gradient-based error matrix*

$$E_G(t) = (I - V(t)A)A^{\mathrm{T}}.$$

initiates the $\mathrm{GGNN}(I, AA^{\mathrm{T}}, A^{\mathrm{T}})$ *design.*

The gain parameter of the model is $\gamma = 100$, *and the initial state is* $V(0) = 0$ *with a stop time* $t = 0.00001$.

The Frobenius norms of the error matrix $E(t)$ *generated by the linear GNN and GGNN models for different values of* γ ($\gamma = 10^2, \gamma = 10^3, \gamma = 10^6$) *are shown in Figure 7a–c. The graphs in these figures confirm an increase in the convergence speed, which is caused by the increase in the gain parameter* γ. *Because of that, the considered time intervals are* $[0, 10^{-2}]$, $[0, 10^{-3}]$ *and* $[0, 10^{-6}]$, *respectively. In all three scenarios, a faster convergence of the GGNN model is observable compared to the GNN design. The values of the norm* $\|E_G\|_F$ *generated by both the GNN and GGNN models with linear and two nonlinear activation functions are shown in Figure 8a–c. Like the conclusion in the previous example, the perception is that the GGNN converges faster compared to the GNN model.*

In addition, the graphs in Figure 8b,c, corresponding to the power-sigmoid and smooth power-sigmoid AFs, respectively, show a certain level of instability in convergence, as well as an increase in the value of $\|E_G(t)\|_F$.

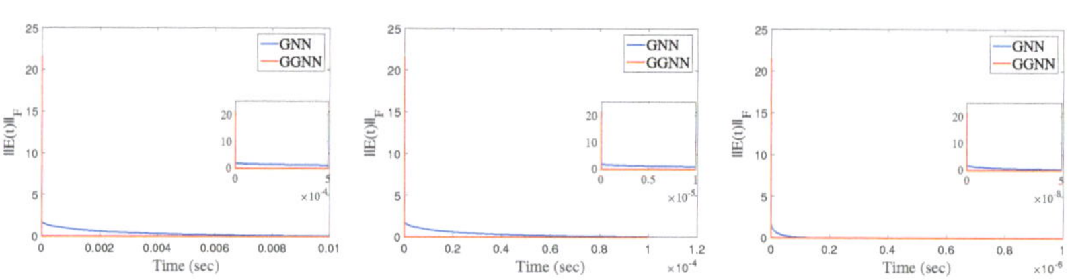

(a) (b) (c)

Figure 7. **(a)** $\gamma = 10, t \in [0, 10^{-2}]$. **(b)** $\gamma = 10^3, t \in [0, 10^{-3}]$. **(c)** $\gamma = 10^6, t \in [0, 10^{-6}]$. $\|E(t)\|_F$ for different γ in $\mathrm{GGNN}(I, AA^{\mathrm{T}}, A^{\mathrm{T}})$ compared to $\mathrm{GNN}(I, A, I)$ in Example 3.

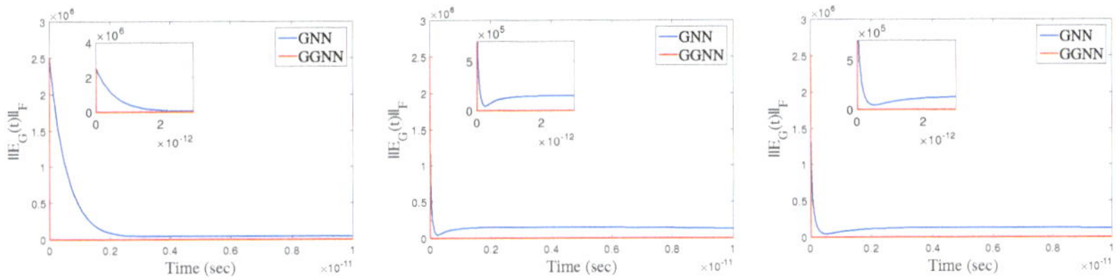

(**a**) (**b**) (**c**)

Figure 8. (**a**) Linear activation. (**b**) Power-sigmoid activation. (**c**) Smooth power–sigmoid activation. $\|E_G(t)\|_F$ in GGNN$(I, AA^{\mathrm{T}}, A^{\mathrm{T}})$ compared to GNN(I, A, I) in Example 3.

Example 4. *Consider the matrices*

$$A = \begin{bmatrix} 15 & -352 & -45 & -238 & 42 \\ -5 & 14 & 8 & 132 & -65 \\ 235 & -65 & 44 & 350 & -73 \end{bmatrix}, \ D = \begin{bmatrix} -4 & 4 & 16 \\ 3 & 1 & -9 \\ 1 & -7 & 2 \\ 2 & 2 & -4 \\ 4 & 1 & -5 \end{bmatrix}, \ A_1 = DA,$$

which dissatisfy $\operatorname{rank}(A_1) = \operatorname{rank}(D) = 3$. *Now, we apply the GNN and GGNN formulae to solve the matrix equation* $A_1X = D$. *The standard error function is defined as* $E(t) = D - A_1V(t)$. *So, we consider* GNN(A_1, I_3, D). *The error matrix for the corresponding GGNN model is* $E_G(t) = A_1^{\mathrm{T}}(D - A_1V(t))$, *which initiates the* GGNN$(A_1^{\mathrm{T}}A_1, I_3, A_1^{\mathrm{T}}D)$ *flow. The gain parameter of the model is* $\gamma = 10^9$, *and the final time is* $t = 0.00001$. *The zero initial state* $V(0) = 0$ *generates the best approximate solution* $X = A_1^{\dagger}D = (DA)^{\dagger}D$ *of the matrix equation* $A_1X = D$, *given by*

$$X = A_1^{\dagger}D = \begin{bmatrix} -\frac{133851170015}{180355524917879} & -\frac{1648342203725}{180355524917879} & \frac{608888775010}{180355524917879} \\ -\frac{508349079720}{180355524917879} & -\frac{691967699675}{180355524917879} & -\frac{48398092277}{180355524917879} \\ -\frac{68130232042}{180355524917879} & -\frac{242513061343}{180355524917879} & \frac{82710890618}{180355524917879} \\ -\frac{31936168532}{180355524917879} & \frac{727110260384}{180355524917879} & \frac{134047117682}{180355524917879} \\ -\frac{172434574901}{180355524917879} & -\frac{1350198643304}{180355524917879} & \frac{225136761416}{180355524917879} \end{bmatrix}$$

$$\approx \begin{bmatrix} -0.000742 & -0.00914 & 0.00338 \\ -0.00282 & -0.00384 & -0.000268 \\ -0.000378 & -0.00134 & 0.000459 \\ -0.000177 & 0.00403 & 0.000743 \\ -0.000956 & -0.00749 & 0.00125 \end{bmatrix}.$$

The Frobenius norms of the error matrix $E(t) = D - A_1V(t)B$ *in the GNN and GGNN models for both linear and nonlinear activation functions are shown in Figure 9a–c, and the error matrix* $E_G(t) = A_1^{\mathrm{T}}(D - A_1V(t))$ *in both models for linear and nonlinear activation functions are shown in Figure 10a–c. It is observable that the GGNN converges faster than GNN.*

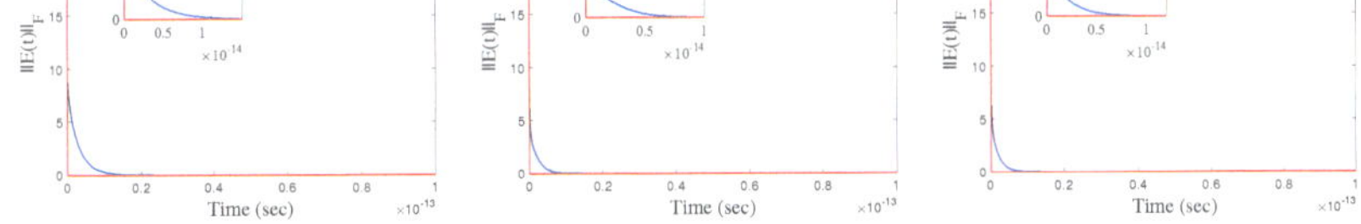

(**a**) (**b**) (**c**)

Figure 9. (**a**) Linear activation. (**b**) Power-sigmoid activation. (**c**) Smooth power–sigmoid activation. $\|E(t)\|_F$ in GGNN$(A_1^{\mathrm{T}}A_1, I_3, A_1^{\mathrm{T}}D)$ compared to GNN(A_1, I_3, D) in Example 4.

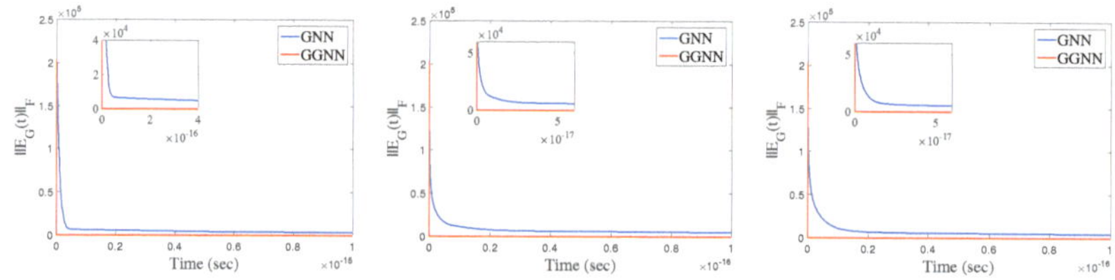

(a) (b) (c)

Figure 10. (**a**) Linear activation. (**b**) Power-sigmoid activation. (**c**) Smooth power–sigmoid activation. $\|E_G(t)\|_F$ in GGNN$(A_1^T A_1, I_3, A_1^T D)$ compared to GNN(A_1, I_3, D) in Example 4.

Example 5. *Tables 1 and 2 show the results obtained during experiments we conducted with nonsquared matrices, where $m \times n$ is the dimension of the matrix. Table 1 lists the input data that were used to perform experiments with the Simulink model and generated the results in Table 2. The best cases in Table 2 are marked in bold text.*

Table 1. Input data.

Matrix A			Matrix B			Matrix D			Input and Residual Norm		
m	n	rank(A)	p	q	rank(B)	m	q	rank(D)	γ	t_f	$\|\|AA^{\dagger}DB^{\dagger}B-D\|\|_F$
10	8	8	9	7	7	10	7	7	10^4	0.5	1.051
10	8	6	9	7	7	10	7	7	10^4	0.5	1.318
10	8	6	9	7	5	10	7	7	10^4	0.5	1.81
10	8	6	9	7	5	10	7	5	10^4	5	2.048
10	8	1	9	7	2	10	7	1	10^4	5	2.372
20	10	10	8	5	5	20	5	5	10^6	5	1.984
20	10	5	8	5	5	20	5	5	10^6	5	2.455
20	10	5	8	5	2	20	5	5	10^6	1	3.769
20	10	2	8	5	2	20	5	2	10^6	1	2.71
20	15	15	5	2	2	20	2	2	10^8	1	1.1
20	15	10	5	2	2	20	2	2	10^8	1	1.158
20	15	10	5	2	1	20	2	2	10^8	1	2.211
20	15	5	5	2	1	20	2	2	10^8	1	1.726

Table 2. Experimental results based on data presented in Table 1.

$\|\|E(t)\|\|_F$(GNN)	$\|\|E(t)\|\|_F$(GGNN)	$\|\|E_G(t)\|\|_F$(GNN)	$\|\|E_G(t)\|\|_F$(GGNN)	CPU(GNN)	CPU(GGNN)
1.051	1.094	$\mathbf{2.52 \times 10^{-9}}$	0.02524	**5.017148**	13.470995
1.318	1.393	$\mathbf{3.122 \times 10^{-7}}$	0.03661	22.753954	**10.734163**
1.811	1.899	**0.0008711**	0.03947	15.754537	**15.547785**
2.048	2.082	$\mathbf{1.96 \times 10^{-10}}$	0.00964	**9.435709**	17.137916
2.372	**2.3722**	$\mathbf{1.7422 \times 10^{-15}}$	2.003×10^{-15}	21.645386	**13.255210**
1.984	**1.984**	2.288×10^{-14}	$\mathbf{9.978 \times 10^{-15}}$	21.645386	**13.255210**
2.455	**2.455**	1.657×10^{-11}	$\mathbf{1.693 \times 10^{-14}}$	50.846893	**19.059385**
3.769	**3.769**	6.991×10^{-11}	$\mathbf{4.071 \times 10^{-14}}$	42.184748	**13.722390**
2.71	**2.71**	1.429×10^{-14}	$\mathbf{1.176 \times 10^{-14}}$	148.484258	**13.527065**
1.1	**1.1**	1.766×10^{-13}	$\mathbf{5.949 \times 10^{-15}}$	218.169376	**17.5666568**
1.158	**1.158**	2.747×10^{-10}	$\mathbf{2.981 \times 10^{-13}}$	45.505618	**12.441782**
2.211	**2.211**	7.942×10^{-12}	$\mathbf{8.963 \times 10^{-14}}$	194.605133	**14.117241**
1.726	**1.726**	8.042×10^{-15}	$\mathbf{3.207 \times 10^{-15}}$	22.340501	**11.650829**

The numerical results arranged in Table 2 are divided into two parts by a horizontal line. The upper part corresponds to the test matrices of dimensions ≤ 10, while the lower part corresponds to the dimensions $m, n \geq 10$. Considering the first two columns, it is observable from the upper part that the GGNN generates smaller values $||E(t)||_F$ compared to the GGNN. The values of $||E(t)||_F$ in the lower part generated by the GNN and GGNN are equal. Considering the third and fourth columns, it is observable from the upper part that the GGNN generates smaller values $||E_G(t)||_F$ compared to the GGNN. On the other hand, the values of $||E_G(t)||_F$ in the lower part, generated by the GGNN, are smaller than the corresponding values generated by the GNN. The last two columns show that the GGNN requires less CPU time compared to the GNN. The general conclusion is that the GGNN model is more efficient in rank-deficient test matrices of larger order $m, n \geq 10$.

5. Mixed GGNN-GZNN Model for Solving Matrix Equations

The gradient-based error matrix for solving the matrix equation $AX = B$ is defined by

$$E_{G_{A,I,B}}(t) = A^{\mathrm{T}}(AV(t) - B).$$

The GZNN design (14) corresponding to the error matrix $E_{A,I,B}$, designated GZNN(A, I, B), is of the form:

$$\dot{E}_{G_{A,I,B}}(t) = -\gamma\mathcal{F}\Big(A^{\mathrm{T}}(AV(t) - B)\Big). \tag{22}$$

Now, the scalar-valued norm-based error function corresponding to $E_{G_{A,I,B}}(t)$ is given by

$$\varepsilon(t) = \varepsilon(V(t)) = \frac{1}{2}||E_{G_{A,I,B}}(t)||_F = \frac{||A^{\mathrm{T}}(AV(t) - B)||_F}{2}.$$

The following dynamic state equation can be derived using the GGNN(A, I, B) design formula based on (10):

$$\dot{V}(t) = -\gamma A^{\mathrm{T}}A\mathcal{F}\Big(A^{\mathrm{T}}(AV(t) - B)\Big). \tag{23}$$

Further, using a combination of $\dot{E}_{G_{A,I,B}}(t) = A^{\mathrm{T}}A\dot{V}(t)$ and the GNN dynamics (23), it follows that

$$\dot{E}_{G_{A,I,B}}(t) = A^{\mathrm{T}}A\dot{V}(t) = -\gamma A^{\mathrm{T}}AA^{\mathrm{T}}A\mathcal{F}\Big(A^{\mathrm{T}}(AV(t) - B)\Big). \tag{24}$$

The next step is to define the new hybrid model based on the summation of the right-hand sides in (22) and (24), as follows:

$$\dot{E}_{G_{A,I,B}}(t) = -\gamma\Big(\Big(A^{\mathrm{T}}A\Big)^2 + I\Big)\mathcal{F}\Big(A^{\mathrm{T}}(AV(t) - B)\Big). \tag{25}$$

The model (25) is derived from the combination of the model GGNN(A, I, B) and the model GZNN(A, I, B). Hence, it is equally justified to use the term Hybrid GGNN (abbreviated HGGNN) and Hybrid GZNN (abbreviated HGZNN) model. But model (25) is implicit, so it is not a type of GGNN dynamics. On the other hand, it is designed for time-invariant matrices, which is not in accordance with the common nature of GZNN models, because usually, the GZNN is used in the time-varying case. A formal comparison of (25) and GZNN(A, I, B) reveals that both these methods possess identical left-hand sides, and the right-hand side of (25) can be derived by multiplying the right-hand side of GZNN(A, I, B) by the term $(A^{\mathrm{T}}A)^2 + I$.

Formally, (25) is closer to GZNN dynamics, so we will denote the model (25) by HGZNN(A, I, B), considering that this model is not the exact GZNN neural dynamics and is applicable to time-invariant case. This is the case of the constant coefficient matrices A, I and B. Figure 11 represents the Simulink implementation of HGZNN(A, I, B) dynamics (25).

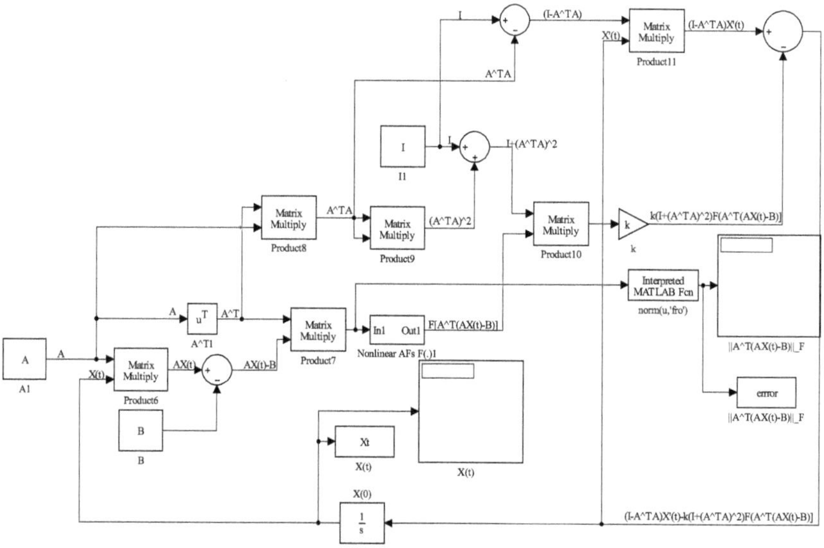

Figure 11. Simulink implementation of (25).

Now, we will take into account the process of solving the matrix equation $XC = D$. The error matrix for this equation is defined by

$$E_{G_{I,C,D}}(t) = (V(t)C - D)C^{\mathrm{T}}.$$

The GZNN design (14) corresponding to the error matrix $E_{I,C,D}$, denoted by $\mathrm{GZNN}(I,C,D)$, is of the form:

$$\dot{E}_{G_{I,C,D}}(t) = \dot{V}CC^{\mathrm{T}} = -\gamma\mathcal{F}\Big((V(t)C - D)C^{\mathrm{T}}\Big). \tag{26}$$

On the other hand, the GGNN design formula (10) produces the following dynamic state equation:

$$\dot{V}(t) = -\gamma\mathcal{F}\Big((V(t)C - D)C^{\mathrm{T}}\Big)CC^{\mathrm{T}},\ V(0) = V_0. \tag{27}$$

The GGNN model (27) is denoted by $\mathrm{GGNN}(I,C,D)$. It implies

$$\dot{E}_{G_{I,C,D}}(t) = \dot{V}(t)CC^{\mathrm{T}} = -\gamma\mathcal{F}\Big((V(t)C - D)C^{\mathrm{T}}\Big)CC^{\mathrm{T}}CC^{\mathrm{T}}. \tag{28}$$

A new hybrid model based on the summation of the right-hand sides in (26) and (28) can be proposed as follows:

$$\dot{E}_{G_{I,C,D}}(t) = -\gamma\mathcal{F}\Big((V(t)C - D)C^{\mathrm{T}}\Big)\Big(I + \left(CC^{\mathrm{T}}\right)^2\Big). \tag{29}$$

The Model (29) will be denoted by $\mathrm{HGZNN}(I,C,D)$. This is the case with the constant coefficient matrices I, C and D.

For the purposes of the proof of the following results, we will use $ECR(\mathcal{M})$ to denote the exponential convergence rate of the model $\mathcal{M}$. With $\lambda_{\min}(K)$ and $\lambda_{\max}(K)$, we denote the smallest and largest eigenvalues of the matrix K, respectively. Continuing the previous work, we use three types of activation functions $\mathcal{F}$: linear, power-sigmoid and smooth power-sigmoid.

The following theorem determines the equilibrium state of $\mathrm{HGZNN}(A,I,B)$ and defines its global exponential convergence.

Theorem 3. *Let $A \in \mathbb{R}^{k\times n}, B \in \mathbb{R}^{k\times m}$ be given and satisfy $AA^{\dagger}B = B$, and let $V(t) \in \mathbb{R}^{n\times m}$ be the state matrix of (25), where $\mathcal{F}$ is defined by f_{lin}, f_{ps} or f_{sps}.*

(a) *Then, $V(t)$ achieves global convergence and satisfies $AV(t) \to B$ when $t \to +\infty$, starting from any initial state $X(0) \in \mathbb{R}^{n\times m}$. The state matrix $V(t) \in \mathbb{R}^{n\times m}$ of* HGZNN(A, I, B) *is stable in the sense of Lyapunov.*

(b) *The exponential convergence rate of the* HGZNN(A, I, B) *model* (25) *in the linear case is equal to*

$$ECR(\text{HGZNN}(A, I, B)) = \gamma\left(1 + \sigma^4_{\min}(A)\right), \tag{30}$$

where $\sigma_{\min}(A) = \lambda_{\min}(A^{\mathrm{T}}A)$ is the minimum singular value of A.

(c) *The activation state variable matrix $V(t)$ of the model* HGZNN(A, I, B) *is convergent when $t \to +\infty$ with the equilibrium state matrix*

$$V(t) \to \tilde{V}_{V(0)} = A^{\dagger}B + (I - A^{\dagger}A)V(0). \tag{31}$$

Proof. (a) The assumption $AA^{\dagger}B = B$ provides the solvability of the matrix equation $AX = B$.

The appropriate Lyapunov function is defined as

$$\mathcal{L}(t) = \frac{1}{2}||E_{G_{A,I,B}}(t)||_F^2 = \frac{1}{2}\mathrm{Tr}\left(\left(E_{G_{A,I,B}}(t)\right)^{\mathrm{T}} E_{G_{A,I,B}}(t)\right).$$

Hence, from (25) and $\mathrm{d}\,\mathrm{Tr}(V^{\mathrm{T}}V) = 2\mathrm{Tr}(V^{\mathrm{T}}\mathrm{d}V)$, it holds that

$$\begin{aligned}
\dot{\mathcal{L}}(t) &= \frac{1}{2}\frac{\mathrm{d}}{\mathrm{d}t}\mathrm{Tr}\left(\left(E_{G_{A,I,B}}(t)\right)^{\mathrm{T}} E_{G_{A,I,B}}(t)\right) \\
&= \mathrm{Tr}\left(\left(E_{G_{A,I,B}}(t)\right)^{\mathrm{T}} \dot{E}_{A,I,B}(t)\right) \\
&= \mathrm{Tr}\left(\left(E_{G_{A,I,B}}(t)\right)^{\mathrm{T}}\left(-\gamma\left(\left(A^{\mathrm{T}}A\right)^2 + I\right)\mathcal{F}\left(E_{G_{A,I,B}}(t)\right)\right)\right) \\
&= -\gamma\mathrm{Tr}\left(\left(\left(A^{\mathrm{T}}A\right)^2 + I\right)\mathcal{F}\left(E_{G_{A,I,B}}(t)\right)\left(E_{G_{A,I,B}}(t)\right)^{\mathrm{T}}\right).
\end{aligned}$$

According to similar results from [45], one can verify the following inequality:

$$\dot{\mathcal{L}}(t) \leq -\gamma\mathrm{Tr}\left(\left(\left(A^{\mathrm{T}}A\right)^2 + I\right)E_{G_{A,I,B}}(t)\left(E_{G_{A,I,B}}(t)\right)^{\mathrm{T}}\right).$$

We also consider the following inequality from [46], which is valid for a real symmetric matrix K and a real symmetric positive-semidefinite matrix L of the same size:

$$\lambda_{\min}(K)\mathrm{Tr}(L) \leq \mathrm{Tr}(KL) \leq \lambda_{\max}(K)\mathrm{Tr}(L). \tag{32}$$

Now, the following can be chosen: $K = \left(A^{\mathrm{T}}A\right)^2 + I$ and $L = E_{G_{A,I,B}}(t)\left(E_{G_{A,I,B}}(t)\right)^{\mathrm{T}}$. Consider $\lambda_{\min}\left(\left(A^{\mathrm{T}}A\right)^2\right) = \lambda^2_{\min}(A^{\mathrm{T}}A) = \sigma^4_{\min}(A)$, where $\lambda_{\min}(A)$ is the minimum eigenvalue of A, and $\sigma_{\min}(A) = \sqrt{\lambda_{\min}(A^{\mathrm{T}}A)}$ is the minimum singular value of A. Then, $1 + \sigma^4_{\min}(A) \geq 1$ is the minimum nonzero eigenvalue of $\left(A^{\mathrm{T}}A\right)^2 + I$, which implies

$$\dot{\mathcal{L}}(t) \leq -\gamma\left(1 + \sigma^4_{\min}(A)\right)\mathrm{Tr}\left(E_{G_{A,I,B}}(t)\left(E_{G_{A,I,B}}(t)\right)^{\mathrm{T}}\right). \tag{33}$$

From (33), it can be concluded

$$\dot{\mathcal{L}}(t)\begin{cases} <0 & \text{if } E_{G_{A,I,B}}(t) \neq 0 \\ =0 & \text{if } E_{G_{A,I,B}}(t) = 0. \end{cases} \tag{34}$$

According to (34), the Lyapunov stability theory confirms that $E_{A,I,B}(t) = AV(t) - B = 0$ is a globally asymptotically stable equilibrium point of the HGZNN(A, I, B) model (25). So, $E_{A,I,B}(t)$ converges to the zero matrix, i.e., $AV(t) \to B$, from any initial state $X(0)$.

(b) From (a), it follows that

$$\begin{aligned} \dot{\mathcal{L}} &\leq -\gamma\left(1+\sigma_{\min}^4(A)\right)\mathrm{Tr}\left(\left(E_{G_{A,I,B}}(t)\right)^{\mathrm{T}} E_{G_{A,I,B}}(t)\right) \\ &= -\gamma\left(1+\sigma_{\min}^4(A)\right)||E_{G_{A,I,B}}(t)||_F^2 \\ &= -\frac{\gamma}{2}\left(1+\sigma_{\min}^4(A)\right)\mathcal{L}(t). \end{aligned}$$

This implies

$$\begin{aligned} \mathcal{L} &\leq \mathcal{L}(0)e^{-\gamma(1+\sigma_{\min}^4(A))t} \iff \\ ||E_{G_{A,I,B}}(t)||_F^2 &\leq ||E_{G_{A,I,B}}(0)||_F^2\, \mathrm{e}^{-\gamma(1+\sigma_{\min}^4(A))} \iff \\ ||E_{G_{A,I,B}}(t)||_F &\leq ||E_{G_{A,I,B}}(0)||_F\, \mathrm{e}^{-\gamma/2(1+\sigma_{\min}^4(A))}, \end{aligned}$$

which confirms the convergence rate (30) of HGZNN(A, I, B).

(c) This part of the proof can be verified with the particular case $B := I, D := B$ of Theorem 2.

□

Theorem 4. *Let $C \in \mathbb{R}^{m\times l}, D \in \mathbb{R}^{n\times l}$ be given and satisfy $DC^\dagger C = D$, and let $V(t) \in \mathbb{R}^{n\times m}$ be the state matrix of* (29)*, where $\mathcal{F}$ is defined by f_{lin}, f_{ps} or f_{sps}.*

(a) *Then, $V(t)$ achieves global convergence $V(t)C \to D$ when $t \to +\infty$, starting from any initial state $V(0) \in \mathbb{R}^{n\times m}$. The state matrix $V(t) \in \mathbb{R}^{n\times m}$ of* HGZNN(I, C, D) *is stable in the sense of Lyapunov.*

(b) *The exponential convergence rate of the* HGZNN(I, C, D) *model* (29) *in the linear case is equal to*

$$ECR(\mathrm{HGZNN}(I,C,D)) = \gamma\left(1+\sigma_{min}^4(C)\right). \tag{35}$$

(c) *The activation state variable matrix $V(t)$ of the model* HGZNN(I, C, D) *is convergent when $t \to +\infty$ with the equilibrium state matrix*

$$V(t) \to \tilde{V}_{V(0)} = DC^\dagger + V(0)(I - CC^\dagger). \tag{36}$$

Proof. (a) The assumption $DC^\dagger C = D$ ensures the solvability of the matrix equation $XC = D$.

Let us define the Lyapunov function by

$$\mathcal{L}(t) = \frac{1}{2}||E_{G_{I,C,D}}(t)||_F^2 = \frac{1}{2}\mathrm{Tr}\left(\left(E_{G_{I,C,D}}(t)\right)^{\mathrm{T}} E_{G_{I,C,D}}(t)\right).$$

Hence, from (29) and $\mathrm{d}\,\mathrm{Tr}(X^{\mathrm{T}}X) = 2\mathrm{Tr}(X^{\mathrm{T}}\mathrm{d}X)$, it holds that

$$\begin{aligned}\dot{\mathcal{L}}(t) &= \frac{1}{2}\frac{\mathrm{d}}{\mathrm{d}t}\mathrm{Tr}\Big(\big(E_{G_{I,C,D}}(t)\big)^{\mathrm{T}}E_{G_{I,C,D}}(t)\Big)\\ &= \mathrm{Tr}\Big(\big(E_{G_{I,C,D}}(t)\big)^{\mathrm{T}}\dot{E}_{G_{I,C,D}}(t)\Big)\\ &= \mathrm{Tr}\Big(\big(E_{G_{I,C,D}}(t)\big)^{\mathrm{T}}\Big(-\gamma\Big(\big(CC^{\mathrm{T}}\big)^2+I\Big)\mathcal{F}\big(E_{G_{I,C,D}}(t)\big)\Big)\Big)\\ &= -\gamma\mathrm{Tr}\Big(\Big(\big(CC^{\mathrm{T}}\big)^2+I\Big)\mathcal{F}\big(E_{G_{I,C,D}}(t)\big)\big(E_{G_{I,C,D}}(t)\big)^{\mathrm{T}}\Big).\end{aligned}$$

Following the principles from [45], one can verify the following inequality:

$$\dot{\mathcal{L}}(t) \le -\gamma\mathrm{Tr}\Big(\Big(\big(CC^{\mathrm{T}}\big)^2+I\Big)E_{G_{I,C,D}}(t)\big(E_{G_{I,C,D}}(t)\big)^{\mathrm{T}}\Big).$$

Consider the inequality (32) with the particular settings $K = \big(CC^{\mathrm{T}}\big)^2+I$, $L = E_{G_{I,C,D}}(t)\big(E_{G_{I,C,D}}(t)\big)^{\mathrm{T}}$. Let $\lambda_{\min}\Big(\big(CC^{\mathrm{T}}\big)^2\Big)$ be the minimum eigenvalue of $\big(CC^{\mathrm{T}}\big)^2$. Then, $1+\sigma^4_{\min}(\mathrm{C})) \ge 1$ is the minimal nonzero eigenvalue of $\big(CC^{\mathrm{T}}\big)^2+I$, which implies

$$\dot{\mathcal{L}}(t) \le -\gamma\big(1+\sigma^4_{\min}(C)\big)\mathrm{Tr}\Big(E_{G_{I,C,D}}(t)\big(E_{G_{I,C,D}}(t)\big)^{\mathrm{T}}\Big). \tag{37}$$

From (37), it can be concluded

$$\dot{\mathcal{L}}(t)\begin{cases} <0 & \text{if } E_{G_{I,C,D}}(t)\neq 0\\ =0 & \text{if } E_{G_{I,C,D}}(t)=0.\end{cases} \tag{38}$$

According to (38), the Lyapunov stability theory confirms that $E_{G_{I,C,D}}(t) = V(t)C - D = 0$ is a globally asymptotically stable equilibrium point of the HGZNN(A,I,B) model (29). So, $E_{G_{I,C,D}}(t)$ converges to the zero matrix, i.e., $V(t)C \to D$, from any initial state $V(0)$.

(b) From (a), it follows

$$\begin{aligned}\dot{\mathcal{L}} &\le -\gamma\big(1+\sigma^4_{\min}(\mathrm{C})\big)\mathrm{Tr}\Big(\big(E_{G_{I,C,D}}(t)\big)^{\mathrm{T}}E_{G_{I,C,D}}(t)\Big)\\ &= -\gamma\big(1+\sigma^4_{\min}(\mathrm{C})\big)||E_{G_{I,C,D}}(t)||_F^2\\ &= -\frac{\gamma}{2}\big(1+\sigma^4_{\min}(\mathrm{C})\big)\mathcal{L}(t).\end{aligned}$$

This implies

$$\begin{aligned}\mathcal{L} \le \mathcal{L}(0)e^{-2\gamma(1+\sigma^4_{\min}(\mathrm{C}))t} &\iff\\ ||E_{G_{I,C,D}}(t)||_F^2 \le ||E_{G_{I,C,D}}(0)||_F^2 e^{-2\gamma(1+\sigma^4_{\min}(\mathrm{C}))} &\iff\\ ||E_{G_{I,C,D}}(t)||_F \le ||E_{G_{I,C,D}}(0)||_F e^{-\gamma(1+\sigma^4_{\min}(\mathrm{C}))},&\end{aligned}$$

which confirms the convergence rate (35) of HGZNN(I,C,D).

(c) This part of the proof can be verified with the particular case $A := I, B := C$ of Theorem 2.

□

Corollary 1. (a) *Let the matrices* $A \in \mathbb{R}^{k\times n}, B \in \mathbb{R}^{k\times m}$ *be given and satisfy* $AA^{\dagger}B = B$, *and let* $V(t) \in \mathbb{R}^{n\times m}$ *be the state matrix of* (25), *with an arbitrary nonlinear activation* $\mathcal{F}$. *Then,* $ECR(\mathrm{GZNN}(A,I,B)) = \gamma$ *and* $ECR(\mathrm{GGNN}(A,I,B)) = \gamma\sigma_{\min}(A)$.
(b) *Let the matrices* $C \in \mathbb{R}^{m\times l}, D \in \mathbb{R}^{n\times l}$ *be given and satisfy* $DC^{\dagger}C = D$, *and let* $V(t) \in \mathbb{R}^{n\times m}$ *be the state matrix of* (29) *with an arbitrary nonlinear activation* $\mathcal{F}$. *Then,* $ECR(\mathrm{GZNN}(I,C,D)) = \gamma$ *and* $ECR(\mathrm{GGNN}(I,C,D)) = \gamma\sigma_{\min}(C)$.

From Theorem 3 and Corollary 1(a), it follows that

$$\frac{ECR(\mathrm{HGZNN}(A,I,B))}{ECR(\mathrm{GZNN}(A,I,B))} = 1+\sigma^4_{\min}(A) \geq 1. \tag{39}$$

$$\frac{ECR(\mathrm{HGZNN}(A,I,B))}{ECR(\mathrm{GGNN}(A,I,B))} = \frac{1+\sigma^4_{\min}(A)}{\sigma^2_{\min}(A)} > 1. \tag{40}$$

$$\frac{ECR(\mathrm{GZNN}(A,I,B))}{ECR(\mathrm{GGNN}(A,I,B))} = \frac{1}{\sigma^2_{\min}(A)}\begin{cases} <1, & \sigma_{\min}(A) > 1 \\ \geq 1, & \sigma_{\min}(A) \leq 1 \end{cases}. \tag{41}$$

Similarly, according to Theorem 4 and Corollary 1(b), it can be concluded that

$$\frac{ECR(\mathrm{HGZNN}(I,C,D))}{ECR(\mathrm{GZNN}(I,C,D))} = 1+\sigma^4_{\min}(C) \geq 1. \tag{42}$$

$$\frac{ECR(\mathrm{HGZNN}(I,C,D))}{ECR(\mathrm{GGNN}(I,C,D))} = \frac{1+\sigma^4_{\min}(C)}{\sigma^2_{\min}(C)} > 1. \tag{43}$$

$$\frac{ECR(\mathrm{GZNN}(I,C,D))}{ECR(\mathrm{GGNN}(I,C,D))} = \frac{1}{\sigma^2_{\min}(C)}\begin{cases} <1, & \sigma_{\min}(C) > 1 \\ \geq 1, & \sigma_{\min}(C) \leq 1 \end{cases}. \tag{44}$$

Remark 1. (a) *According to* (40), *it follows that* $ECR(\mathrm{HGZNN}(A,I,B)) > ECR(\mathrm{GZNN}(A,I,B))$. *According to* (39), *it is obtained*

$$ECR(\mathrm{HGZNN}(A,I,B))\begin{cases} = ECR(\mathrm{GZNN}(A,I,B)), & \sigma_{\min}(A) = 0 \\ > ECR(\mathrm{GZNN}(A,I,B)), & \sigma_{\min}(A) > 0. \end{cases}$$

According to (41), *it follows*

$$ECR(\mathrm{GZNN})(\mathrm{A,I,B})\begin{cases} < ECR(\mathrm{GGNN}(A,I,B)), & \sigma_{\min}(A) > 1 \\ \geq ECR(\mathrm{GGNN}(A,I,B)), & \sigma_{\min}(A) \leq 1 \end{cases}.$$

As a result, the following conclusions follow:

- $\mathrm{HGZNN}(A,I,B)$ *is always faster than* $\mathrm{GGNN}(A,I,B)$;
- $\mathrm{HGZNN}(A,I,B)$ *is faster than* $\mathrm{GZNN}(A,I,B)$ *in the case where* $\sigma_{\min}(A) > 0$;
- $\mathrm{GZNN}(A,I,B)$ *is faster than* $\mathrm{GGNN}(A,I,B))$ *in the case where* $\sigma_{\min}(A) < 1$.

(b) *According to* (43), *it follows that* $ECR(\mathrm{HGZNN}(I,C,D)) > ECR(\mathrm{GZNN}(I,C,D))$. *According to* (42), *it follows that*

$$ECR(\mathrm{HGZNN}(I,C,D))\begin{cases} = ECR(\mathrm{GZNN}(I,C,D)), & \sigma_{\min}(C) = 0 \\ > ECR(\mathrm{GZNN}(I,C,D)), & \sigma_{\min}(C) > 0. \end{cases}$$

According to (41) *and* (44), *it can be verified*

$$ECR(\mathrm{GZNN})(\mathrm{I,C,D})\begin{cases} < ECR(\mathrm{GGNN}(I,C,D)), & \sigma_{\min}(C) > 1 \\ \geq ECR(\mathrm{GGNN}(I,C,D)), & \sigma_{\min}(C) \leq 1 \end{cases}.$$

As a result, the following conclusions follow:

- HGZNN(I, C, D) *is always faster than* GGNN(I, C, D);
- HGZNN(I, C, D) *is faster than* GZNN(I, C, D) *in the case where* $\sigma_{\min}(C) > 0$;
- GZNN(I, C, D) *is faster than* GGNN$(I, C, D))$ *in the case where* $\sigma_{\min}(C) < 1$.

Remark 2. *The particular HGZNN$(A^{\mathrm{T}}A, I, A^{\mathrm{T}})$ and GGNN$(A^{\mathrm{T}}A, I, A^{\mathrm{T}})$ designs define the corresponding modifications of the improved GNN design proposed in [26] if $A^{\mathrm{T}}A$ is invertible. In the dual case, HGZNN$(I, CC^{\mathrm{T}}, C^{\mathrm{T}})$ and GGNN$(I, CC^{\mathrm{T}}, C^{\mathrm{T}})$ define the corresponding modifications of the improved GNN design proposed in [26] if CC^{T} is invertible.*

Regularized HGZNN Model for Solving Matrix Equations

The convergence of HGZNN(A, I, B) (resp. HGZNN(I, C, D)), as well as GGNN(A, I, B) (resp. GGNN(I, C, D)), can be improved in the case where $\sigma_{\min}(A) > 0$ (resp. $\sigma_{\min}(C) > 0$). There exist two possible situations when the acceleration terms $A^{\mathrm{T}}A$ and CC^{T} improve the convergence. The first case assumes the invertibility of A (resp. C), and the second case assumes the left invertibility of A (resp. right invertibility of C). Still, in some situations, the matrices A and C could be rank-deficient. Hence, in the case where A and C are square and singular, it is useful to use the invertible matrices $A_1 := A + \lambda I$ and $C_1 := C + \lambda I$, $\lambda > 0$ instead of A and C and to consider the models HGZNN(A_1, I, B) and HGZNN(I, C_1, D). The following presents the convergence results considering the nonsingularity of A_1 and C_1.

Corollary 2. *Let $A \in \mathbb{R}^{n\times n}$, $B \in \mathbb{R}^{n\times m}$ be given and $V(t) \in \mathbb{R}^{n\times m}$ be the state matrix of (25), where $\mathcal{F}$ is defined by f_{lin}, f_{ps} or f_{sps}. Let $\lambda > 0$ be a selected real number. Then, the following statements are valid:*

(a) *The state matrix $V(t) \in \mathbb{R}^{n\times m}_r$ of the model* HGZNN(A_1, I, B) *converges globally to*

$$\tilde{V}_{V(0)} = A_1^{-1}B,$$

when $t \to +\infty$, starting from any initial state $X(0) \in \mathbb{R}^{n\times m}$, and the solution is stable in the sense of Lyapunov.

(b) *The exponential convergence rate of* HGZNN(A_1, I, B) *in the case where $\mathcal{F} = I$ is equal to*

$$ECR(\mathrm{HGZNN}(A_1, I, B)) = \gamma\left(1 + \sigma^4_{\min}(A + \lambda I)\right).$$

(c) *Let $\tilde{V}_{V(0)}$ be the limiting value of $V(t)$ when $t \to +\infty$. Then,*

$$\lim_{\lambda\to 0} \tilde{V}_{V(0)} = \lim_{\lambda\to 0}(A + \lambda I)^{-1}B. \tag{45}$$

Proof. Since $A + \lambda I$ is invertible, it follows that $V = (A + \lambda I)^{-1}B$.

From (31) and the invertibility of $A + \lambda I$, we conclude the validity of (a). In this case, it follows that

$$\begin{aligned}\tilde{V}_{V(0)} &= (A + \lambda I)^{-1}B + (I - (A + \lambda I)^{-1}(A + \lambda I))V(0) \\ &= (A + \lambda I)^{-1}B + (I - I)V(0) \\ &= (A + \lambda I)^{-1}B.\end{aligned}$$

The part (b) is proved analogously to the proof of Theorem 3. The last part (c) follows from (a). □

Corollary 3. *Let* $C \in \mathbb{R}^{m\times m}$, $D \in \mathbb{R}^{n\times m}$ *be given and* $V(t) \in \mathbb{R}^{n\times m}$ *be the state matrix of* (29), *where* $\mathcal{F} = I, \mathcal{F} = \mathcal{F}_{ps}$ *or* $\mathcal{F} = \mathcal{F}_{sps}$. *Let* $\lambda > 0$ *be a selected real number. Then, the following statements are valid:*

(a) *The state matrix* $V(t) \in \mathbb{R}_r^{n\times m}$ *of* HGZNN(I, C_1, D) *converges globally to*

$$\tilde{V}_{V(0)} = D(C + \lambda I)^{-1},$$

when $t \to +\infty$, *starting from any initial state* $X(0) \in \mathbb{R}^{n\times m}$, *and the solution is stable in the sense of Lyapunov.*

(b) *The exponential convergence rate of* HGZNN(I, C_1, D) *in the case where* $\mathcal{F} = I$ *is equal to*

$$ECR(\text{HGZNN}(I, C_1, D)) = \gamma\Big(1 + \sigma^4_{\min}(1)\Big).$$

(c) *Let* $\tilde{V}_{V(0)}$ *be the limiting value of* $V(t)$ *when* $t \to +\infty$. *Then,*

$$\lim_{\lambda\to 0} \tilde{V}_{V(0)} = \lim_{\lambda\to 0} D(C + \lambda I)^{-1}. \quad (46)$$

Proof. It can be proved analogously to Corollary 2. □

Remark 3. (a) *According to* (40), *it can be concluded that*

$$ECR(\text{HGZNN}(A_1, I, B)) > ECR(\text{GZNN}(A_1, I, B)).$$

Based on (39) *it can be concluded*

$$ECR(\text{HGZNN}(A_1, I, B)) > ECR(\text{GZNN}(A_1, I, B)).$$

According to (41), *one concludes*

$$ECR(\text{GZNN}(A_1, I, B)) < ECR(\text{GGNN}(A_1, I, B)).$$

(b) *According to* (43), *it can be concluded*

$$ECR(\text{HGZNN}(I, C_1, D)) > ECR(\text{GZNN}(I, C_1, D)).$$

According to (42), *it follows*

$$ECR(\text{HGZNN}(I, C_1, D)) > ECR(\text{GZNN}(I, C_1, D)).$$

Based on (41) *and* (44), *it can be concluded*

$$ECR(\text{GZNN}(I, C_1, D)) < ECR(\text{GGNN}(I, C_1, D)).$$

6. Numerical Examples on Hybrid Models

In this section, numerical examples are presented based on the Simulink implementation of the HGZNN formula. The previously mentioned three types of activation functions $f(\cdot)$ in (11), (12) and (13) will be used in the following examples. The parameters γ, the initial state $V(0)$ and the parameters ρ and ϱ of the nonlinear activation functions (12) and (13) are entered directly into the model, while the matrices A, B, C and D are defined from the workspace. We assume that $\rho = \varrho = 3$ in all examples. The ordinary differential equation solver in the configuration parameters is ode15s.

We present numerical examples in which we compare Frobenius norms $||E_G||_F$ and $||A^{-1}B - V(t)||_F$, which are generated by HGZNN, GZNN and GGNN.

Example 6. *Consider the matrix*

$$A = \begin{bmatrix} 0.49 & 0.276 & 0.498 & 0.751 & 0.959 \\ 0.446 & 0.68 & 0.96 & 0.255 & 0.547 \\ 0.646 & 0.655 & 0.34 & 0.506 & 0.139 \\ 0.71 & 0.163 & 0.585 & 0.699 & 0.149 \\ 0.755 & 0.119 & 0.224 & 0.891 & 0.258 \end{bmatrix}.$$

In this example, we compare the HGZNN(A, I, I) model with GZNN(A, I, I) and GGNN(A, I, I), considering all three types of activation functions. The gain parameter of the model is $\gamma = 10^6$, the initial state $V(0) = 0$, and the final time is $t = 0.00001$.

The Frobenius norm of the error matrix E_G in the HGZNN, GZNN and GGNN models for both linear and nonlinear activation functions are shown in Figure 12a–c, and the error matrices $A^{-1}B - V(t)$ of both models for linear and nonlinear activation functions are shown in Figure 13a–c. On each graph, the Frobenius norm of the error from the HGZNN formula vanishes faster to zero than those from the GZNN and GGNN models.

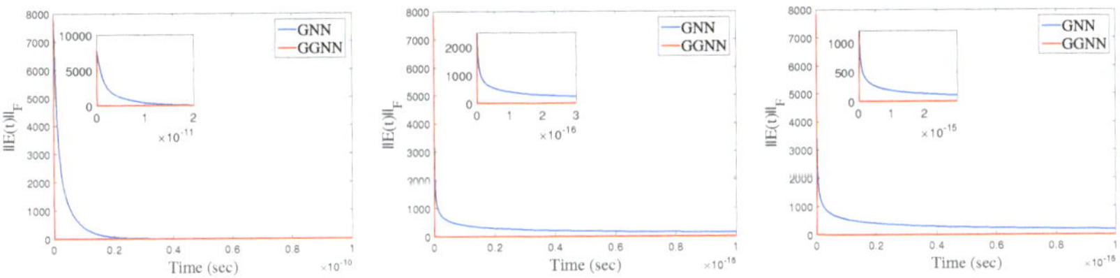

(a) (b) (c)

Figure 12. (**a**) Linear activation. (**b**) Power-sigmoid activation. (**c**) Smooth power–sigmoid activation. $\|E_{A,I,B}\|_F$ of HGZNN(A, I, I) compared to GGNN(A, I, I) and GZNN(A, I, I) in Example 6.

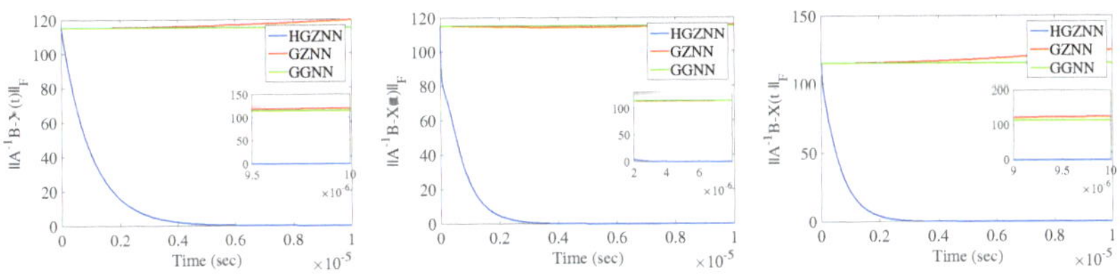

(a) (b) (c)

Figure 13. (**a**) Linear activation. (**b**) Power–sigmoid activation. (**c**) Smooth power–sigmoid activation. $\|A^{-1}B - V(t)\|_F$ of HGZNN(A, I, I) compared to GGNN(A, I, I) and GZNN(A, I, I) in Example 6.

Example 7. *Consider the matrices*

$$A = \begin{bmatrix} 0.0818 & 0.0973 & 0.0083 & 0.0060 & 0.0292 & 0.0372 \\ 0.0818 & 0.0649 & 0.0133 & 0.0399 & 0.0432 & 0.0198 \\ 0.0722 & 0.0800 & 0.0173 & 0.0527 & 0.0015 & 0.0490 \\ 0.0150 & 0.0454 & 0.0391 & 0.0417 & 0.0984 & 0.0339 \\ 0.0660 & 0.0432 & 0.0831 & 0.0657 & 0.0167 & 0.0952 \\ 0.0519 & 0.0825 & 0.0803 & 0.0628 & 0.0106 & 0.0920 \end{bmatrix},$$

$$B = \begin{bmatrix} 0.1649 & 0.1813 & 0.0851 & 0.1197 & 0.0138 & 0.1437 & 0.1558 \\ 0.1965 & 0.1759 & 0.0625 & 0.0942 & 0.0639 & 0.1937 & 0.0847 \\ 0.1460 & 0.1636 & 0.0323 & 0.1392 & 0.1062 & 0.1063 & 0.0182 \\ 0.0688 & 0.0521 & 0.0358 & 0.1400 & 0.1309 & 0.0650 & 0.0533 \\ 0.1168 & 0.1189 & 0.0846 & 0.1277 & 0.0815 & 0.0211 & 0.0307 \\ 0.0216 & 0.0045 & 0.0188 & 0.0067 & 0.1640 & 0.1222 & 0.0562 \end{bmatrix}.$$

In this example, we compare the HGZNN(A, I, B) model with GZNN(A, I, B) and GGNN(A, I, B), considering all three types of activation functions. The gain parameter of the model is $\gamma = 1000$, the initial state $V(0) = 0$, and the final time is $t = 0.01$.

The elementwise trajectories of the state variable are shown with red lines in Figure 14a–c, for linear, power-sigmoid and smooth power-sigmoid activation functions, respectively. The solid red lines corresponding to HGZNN(A, I, B) converge to the black dashed lines of the theoretical solution X. It is observable that the trajectories indicate the usual convergence behavior, so the system is globally asymptotically stable. The error matrices E_G of the HGZNN, GZNN and GGNN models for both linear and nonlinear activation functions are shown in Figure 15a–c, and the residual matrices $A^{-1}B - X(t)$ of both models for linear and nonlinear activation functions are shown in Figure 16a–c. In each graph, for both error cases, the Frobenius norm of the error of the HGZNN formula is similar to the Frobenius norm of the error of the GZNN model, and they both converges faster to zero than the GGNN model.

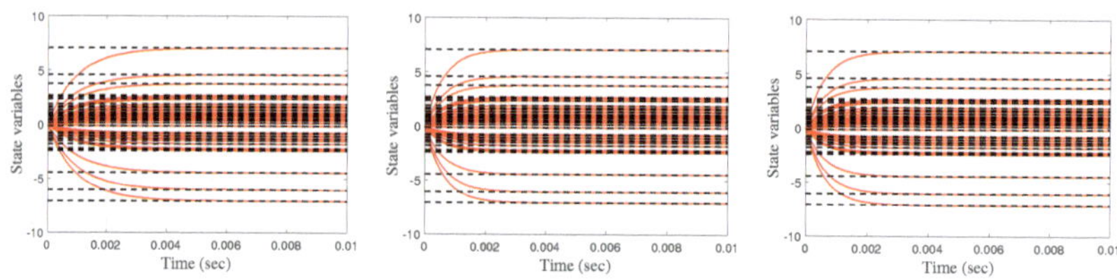

(a) (b) (c)

Figure 14. (**a**) Linear activation. (**b**) Power-sigmoid activation. (**c**) Smooth power–sigmoid activation. Elementwise convergence trajectories of the HGZNN(A, I, B) network in Example 7.

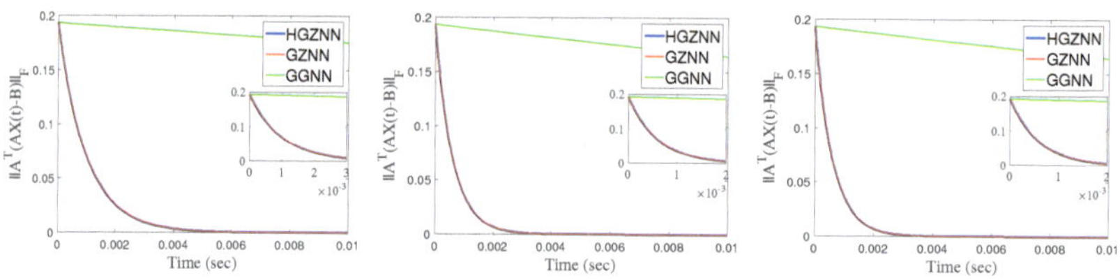

(a) (b) (c)

Figure 15. (**a**) Linear activation. (**b**) Power-sigmoid activation. (**c**) Smooth power–sigmoid activation. $\|E_{A,I,B}\|_F$ of HGZNN(A, I, B) compared to GGNN(A, I, B) and GZNN(A, I, B) in Example 7.

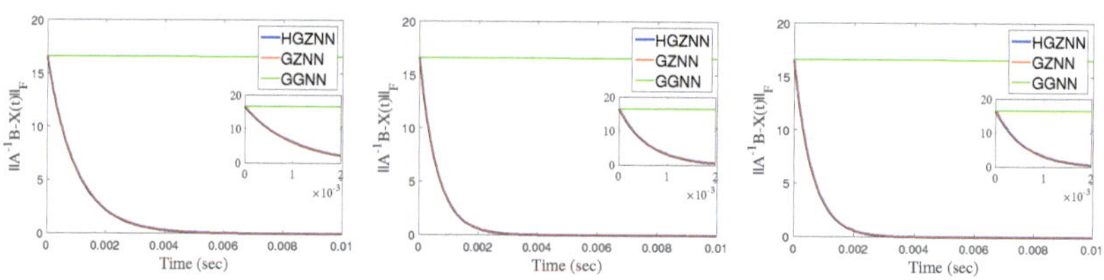

(a) (b) (c)

Figure 16. (**a**) Linear activation. (**b**) Power-sigmoid activation. (**c**) Smooth power–sigmoid activation. Frobenius norm of error matrix $A^{-1}B - X(t)$ of HGZNN(A, I, B) compared to GGNN(A, I, B) and GZNN(A, I, B) in Example 7.

Remark 4. *In this remark, we analyze the answer to the question, "how are the system parameters selected to obtain better performance?" The answer is complex and consists of several parts.*

1. *The gain parameter γ is the parameter with the most influence on the behavior of the observed dynamic systems. The general rule is "the parameter γ should be selected as large as possible". The numerical confirmation of this fact is investigated in Figure 7.*

2. *The influence of γ and AFs is indisputable. The larger the value of γ, the faster the convergence. And, clearly, AFs increase convergence compared to the linear models. In the presented numerical examples, we investigate the influence of three AFs: linear, power-sigmoid and smooth power-sigmoid.*
3. *The right question is as follows: what makes the* GGNN *better than the* GNN *under fair conditions that assume an identical environment during testing? Numerical experiments show better performance of the* GGNN *design compared to the* GNN *with respect to all three tested criteria: $\|E(t)\|_F$, $\|E_G(t)\|_F$ and $\|V(t) - V^*\|_F$. Moreover, Table 2 in Example 5 is aimed at convergence analysis. The general conclusion from the numerical data arranged in Table 2 is that the GGNN model is more efficient compared to the GNN in rank-deficient test matrices of larger order $m, n \geq 10$.*
4. *The convergence rate of the linear hybrid model* $\mathrm{HGZNN}(A, I, B))$ *depends on γ and the singular value $\sigma_{\min}(A)$, while the convergence rate of the hybrid model* $\mathrm{HGZNN}(I, C, D)$ *depends on γ and $\sigma_{\min}(C)$.*
5. *The convergence of the linear regularized hybrid model* $\mathrm{HGZNN}(A + \lambda I, I, B))$ *depends on γ, $\sigma_{\min}(A)$ and the regularization parameter $\lambda > 0$, while the convergence of the linear regularized hybrid model* $\mathrm{HGZNN}(I, C + \lambda I, D))$ *depends on γ, $\sigma_{\min}(C)$ and λ.*

In conclusion, it is reasonable to analyze the system parameter selections to obtain better performance. But the best performance is not defined.

7. Conclusions

We show that the error functions which make the basis of GNN and ZNN dynamical evolutions can be defined using the gradient of the Frobenius norm of the traditional error function $E(t)$. The result of such a strategy is the usage of the error function $E_G(t)$ for the basis of GNN dynamics, which results in the proposed GGNN model. The results related to the GNN model (called $\mathrm{GNN}(A, B, D)$) for solving the general matrix equation $AXB = D$ are extended in the GGNN model (called $\mathrm{GGNN}(A, B, D)$) in both theoretical and computational directions. In a theoretical sense, the convergence of the defined GGNN model is considered. It is shown that the neural state matrix $V(t)$ of the $\mathrm{GGNN}(A, B, D)$ model asymptotically converges to the solution of the matrix equation $AXB = D$ for an arbitrary initial state matrix $V(0)$ and coincides with the general solution of the linear matrix equation. A number of applications of GNN(A, B, D) are considered. All applications are globally convergent. Several particular appearances of the general matrix equation are observed and applied for computing various classes of generalized inverses. Illustrative numerical examples and simulation results were obtained using Matlab Simulink implementation and are presented to demonstrate the validity of the derived theoretical results. The influence of various nonlinear activations on the GNN models is considered in both the theoretical and computational directions. From the presented examples, it can be concluded that the GGNN model is faster and has a smaller error compared to the GNN model.

Further research can be oriented to the definition of finite-time convergent GGNN or GZNN models, as well as the definition of a noise-tolerant GGNN or GZNN design.

Author Contributions: Conceptualization, P.S.S. and G.V.M.; methodology, P.S.S., N.T., D.G. and V.S.; software, D.G., V.L.K. and N.T.; validation, G.V.M., M.J.P. and P.S.S.; formal analysis, M.J.P., N.T. and D.G.; investigation, M.J.P., G.V.M. and P.S.S.; resources, D.G., N.T., V.L.K. and V.S.; data curation, M.J.P., V.L.K., V.S., D.G. and N.T.; writing—original draft preparation, P.S.S., D.G. and N.T.; writing—review and editing, M.J.P. and G.V.M.; visualization, D.G. and N.T.; supervision, G.V.M.; project administration, M.J.P.; funding acquisition, G.V.M., M.J.P. and P.S.S. All authors have read and agreed to the published version of the manuscript.

Funding: This work was supported by the Ministry of Science and Higher Education of the Russian Federation (Grant No. 075-15-2022-1121).

Data Availability Statement: Data results are available on reader request.

Acknowledgments: Predrag Stanimirović is supported by the Science Fund of the Republic of Serbia (No. 7750185, Quantitative Automata Models: Fundamental Problems and Applications—QUAM).

Dimitrios Gerontitis receives financial support from the "Savas Parastatidis" named scholarship granted provided by the Bodossaki Foundation. Milena J. Petrović acknowledges support from a project supported by Ministry of Education and Science of Republic of Serbia, Grant No. 174025.

Conflicts of Interest: The authors declare no conflicts of interest. The funders had no role in the design of the study; in the collection, analyses or interpretation of the data; in the writing of the manuscript, or in the decision to publish the results.

References

1. Zhang, Y.; Chen, K. Comparison on Zhang neural network and gradient neural network for time-varying linear matrix equation $AXB = C$ solving. In Proceedings of the 2008 IEEE International Conference on Industrial Technology, Chengdu, China, 21–24 April 2008; pp. 1–6. [CrossRef]
2. Zhang, Y.; Yi, C.; Guo, D.; Zheng, J. Comparison on Zhang neural dynamics and gradient-based neural dynamics for online solution of nonlinear time-varying equation. *Neural Comput. Appl.* **2011**, *20*, 1–7. [CrossRef]
3. Zhang, Y.; Xu, P.; Tan, L. Further studies on Zhang neural-dynamics and gradient dynamics for online nonlinear equations solving. In Proceedings of the 2009 IEEE International Conference on Automation and Logistics, Shenyang, China, 5–7 August 2009; pp. 566–571. [CrossRef]
4. Ben-Israel, A.; Greville, T.N.E. *Generalized Inverses: Theory and Applications*, 2nd ed.; CMS Books in Mathematics; Springer: New York, NY, USA, 2003.
5. Wang, G.; Wei, Y.; Qiao, S. *Generalized Inverses: Theory and Computations*; Science Press, Springer: Beijing, China, 2018.
6. Dash, P.; Zohora, F.T.; Rahaman, M.; Hasan, M.M.; Arifuzzaman, M. Usage of Mathematics Tools with Example in Electrical and Electronic Engineering. *Am. Sci. Res. J. Eng. Technol. Sci. (ASRJETS)* **2018**, *46*, 178–188.
7. Qin, F.; Lee, J. Dynamic methods for missing value estimation for DNA sequences. In Proceedings of the 2010 International Conference on Computational and Information Sciences, IEEE, Chengdu, China, 9–11 July 2010; pp. 442–445. [CrossRef]
8. Soleimani, F.; Stanimirović, P.S.; Soleimani, F. Some matrix iterations for computing generalized inverses and balancing chemical equations. *Algorithms* **2015**, *8*, 982–998. [CrossRef]
9. Udawat, B.; Begani, J.; Mansinghka, M.; Bhatia, N.; Sharma, H.; Hadap, A. Gauss Jordan method for balancing chemical equation for different materials. *Mater. Today Proc.* **2022**, *51*, 451–454. [CrossRef]
10. Doty, K.L.; Melchiorri, C.; Bonivento, C. A theory of generalized inverses applied to robotics. *Int. J. Robot. Res.* **1993**, *12*, 1–19. [CrossRef]
11. Li, L.; Hu, J. An efficient second-order neural network model for computing the Moore–Penrose inverse of matrices. *IET Signal Process.* **2022**, *16*, 1106–1117. [CrossRef]
12. Wang, X.; Tang, B.; Gao, X.G.; Wu, W.H. Finite iterative algorithms for the generalized reflexive and anti-reflexive solutions of the linear matrix equation $AXB = C$. *Filomat* **2017**, *31*, 2151–2162. [CrossRef]
13. Ding, F.; Chen, T. Gradient based iterative algorithms for solving a class of matrix equations. *IEEE Trans. Autom. Control* **2005**, *50*, 1216–1221. [CrossRef]
14. Ding, F.; Zhang, H. Gradient-based iterative algorithm for a class of the coupled matrix equations related to control systems. *IET Control Theory Appl.* **2014**, *8*, 1588–1595. [CrossRef]
15. Zhang, H. Quasi gradient-based inversion-free iterative algorithm for solving a class of the nonlinear matrix equations. *Comput. Math. Appl.* **2019**, *77*, 1233–1244. [CrossRef]
16. Wang, J. Recurrent neural networks for computing pseudoinverses of rank-deficient matrices. *SIAM J. Sci. Comput.* **1997**, *18*, 1479–1493. [CrossRef]
17. Fa-Long, L.; Zheng, B. Neural network approach to computing matrix inversion. *Appl. Math. Comput.* **1992**, *47*, 109–120. [CrossRef]
18. Wang, J. A recurrent neural network for real-time matrix inversion. *Appl. Math. Comput.* **1993**, *55*, 89–100. [CrossRef]
19. Wang, J. Recurrent neural networks for solving linear matrix equations. *Comput. Math. Appl.* **1993**, *26*, 23–34. [CrossRef]
20. Wei, Y. Recurrent neural networks for computing weighted Moore–Penrose inverse. *Appl. Math. Comput.* **2000**, *116*, 279–287. [CrossRef]
21. Xiao, L.; Zhang, Y.; Li, K.; Liao, B.; Tan, Z. FA novel recurrent neural network and its finite-time solution to time-varying complex matrix inversion. *Neurocomputing* **2019**, *331*, 483–492. [CrossRef]
22. Yi, C.; Chen, Y.; Lu, Z. Improved gradient-based neural networks for online solution of Lyapunov matrix equation. *Inf. Process. Lett.* **2011**, *111*, 780–786. [CrossRef]
23. Yi, C.; Qiao, D. Improved neural solution for the Lyapunov matrix equation based on gradient search. *Inf. Process. Lett.* **2013**, *113*, 876–881.
24. Xiao, L.; Li, K.; Tan, Z.; Zhang, Z.; Liao, B.; Chen, K.; Jin, L.; Li, S. Nonlinear gradient neural network for solving system of linear equations. *Inf. Process. Lett.* **2019**, *142*, 35–40. [CrossRef]
25. Xiao, L. A finite-time convergent neural dynamics for online solution of time-varying linear complex matrix equation. *Neurocomputing* **2015**, *167*, 254–259. [CrossRef]

26. Lv, X.; Xiao, L.; Tan, Z.; Yang, Z.; Yuan, J. Improved Gradient Neural Networks for solving Moore–Penrose Inverse of full-rank matrix. *Neural Process. Lett.* **2019**, *50*, 1993–2005. [CrossRef]
27. Wang, J. Electronic realisation of recurrent neural network for solving simultaneous linear equations. *Electron. Lett.* **1992**, *28*, 493–495. [CrossRef]
28. Zhang, Y.; Chen, K.; Tan, H.Z. Performance analysis of gradient neural network exploited for online time-varying matrix inversion. *IEEE Trans. Autom. Control.* **2009**, *54*, 1940–1945. [CrossRef]
29. Wang, J.; Li, H. Solving simultaneous linear equations using recurrent neural networks. *Inf. Sci.* **1994**, *76*, 255–277. [CrossRef]
30. Tan, Z.; Chen, H. Nonlinear function activated GNN versus ZNN for online solution of general linear matrix equations. *J. Frankl. Inst.* **2023**, *360*, 7021–7036. [CrossRef]
31. Tan, Z.; Hu, Y.; Chen, K. On the investigation of activation functions in gradient neural network for online solving linear matrix equation. *Neurocomputing* **2020**, *413*, 185–192. [CrossRef]
32. Tan, Z. Fixed-time convergent gradient neural network for solving online sylvester equation. *Mathematics* **2022**, *10*, 3090. [CrossRef]
33. Wang, D.; Liu, X.-W. A gradient-type noise-tolerant finite-time neural network for convex optimization. *Neurocomputing* **2022**, *49*, 647–656. [CrossRef]
34. Stanimirović, P.S.; Petković, M.D. Gradient neural dynamics for solving matrix equations and their applications. *Neurocomputing* **2018**, *306*, 200–212. [CrossRef]
35. Stanimirović, P.S.; Katsikis, V.N.; Li, S. Hybrid GNN-ZNN models for solving linear matrix equations. *Neurocomputing* **2018**, *316*, 124–134. [CrossRef]
36. Sowmya, G.; Thangavel, P.; Shankar, V. A novel hybrid Zhang neural network model for time-varying matrix inversion. *Eng. Sci. Technol. Int. J.* **2022**, *26*, 101009. [CrossRef]
37. Wu, W.; Zheng, B. Improved recurrent neural networks for solving Moore–Penrose inverse of real-time full-rank matrix. *Neurocomputing* **2020**, *418*, 221–231. [CrossRef]
38. Zhang, Y.; Wang, C. Gradient-Zhang neural network solving linear time varying equations. In Proceedings of the 2022 IEEE 17th Conference on Industrial Electronics and Applications (ICIEA), Chengdu, China, 16–19 December 2022; pp. 396–403. [CrossRef]
39. Wang, C., Zhang, Y. Theoretical Analysis of Gradient-Zhang Neural Network for Time-Varying Equations and Improved Method for Linear Equations. In *Neural Information Processing;* ICONIP 2023, Lecture Notes in Computer Science; Luo, B., Cheng, L., Wu, Z.G., Li, H., Li, C., Eds.; Springer: Singapore, 2024; Volume 14447. [CrossRef]
40. Stanimirović, P.S.; Mourtas, S.D.; Katsikis, V.N.; Kazakovtsev, L.A. Krutikov, V.N. Recurrent neural network models based on optimization methods. *Mathematics* **2022**, *10*, 4292. [CrossRef]
41. Nocedal, J.; Wright, S. *Numerical Optimization;* Springer: New York, NY, USA, 1999.
42. Stanimirović, P.S.; Petković, M.D.; Gerontitis, D. Gradient neural network with nonlinear activation for computing inner inverses and the Drazin inverse. *Neural Process. Lett.* **2017**, *48*, 109–133. [CrossRef]
43. Smoktunowicz, A.; Smoktunowicz, A. Set-theoretic solutions of the Yang–Baxter equation and new classes of *R*-matrices. *Linear Algebra Its Appl.* **2018**, *546*, 86–114. [CrossRef]
44. Baksalary, O.M.; Trenkler, G. On matrices whose Moore–Penrose inverse is idempotent. *Linear Multilinear Algebra* **2022**, *70*, 2014–2026. [CrossRef]
45. Wang, X.Z.; Ma, H.; Stanimirović, P.S. Nonlinearly activated recurrent neural network for computing the Drazin inverse. *Neural Process. Lett.* **2017**, *46*, 195–217. [CrossRef]
46. Wang, S.D.; Kuo, T.S.; Hsu, C.F. Trace bounds on the solution of the algebraic matrix Riccati and Lyapunov equation. *IEEE Trans. Autom. Control* **1986**, *31*, 654–656. [CrossRef]

axioms

MDPI

Article

Hyper-Heuristic Approach for Tuning Parameter Adaptation in Differential Evolution

Vladimir Stanovov [1,2,*], Lev Kazakovtsev [1,2,*] and Eugene Semenkin [1,2]

[1] Laboratory "Hybrid Methods of Modelling and Optimization in Complex Systems", Siberian Federal University, Krasnoyarsk 660074, Russia; eugenesemenkin@yandex.ru

[2] Institute of Informatics and Telecommunication, Reshetnev Siberian State University of Science and Technology, Krasnoyarsk 660037, Russia

* Correspondence: vladimirstanovov@yandex.ru (V.S.); levk@bk.ru (L.K.)

Abstract: Differential evolution (DE) is one of the most promising black-box numerical optimization methods. However, DE algorithms suffer from the problem of control parameter settings. Various adaptation methods have been proposed, with success history-based adaptation being the most popular. However, hand-crafted designs are known to suffer from human perception bias. In this study, our aim is to design automatically a parameter adaptation method for DE with the use of the hyper-heuristic approach. In particular, we consider the adaptation of scaling factor F, which is the most sensitive parameter of DE algorithms. In order to propose a flexible approach, a Taylor series expansion is used to represent the dependence between the success rate of the algorithm during its run and the scaling factor value. Moreover, two Taylor series are used for the mean of the random distribution for sampling F and its standard deviation. Unlike most studies, the Student's t distribution is applied, and the number of degrees of freedom is also tuned. As a tuning method, another DE algorithm is used. The experiments performed on a recently proposed L-NTADE algorithm and two benchmark sets, CEC 2017 and CEC 2022, show that there is a relatively simple adaptation technique with the scaling factor changing between 0.4 and 0.6, which enables us to achieve high performance in most scenarios. It is shown that the automatically designed heuristic can be efficiently approximated by two simple equations, without a loss of efficiency.

Keywords: numerical optimization; differential evolution; parameter adaptation; hyper-heuristic

MSC: 90C26; 90C59; 68T20

1. Introduction

Single-objective numerical optimization methods for black-box problems represent a direction that is thoroughly studied in the evolutionary computation (EC) area. The reason for this is that evolutionary algorithms do not require any specific information about the target function except the possibility to calculate it, i.e., they are zero-order methods. First attempts to solve such problems with evolutionary algorithms were made with the classical Genetic Algorithm (GA), which searched the binary space [1]; however, later, more efficient approaches were proposed, including simulated binary crossover [2], as well as other nature-inspired methods, such as Particle Swarm Optimization [3]. However, in recent years, most of the researchers' attention is toward the differential evolution (DE) algorithm [4].

The reasons for DE's popularity are diverse and include simplicity in both understanding and realization and high performance across many domains and applications [5–7]. The high performance of DE is due to its implicit adaptation to the function landscape, which originates from the main idea—difference-based mutation. However, the performance of DE comes with a drawback: the few parameters of the algorithm, namely, the population size N, scaling factor F and crossover rate Cr, should be carefully tuned, and most of the research on DE is focused on determining the best possible ways of tuning these parameters during the algorithm's work [8].

This study focuses on finding a method for the automatic tuning of the most sensitive parameter, scaling factor F. Today, the most popular adaptation technique is success history-based adaptation (SHA), proposed 10 years ago in the SHADE algorithm [9]. However, despite the gradual improvements [10], there are possibilities to design even better adaptation methods. This paper is a follow-up work to a recent study [11], where success rate-based adaptation was proposed, and the surrogate-assisted search for Taylor series coefficients for F, Cr and N was performed using the Efficient Global Optimization (EGO) algorithm [12]. Here, a similar hyper-heuristic approach is considered; however, instead of EGO, another differential evolution is applied on the upper level, and additional parameters are introduced to increase the flexibility of the approach. In particular, the scale parameter of Student's t random distribution for sampling F values is also tuned, as well as the number of degrees of freedom. The experiments, performed with the L-NTADE algorithm [13] on two sets of test problems taken from the Congress on Evolutionary Computation (CEC) competition on numerical optimization 2017 [14] and CEC 2022 [15], demonstrated that the new approach enables us to find simpler and more efficient adaptation techniques.

The main contributions of this study can be outlined as follows:

1. Setting the lower and upper border for the Taylor series when tuning the curve parameters for success rate-based scaling factor sampling improves flexibility and allows for finding a simpler dependence;
2. The number of degrees of freedom, found by the proposed approach, places the Student's distribution between the usually applied normal and Cauchy distributions;
3. The DE algorithm applied instead of the EGO algorithm on the upper level is capable of finding efficient solutions, despite the problem complexity and dimension;
4. The Friedman ranking procedure, used instead of the total standard score for heuristics comparison during a search, is a good alternative with comparable performance and does not require any baseline results;
5. The designed heuristic for scaling factor adaptation is simple and can be efficiently applied to many other DE variants.

The rest of this paper is organized as follows. The next section describes the background studies; in the third section, the related works are discussed; in the fourth section, the proposed approach is described; the fifth section contains the experiments and results; and the sixth section contains the discussion, followed by the conclusion.

2. Background

2.1. Differential Evolution

The numerical optimization problem in a single-objective case consists of the search space $X \subseteq R^D$, real-valued function f: $X \rightarrow R$ and a set of bound constraints:

$$\min_{x} f(x), \tag{1}$$

subject to $x_{lb,j} < x_j < x_{ub,j}$ $j = 1, \ldots, D$, where x_{lb} is the vector of the lower boundaries, x_{ub} is the vector of the upper boundaries and D is the problem dimension. As bound constraints are easily satisfied, such problems are often called unconstrained. In this study, the black-box scenario is considered, which means that there is no information about the structure or properties of the function $f(x)$, so that it can be multimodal, non-convex, ill-conditioned, etc. The gradient is also not available.

Differential evolution starts by initializing a set of N D-dimensional vectors $x_i = (x_{i,1}, x_{i,2}, \ldots, x_{i,D}), i = 1, \ldots, N$ randomly using uniform distribution within $[x_{lb,j}, x_{ub,j}]$, $j = 1, \ldots, D$.

After initialization, the main loop of the algorithm starts with the first operation called the difference-based mutation. There are many known mutation strategies, such as rand/1, rand/2, best/1 and current-to-rand/1, but the most popular is the current-to-pbest/1 strategy:

$$v_{i,j} = x_{i,j} + F \times (x_{pbest,j} - x_{i,j} + x_{r1,j} - x_{r2,j}), \tag{2}$$

where F is the scaling factor parameter, v_i is the newly generated mutant vector, $r1$ and $r2$ are the uniformly randomly chosen indexes of the vectors in the range $[1, N]$ and $pbest$ is chosen from the best $p\%$ of the individuals, $i = 1, \ldots, N$, $j = 1, \ldots, D$. Same as most evolutionary algorithms, DE relies on two variation operations: mutation and crossover. The crossover mixes the genetic information of the target vector x_i and the newly generated mutant vector v_i; as a result, the trial vector u_i is generated. The most popular scheme is the binomial crossover, which works as follows:

$$u_{i,j} = \begin{cases} v_{i,j}, & \text{if } rand(0,1) < Cr \text{ or } j = jrand \\ x_{i,j}, & \text{otherwise} \end{cases}. \tag{3}$$

where Cr is the crossover rate parameter, and $jrand$ is a random index in $[1, D]$ required to make sure that at least one solution is taken from the mutant vector. The trial vector is checked to be within the search boundaries; one of the popular methods to perform this is called the midpoint target:

$$u_{i,j} = \begin{cases} \frac{x_{lb,j}+x_{i,j}}{2}, & \text{if } v_{i,j} < x_{lb,j} \\ \frac{x_{ub,j}+x_{i,j}}{2}, & \text{if } v_{i,j} > x_{ub,j} \\ u_{i,j}, & \text{otherwise} \end{cases}. \tag{4}$$

After this step, the trial vector is evaluated using target function $f(x)$ and compared to the target vector x_i in the selection step:

$$x_i = \begin{cases} u_i, & \text{if } f(u_i) \leq f(x_i) \\ x_i, & \text{if } f(u_i) > f(x_i) \end{cases}. \tag{5}$$

At the end of the generation, some of the individuals may be replaced, and due to the selection step, the average fitness either increases or stays the same.

2.2. Parameter Adaptation in Differential Evolution

As mentioned in the Introduction, most of the works on DE are directed toward parameter adaptation and control methods [8]. The reason for this is that DE is highly sensitive to the F and Cr settings, and one of the earliest studies that considered this problem was [16], where the authors proposed the jDE algorithm with the parameter values adapted as follows:

$$F_{i,t+1} = \begin{cases} random(F_l, F_u), & \text{if } random(0,1) < \tau_1, \\ F_{i,t}, & \text{otherwise}, \end{cases} \tag{6}$$

$$CR_{i,t+1} = \begin{cases} random(0,1), & \text{if } random(0,1) < \tau_2, \\ CR_{i,t}, & \text{otherwise}, \end{cases} \tag{7}$$

where F_l and F_u are the lower and upper boundaries for F, and τ_1 and τ_2 control the frequency of the F and Cr changes, usually set to 0.1. If the trial vector is better, then the new parameter values are saved. The modifications of jDE have proven themselves to be highly competitive, for example, jDE100 [17] and j2020 [18] demonstrated high efficiency on bound-constrained test problems.

Despite the efficiency of jDE, nowadays, success history-based adaptation is one of the widely used methods [9], based on the originally proposed JADE algorithm [19]. Here, the working principle of SHA will be described.

Success history-based adaptation tunes both the scaling factor F and crossover rate Cr. At the initialization step, a set of H memory cells $M_{F,h}$ and $M_{Cr,h}$ is created, each containing a constant value, such as 0.5. The values in the memory cells are used to sample the F and Cr values to be used in the mutation and crossover as follows:

$$\begin{cases} F = randc(M_{F,k}, 0.1) \\ Cr = randn(M_{Cr,k}, 0.1) \end{cases}. \tag{8}$$

where $randc(m,s)$ is a Cauchy-distributed random value with location parameter m and scale parameter s; $randn(m,s)$ is a normally distributed random value with mean m and standard deviation s. In the SHADE algorithm, if the sampled $F < 0$, then it is generated again, and if $F > 1$, it is set to 1. The Cr value is simply truncated to a $[0,1]$ interval. The index k of the memory cell to be used is generated randomly in $[1,H]$. Note that the Cauchy distribution has "heavier tails", i.e., it generates larger and smaller values more often compared to normal distribution—this gives more diverse F values.

During every selection step, if the newly generated trial vector u_i is better than x_i, then the F and Cr values are stored in S_F and S_{Cr}, as well as the improvement value $\Delta f = |f(x_i) - f(u_i)|$ stored in $S_{\Delta f}$. At the end of the generation, the new values updating the memory cells are calculated using the weighted Lehmer mean:

$$mean_{wL,F} = \frac{\sum_{j=1}^{|S_F|} w_j S_{F,j}^2}{\sum_{j=1}^{|S_F|} w_j S_{F,j}}, mean_{wL,Cr} = \frac{\sum_{j=1}^{|S_{Cr}|} w_j S_{Cr,j}^2}{\sum_{j=1}^{|S_{Cr}|} w_j S_{Cr,j}}, \tag{9}$$

where $w_j = \frac{S_{\Delta f_j}}{\sum_{k=1}^{|S|} S_{\Delta f_k}}$. Two values are calculated, i.e., one using S_F and another using S_{Cr}. The memory cell with index h, iterated from 1 to H every generation, is updated as follows:

$$\begin{cases} M_{F,k} = 0.5(M_{F,k} + mean_{wL,F}) \\ M_{Cr,k} = 0.5(M_{Cr,k} + mean_{wL,Cr}) \end{cases}, \tag{10}$$

The SHA confirm and modify. Following highlights are same issue. method uses biased parameter adaptation, i.e., in the Lehmer mean in the nominator, the successful values are squared; thus, the mean is shifted toward larger values. In this study, the Lehmer mean was modified by introducing an additional parameter pm:

$$mean_{wL,F} = \frac{\sum_{j=1}^{|S_F|} w_j S_{F,j}^{pm}}{\sum_{j=1}^{|S_F|} w_j S_{F,j}^{pm-1}}, mean_{wL,Cr} = \frac{\sum_{j=1}^{|S_{Cr}|} w_j S_{Cr,j}^{pm}}{\sum_{j=1}^{|S_{Cr}|} w_j S_{Cr,j}^{pm-1}}. \tag{11}$$

Increasing the pm parameter leads to more skewed means toward larger values. The standard setting in L-SHADE is $pm = 2$, and it is shown that increasing this value and generating a larger F may lead to much better results in high-dimensional problems.

For the population size N, the third main parameter of DE, the following technique was proposed in the L-SHADE algorithm [20]:

$$N_{g+1} = round\left(\frac{N_{min} - N_{max}}{NFE_{max}} NFE\right) + N_{max}, \tag{12}$$

where NFE is the current number of target function evaluations, NFE_{max} is the total available computational resource, N_{max} and N_{min} are the initial and final number of individuals and g is the generation number. This method called linear population size reduction (LPSR) has the main idea of spreading across the search space at the beginning and concentrating at the end of the search. LPSR allows for achieving significant improvements in performance, if the computational resource limit is known. In such a scenario, it makes sense to use a broader search at the beginning and more concentrated effort at the end. That is, if the computational resource is running out, it is better to converge to at least some good solution quickly with a small population rather than continuing a broad and slow search, hoping to get to the global optimum. Although the usage of LPSR may seem to contradict the global optimization setup, in a recent competition on global numerical optimization with unlimited resources [21], it was shown that algorithms with LPSR have some of the best performance characteristics.

In [22], it was shown that adding tournament or rank-based selection strategies to sample the indexes of individuals for further mutation may be beneficial. The exponential rank-based selection was implemented by selecting an individual depending on its fitness in a sorted array, with the ranks assigned as follows:

$$rank_i = e^{\frac{-kp \cdot i}{N}}, \tag{13}$$

where kp is the parameter controlling the pressure, and i is the individual number. Larger ranks are assigned to better individuals, and a discrete distribution is used for selection.

The L-SHADE algorithm has become very popular among DE methods, and most of the prize-winning algorithms since 2014 are its variants and modifications, including jSO with specific adaptation rules [23], L-SHADE-RSP with selective pressure [24], DB-LSHADE with distance-based adaptation [25] and a recently proposed L-NTADE [13], which also relies on SHA and LPSR. There are other techniques, for example, the jDE algorithm [16] and its modifications, such as j100 [17] and j2020 [18], that have shown competitive results, but they are not as popular as SHADE. Nevertheless, in [11,26], it was shown that more efficient adaptation techniques can be proposed.

Other modifications of modern DE include the Gaussian–Cauchy mutation [27], modifications for binary search space [28], population regeneration in the case of premature convergence [29] and using an ensemble of mutation and crossover operators [30].

2.3. L-NTADE Algorithm

As a baseline approach, here the recently proposed L-NTADE algorithm [13] is considered. The main idea of L-NTADE is to diverge from the relatively general scheme of modern DE, where a single population is present, with an optional external archive of inferior solutions. Unlike these methods, L-NTADE uses two populations, one containing the best N individuals in x_i^{top} found throughout the search and another containing the latest improved solutions in x_i^{new}, $i = 1, 2, \ldots N$. The mutation strategy used in L-NTADE is a modification of the current-to-pbest called r-new-to-ptop/n/t, with individuals taken from the top and newest populations as follows:

$$v_{i,j} = x_{r1,j}^{new} + F \times (x_{pbest,j}^{top} - x_{i,j}^{new}) + F \times (x_{r2,j}^{new} - x_{r3,j}^{top}), \tag{14}$$

where $r1$ and $r3$ are random indexes, sampled with uniform distribution, and $r2$ is sampled with rank-based selective pressure, with ranks assigned as $rank_i = e^{\frac{-kp \cdot i}{N}}$, wherein kp is a parameter. More detailed research on the effects of selective pressure in DE is given in [22]. The $pbest$ index is chosen from the p% best solutions from the top population. Note that unlike current-to-pbest, the basic solution is not the same as in the first difference, i.e., index $r1$ is different from i—in this sense, r-new-to-ptop/n/t is more similar to the rand/1 mutation.

The crossover step in L-NTADE is unchanged, i.e., the classical binomial crossover is applied, whereas the selection step is changed significantly:

$$x_{nc} = \begin{cases} u_i, & \text{if } f(u_i) \le f(x_{r1}^{new}) \\ x_{nc}, & \text{if } f(u_i) > f(x_{r1}^{new}) \end{cases}. \tag{15}$$

where nc is iterated from 1 to N. The newly generated trial vector is compared not to the target vector x_i but to the basic vector x_{r1}, which was chosen randomly. Moreover, a different individual with index nc is replaced as a result. This gives the effect of a continuous update of the newest individuals' population. At the same time, to preserve the best solutions, the top population is updated in the following order. All the successful trial vectors u_i are stored into a temporary population x^{temp}, and at the end of the generation, a joined set of x^{temp} and x^{top} is formed, sorted by fitness, and the best N individuals are chosen to stay in x^{top}. The population size control in L-NTADE is realized using the LPSR method, with both the newest and top population reducing the size in the same way.

2.4. Hyper-Heuristic Approach

The development of meta-heuristic approaches nowadays is mainly performed by researchers manually, i.e., new ideas are proposed, implemented and tested. However, the idea of automating this process has been discussed in the literature for several years. In particular, the so-called hyper-heuristic approach (HH) is considered [31], when some method, such as, for example, genetic programming (GP), is used to design new operators or even entire algorithms. There exist generative hyper-heuristics and selection hyper-heuristics, with the last used to configure a meta-heuristic algorithm. The generative hyper-heuristics are sometimes referred to as the automated design of algorithms (ADAs) or genetic improvement (GI) [32]. With modern computational capabilities, the HH approach opens possibilities of discovering new algorithmic ideas in an automated manner, thus significantly moving the whole field further. More details on the application of HH are given in the next section.

3. Related Work

Differential evolution is a highly competitive numerical optimizer, which has proven its efficiency across a variety of applications. Moreover, in the last 10 years, competitions on numerical optimization have been won by DE or its hybrids with other methods, such as CMA-ES (for example, the LSHADE-SPACMA performed well on the CEC 2017 benchmark) [33]. However, despite all these achievements, there is still room for further improvement. Success history adaptation, proposed in SHADE, is a method, which has proven its efficiency, delivering significant improvements.

One of the ways to propose new ideas for parameter adaptation is to use automated search methods. An attempt to create a new parameter adaptation technique with the hyper-heuristic approach was made in [26], where genetic programming for symbolic regression was used to create equations for adapting F and Cr in DE. In particular, it was shown that it is possible to develop relatively simple and yet efficient methods, which are significantly different from success history-based adaptation.

The experiments with the L-NTADE algorithm, aimed at designing new adaptation techniques for an algorithm, whose general scheme is different from L-SHADE, were performed in [34]. In particular, it was found that the success rate, i.e., the number of improvements in the current generation divided by the population size ($SR = \frac{NS}{N}$), is an important source of information for parameter adaptation. This value was included in the study where GP was used [26]; the connection was less obvious there. It is worth mentioning that the success rate SR is rarely used in evolutionary computation for parameter adaptation.

In an attempt to further explore the possible influence of SR and derive the important dependencies, in [11], the surrogate-assisted approach was proposed. In particular, a 10th-order Taylor series expansion was used to allow for a flexible tuning of the curve, which uses SR to determine the mean value for sampling F. It was shown that it is possible to find such curves and that the efficiency of DE can be greatly improved. However, this method had several disadvantages. First of all, as a higher-level optimizer, which searches for Taylor series coefficients, the surrogate-assisted method Efficient Global Optimization (EGO) was applied [12]. Although this is a well-performing method, which allowed for finding interesting solutions, it is not very suitable for this particular problem. The main reason is that the evaluation of a set of Taylor series parameters, determining the parameter adaptation technique, is a noisy function, i.e., it requires running an algorithm, which uses random values. The total standard score, used as the target function in [11], is not very suitable for Kriging approximation. Considering these drawbacks, a new approach was developed, which will be described in the next section.

4. Proposed Approach

4.1. Scaling Factor Sampling

The two main ideas of this study are to change the optimization tool, used on the upper level, and to replace the solution evaluation method. The hyper-heuristic approach may use any optimization tool, for example, genetic programming, to search for parameter adaptation techniques directly or EGO to tune the Taylor series parameters. In particular, in this study, the success rate parameter is used as a source of information for tuning the scaling factor parameter F. The success rate is calculated every generation as follows:

$$SR = \frac{NS}{N}, \tag{16}$$

where NS is the number of successful replacements in the selection operation. The main idea of [11] was to use a Taylor series to approximate the dependence between SR and location parameter MF (mean F) for F sampling. The Taylor polynomials are used as function approximations using derivatives; however, as here the true dependence is unknown, the coefficients can be derived via computational experiments. The Taylor expansion is used due to the flexibility of the polynomials. The method consists of calculating the raw value MF_r and then normalizing it to a $[0,1]$ interval and scaling it. The first step is performed as follows:

$$MF_r = c_{m,1} + \sum_{i=2}^{11} c_{m,i}(SR - c_{m,0})^i \tag{17}$$

where $c_{m,i}$, $i = 0,1,\ldots,11$ are the coefficients to be found, and MF_r is a raw, non-normalized value. To perform the normalization, i.e., scale to the $[0,1]$ range, the minimum and maximum values are used:

$$MF_s = \frac{(MF_r - MF_{r,min})}{(MF_{r,max} - MF_{r,min})}, \tag{18}$$

where $MF_{r,min}$ and $MF_{r,max}$ are found by searching (via lattice search with step 0.001) in $SR \in [0,1]$, and MF_s is a scaled value. After this, an additional step is proposed in this study. To allow for a more flexible adaptation, the lower and upper boundaries for the fitted curve should also be tuned and not just set to $[0,1]$. To perform this, the final MF value is calculated as follows:

$$MF = MF_s(c_{m,u} - c_{m,l}) + c_{m,l}, \tag{19}$$

where $c_{m,l}$ and c_u are the lower and upper boundaries for MF. That is, if, say, $c_{m,l} = 0.1$ and $c_{m,u} = 0.7$, then the MF curve, which depends on the success rate SR, will be in the range $[0.1, 0.7]$. This results in a pair of additional parameters added to those that should be optimized. The MF value is then used in Student's t distribution instead of a Cauchy or normal one:

$$F = randt(MF, SF, c_{DoF}), \tag{20}$$

where $randt(m,s,v)$ is a Student's t-distributed random value with a location parameter m, scale parameter s and number of degrees of freedom v; c_{DoF} is another tuned parameter; and SF is a scale parameter (σF). The reason to use Student's distribution is that it is a more general distribution, which is capable of becoming a Cauchy distribution when $v = 1$ and a normal distribution when $v \to \infty$ ($v > 30$ is enough in practice). When v is small, the t distribution is heavy-tailed, i.e., more similar to Cauchy. Modern C++ libraries allow for setting v to an arbitrary positive floating-point value, thus allowing us to tune the distribution arbitrarily. Also, note that sampling F is performed with the following rules:

while $F < 0$, it is sampled again, and if $F > 1$, it is set to 1. Figure 1 shows the comparison of the normal, Cauchy and Student's distribution.

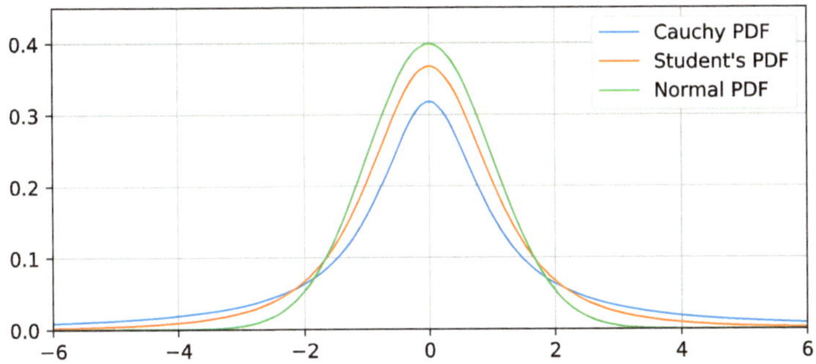

Figure 1. Comparison of normal, Student's ($\nu = 3$) and Cauchy distributions.

To allow for even greater flexibility for the approach, the scale parameter SF is also tuned in the same way as MF. That is, another set of coefficients is used to determine the dependence of SF on the success rate SR. For clarity, we provide below the equations to calculate SF.

$$SF_r = c_{s,1} + \sum_{i=2}^{11} c_{s,i}(SR - c_{s,0})^i \tag{21}$$

$$SF_s = \frac{(SF_r - SF_{r,min})}{(SF_{r,max} - SF_{r,min})}, \tag{22}$$

$$SF = SF_s(c_{s,u} - c_{s,l}) + c_{s,l}, \tag{23}$$

Equations (16)–(18) are the same as (12)–(14), but for a different parameter, and the resulting MF and SF values are used in (15). The search for $SF_{r,min}$ and $SR_{r,max}$ for normalization is performed in the same manner, i.e., with a lattice search with a step value of 0.001. It is important to tune the scale parameter, i.e., the width of the distribution, as it significantly influences the distribution of the sampled F values.

Thus, setting 12 parameters for a Taylor series curve plus two more for lower and upper boundaries gives a total of 14 c_m values for MF. Another 14 are used to set SF and one more to tune the number of degrees of freedom c_{DoF}. This gives a total of 29 numeric values, which should be set in order to determine the adaptation method in a 29-dimensional search space. The search for the optimal set of 29 parameters is described in Section 4.2, where each set of values corresponds to a specific adaptation heuristic, which is evaluated. The search itself is performed by another DE algorithm, L-SRDE.

4.2. Evaluating Designed Heuristics

The evaluation of the designed heuristic is an important step for determining its efficiency, and the evaluation method significantly influences the search for better heuristics. In [11], the idea was to apply statistical tests to evaluate the efficiency of an algorithm with a designed heuristic with a single numeric value. In particular, the baseline results were obtained, i.e., the L-NTADE algorithm was tested with success history parameter adaptation, and then the new results were compared to it. The comparison involved applying the Mann–Whitney statistical test to every function so that the best found target function values were compared. There are 51 independent runs in the CEC 2017 competition benchmark, so comparing two samples of 51 values allowed for using normal approximation (with tie-breaking) for the Mann–Whitney U statistics. That is, for every test function out of 30, the standard Z score was calculated. The total score Z_T was determined as follows:

$$Z_T = \sum_{j=1}^{30} Z_j, \tag{24}$$

where j is the function number. Such a metric gave an averaged evaluation of the adaptation technique, i.e., if two algorithms perform the same on the function, Z_j will be close to 0, but if the heuristic performed better, then $Z_j > 0$, and $Z_j > 2.58$ corresponds to a statistical significance level of $p = 0.01$.

Although such an approach has shown that it is capable of finding efficient solutions, evaluating an adaptation technique across a variety of test functions with a single value creates a bottleneck, i.e., limits the amount of information that the upper-level optimizer receives from testing a newly designed heuristic. In order to overcome this, here, instead of Mann–Whitney tests and the EGO algorithm for optimization, the usage of Friedman ranking and another differential evolution algorithm for tuning coefficients c is proposed. The Friedman ranking is used in the Friedman statistical test to compare not a pair (like in the Mann–Whitney test) but a set of conditions, under which the experiments were performed.

One of the advantages of the classical DE algorithm is that it does not require exact fitness values to work. That is, the selection step only needs to determine if the newly generated individual is better than the target individual with index i. In other words, if there is a method to compare a pair (or rank a population) of solutions, then DE is able to work with this information. Hence, the idea is to use simplified DE to tune the coefficients of the heuristic c_m, c_s and c_{DoF}. The main steps can be described as follows.

1. Initialize the population x^{cur} of 29-dimensional vectors randomly, with N individuals.
2. Pass the parameters c to the L-NTADE algorithm and run it for every set of coefficients.
3. Collect a set of results, i.e., a tensor with dimensions $(N, 30, 51)$.
4. Rank the solutions using Friedman ranking; for this, perform independent ranking for every function and sum the ranks.
5. Begin the main loop of DE and use ranks as fitness values; store N new solutions in the trial population x^{tr}.
6. Evaluate new individuals in x^{tr} by running the L-NTADE algorithms with the corresponding tuning parameters.
7. Join together the results of the current population x^{cur} and x^{tr} and apply Friedman ranking again to the tensor of size $(2 \times N, 30, 51)$.
8. If the rank of the trial individual with index i is better than the rank of the target individual, then perform the replacement.

In this manner, the DE algorithm is applied without evaluating the fitness as a single value but rather ranking the best performing heuristics higher. A similar approach using Friedman ranking was used to evaluate the solutions of GP in [26]. That is, there is no single fitness value on the upper optimization level, while the lower level uses the target function value from the benchmark set as fitness. The flow chart of the proposed method is shown in Figure 2.

The particular DE used on the upper level here was similar to the L-SHADE algorithm but with several important features for parameter tuning. First, the adaptation of Cr was not performed, and Cr was sampled with normal distribution with parameters $m = 0.9$ and $\sigma = 0.1$. The scaling factor was set as $F = randc(SR^{0.25}, 0.1)$, i.e., it depended on the success rate as a 4th-order root. The mutation parameter $pbest = 0.3$, and the $r1$ index in the current-to-pbest mutation strategy was sampled using exponential rank-based selective pressure with ranks assigned as $rank_i = e^{\frac{3 \cdot i}{N}}$. The archive set and the linear population size reduction were also used. This algorithm will be further referred to as L-SRDE (success rate-based DE with LPSR). The exact parameters of all the methods and results are given in the next section.

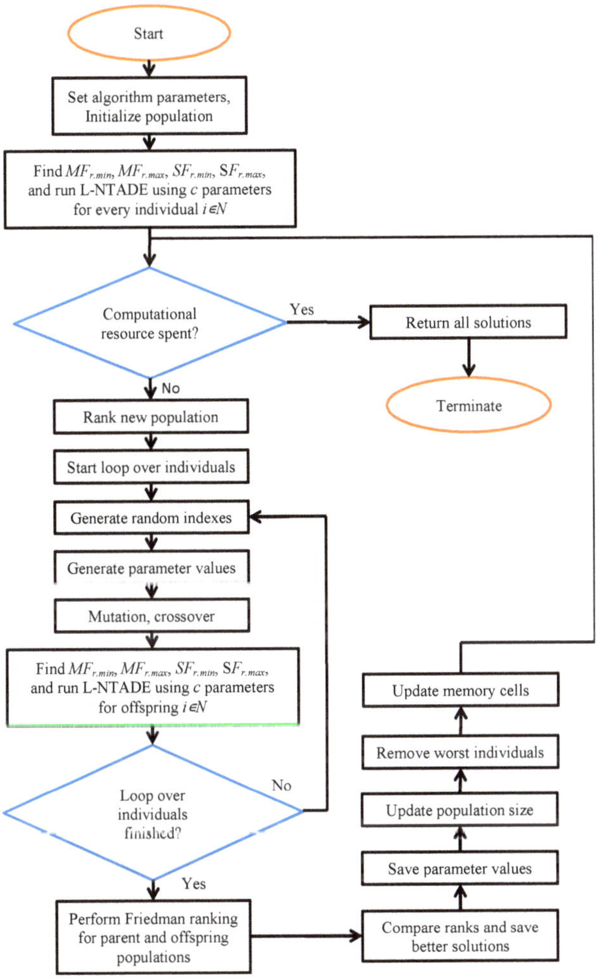

Figure 2. Flow chart of the proposed approach.

5. Experimental Setup and Results

5.1. Benchmark Functions and Parameters

The experiments in this study are divided into two phases. In the training phase, the coefficients c are searched by L-SRDE, and in the test phase, the performance of the found dependencies between the success rate SR and distribution parameters MF, SF and ν is evaluated on different benchmarks.

The two benchmarks used here are the Congress on Evolutionary Computation 2017 single-objective bound-constrained numerical optimization benchmark [14] and the CEC 2022 benchmark [15]. The former has 30 test functions, and according to the competition rules, there should be 51 independent runs made for every function. The dimensions are $D = 10$, 30, 50 and 100, and the available computational resource is limited by the $NFE_{max} = 10,000D$ evaluations. In the CEC 2022 benchmark, there are 12 test functions and 30 independent runs, the dimensions are $D = 10$ and $D = 20$ and the computational resource is bigger and set to 2×10^5 and 1×10^6, respectively.

The CEC 2017 and CEC 2022 benchmarks have different evaluation metrics. In particular, in CEC 2017, the measure of algorithm efficiency is simply the best found function value, whereas in CEC 2022 the number of evaluations is also considered. If an algorithm was able to find the solution (with tolerance level 1×10^{-8}), then the number of evaluations it took on this run is recorded. The algorithms are then compared via the convergence speed and best found value at the same time [35].

In the training phase, the CEC 2017 benchmark is used as it has more diverse functions and a smaller resource, i.e., faster evaluation. The 30-dimensional problems are used, as in the $10D$ case most of the test functions appear to be too simple for the available resource, and the difference between the parameter adaptation methods is small. The ranking of the solutions during the training phase was performed with the criteria from CEC 2022, i.e., both the convergence speed and best function value were considered.

The parameters for L-SRDE were described above, except for the initial population size, which was set to $N_{max} = 25$. The number of function evaluations given to L-SRDE was set to 1000, i.e., there were 1000 heuristics evaluated. The L-NTADE algorithm had the following settings: the initial size of both populations $N_{max} = 20D$; mutation strategy parameter $pb = 0.3$; memory size for SHA $H = 5$; initial memory values $M_{F,r} = 0.3$, $M_{Cr,r} = 1.0$ and $r = 1, 2, \ldots, H$; adaptation bias for the scaling factor in the weighted Lehmer mean $pm = 4$; and selective pressure for the $r2$ index $kp = 3$. These settings were determined in [13] and later used in [11]. When sampling F was replaced by the heuristic, the Cr tuning was still performed by SHA. The search range for c values was set as follows: $c_{m,i} \in [-10, 10]$, $c_{m,l} \in [0, 1]$, $c_{m,u} \in [0, 1]$, $c_{s,i} \in [-10, 10]$, $c_{s,l} \in [0, 1]$, $c_{s,u} \in [0, 1]$, $c_{DoF} \in [0.1, 10]$ and $i = 1, 2, \ldots, 12$. Note that $c_{m,l}$ and $c_{m,u}$ are only named lower and upper for convenience, and in fact, it is possible that $c_{m,l} > c_{m,u}$—this will result in flipping the curve.

The L-SRDE algorithm with Friedman ranking was implemented in Python 3.9, and L-NTADE was written in C++. L-NTADE ran on an OpenMPI-powered cluster of eight AMD Ryzen 3700 PRO processors using Ubuntu Linux 20.04. The python code automatically ran the L-NTADE algorithm and collected the results. The post-processing was also performed in Python 3.9.

5.2. Numerical Results

The training phase resulted in 1000 different heuristics evaluated, and each of them was saved independently. The eight best found heuristics and the corresponding curves are shown in Figure 3, and Table 1 contains the lower and upper c values and number of degrees of freedom ν, as well as the NFE number at which the heuristic was found.

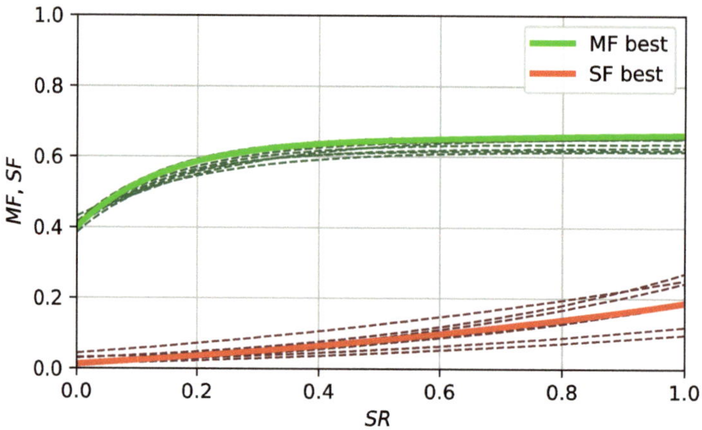

Figure 3. Curves for parameter adaptation designed by EGO for Taylor series, best found function values used in ranking.

Table 1. Parameters of eight best heuristics.

Rank	NFE	c_{DoF}	$c_{m,l}$	$c_{m,u}$	$c_{s,l}$	$c_{s,u}$
1	637	3.635	0.400	0.662	0.013	0.187
2	625	3.369	0.402	0.619	0.008	0.182
3	640	3.453	0.398	0.636	0.018	0.119
4	613	3.353	0.416	0.652	0.030	0.270
5	652	3.543	0.385	0.625	0.013	0.097
6	432	2.981	0.414	0.650	0.043	0.252
7	463	3.472	0.413	0.662	0.013	0.243
8	582	3.197	0.431	0.615	0.031	0.189

As can be seen from Figure 3, the best curves found by L-SRDE are relatively simple, i.e., they all start from around 0.4, and when $SR = 0.2$, then it reaches 0.6. This is similar to some of the known recommendations about setting F, for example, in [36], quote, "A DE control parameter study by Gamperle et al. (2002) explored DE's performance on two of the same test functions that Zaharie used and concluded that F < 0.4 was not useful. In Ali and Törn (2000), C–Si clusters were optimized with F never falling below F = 0.4", end quote [37–39]. Thus, the heuristically found parameters are in line with the observations of DE behavior.

As for the spread parameter SF, its values are smaller than the mostly used $SF = 0.1$. Moreover, there is a dependence between SF and the success rate SR: if the success rate is small, then SF is close to the 0.01–0.05 range, and it increases with an SR up to 0.2. The number of degrees of freedom ν in Student's t-distribution is equal to 3, which places it in between the Cauchy distribution ($\nu = 1$) and normal distribution ($\nu > 30$). The difference between the best eight heuristics is rather small.

As each set of parameters was described by a vector of the results of the tested heuristic on a set of benchmark functions, it is not possible to plot a convergence curve, like for a classical single-objective optimization problem. However, it is possible to rank all the tested heuristics, and Figure 4 shows the ranks of 1000 evaluated heuristics, compared together with the Friedman ranking in the order in which they were evaluated.

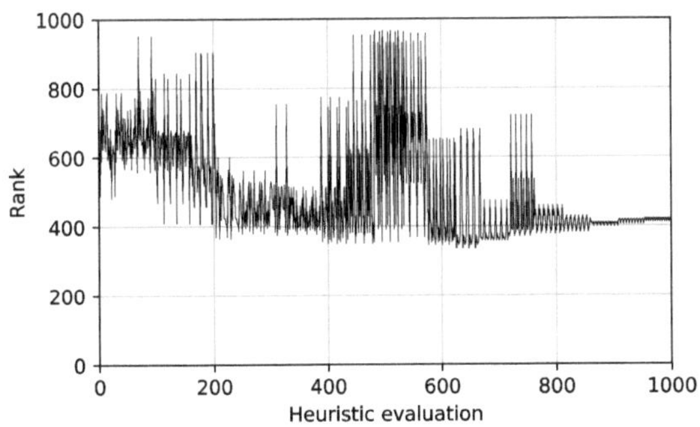

Figure 4. Ranks of the evaluated heuristics

From Figure 4, it can be seen that after 600 evaluations, some of the best heuristics were found, and the rest of the time the algorithm was trying to improve these solutions.

Introducing many hyperparameters into the algorithm may be inefficient, as tuning them is challenging. Such a large number was needed only to allow for significant flexibility of the search, as at the beginning of the experiment we had no knowledge on what the found curves should look like. As Figure 5 shows, the dependence appeared to be relatively simple (represented by two simple equations, which were hand-tuned), so there is no need to use 29 parameters after the learning process.

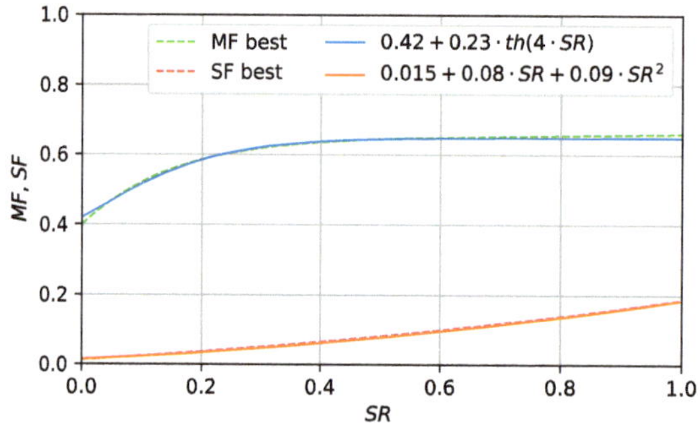

Figure 5. Approximation of best found curves, applied in L-NTADE-AHF.

The *MF* values in Figure 5 are approximated by a hyperbolic tangent function, and the *SF* values are approximated with a quadratic function. A version of L-NTADE with these equations was additionally tested on both benchmarks (denoted as L-NTADE-AHF, L-NTADE with approximated heuristic *F* sampling, and the number of degrees of freedom was set to 3, in accordance with Table 1).

The best heuristic was tested on the whole CEC 2017 benchmark and compared to several alternative approaches. The results are shown in Table 2. For comparison, the Mann–Whitney statistical test was used, and each cell in the table contains the number of wins/ties/losses out of 30 test functions, as well as total standard score Z_T.

Table 2. Mann–Whitney tests of L-NTADE with designed heuristic against alternative approaches, CEC 2017 benchmark, number of wins/ties/losses and total standard score.

Algorithm	10*D*	30*D*	50*D*	100*D*
L-NTADE-HHF vs. LSHADE-SPACMA [33]	11/15/4 (31.38)	17/8/5 (93.37)	15/7/8 (60.70)	17/4/9 (64.55)
L-NTADE-HHF vs. jSO [23]	9/14/7 (14.94)	20/9/1 (147.01)	23/7/0 (192.86)	26/0/4 (184.63)
L-NTADE-HHF vs. EBOwithCMAR [40]	4/16/10 (−39.75)	16/11/3 (102.60)	23/6/1 (162.33)	24/3/3 (174.57)
L-NTADE-HHF vs. L-SHADE-RSP [24]	8/18/4 (11.62)	20/9/1 (138.18)	23/7/0 (183.07)	25/2/3 (172.99)
L-NTADE-HHF vs. NL-SHADE-RSP [41]	12/7/11 (11.54)	23/4/3 (176.22)	30/0/0 (259.17)	29/0/1 (246.89)
L-NTADE-HHF vs. NL-SHADE-LBC [42]	7/19/4 (12.74)	23/7/0 (183.84)	28/2/0 (239.78)	27/2/1 (225.46)
L-NTADE-HHF vs. L-NTADE [13]	11/12/7 (27.52)	17/12/1 (105.74)	23/7/0 (157.15)	26/2/2 (182.49)
L-NTADE-HHF vs. L-NTADE$_{MF}$ [11]	4/26/0 (20.20)	13/16/1 (64.65)	22/8/0 (135.34)	28/1/1 (191.34)
L-NTADE-HHF vs. L-NTADE-AHF	0/30/0 (2.29)	1/29/0 (9.79)	3/27/0 (3.03)	1/29/0 (3.11)

As Table 2 demonstrates, the proposed heuristic, applied to L-NTADE, is capable of outperforming the alternative approaches in almost all cases. The L-NTADE-HHF (hyper-heuristic-based *F* sampling) is better than standard L-NTADE, and the gap in performance increases as the dimension grows. Compared to L-SHADE-RSP, the second best approach from the CEC 2018 competition, L-NTADE-HHF performs similar or better in the 10*D* case and almost always better in the 100*D* case. In 10*D*, the only algorithm that outperformed L-

NTADE-HHF is the EBOwithCMAR approach, but it fails in high-dimensional cases. Also, the comparison to the L-NTADE$_{MF}$ algorithm from [11] shows that the newly designed heuristics are more efficient. Table 3 contains the Friedman ranking of the same algorithms.

Table 3. Friedman ranking of L-NTADE with designed heuristic against alternative approaches, CEC 2017 benchmark.

Algorithm	10*D*	30*D*	50*D*	100*D*	Total
LSHADE-SPACMA [33]	171.12	167.56	137.75	121.96	598.39
jSO [23]	166.36	177.38	183.68	190.26	717.69
EBOwithCMAR [40]	141.15	164.69	172.70	180.51	659.04
L-SHADE-RSP [24]	163.95	171.30	171.71	172.28	679.25
NL-SHADE-RSP [41]	177.54	246.55	285.47	284.82	994.38
NL-SHADE-LBC [42]	165.00	228.15	250.02	247.88	891.05
L-NTADE [13]	175.91	151.82	147.98	152.27	627.99
L-NTADE$_{MF}$ [11]	168.70	126.46	126.62	135.35	557.13
L-NTADE-HHF	160.41	106.62	86.60	81.94	435.57
L-NTADE-AHF	159.86	109.47	87.48	82.71	439.52

The comparison in Table 3 shows a similar picture: in the lower-dimensional case, the L-NTADE-HHF is comparable to other algorithms, but for 50D and 100D, the new algorithm is always better. As for the comparison between L-NTADE-HHF and L-NTADE-AHF with the approximation of the heuristic, the results of these methods are very similar.

Table 4 contains the comparison with the alternative approaches on the CEC 2022 benchmark using the Mann–Whitney tests, and Table 5 contains the Friedman ranking.

For the CEC 2022 benchmark, the top 3 best methods were chosen for comparison, as well as some other algorithms.

Table 4. Mann–Whitney tests of L-NTADE-HHF against the competition top 3, and other approaches, CEC 2022, number of wins/ties/losses and total standard score.

Algorithm	10*D*	20*D*
L-NTADE-HHF vs. APGSK-IMODE [43]	8/2/2 (40.45)	7/1/4 (26.02)
L-NTADE-HHF vs. MLS-LSHADE [44]	8/1/3 (30.45)	5/1/6 (−0.06)
L-NTADE-HHF vs. MadDE [45]	8/2/2 (39.81)	7/1/4 (22.51)
L-NTADE-HHF vs. EA4eigN100 [46]	6/2/4 (4.32)	6/1/5 (4.93)
L-NTADE-HHF vs. NL-SHADE-RSP-MID [47]	5/4/3 (9.61)	5/2/5 (10.61)
L-NTADE-HHF vs. L-SHADE-RSP [24]	7/3/2 (29.80)	5/3/4 (9.54)
L-NTADE-HHF vs. NL-SHADE-RSP [41]	7/2/3 (25.57)	5/3/4 (9.80)
L-NTADE-HHF vs. NL-SHADE-LBC [42]	8/3/1 (36.95)	4/5/3 (13.44)
L-NTADE-HHF vs. L-NTADE [13]	6/5/1 (28.68)	3/5/4 (2.61)
L-NTADE-HHF vs. L-NTADE$_{MF}$ [11]	3/7/2 (3.79)	4/5/3 (6.67)
L-NTADE-HHF vs. L-NTADE-AHF	1/11/0 (7.74)	2/6/4 (−7.54)

Table 4 shows that L-NTADE-HHF is better than most state-of-the-art algorithms and is comparable to EA4eigN100, L-NTADE$_{MF}$ and L-NTADE (in the 20D case). However, the comparison with the Friedman ranking has shown that EA4eigN100, the winner of the CEC 2022 competition, performs better in both the 10D case and 20D case, but L-NTADE-HHF is still second, considering the total ranking. These results show that the designed heuristic is applicable not only to CEC 2017, where the training was performed, but also CEC 2022, where different functions and different computational resources are used. Same as before, the results of L-NTADE-HHF and L-NTADE-AHF are very close, which means that the approximation is working well, and can be used in other algorithms.

Table 5. Friedman ranking of L-NTADE with designed heuristic against alternative approaches, CEC 2022 benchmark.

Algorithm	10*D*	20*D*	Total
APGSK-IMODE [43]	99.73	104.65	204.38
MLS-LSHADE [44]	83.25	63.17	146.42
MadDE [45]	104.92	102.62	207.53
EA4eigN100 [46]	52.73	65.55	118.28
NL-SHADE-RSP-MID [47]	73.28	84.95	158.23
L-SHADE-RSP [24]	83.58	73.85	157.43
NL-SHADE-RSP [41]	104.52	98.07	202.58
NL-SHADE-LBC [42]	72.00	71.40	143.40
L-NTADE [13]	81.12	71.20	152.32
L-NTADE$_{MF}$ [11]	62.03	68.05	130.08
L-NTADE-HHF	58.40	69.92	128.32
L-NTADE-AHF	60.43	62.58	123.02

The presented results demonstrate that the hyper-heuristic approach allowed for finding an efficient parameter adaptation technique, which was able to perform well not only on the set of functions, where the training was performed, i.e., 30-dimensional problems from CEC 2017, but also for different dimensions and a different benchmark, CEC 2022. The overall performance of L-NTADE-HHF is higher than most of the algorithms, and the designed heuristic can be efficiently approximated with relatively simple equations. In the next section, the obtained results and their meaning is discussed in more detail.

6. Discussion

The heuristic for parameter adaptation based on the success rate, found by the L-SRDE algorithm, is relatively simple and straightforward. If the success rate is low, then F should be close to 0.4, and if the success rate is at least 20%, then F should be sampled with a mean of around 0.6. Also, for low success rates, the sampling should be performed with smaller variance, while an increased success rate requires larger variance. For a better understanding of the reasons of the high performance of such a simple method compared to success history adaptation with memory cells and weighted mean, it is worth considering the distributions that are used. For this purpose, in Figure 6, the histograms of six distributions are built, three for the case of a low SR ($MF = 0.4$ and $SF = 0.02$) and three for a high SR ($MF = 0.65$ and $SF = 0.1$). The sample size was 1×10^6 points, and the same procedure as for generating F was used, i.e., while $F < 0$, it is sampled again, and if $F > 1$, it is set to 1.

In Figure 6, in the case of small variance, all three distributions, i.e., normal, Student's and Cauchy, are very compact, i.e., they generate F values close to 0.4. However, it can be seen that the Cauchy distribution has heavier tails, which results in a peak at $F = 1.0$—there is a certain percent of F values, which are larger than 1 and clipped back. Although Cauchy gives more diverse F values, it is not clear if a peak at $F = 1.0$ is a useful thing. In the case when the SR is relatively high, the hyper-heuristic approach proposes increasing the variance. For example, with $MF = 0.65$ and $SF = 0.1$, the normal distribution is much wider, but it still does not reach 0.1 very often. The learned Student's distribution with

$\nu = 3$ encounters clipping at $F = 1.0$ but not as often as it happens with Cauchy distribution. At the same time, Student's distribution is able to also generate small F values quite often.

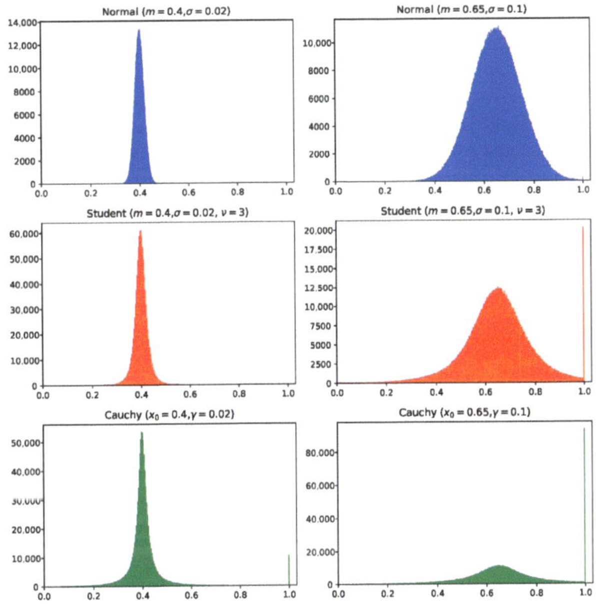

Figure 6. Histograms of sampling F values with various distributions.

Considering the above, it can be concluded that the hyper-heuristic approach was able to find such distribution parameters that the clipping does not happen very often, but the distribution is still wide enough. The fact that the variance changes with the success rate is new and has not been considered in most studies, where it was usually fixed to 0.1 as a small value. The hyper-heuristics have shown that smaller variances can be beneficial, especially if the algorithm is stuck. That is, if the success rate is high, a more wide search with arbitrary F values is allowed, but if the algorithm hits a local optimum, then smaller F values are better. The idea of depending on the success rate was discussed in [11]; the usage of a mutation strategy similar to current-to-pbest makes the algorithm go faster toward one of the p% best individuals (exploitation and faster convergence) when the SR is high and switch to exploration, when the second difference between individuals with indexes $r1$ and $r2$ is more important, if the success rate is low.

The proposed approach is a universal tool for tuning algorithms, designing new adaptation techniques and searching for dependencies between parameters based on extensive experiments. The only drawback is the computational effort required to use such a method. The usage of the Taylor series was dictated by the flexibility, but any other approximation method can be used. Further studies on DE and hyper-heuristics may include the following:

1. Proposing more flexible methods to control the random distribution of F values and tuning them;
2. Reducing the found heuristic to a set of simple rules and equations without many parameters of Taylor series;
3. Applying the new heuristic to other DE-based algorithms and replacing the success history adaptation;
4. Determining the dependence of the Cr parameter on some of the values present in the DE algorithm.

7. Conclusions

In this study, the hyper-heuristic approach was used to generate new parameter adaptation methods for the scaling factor parameter in differential evolution. The training phase resulted in a relatively simple adaptation method, which relies on the success rate value. The comparison of the L-NTADE algorithm with the new heuristic has shown that it is able to outperform alternative approaches on two sets of benchmark problems, and the efficiency of the modification increases in higher dimensions. The hyper-heuristic approach described in this study can be applied to other evolutionary computation methods to search for parameter adaptation procedures. One of the drawbacks of this study is that here only symmetrical distributions were considered for sampling the scaling factor values, but it is possible that skewed distributions may give better results. The skewed distributions have not been used in differential evolution, to the best of our knowledge, and it can be a direction of further studies.

Author Contributions: Conceptualization, V.S. and E.S.; methodology, V.S., L.K. and E.S.; software, V.S.; validation, V.S., L.K. and E.S.; formal analysis, L.K.; investigation, V.S.; resources, E.S. and V.S.; data curation, E.S.; writing—original draft preparation, V.S.; writing—review and editing, V.S. and L.K.; visualization, V.S.; supervision, E.S. and L.K.; project administration, E.S.; funding acquisition, L.K. and V.S. All authors have read and agreed to the published version of the manuscript.

Funding: This work was supported by the Ministry of Science and Higher Education of the Russian Federation (Grant No. 075-15-2022-1121).

Data Availability Statement: Data are contained within the article..

Conflicts of Interest: The authors declare no conflicts of interest.

Abbreviations

The following abbreviations are used in this manuscript:

GA	Genetic Algorithms
GP	Genetic Programming
EC	Evolutionary Computation
DE	Differential Evolution
EGO	Efficient Global Optimization
CEC	Congress on Evolutionary Computation
SHADE	Success History Adaptive Differential Evolution
LPSR	Linear Population Size Reduction
LBC	Linear Bias Change
RSP	Rank-based Selective Pressure
HHF	Hyper-Heuristic Generation of Scaling Factor F
L-NTADE	Linear Population Size Reduction–Newest and Top Adaptive Differential Evolution

References

1. Eshelman, L.J.; Schaffer, J.D. Real-Coded Genetic Algorithms and Interval-Schemata. In *Foundations of Genetic Algorithms*; Elsevier: Amsterdam, The Netherlands, 1992.
2. Deb, K.; Agrawal, R.B. Simulated Binary Crossover for Continuous Search Space. *Complex Syst.* **1995**, *9*, 115–148.
3. Poli, R.; Kennedy, J.; Blackwell, T.M. Particle swarm optimization. *Swarm Intell.* **1995**, *1*, 33–57.
4. Storn, R.; Price, K. Differential evolution – a simple and efficient heuristic for global optimization over continuous spaces. *J. Glob. Optim.* **1997**, *11*, 341–359. [CrossRef]
5. Feoktistov, V. *Differential Evolution in Search of Solutions*; Springer: Berlin/Heidelberg, Germany, 2006.
6. Das, S.; Suganthan, P. Differential evolution: A survey of the state-of-the-art. *IEEE Trans. Evol. Comput.* **2011**, *15*, 4–31. [CrossRef]
7. Das, S.; Mullick, S.; Suganthan, P. Recent advances in differential evolution—An updated survey. *Swarm Evol. Comput.* **2016**, *27*, 1–30. [CrossRef]
8. Al-Dabbagh, R.D.; Neri, F.; Idris, N.; Baba, M.S.B. Algorithmic design issues in adaptive differential evolution schemes: Review and taxonomy. *Swarm Evol. Comput.* **2018**, *43*, 284–311.

9. Tanabe, R.; Fukunaga, A. Success-history based parameter adaptation for differential evolution. In Proceedings of the IEEE Congress on Evolutionary Computation, Cancun, Mexico, 20–23 June 2013; IEEE Press: Piscataway, NJ, USA, 2013; pp. 71–78. [CrossRef]
10. Piotrowski, A.P.; Napiorkowski, J.J. Step-by-step improvement of JADE and SHADE-based algorithms: Success or failure? *Swarm Evol. Comput.* **2018**, *43*, 88–108. [CrossRef]
11. Stanovov, V.; Semenkin, E. Surrogate-Assisted Automatic Parameter Adaptation Design for Differential Evolution. *Mathematics* **2023**, *11*, 2937. [CrossRef]
12. Jones, D.R.; Schonlau, M.; Welch, W.J. Efficient Global Optimization of Expensive Black-Box Functions. *J. Glob. Optim.* **1998**, *13*, 455–492. [CrossRef]
13. Stanovov, V.; Akhmedova, S.; Semenkin, E. Dual-Population Adaptive Differential Evolution Algorithm L-NTADE. *Mathematics* **2022**, *10*, 4666. [CrossRef]
14. Awad, N.; Ali, M.; Liang, J.; Qu, B.; Suganthan, P. *Problem Definitions and Evaluation Criteria for the CEC 2017 Special Session and Competition on Single Objective Bound Constrained Real-Parameter Numerical Optimization*; Technical Report; Nanyang Technological University: Singapore, 2016.
15. Kumar, A.; Price, K.; Mohamed, A.K.; Suganthan, P.N. *Problem Definitions and Evaluation Criteria for the CEC 2022 Special Session and Competition on Single Objective Bound Constrained Numerical Optimization*; Technical Report; Nanyang Technological University: Singapore, 2021.
16. Brest, J.; Greiner, S.; Boškovic, B.; Mernik, M.; Žumer, V. Self-adapting control parameters in differential evolution: A comparative study on numerical benchmark problems. *IEEE Trans. Evol. Comput.* **2006**, *10*, 646–657. [CrossRef]
17. Brest, J.; Maucec, M.; Bovsković, B. The 100-Digit Challenge: Algorithm jDE100. In Proceedings of the 2019 IEEE Congress on Evolutionary Computation (CEC), Wellington, New Zealand, 10–13 June 2019; pp. 19–26.
18. Brest, J.; Maucec, M.; Bosković, B. Differential Evolution Algorithm for Single Objective Bound-Constrained Optimization: Algorithm j2020. In Proceedings of the 2020 IEEE Congress on Evolutionary Computation (CEC), Glasgow, UK, 19–24 July 2020; pp. 1–8.
19. Zhang, J.; Sanderson, A.C. JADE: Adaptive Differential Evolution with Optional External Archive. *IEEE Trans. Evol. Comput.* **2009**, *13*, 945–958. [CrossRef]
20. Tanabe, R.; Fukunaga, A. Improving the search performance of SHADE using linear population size reduction. In Proceedings of the IEEE Congress on Evolutionary Computation, CEC, Beijing, China, 6–11 July 2014; pp. 1658–1665. [CrossRef]
21. Price, K.V.; Awad, N.H.; Ali, M.Z.; Suganthan, P.N. *The 2019 100-Digit Challenge on Real-Parameter, Single Objective Optimization: Analysis of Results*; Technical Report; Nanyang Technological University: Singapore, 2019.
22. Stanovov, V.; Akhmedova, S.; Semenkin, E. Selective Pressure Strategy in differential evolution: Exploitation improvement in solving global optimization problems. *Swarm Evol. Comput.* **2019**, *50*, 100463.
23. Brest, J.; Maučec, M.; Boškovic, B. Single objective real-parameter optimization algorithm jSO. In *Proceedings of the IEEE Congress on Evolutionary Computation, Donostia, Spain, 5–8 June 2017*; IEEE Press: Hoboken, NJ, USA, 2017; pp. 1311–1318. [CrossRef]
24. Stanovov, V.; Akhmedova, S.; Semenkin, E. LSHADE Algorithm with Rank-Based Selective Pressure Strategy for Solving CEC 2017 Benchmark Problems. In Proceedings of the 2018 IEEE Congress on Evolutionary Computation (CEC), Rio de Janeiro, Brazil, 8–13 July 2018; pp. 1–8.
25. Viktorin, A.; Senkerik, R.; Pluhacek, M.; Kadavy, T.; Zamuda, A. Distance based parameter adaptation for Success-History based Differential Evolution. *Swarm Evol. Comput.* **2019**, *50*, 100462. [CrossRef]
26. Stanovov, V.; Akhmedova, S.; Semenkin, E. The automatic design of parameter adaptation techniques for differential evolution with genetic programming. *Knowl. Based Syst.* **2022**, *239*, 108070. [CrossRef]
27. Chen, X.; Shen, A. Self-adaptive differential evolution with Gaussian–Cauchy mutation for large-scale CHP economic dispatch problem. *Neural Comput. Appl.* **2022**, *34*, 11769–11787. [CrossRef]
28. Santucci, V.; Baioletti, M.; Bari, G.D. An improved memetic algebraic differential evolution for solving the multidimensional two-way number partitioning problem. *Expert Syst. Appl.* **2021**, *178*, 114938.
29. Yang, M.; Cai, Z.; Li, C.; Guan, J. An improved adaptive differential evolution algorithm with population adaptation. In Proceedings of the Annual Conference on Genetic and Evolutionary Computation, Amsterdam, The Netherlands, 6–10 July 2013.
30. Yi, W.; Chen, Y.; Pei, Z.; Lu, J. Adaptive differential evolution with ensembling operators for continuous optimization problems. *Swarm Evol. Comput.* **2021**, *69*, 100994. [CrossRef]
31. Burke, E.; Hyde, M.; Kendall, G.; Ochoa, G.; Özcan, E.; Woodward, J. A Classification of Hyper-Heuristic Approaches: Revisited. In *Handbook of Metaheuristics*; Springer International Publishing: Cham, Switzerland, 2019; pp. 453–477. [CrossRef]
32. Haraldsson, S.O.; Woodward, J. Automated design of algorithms and genetic improvement: Contrast and commonalities. In Proceedings of the Companion Publication of the 2014 Annual Conference on Genetic and Evolutionary Computation, Vancouver, BC, Canada, 12–16 July 2014.
33. Mohamed, A.; Hadi, A.A.; Fattouh, A.; Jambi, K. LSHADE with semi-parameter adaptation hybrid with CMA-ES for solving CEC 2017 benchmark problems. In Proceedings of the 2017 IEEE Congress on Evolutionary Computation (CEC), Donostia, Spain, 5–8 June 2017; pp. 145–152.

34. Stanovov, V.; Semenkin, E. Genetic Programming for Automatic Design of Parameter Adaptation in Dual-Population Differential Evolution. In Proceedings of the Companion Conference on Genetic and Evolutionary Computation, Lisbon, Portugal, 15–19 July 2023.
35. Price, K.V.; Kumar, A.; Suganthan, P.N. Trial-based dominance for comparing both the speed and accuracy of stochastic optimizers with standard non-parametric tests. *Swarm Evol. Comput.* **2023**, *78*, 101287. [CrossRef]
36. Price, K.; Storn, R.; Lampinen, J. *Differential Evolution: A Practical Approach to Global Optimization*; Springer: Berlin/Heidelberg, Germany, 2005.
37. Gamperle, R.; Muller, S.; Koumoutsakos, A. A Parameter Study for Differential Evolution. *Adv. Intell. Syst. Fuzzy Syst. Evol. Comput.* **2002**, *10*, 293–298.
38. Zaharie, D. Critical values for the control parameters of differential evolution algorithms. *Crit. Values Control Parameters Differ. Evol. Algorithmss* **2002**, *2*, 62–67.
39. Ali, M.; Törn, A. Optimization of Carbon and Silicon Cluster Geometry for Tersoff Potential using Differential Evolution. In *Optimization in Computational Chemistry and Molecular Biology: Local and Global Approaches*; Springer: Berlin/Heidelberg, Germany, 2000. [CrossRef]
40. Kumar, A.; Misra, R.K.; Singh, D. Improving the local search capability of Effective Butterfly Optimizer using Covariance Matrix Adapted Retreat Phase. In Proceedings of the 2017 IEEE Congress on Evolutionary Computation (CEC), Donostia, Spain, 5–8 June 2017; pp. 1835–1842.
41. Stanovov, V.; Akhmedova, S.; Semenkin, E. NL-SHADE-RSP Algorithm with Adaptive Archive and Selective Pressure for CEC 2021 Numerical Optimization. In Proceedings of the 2021 IEEE Congress on Evolutionary Computation (CEC), Kraków, Poland, 28 June–1 July 2021; pp. 809–816. [CrossRef]
42. Stanovov, V.; Akhmedova, S.; Semenkin, E. NL-SHADE-LBC algorithm with linear parameter adaptation bias change for CEC 2022 Numerical Optimization. In Proceedings of the 2022 IEEE Congress on Evolutionary Computation (CEC), Padua, Italy, 18–23 July 2022.
43. Mohamed, A.W.; Hadi, A.A.; Agrawal, P.; Sallam, K.M.; Mohamed, A.K. Gaining-Sharing Knowledge Based Algorithm with Adaptive Parameters Hybrid with IMODE Algorithm for Solving CEC 2021 Benchmark Problems. In Proceedings of the 2021 IEEE Congress on Evolutionary Computation (CEC), Kraków, Poland, 28 June–1 July 2021; pp. 841–848.
44. Cuong, L.V.; Bao, N.N.; Binh, H.T.T. *Technical Report: A Multi-Start Local Search Algorithm with L-SHADE for Single Objective Bound Constrained Optimization*; Technical Report; SoICT, Hanoi University of Science and Technology: Hanoi, Vietnam, 2021.
45. Biswas, S.; Saha, D.; De, S.; Cobb, A.D.; Das, S.; Jalaian, B. Improving Differential Evolution through Bayesian Hyperparameter Optimization. In Proceedings of the 2021 IEEE Congress on Evolutionary Computation (CEC), Kraków, Poland, 28 June–1 July 2021; pp. 832–840.
46. Bujok, P.; Kolenovsky, P. Eigen Crossover in Cooperative Model of Evolutionary Algorithms Applied to CEC 2022 Single Objective Numerical Optimisation. In Proceedings of the 2022 IEEE Congress on Evolutionary Computation (CEC), Padua, Italy, 18–23 July 2022.
47. Biedrzycki, R.; Arabas, J.; Warchulski, E. A Version of NL-SHADE-RSP Algorithm with Midpoint for CEC 2022 Single Objective Bound Constrained Problems. In Proceedings of the 2022 IEEE Congress on Evolutionary Computation (CEC), Padua, Italy, 18–23 July 2022.

axioms

MDPI

Article

An Efficient Subspace Minimization Conjugate Gradient Method for Solving Nonlinear Monotone Equations with Convex Constraints

Taiyong Song and Zexian Liu *

School of Mathematics and Statistics, Guizhou University, Guiyang 550025, China; gs.tysong21@gzu.edu.cn
* Correspondence: zxliu6@gzu.edu.cn

Abstract: The subspace minimization conjugate gradient (SMCG) methods proposed by Yuan and Store are efficient iterative methods for unconstrained optimization, where the search directions are generated by minimizing the quadratic approximate models of the objective function at the current iterative point. Although the SMCG methods have illustrated excellent numerical performance, they are only used to solve unconstrained optimization problems at present. In this paper, we extend the SMCG methods and present an efficient SMCG method for solving nonlinear monotone equations with convex constraints by combining it with the projection technique, where the search direction is sufficiently descent.Under mild conditions, we establish the global convergence and R-linear convergence rate of the proposed method. The numerical experiment indicates that the proposed method is very promising.

Keywords: nonlinear monotone equations; subspace minimization conjugate gradient method; convex constraints; global convergence; R-linear convergence rate

MSC: 90C06; 65K

1. Introduction

We consider the following nonlinear equations with convex constraints:

$$F(x) = 0, \quad x \in \Omega, \tag{1}$$

where $\Omega \subset \mathbb{R}^n$ is a non-empty closed convex set and $F : \mathbb{R}^n \to \mathbb{R}^n$ is a continuous mapping that satisfies the monotonicity condition

$$\langle F(x) - F(y), x - y \rangle \geq 0, \tag{2}$$

for all $x, y \in \mathbb{R}^n$. It is easy to verify that the solution set of problem (1) is convex under condition (2).

Nonlinear equations have numerous practical applications, e.g., machinery manufacturing problems [1], neural networks [2], economic equilibrium problems [3], image recovery problems [4], and so on. In the context of many practical applications, problem (1) has attracted a substantial number of scholars to put forward more effective iterative methods to find solutions, such as Newton's method, quasi-Newton methods, trust region methods, Levenberg–Marquardt methods, or their variants ([5–9]). Although these methods are very popular and have fast convergence at an adequately good initial point, they are not suitable for solving large-scale nonlinear equations due to the calculation and storage of the Jacobian matrix or its approximation.

Due to its simple form and low memory requirement, conjugate gradient (CG) methods are used to solve problem (1) by combining them with projection technology proposed by Solodov and Svaiter [10] (see [11,12]). Xiao and Zhu [13] extended the famous CG_DESCENT method [14] for solving nonlinear monotone equations with convex constraints due to its effectiveness. Liu and Li [15] presented an efficient projection method for solving convex constrained monotone nonlinear equations, which can be viewed as another extension of the CG_DESCENT method [14] and was used to solve the sparse signal reconstruction in compressive sensing. Based on the Dai–Yuan (DY) method [16], Liu and Feng [17] presented an efficient derivative-free iterative method and established its Q-linear convergence rate of the proposed method under the local error bound condition. By minimizing the distance between relative matrix and the self-scaling memoryless BFGS method in the Frobenius norm, Gao et al. [18] proposed an adaptive projection method for solving nonlinear equations and applied it to recover a sparse signal from incomplete and contaminated sampling measurements. Based on [19], Li and Zheng [20] proposed two effective derivative-free methods for solving large-scale nonsmooth monotone nonlinear equations. Waziri et al. [21] proposed two DY-type iterative methods for solving (1). By using the projection method [10], Abdulkarim et al. [22] introduced two classes of three-term methods for solving (1) and established the global convergence under a weaker monotonicity condition.

The subspace minimization conjugate gradient (SMCG) methods proposed by Yuan and Stoer [23] are generalizations of the traditional CG methods and are a class of iterative methods for unconstrained optimization. The SMCG methods have illustrated excellent numerical performance and have also received much attention recently. However, the SMCG methods are only used to solve unconstrained optimization at present. Therefore, it is very interesting to study the SMCG methods for solving nonlinear equations with convex constraints. In this paper, we propose an efficient SMCG method for solving nonlinear monotone equations with convex constraints by combining it with the projection technology, where the search direction is in a sufficient descent. Under suitable conditions, the global convergence and the convergence rate of the proposed method are established. The numerical experiment is conducted, which indicates that the proposed method is superior to some efficient conjugate gradient methods.

The remainder of this paper is organized as follows. In Section 2, an efficient SMCG method for solving nonlinear monotone equations with convex constraints is presented. We prove the global convergence and the convergence rate of the proposed method in Section 3. In Section 4, the conducted numerical experiment is discussed to verify the effectiveness of the proposed method. The conclusion is presented in Section 5.

2. The SMCG Method for Solving Nonlinear Monotone Equations with Convex Constraints

In this section, we first review the SMCG methods for unconstrained optimization, and then propose an efficient SMCG method for solving (1) by combining it with the projection technique and exploit some of its important properties.

2.1. The SMCG Method for Unconstrained Optimization

We review the SMCG methods here.

The SMCG methods were proposed by Yuan and Stoer [23] to solve the unconstrained optimization problem

$$\min_{x \in R^n} f(x),$$

where $f : \mathbb{R}^n \to \mathbb{R}$ is continuously differentiable. The SMCG methods are of the form $x_{k+1} = x_k + \alpha_k \hat{d}_k$, where α_k is the stepsize and $\hat{d}_k$ is the search direction, which are generated by minimizing the quadratic approximate models of the objective function f at the current iterative point x_k in the subspace $\Omega_k = \mathrm{Span}\{\hat{d}_{k-1}, g_k\}$, namely

$$\min_{\hat{d}\in\Omega_k} m_k\left(\hat{d}\right)=g_k^T\hat{d}+\frac{1}{2}\hat{d}^T B_k\hat{d}, \tag{3}$$

where B_k is an approximation to the Hessian matrix and is required to satisfy the quasi-Newton equation $B_k\hat{s}_{k-1} = \hat{y}_{k-1}$, $\hat{s}_{k-1} = x_{k+1} - x_k = \alpha_k\hat{d}_k$, $g_k = \nabla f(x_k)$.

In the following, we consider the case that $\hat{d}_{k-1}$ and g_k are not collinear. Since the vector $\hat{d}_k$ in $\Omega_k = \text{Span}\{\hat{d}_{k-1}, g_k\}$ can be expressed as

$$\hat{d}_k=\mu_k g_k+\nu_k\hat{s}_{k-1}, \tag{4}$$

where $\mu_k, \nu_k \in \mathbb{R}$, by substituting (4) into (3), we obtain

$$\min_{(\mu_k,\nu_k)\in\mathbb{R}^2} \Phi(\mu_k,\nu_k) = \begin{pmatrix} ||g_k||^2 \\ g_k^T\hat{s}_{k-1} \end{pmatrix}^T \begin{pmatrix} \mu_k \\ \nu_k \end{pmatrix} + \frac{1}{2}\begin{pmatrix} \mu_k \\ \nu_k \end{pmatrix}^T \begin{pmatrix} g_k^T B_k g_k & g_k^T B_k\hat{s}_{k-1} \\ \hat{s}_{k-1}^T B_k g_k & \hat{s}_{k-1}^T B_k\hat{s}_{k-1} \end{pmatrix} \begin{pmatrix} \mu_k \\ \nu_k \end{pmatrix}. \tag{5}$$

When B_k is positive definite, by imposing $\nabla\Phi(\mu_k,\nu_k) = (0,0)$, we obtain the optimal solution of subproblem (5) (for more details, please see [23]):

$$\begin{pmatrix} \mu_k^* \\ \nu_k^* \end{pmatrix}=\frac{1}{\Delta_k}\begin{pmatrix} g_k^T\hat{y}_{k-1}g_k^T\hat{s}_{k-1} - \hat{s}_{k-1}^T\hat{y}_{k-1}||g_k||^2 \\ g_k^T\hat{y}_{k-1}||g_k||^2 - \rho_k g_k^T\hat{s}_{k-1} \end{pmatrix}, \tag{6}$$

where $\Delta_k = \rho_k\hat{s}_{k-1}^T\hat{y}_{k-1} - \left(g_k^T\hat{y}_{k-1}\right)^2$, $\rho_k = g_k^T B_k g_k$, $\hat{y}_{k-1} = g_{k+1} - g_k$.

An important property about the SMCG methods was given by Dai and Kou [24] in 2016. They established the two-dimensional finite termination property of the SMCG methods and presented some Barzilai–Borwein conjugate gradient (BBCG) methods with different ρ_k values, and the most efficient one is

$$\rho_k^{BBCG3} = \frac{3||g_k||^2||\hat{y}_{k-1}||^2}{2\hat{s}_{k-1}^T\hat{y}_{k-1}}. \tag{7}$$

Motivated by the SMCG methods [23] and ρ_k^{BBCG3}, Liu and Liu [25] extended the BBCG3 method to general unconstrained optimization and presented an efficient subspace minimization conjugate gradient method (SMCG_BB). Since then, a lot of SMCG methods [26–28] have been proposed for unconstrained optimization. The SMCG methods are very efficient and have received much attention.

2.2. The SMCG Method for Solving (1) *and Its Some Important Properties*

We will extend the SMCG methods for unconstrained optimization for solving (1) by combining it with the projection technique and exploit some important properties of the search direction in the subsection. The motivation behind we extend the SMCG methods for unconstrained optimization to solve (1) is that the SMCG methods have the following characteristics: (i) The search directions of the SMCG methods are parallel to those of the traditional CG methods when the exact line search is performed, and thus reduce to the traditional CG methods when the exact line search is performed. It implies that the SMCG methods can inherit the finite termination property of the traditional CG methods for convex quadratic minimization. (ii) The search directions of the SMCG methods are generated by solving (3) over the whole two-dimensional subspace $\Omega_k = \text{Span}\{\hat{d}_{k-1}, g_k\}$, while those of the traditional CG methods are $\hat{d}_k = -g_k + \beta_k\hat{d}_{k-1}$, where β_k is called the conjugate parameter. Obviously, the search directions of the traditional CG methods are derived in the special subset of Ω_k to make them possess the conjugate property. As a result, the SMCG methods have more choices and thus have more potential in theoretical properties and numerical performance. In theory, the SMCG methods without the exact line search can possess the finite termination property when solving two-dimensional strictly convex quadratic minimization problems [24], while this is impossible for the traditional

CG methods when the line search is not exact. In numerical performance, the numerical results in [25–28] indicated that the SMCG methods are very efficient.

For simplicity, we abbreviate $F(x_k)$ as F_k in the following. We are particularly interested in the SMCG methods proposed by Yuan and store [23], where the search directions are given by

$$\hat{d}_k = \mu_k^* g_k + \nu_k^* \hat{s}_{k-1}, \tag{8}$$

where μ_k^* and ν_k^* are determined by (6). For the choice of ρ_k in (6), we take the form (7) due to its effectiveness [24]. Therefore, based on (8) and (7), the search direction of the SMCG method for solving problem (1) can be arranged as

$$\bar{d}_k = \frac{1}{\Delta_k}\left[\left(F_k^T y_{k-1} F_k^T s_{k-1} - s_{k-1}^T y_{k-1}\|F_k\|^2\right)F_k + \left(F_k^T y_{k-1}\|F_k\|^2 - \rho_k F_k^T s_{k-1}\right)s_{k-1}\right], \tag{9}$$

where $y_{k-1} = \bar{y}_{k-1} + r s_{k-1}$, $\bar{y}_{k-1} = F(x_k) - F_{k-1}$, $s_{k-1} = x_k - x_{k-1}$, $\Delta_k = \rho_k s_{k-1}^T y_{k-1} - \left(F_k^T y_{k-1}\right)^2$, $\rho_k = \frac{3||F_k||^2||y_{k-1}||^2}{2s_{k-1}^T y_{k-1}}$.

In order to analyze some properties of the search direction, the search direction will be reset as $-F_k$ when $s_{k-1}^T y_{k-1} < \xi_1||y_{k-1}||^2$, where $\xi_1 > 0$. Therefore, the search direction is truncated as

$$d_k = \begin{cases} \bar{d}_k, & \text{if } s_{k-1}^T y_{k-1} \geq \xi_1||y_{k-1}||^2 , \\ -F_k, & \text{otherwise,} \end{cases} \tag{10}$$

where $\bar{d}_k$ is given by (9).

The projection technique, which will be used in the proposed method, is described as follows.

By setting $z_k = x_k + \alpha_k d_k$ as a trial point, we define a hyperplane

$$H_k = \{x \in \mathbb{R}^n | \langle F(z_k), x - z_k\rangle = 0\},$$

which strictly separates x_k from the zero points of $F(x)$ in (1). The projection operator is a mapping from R^n to the non-empty closed subset Ω :

$$P_\Omega[x] = \arg\min\{||x-y|| | y \in \Omega\},$$

which enjoys the non-expansive property

$$||P_\Omega[x] - y|| \leq ||x-y||, \ \forall y \in \Omega.$$

Solodov and Svaiter [10] showed that the next iterative point x_{k+1} is the projection of x_k onto H_k, namely

$$x_{k+1} = x_k - \frac{\langle F(z_k), x_k - z_k\rangle}{||F(z_k)||^2} F(z_k).$$

By combining (10) with the projection technique, we present an SMCG method for solving (1), which is described in detail as follows.

The following lemma indicates that the search direction d_k satisfies the sufficient descent property.

Lemma 1. *The search direction $\{d_k\}$ generated by Algorithm 1 always satisfies the sufficient descent condition*

$$d_k^T F_k \leq -C||F_k||^2, \tag{11}$$

for all $k \geq 0$.

Proof. According to (10), we know that (11) holds with $C = 1$ if $s_{k-1}^T y_{k-1} < \xi_1||y_{k-1}||^2$. We next consider the opposite situation. It follows that

$$
\begin{aligned}
d_k^T F_k &= \frac{1}{\Delta_k}[\left(F_k^T y_{k-1} F_k^T s_{k-1} - s_{k-1}^T y_{k-1}||F_k||^2\right) F_k + \left(F_k^T y_{k-1}||F_k||^2 - \rho_k F_k^T s_{k-1}\right) s_{k-1}]^T F_k \\
&= -\frac{||F_k||^4}{\Delta_k}\left[s_{k-1}^T y_{k-1} - 2F_k^T y_{k-1}\frac{F_k^T s_{k-1}}{||F_k||^2} + \rho_k\left(\frac{F_k^T s_{k-1}}{||F_k||^2}\right)^2\right] \\
&\triangleq -\frac{||F_k||^4}{\Delta_k}\cdot\eta_k \le -\frac{||F_k||^4}{\Delta_k}\cdot\frac{\Delta_k}{\rho_k} = -\frac{||F_k||^4}{\rho_k},
\end{aligned}
\tag{12}
$$

where the inequality comes from the fact that treating η_k as a one variable function of $\frac{F_k^T s_{k-1}}{||F_k||^2}$ and minimizing it can yield $\eta_k \ge \frac{\Delta_k}{\rho_k}$. Consequently, by the choice of ρ_k and (10), it holds that

$$
d_k^T F_k \le -\frac{||F_k||^4}{\rho_k} \le -\frac{2s_{k-1}^T y_{k-1}}{3||y_{k-1}||^2}||F_k||^2 \le -\frac{2\xi_1}{3}||F_k||^2.
$$

In sum, (11) holds with $C = \min\left\{1, \frac{2\xi_1}{3}\right\}$. The proof is completed. □

Algorithm 1 Subspace Minimization Conjugate Gradient Method for Solving (1)

Step 0. Initialization. Select $x_0 \in \mathbb{R}^n$, $\varepsilon > 0$, $0 < \sigma < 1$, $\xi \in (0,1)$, $\rho \in (0,1)$, $\kappa \in (0,2)$. Set $k = 0$.
Step 1. If $||F_k|| \le \varepsilon$, stop. Otherwise, compute search direction d_k by (10).
Step 2. Let $z_k = x_k + \alpha_k d_k$, where $\alpha_k = \max\{\xi\rho^i | i = 0,1,2,3,\cdots\}$ is determined by

$$
-\langle F(x_k + \alpha_k d_k), d_k\rangle \ge \sigma\alpha_k||F(x_k + \alpha_k d_k)||||d_k||^2, \tag{13}
$$

Step 3. If $z_k \in \Omega$ and $||F(z_k)|| \le \varepsilon$, $x_{k+1} = z_k$, then stop. Otherwise, we determine x_{k+1} by

$$
x_{k+1} = P_\Omega[x_k - \kappa\lambda_k F(z_k)],
$$

where

$$
\lambda_k = \frac{\langle F(z_k), x_k - z_k\rangle}{||F(z_k)||^2}.
$$

Step 4. Set $k = k + 1$ and go to Step 1.

Lemma 2. *Let the sequences $\{d_k\}$ and $\{x_k\}$ be generated by Algorithm 1, then there always exists a stepsize α_k satisfying the line search* (13).

Proof. We prove it by contradiction. Suppose that inequality (13) does not hold for any positive integer i at the k-th iteration, we can determine that

$$
-\left\langle F(x_k + \beta\rho^i d_k), d_k\right\rangle < \sigma\beta\rho^i\left\|F(x_k + \beta\rho^i d_k)\right\|||d_k||^2. \tag{14}
$$

By taking $i \to \infty$, it follows from the continuity of F and $\rho \in (0,1)$ that

$$
-F(x_k)^T d_k \le 0, \tag{15}
$$

which contradicts (11). The proof is completed. □

3. Convergence Analysis

In this section, we will establish the global convergence and the convergence rate of Algorithm 1.

3.1. Global Convergence

We first perform the following assumptions.

Assumption 1. *There is a solution $x^* \in \Omega^*$ such that $F(x^*) = 0$.*

Assumption 2. *The mapping F is continuous and monotone.*

By utilizing (2), we can obtain

$$s_{k-1}^T y_{k-1} = s_{k-1}^T(\bar{y}_{k-1} + r s_{k-1}) = s_{k-1}^T(F(x_k) - F(x_{k-1})) + r s_{k-1}^T s_{k-1} \geq r||s_{k-1}||^2 > 0. \tag{16}$$

The next lemma indicates that sequence $\{||x_k - x^*||\}$ generated by Algorithm 1 is Fejèr monotone with respect to Ω.

Lemma 3. *Suppose that Assumptions 1 and 2 hold, and $\{x_k\}$ and $\{z_k\}$ are generated by Algorithm 1. Then, it holds that*

$$||x_{k+1} - x^*||^2 \leq ||x_k - x^*||^2 - \kappa(2-\kappa)\sigma^2||x_k - z_k||^4, \ \ \forall x^* \in \Omega^*. \tag{17}$$

Moreover, the sequence $\{x_k\}$ is bounded and

$$\sum_{k=0}^{\infty} ||x_k - z_k||^4 < +\infty. \tag{18}$$

Proof. From (2), the following holds:

$$\langle F(z_k), x_k - x^* \rangle \geq \langle F(z_k), x_k - z_k \rangle, \forall x^* \in \Omega^*,$$

which, together with (13), implies that

$$\langle F(z_k), x_k - z_k \rangle \geq \sigma\alpha_k^2 ||F(z_k)|| ||d_k||^2 \geq 0.$$

As a result, we have

$$\begin{aligned}
||x_{k+1} - x^*||^2 &= P_\Omega[x_k - \kappa\lambda_k F(z_k) - x^*] \leq ||x_k - \kappa\lambda_k F(z_k) - x^*||^2 \\
&= ||x_k - x^*||^2 - 2\kappa\lambda_k\langle F(z_k), x_k - x^* \rangle + ||\kappa\lambda_k F(z_k)||^2 \\
&\leq ||x_k - x^*||^2 - 2\kappa\lambda_k\langle F(z_k), x_k - z_k \rangle + ||\kappa\lambda_k F(z_k)||^2 \\
&= ||x_k - x^*||^2 - \kappa(2-\kappa)\frac{\langle F(z_k), x_k - z_k \rangle^2}{||F(z_k)||^2} \\
&\leq ||x_k - x^*||^2 - \kappa(2-\kappa)\sigma^2||x_k - z_k||^4.
\end{aligned}$$

□

It follows that the sequence $||x_k - x^*||$ is non-increasing and thus, the sequence $\{x_k\}$ is bounded. We also have

$$\kappa(2-\kappa)\sigma^2 \sum_{k=0}^{\infty} ||x_k - z_k||^4 < ||x_0 - x^*||^2 < +\infty.$$

By the definition of $\{z_k\}$, we can determine that

$$\lim_{k\to\infty} ||x_k - z_k|| = \lim_{k\to\infty} \alpha_k ||d_k|| = 0. \tag{19}$$

The following lemma is proved only based on the continuity assumption on F.

Lemma 4. *Suppose that $\{d_k\}$ is generated by Algorithm 1. Then, for all $k \geq 0$, we have*

$$C||F_k|| \leq ||d_k|| \leq C_3||F_k||, \tag{20}$$

where $0 < C < C_3$.

Proof. From (11) and by utilizing the Cauchy–Schwartz inequality, it follows that

$$||d_k|| \geq C||F_k||. \tag{21}$$

In the following, we consider two cases: when (i) $s_{k-1}^T y_{k-1} \geq \xi_1 ||y_{k-1}||^2$ holds, we have

$$\left|\frac{1}{\Delta_k}\right| = \frac{1}{\left|\rho_k s_{k-1}^T y_{k-1} - (F_k^T y_{k-1})^2\right|} = \frac{1}{\left|\frac{3}{2}||y_{k-1}||^2||F_k||^2 - (F_k^T y_{k-1})^2\right|} \leq \frac{2}{||y_{k-1}||^2||F_k||^2}. \tag{22}$$

Therefore, by (10), (16) and (22), as well as the Cauchy–Schwarz inequality, we obtain

$$\begin{aligned}
||d_k|| &= \left|\frac{1}{\Delta_k}\right| \cdot \left|\left|[(F_k^T y_{k-1} F_k^T s_{k-1} - s_{k-1}^T y_{k-1}||F_k||^2)F_k + (F_k^T y_{k-1}||F_k||^2 - \frac{3||y_{k-1}||^2||F_k||^2}{2s_{k-1}^T y_{k-1}} F_k^T s_{k-1})s_{k-1}]\right|\right| \\
&\leq \left|\frac{1}{\Delta_k}\right| \cdot [\left|\left|F_k^T y_{k-1} F_k^T s_{k-1}\right|\right| ||F_k|| + \left|\left|s_{k-1}^T y_{k-1}\right|\right| ||F_k||^3 \\
&+ \left|\left|F_k^T y_{k-1}\right|\right| ||F_k||^2 ||s_{k-1}|| + \frac{3||y_{k-1}||^2||F_k||^2}{2s_{k-1}^T y_{k-1}} \left|\left|F_k^T s_{k-1}\right|\right| ||s_{k-1}||] \\
&\leq \frac{2}{||y_{k-1}||^2||F_k||^2} \cdot [3||s_{k-1}|| \, ||y_{k-1}|| \, ||F_k||^3 + \frac{3}{2s_{k-1}^T y_{k-1}} ||y_{k-1}||^2 ||s_{k-1}||^2 ||F_k||^3] \\
&= \left(\frac{6||s_{k-1}||}{||y_{k-1}||} + \frac{3}{s_{k-1}^T y_{k-1}} ||s_{k-1}||^2\right) ||F_k|| \\
&= \left(\frac{6||s_{k-1}||^2}{||s_{k-1}|| \, ||y_{k-1}||} + \frac{3}{s_{k-1}^T y_{k-1}} ||s_{k-1}||^2\right) ||F_k|| \\
&\leq \left(\frac{6||s_{k-1}||^2}{s_{k-1}^T y_{k-1}} + \frac{3}{s_{k-1}^T y_{k-1}} ||s_{k-1}||^2\right) ||F_k|| \\
&\leq \frac{9||s_{k-1}||^2}{s_{k-1}^T y_{k-1}} ||F_k|| \\
&\leq \frac{9}{r} ||F_k||.
\end{aligned} \tag{23}$$

(ii) $s_{k-1}^T y_{k-1} < \xi_1 ||y_{k-1}||^2$ or $k = 0$, $||d_k|| = ||F_k||$. In sum, (20) holds for all $k \geq 0$ with $C_3 = \max\{\frac{9}{r}, 1\}$ and C in (11). The proof is completed. □

In the following theorem, we establish the global convergence of Algorithm 1.

Theorem 1. *Suppose that Assumption 2 holds, and the sequences $\{x_k\}$ and $\{z_k\}$ are generated by Algorithm 1. Then, the following holds:*

$$\lim_{k \to \infty} \inf ||F_k|| = 0. \tag{24}$$

Proof. We prove it by contradiction. Suppose that (24) does not hold, i.e., there exists a constant $r > 0$ such that $||F_k|| \geq r$, $\forall k \geq 0$. Together with (21), it implies that

$$||d_k|| \geq Cr, \forall k \geq 0. \tag{25}$$

By utilizing (19) and (25), we can determine that $\lim_{k\to\infty} \alpha_k = 0$. By $\alpha_k = \beta\rho^{i_k}$ and the line search (13), for a large enough k, we can determine that

$$-\left\langle F(x_k + \beta\rho^{i_{k-1}} d_k), d_k \right\rangle < \sigma\beta\rho^{i_{k-1}} \left\| F(x_k + \beta\rho^{i_{k-1}} d_k) \right\| \|d_k\|^2. \tag{26}$$

It follows from (20) and $||F_k|| \geq r$ that the sequence $\{d_k\}$ is bounded. Together with the boundedness of $\{x_k\}$, we know that there exist convergent subsequences for both $\{x_k\}$ and $\{d_k\}$. Without the loss of generality, we assume that the two sequences $\{x_k\}$ and $\{d_k\}$ are convergent. Hence, taking limits on (26) yields

$$-\langle F(\bar{x}), \bar{d} \rangle < 0, \tag{27}$$

where $\bar{x}$ and $\bar{d}$ are the corresponding limit points. By taking limits on both sides of (11), we obtain

$$-\langle F(\bar{x}), \bar{d} \rangle \geq C \|F(\bar{x})\|^2. \tag{28}$$

It follows from (27) and (28) that $\|F(\bar{x})\| = 0$, which contradicts $||F_k|| \geq r$. Therefore, we obtain (24). The proof is completed. □

3.2. R-Linear Convergence Rate

We begin to analyze the Q-linear convergence and R-linear convergence of Algorithm 1. We say that a method enjoys Q-linear convergence to mean that its iterative sequence $\{x_k\}$ satisfies $\limsup_{n\to\infty} \frac{\|x_{n+1}-x^*\|}{\|x_n - x^*\|} \leq \phi$, where $\phi \in (0,1)$; we say that a method enjoys R-linear convergence to mean that for its iterative sequence $\{x_k\}$, there exists two positive constants $m \in (0,\infty), q \in (0,1)$ such that $\|x_n - x^*\| \leq mq^k$ holds (See [29]).

Assumption 3. *For any $x^* \in \Omega^*$, there exist constant $\omega \in (0,1)$ and $\delta > 0$ such that*

$$\omega dist(x, \Omega^*) \leq \|F(x)\|^2, \ \forall x \in N(x^*, \delta), \tag{29}$$

where $dist(x,\Omega^*)$ denotes the distance from x to the solution set Ω^*, and $N(x^*,\delta) = \{x \in \Omega | \|x - x^*\| \leq \delta\}$.

Theorem 2. *Suppose that Assumptions 2 and 3 hold, and let the sequence $\{x_k\}$ be generated by Algorithm 1. Then, the sequence $dist\{x_k, \Omega^*\}$ is Q-linearly convergent to 0 and the sequence $\{x_k\}$ is R-linearly convergent to $\bar{x} \in \Omega^*$.*

Proof. By setting $u_k := \arg\min\{\|x_k - u\| | u \in \Omega^*\}$, we know that u_k is the nearest solution from x_k, i.e.,

$$\|x_k - u_k\| = dist(x_k, \Omega^*).$$

From (17), (21) and (29), for $u_k \in \Omega^*$, we have

$$\begin{aligned} dist(x_{k+1}, \Omega^*)^2 &= \|x_{k+1} - u_k\|^2 \\ &\leq dist(x_k, \Omega^*)^2 - \sigma^2 \|\alpha_k d_k\|^4 \\ &\leq dist(x_k, \Omega^*)^2 - \sigma^2 \alpha_k^4 C^4 \|F_k\|^4 \\ &\leq dist(x_k, \Omega^*)^2 - \sigma^2 \omega^2 \alpha_k^4 C^4 dist(x_k, \Omega^*)^2 \\ &= \left(1 - \sigma^2 \omega^2 \alpha_k^4 C^4\right) dist(x_k, \Omega^*)^2, \end{aligned}$$

which, together with $\sigma \in (0,1)$, $\omega \in (0,1)$, $\alpha_k \in [0,1]$, and $C \in [0,1]$ implies that the sequence $dist(x_k, \Omega^*)$ is Q-linearly convergent to 0. If $dist(x_k, \Omega^*)$ has this property, then the sequence $\{x_k\}$ is R-linearly convergent to $\bar{x} \in \Omega^*$. The proof is completed. □

4. Numerical Experiments

In this section, the numerical experiment is conducted to compare the performance of Algorithm 1 with that of the HTTCGP method [30], the PDY method [17], the MPRPA method [18], and the PCG method [15], which are very effective types of projection algorithm for solving (1). All codes of the test methods were implemented in MATLAB R2019a and were run on an HP personal desktop computer with Intel(R) Core(TM) i5-10500 CPU 3.10 GHz, 8.00 GB RAM, and Windows 10 operation system.

In Algorithm 1, we choose the following the parameter values:

$$\rho = 0.53, \sigma = 0.0001, \xi = 0.55, \xi_1 = 10^{-7}, \xi = 0.55, \kappa = 1.9\ , r = 0.1.$$

The parameters of the other four test algorithms use the default values from [15,17,18,30], respectively. In the numerical experiment, all test methods are terminated if the iteration exceeds 10,000, or if the function value of the current iterations satisfies the condition $\|F(x_k)\| \leq 10^{-5}$.

Denote

$$F(x) = (F_1(x), F_2(x), \cdots, F_n(x))^T.$$

The test problems are given as follows.

Problem 1. *This problem is a logarithmic function with* $\Omega = \{x \in \mathbb{R}^n | x_i > -1\}$ *[17], i.e.,*

$$F_i(x) = ln(x_i + 1) - \frac{x_i}{n}, i = 1, 2, 3, \cdots, n.$$

Problem 2. *This problem is a discrete boundary value problem with* $\Omega = \mathbb{R}^n_+$ *[17], i.e.,*

$$\begin{aligned} F_1(x) &= 2x_1 + 0.5h^2(x_1 + h)^3 - x_2, \\ F_i(x) &= 2x_i + 0.5h^2(x_i + ih)^3 - x_{i-1} + x_{i+1}, \\ F_n(x) &= 2x_n + 0.5h^2(x_n + nh)^3 - x_{n-1}, \end{aligned}$$

where $h = \frac{1}{n+1}, i = 2, 3, \cdots, n-1$.

Problem 3. *This problem is a trigexp funtion with* $\Omega = \mathbb{R}^n_+$ *[17], i.e.,*

$$\begin{aligned} F_1(x) &= 3x_1^3 + 2x_2 - 5 + \sin(x_1 - x_2)\sin(x_1 + x_2), \\ F_i(x) &= -x_{i-1}e^{(x_{i-1} - x_i)} + x_i(4 + 3x_i^2) + 2x_{i+1} + \sin(x_{i-1} - x_i)\sin(x_{i-1} + x_i) - 8, \\ F_n(x) &= -x_{n-1}e^{(x_{n-1} - x_n)} + 4x_n - 3, \end{aligned}$$

where $i = 2, 3, \cdots, n-1$.

Problem 4. *This problem is a tridiagonal exponential problem with* $\Omega = \mathbb{R}^n_+$ *[17], i.e.,*

$$F_i(x) = e^{x_i} - 1,$$

where $i = 1, 2, \cdots, n$.

Problem 5. *This problem is problem 4.6 in [17] with* $\Omega = \mathbb{R}^n_+$*, i.e.,*

$$F_i(x) = x_i - 2\sin|x_i - 1|,$$

where $i = 1, 2, \cdots, n$.

Problem 6. *This problem is problem 4.7 in [17], i.e.,*

$$\begin{aligned} F_1(x) &= 2.5x_1 + x_2 - 1, \\ F_i(x) &= x_{i-1} + 2.5x_i + x_{i+1} - 1, \\ F_n(x) &= x_{n-1} + 2.5x_n - 1, \end{aligned}$$

where $\Omega = \{x \in \mathbb{R}^n | x \geq -3\}, i = 2, 3, \cdots, n-1.$

Problem 7. *This problem is problem 4.8 in [17], i.e.,*

$$F_i(x) = 2x_i - \sin(x_i),$$

where $\Omega = \{x \in \mathbb{R}^n | x \geq -2\}, i = 1, 2, \cdots, n.$

Problem 8. *This problem is problem 3 in [31], i.e.,*

$$\begin{aligned} F_1(x) &= x_1 - e^{\cos\left(\frac{x_1+x_2}{n+1}\right)}, \\ F_i(x) &= x_i - e^{\cos\left(\frac{x_{i-1}+x_i+x_{i+1}}{n+1}\right)}, \\ F_n(x) &= x_n - e^{\cos\left(\frac{x_{n-1}+x_n}{n+1}\right)}, \end{aligned}$$

where $\Omega = \mathbb{R}^n_+, i = 2, \cdots, n-1.$

Problem 9. *This problem is problem 4.3 in [32], i.e.,*

$$F_i(x) = \frac{i}{n} e^{x_i} - 1,$$

where $\Omega = \mathbb{R}^n_+, i = 1, 2, \cdots, n.$

Problem 10. *This problem is problem 4.8 in [32], i.e.,*

$$F_i(x) = (e^{x_i})^2 + 3 \sin x_i \cos x_i - 1,$$

where $\Omega = \mathbb{R}^n_+, i = 1, 2, \cdots, n.$

Problem 11. *This problem is problem 4.5 in [32], i.e.,*

$$\begin{aligned} F_1(x) &= x_1 - e^{\cos\left(\frac{x_1+x_2}{2}\right)}, \\ F_i(x) &= x_i - e^{\cos\left(\frac{x_{i-1}+x_i+x_{i+1}}{i}\right)}, \\ F_n(x) &= x_n - e^{\cos\left(\frac{x_{n-1}+x_n}{n}\right)}, \end{aligned}$$

where $\Omega = \mathbb{R}^n_+, i = 2, \cdots, n-1.$

Problem 12. *This problem is problem 5 in [31], i.e.,*

$$\begin{aligned} F_1(x) &= e^{x_1} - 1, \\ F_i(x) &= e^{x_i} + x_{i-1} - 1, \end{aligned}$$

where $\Omega = \mathbb{R}^n_+, i = 2, \cdots, n-1.$

Problem 13. *This problem is problem 6 in [31], i.e.,*

$$\begin{aligned} F_1(x) &= 2x_1 - x_2 + e^{x_1} - 1, \\ F_i(x) &= -x_{i-1} + 2x_i - x_{i+1} + e^{x_i} - 1, \\ F_n(x) &= -x_{n-1} + 2x_n + e^{x_n} - 1, \end{aligned}$$

where $\Omega = \mathbb{R}^n_+, i = 2, \cdots, n-1.$

Problem 14. *This problem is problem 4.3 in [20], i.e.,*

$$\begin{aligned} F_1(x) &= x_1(2x_1^2 + 2x_2^2) - 1, \\ F_i(x) &= x_i(2x_{i-1}^2 + 2x_i^2 + 2x_{i+1}^2) - 1, \\ F_n(x) &= x_n(2x_{n-1}^2 + 2x_n^2) - 1, \end{aligned}$$

where $\Omega = \mathbb{R}_+^n, i = 2, \cdots, n-1.$

Problem 15. *This problem is a complementarity problem in [20],i.e.,*

$$F_i(x) = (x_i - 1)^2 - 1.01,$$

where $\Omega = \mathbb{R}_+^n, i = 1, 2, \cdots, n.$

The above 15 problems with different dimensions ($n = 1000, 5000, 10{,}000$, and $50{,}000$) are used to test the five test methods, as well as different initial points $x_0 = a_1 * ones(n,1)$, where $a_1 = 0.1, 0.2, 0.5, 0.12, 0.15, 2.0$, and $m = ones(n,1)$. Some of the numerical results are listed in Table 1, where "Al" represents Algorithm 1, "Pi" $(i = 1, 2, \cdots, 15)$ stands for the i-th test problem listed above, and "Ni" and "NF" denote the number of iterations and the number of function calculations, respectively. Other numerical results are available at https://www.cnblogs.com/888-0516-2333/p/18026523 (accessed on 6 January 2024).

Table 1. The numerical results (n = 10,000).

P	x_0	Al	PDY	HTTCGP	MPRPA	PCG	x_0	Al	HTTCGP	PDY	MPRPA	PCG
		Ni/NF	Ni/NF	Ni/NF	Ni/NF	Ni/NF		Ni/NF	Ni/NF	Ni/NF	Ni/NF	Ni/NF
P1	0.1 m	4\9	14\31	3\7	28\57	9\23	1.2 m	8\17	14\31	5\11	34\69	11\27
	0.2 m	5\11	14\31	3\7	29\59	8\20	1.5 m	8\17	20\42	5\11	35\71	9\22
	0.5 m	6\13	18\39	4\9	31\63	10\25	2.0 m	8\17	15\33	6\14	36\73	11\27
P2	0.1 m	4\10	7\23	6\19	12\25	10\36	1.2 m	5\11	8\25	7\22	13\27	9\32
	0.2 m	4\10	7\23	6\19	12\25	10\36	1.5 m	6\13	8\25	7\22	13\27	9\32
	0.5 m	3\8	6\20	5\16	9\19	8\29	2.0 m	6\13	8\25	8\25	14\29	10\35
P3	0.1 m	19\39	16\42	26\72	42\85	16\39	1.2 m	17\35	27\81	49\126	37\75	18\52
	0.2 m	19\39	19\49	31\83	42\85	16\39	1.5 m	19\40	20\58	41\109	33\67	17\46
	0.5 m	19\39	22\57	28\80	41\83	18\48	2.0 m	18\38	32\148	46\121	34\70	19\59
P4	0.1 m	22\46	24\97	50\172	77\170	19\77	1.2 m	29\60	32\129	53\185	92\205	22\89
	0.2 m	24\50	26\105	52\179	83\184	20\81	1.5 m	30\62	33\133	53\185	92\205	22\89
	0.5 m	26\54	30\121	59\202	86\191	21\85	2.0 m	31\64	34\137	54\189	95\212	23\93
P5	0.1 m	1\3	1\4	20\61	27\55	9\24	1.2 m	1\4	1\5	23\71	30\61	11\31
	0.2 m	1\3	1\4	21\64	29\59	9\24	1.5 m	1\4	1\5	23\71	29\59	11\31
	0.5 m	1\3	1\4	22\67	30\61	10\27	2.0 m	1\4	1\6	24\76	31\64	10\28
P6	0.1 m	5\11	6\20	7\22	12\25	9\32	1.2 m	6\13	7\22	7\22	13\27	9\32
	0.2 m	5\11	6\20	6\19	12\25	8\29	1.5 m	5\11	6\20	7\22	13\27	10\35
	0.5 m	3\8	6\20	5\16	9\19	8\29	2.0 m	6\14	7\22	8\25	14\29	10\34
P7	0.1 m	8\18	11\36	16\57	17\35	17\65	1.2 m	6\13	10\31	18\70	12\25	11\42
	0.2 m	8\20	10\33	15\54	16\33	20\78	1.5 m	6\13	10\31	20\79	11\23	15\59
	0.5 m	7\15	11\33	18\68	14\29	18\69	2.0 m	3\8	7\23	17\69	8\17	15\61
P8	0.1 m	5\11	7\19	20\61	28\57	10\26	1.2 m	7\15	13\31	24\73	32\65	10\26
	0.2 m	5\11	7\19	21\64	29\59	10\26	1.5 m	7\15	14\33	24\74	32\65	10\26
	0.5 m	6\13	6\16	23\70	31\63	10\26	2.0 m	8\17	14\33	25\77	32\65	11\29
P9	0.1 m	6\13	9\24	26\80	34\69	12\31	1.2 m	6\13	9\24	24\73	33\67	11\29
	0.2 m	6\13	9\24	26\80	34\69	12\31	1.5 m	6\13	9\24	24\73	32\65	11\29
	0.5 m	6\13	9\24	25\77	34\69	12\31	2.0 m	6\13	9\24	23\70	31\63	10\26
P10	0.1 m	51\105	40\192	197\816	13\40	68\311	1.2 m	27\57	26\143	147\617	14\43	52\241
	0.2 m	51\105	31\159	187\774	13\40	71\324	1.5 m	31\65	36\180	121\512	14\43	43\201
	0.5 m	29\61	26\131	181\752	14\43	62\285	2.0 m	34\71	35\174	132\557	16\49	43\201

Table 1. *Cont.*

P	x_0	A1	PDY	HTTCGP	MPRPA	PCG	x_0	A1	HTTCGP	PDY	MPRPA	PCG
		Ni/NF	Ni/NF	Ni/NF	Ni/NF	Ni/NF		Ni/NF	Ni/NF	Ni/NF	Ni/NF	Ni/NF
P11	0.1 m	1\5	1\7	16\81	23\93	10\51	1.2 m	1\4	1\4	18\92	24\97	1\5
	0.2 m	1\5	1\7	17\86	24\97	10\51	1.5 m	1\7	1\3	18\93	1\4	1\3
	0.5 m	1\5	1\3	17\86	25\101	1\3	2.0 m	1\6	1\8	19\100	1\4	2\11
P12	0.1 m	20\41	18\75	95\306	25\51	44\152	1.2 m	21\43	15\60	73\233	28\57	43\149
	0.2 m	20\41	15\59	95\306	24\49	44\152	1.5 m	21\43	15\61	65\210	26\53	24\85
	0.5 m	20\41	17\67	98\315	25\51	44\152	2.0 m	18\37	20\76	92\293	23\47	38\131
P13	0.1 m	30\62	24\119	182\741	83\246	99\442	1.2 m	37\76	27\136	216\880	104\333	127\641
	0.2 m	34\70	25\124	188\761	88\261	98\440	1.5 m	37\77	28\157	226\963	85\284	79\389
	0.5 m	34\71	26\133	191\786	96\288	101\458	2.0 m	3\80	25\127	210\872	120\454	3\48
P14	0.1 m	54\111	31\163	101\430	129\416	14\70	1.2 m	47\99	28\152	61\269	167\533	18\94
	0.2 m	40\82	42\260	125\530	184\582	17\85	1.5 m	55\120	27\158	91\393	157\505	18\96
	0.5 m	49\101	31\159	123\522	177\563	17\86	2.0 m	52\115	34\177	138\588	147\473	22\119
P15	0.1 m	34\72	22\177	39\245	16\80	20\140	1.2 m	21\47	20\165	48\306	15\76	16\113
	0.2 m	31\66	23\185	35\218	16\80	18\126	1.5 m	31\67	22\184	48\311	18\91	43\291
	0.5 m	28\60	23\162	42\262	17\86	18\127	2.0 m	24\54	19\155	58\361	16\82	17\121

The performance profiles proposed by Dolan and Moré [33] are used to compare the numerical performance of the test methods in terms of Ni, NF, and T, respectively. We explain the performance profile by taking the number of iterations as an example. Denote the test set and the set of algorithms by P and A, respectively. We assume that we have n_a algorithms and n_p problems. For each problem with $p \in P$ and algorithm $a \in A$, $t_{p,a}$ represents the number of iterations required to solve problem p by algorithm a. We use the performance ratio

$$r_{p,a} = \frac{t_{p,a}}{\min\{t_{p,a} | a \in A\}}$$

to compare the performance on problem p by solver a with the best performance by any algorithm on this problem. To obtain an overall assessment of the performance of the algorithm, we define

$$\rho_a(\tau) = \frac{1}{n_p} size\{p \in P | r_{p,a} \leq \tau\},$$

which is the probability for algorithm $a \in A$ that a performance ratio $r_{p,a}$ is within a factor $\tau_a \in \mathbb{R}$ of the best possible ratio and reflects the numerical performance of algorithm a relative to the other test algorithms in A. Obviously, algorithms with large probability $p_a(\tau)$ are to be preferred. Therefore, in the figure plotted with these $\rho_a(\tau)$ of the test methods, the higher the curve is, the better the corresponding algorithm a performs.

As shown in Figure 1, we observe that, in terms of the number of iterations, Algorithm 1 is the best, followed by the HTTCGP, MPRPA, and PCG methods, and the PDY method is the worst. Figure 2 indicates that Algorithm 1 has significant improvement over the other four test methods in terms of the number of function calculations, since it successfully solves about 78% of test problems with the least number of function calculations, while the percentages of the other four methods are all less than 10%. As for the reason for the significant improvement in terms of NF, it is due to the fact that the search direction of Algorithm 1 is generated by minimizing the quadratic approximate model in the two-dimensional subspace $\Omega_k = \text{Span}\{\hat{d}_{k-1}, g_k\}$, which implies that the search direction has new parameters corresponding to F_k and thus results in that it requires less function calculations in Step 2. This is also the advantage of the SMCG methods compared with other CG methods. We can see from Figure 3 that Algorithm 1 is much faster than the other four test methods.

The numerical experiment indicates Algorithm 1 is superior to the the other four test methods.

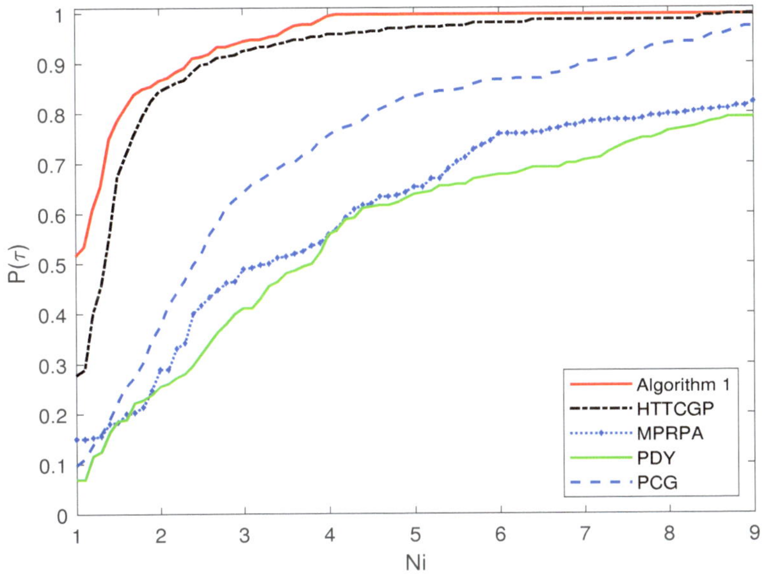

Figure 1. Performance profilesof the five algorithms with respect to number of iterations (Ni).

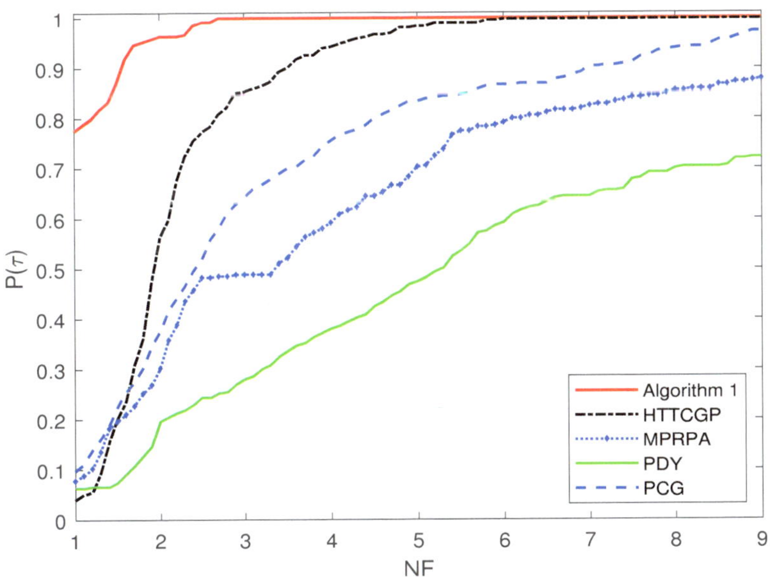

Figure 2. Performance profiles of the five algorithms with respect to number of function evaluations (NF).

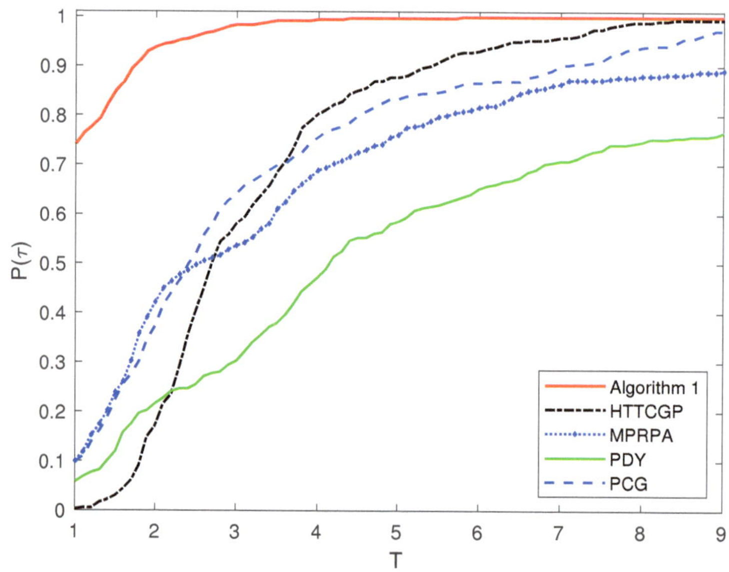

Figure 3. Performance profiles of the five algorithms with respect to CPU time (T).

5. Conclusions

In this paper, an efficient SMCG method is presented for solving nonlinear monotone equations with convex constraints. The sufficient descent property of the search direction is analyzed, and the global convergence and convergence rate of the proposed algorithm are established under suitable assumptions. The numerical results confirm the effectiveness of the proposed method.

The SMCG method has illustrated a good numerical performance for solving nonlinear monotone equations with convex constraints. There is a wide research gap with regard to studying the SMCG methods for solving nonlinear monotone equations with convex constraints, including exploiting suitable quadratic or non-quadratic approximate models to derive new search directions. This is also our future research focus.

Author Contributions: Conceptualization, T.S. and Z.L.; methodology, T.S. and Z.L.; software, T.S. and Z.L.; validation, T.S. and Z.L.; formal analysis, T.S. and Z.L.; investigation, T.S. and Z.L.; resources, T.S. and Z.L.; data curation, T.S. and Z.L.; writing—original draft preparation, T.S.; writing—review and editing, Z.L.; visualization, T.S. and Z.L.; supervision, T.S. and Z.L.; project administration, T.S. and Z.L.; funding acquisition, Z.L.. All authors have read and agreed to the published version of the manuscript.

Funding: This research was supported by National Science Foundation of China (No. 12261019), Guizhou Science Foundation (No. QHKJC-ZK[2022]YB084).

Institutional Review Board Statement: Not applicable.

Informed Consent Statement: Not applicable.

Data Availability Statement: Data are contained within the article and corresponding link.

Acknowledgments: We would like to thank the Associate Editor and the anonymous referees for their valuable comments and suggestions.

Conflicts of Interest: The authors declare no competing interests.

References

1. Guo, D.S.; Nie, Z.Y.; Yan, L.C. The application of noise-tolerant ZD design formula to robots' kinematic control via time-varying nonlinear equations solving. *IEEE Trans. Syst. Man Cybern. Syst.* **2017**, *48*, 2188–2197 . [CrossRef]
2. Shi, Y.; Zhang, Y. New discrete-time models of zeroing neural network solving systems of time-variant linear and nonlinear inequalities. *IEEE Trans. Syst. Man Cybern. Syst.* **2017**, *50*, 565–576. [CrossRef]
3. Dirkse, S.P.; Ferris, M.C. MCPLIB: A collection of nonlinear mixed complementarity problems. *Optim. Methods Softw.* **1995**, *5*, 319–345. [CrossRef]
4. Xiao, Y.H.; Wang, Q.Y.; Hu, Q.J. Non-smooth equations based methods for l1-norm problems with applications to compressed sensing. *Nonlinear Anal.* **2011**, *74*, 3570–3577. [CrossRef]
5. Yuan, Y.X. Subspace methods for large scale nonlinear equations and nonlinear least squares. *Optim. Eng.* **2009**, *10*, 207–218. [CrossRef]
6. Ahmad, F.; Tohidi, E.; Carrasco, J.A. A parameterized multi-step Newton method for solving systems of nonlinear equations. *Numer. Algorithms* **2016**, *71*, 631–653. [CrossRef]
7. Lukšan, L.; Vlček, J. New quasi-Newton method for solving systems of nonlinear equations. *Appl. Math.* **2017**, *62*, 121–134. [CrossRef]
8. Yu, Z. On the global convergence of a Levenberg-Marquardt method for constrained nonlinear equations. *JAMC* **2004**, *16*, 183–194. [CrossRef]
9. Zhang, J.L.; Wang, Y. A new trust region method for nonlinear equations. *Math. Methods Oper. Res.* **2003**, *58*, 283–298. [CrossRef]
10. Solodov, M.V.; Svaiter, B.F. A globally convergent inexact Newton method for systems of monotone equations. In *Reformulation: Nonsmooth, Piecewise Smooth, Semismooth and Smoothing Methods*; Fukushima, M., Qi, L., Eds.; Kluwer Academic: Boston, MA, USA, 1998; pp. 355–369. [Crossref]
11. Zheng, Y.; Zheng, B. Two new Dai–Liao-type conjugate gradient methods for unconstrained optimization problems. *J. Optim. Theory Appl.* **2017**, *175*, 502–509. [CrossRef]
12. Li, M.; Liu, H.W.; Liu, Z.X. A new family of conjugate gradient methods for unconstrained optimization. *J. Appl. Math. Comput.* **2018**, *58*, 219–234. [CrossRef]
13. Xiao, Y.H.; Zhu, H. A conjugate gradient method to solve convex constrained monotone equations with applications in compressive sensing. *J. Math. Anal. Appl.* **2013**, *405*, 310–319. [CrossRef]
14. Hager, H.H.; Zhang, H. A new conjugate gradient method with guaranteed descent and an efficient line search. *SIAM J. Optim.* **2005**, *16*, 170–192. [CrossRef]
15. Liu, J.K.; Li, S.J. A projection method for convex constrained monotone nonlinear equations with applications. *Comput. Math. Appl.* **2015**, *70*, 2442–2453. [CrossRef]
16. Dai, Y.H.; Yuan, Y.X. A nonlinear conjugate gradient with a strong global convergence property. *SIAM J. Optim.* **1999**, *10*, 177–182. [CrossRef]
17. Liu, J.K.; Feng, Y.M. A derivative free iterative method for nonlinear monotone equations with convex constraints. *Numer. Algorithms* **2019**, *82*, 245–262. [CrossRef]
18. Gao, P.T.; He, C.J.; Liu, Y. An adaptive family of projection methods for constrained monotone nonlinear equations with applications. *Appl. Math. Comput.* **2019**, *359*, 1–16. [CrossRef]
19. Bojari, S.; Eslahchi, M.R. Two families of scaled three-term conjugate gradient methods with sufficient descent property for nonconvex optimization. *Numer. Algorithms* **2020**, *83*, 901–933. [CrossRef]
20. Li, Q.; Zheng, B. Scaled three-term derivative-free methods for solving large-scale nonlinear monotone equations. *Numer. Algorithms* **2021**, *87*, 1343–1367. [CrossRef]
21. Waziri, M.Y., Ahmed, K. Two Descent Dai-Yuan Conjugate Gradient Methods for Systems of Monotone Nonlinear Equations. *J. Sci. Comput.* **2022**, *90*, 36. [CrossRef]
22. Ibrahim, A.H.; Alshahrani, M.; Al-Homidan, S. Two classes of spectral three-term derivative-free method for solving nonlinear equations with application. *Numer. Algorithms* **2023**. [CrossRef]
23. Yuan, Y.X.; Stoer, J. A subspace study on conjugate gradient algorithms. *Z. Angew. Math. Mech.* **1995**, *75*, 69–77. [CrossRef]
24. Dai, Y.H.; Kou, C.X. A Barzilai-Borwein conjugate gradient method. *Sci. China Math.* **2016**, *59*, 1511–1524. [CrossRef]
25. Liu, H.W.; Liu, Z.X. An efficient Barzilai–Borwein conjugate gradient method for unconstrained optimization. *J. Optim. Theory Appl.* **2019**, *180*, 879–906. [CrossRef]
26. Li, Y.F.; Liu, Z.X.; Liu, H.W. A subspace minimization conjugate gradient method based on conic model for unconstrained optimization. *Comput. Appl. Math.* **2019**, *38*, 16. [CrossRef]
27. Zhao, T.; Liu, H.W.; Liu, Z.X. New subspace minimization conjugate gradient methods based on regularization model for unconstrained optimization. *Numer. Algorithms* **2021**, *87*, 1501–1534. [CrossRef]
28. Wang, T.; Liu, Z.; Liu, H. A new subspace minimization conjugate gradient method based on tensor model for unconstrained optimization. *Int. J. Comput. Math.* **2019**, *96*, 1924–1942. [CrossRef]
29. Ortega, J.M.; Rheinboldt, W.C. *Iterative Solution of Nonlinear Equation in Several Variables*; Academic Press: New York, NY, USA; London, UK, 1970.
30. Yin, J.H.; Jian, J.B.; Jiang, X.Z.; Liu, M.X; Wang, L.Z. A hybrid three-term conjugate gradient projection method for constrained nonlinear monotone equations with applications. *Numer. Algorithms* **2021**, *88*, 389–418. [CrossRef]

31. Ou, Y.G.; Li, J.Y. A new derivative-free SCG-type projection method for nonlinear monotone equations with convex constraints. *J. Appl. Math. Comput.* **2018**, *56*, 195–216. [CrossRef]
32. Ma, G.D.; Jin, J.C.; Jian, J.B.; Yin, J.H.; Han, D.L. A modified inertial three-term conjugate gradient projection method for constrained nonlinear equations with applications in compressed sensing. *Numer. Algorithms* **2023**, *92*, 1621–1653. [CrossRef]
33. Dolan, E.D.; More, J.J. Benchmarking optimization software with performance profiles. *Math. Program* **2002**, *91*, 201–213. [CrossRef]

axioms

MDPI

Article

An Efficient Penalty Method without a Line Search for Nonlinear Optimization

Assma Leulmi

Department of Mathematics, Ferhat Abbas University of Setif-1, Setif 19137, Algeria; as_smaleulmi@yahoo.fr or assma.leulmi@univ-setif.dz

Abstract: In this work, we integrate some new approximate functions using the logarithmic penalty method to solve nonlinear optimization problems. Firstly, we determine the direction by Newton's method. Then, we establish an efficient algorithm to compute the displacement step according to the direction. Finally, we illustrate the superior performance of our new approximate function with respect to the line search one through a numerical experiment on numerous collections of test problems.

Keywords: interior point methods; logarithmic penalty method; line search; approximate functions; nonlinear optimization

MSC: 90C25; 90C30; 90C51

1. Introduction

The nonlinear optimization is a fundamental subject in the modern optimization literature. It focuses on the problem of optimizing an objective function in the presence of inequality and/or equality constraints. Furthermore, the optimization problem is obviously linear if all the functions are linear, otherwise it is called a nonlinear optimization problem.

This research field is motivated by the fact that it arises in various problems encountered in practice, such as business administration, economics, agriculture, mathematics, engineering, and physical sciences.

In our knowledge, Frank and Wolfe are the deans in nonlinear optimization problems. They established a powerful algorithm in [1] to solve them. Later, they used another method in [2] based on the application of the Simplex method on the nonlinear problem after converting it to a linear one.

This pioneer work inspired many authors to propose and develop several methods and techniques to solve this class of problems. We refer to [3,4] for interior point methods to find the solution of nonlinear optimization problems with a high dimension.

In order to make this theory applicable in practice, other methods are designed on the linear optimization history, among robust algorithms with polynomial complexity. In this perception, Khachian succeeded in 1979 to introduce a new ellipsoid method from approaches applied originally to nonlinear optimization.

Interior point methods outperform the Simplex ones, and they have recently been the subject of several monographs including Bonnans and Gilbert [5], Evtushenko and Zhadan [6], Nesterov and Emirovski [7], and Wright [8] and Ye [9].

Interior point methods can be classified into three different groups as follows: projective methods and their alternatives as in Powell [10] and Rosen [11,12], central trajectory methods (see Ouriemchi [13] and Forsgren et al. [14]), and barrier/penalty methods, where majorant functions were originally proposed by Crouzeix and Merikhi [15] to solve a semidefinite optimization problem. Inspired by this work, Menniche and Benterki [16] and Bachir Cherif and Merikhi [17] applied this idea to linear and nonlinear optimizations, respectively.

A majorant function for the penalty method in convex quadratic optimization was proposed by Chaghoub and Benterki [18]. On the other hand, A. Leulmi et al. [19,20] used new minorant functions for semidefinite optimization, and this idea was extended to linear programming by A. Leulmi and S. Leulmi in [21].

As far as we know, our new approximate function has not been studied in the nonlinear optimization literature. These approximate functions are more convenient and efficient than the line search method for rapidly computing the displacement step.

Therefore, in our work, we aim to optimize a nonlinear problem based on prior efforts. Thus, we propose a straightforward and effective barrier penalty method using new minorant functions.

More precisely, we first introduce the position of the problem and its perturbed problem with the results of convergence in Sections 2 and 3 of our paper. Then, in Section 4, we establish the solution of the perturbed problem by finding new minorant functions. Section 5 is devoted to presenting a concise description of the algorithm and to illustrating the outperformance of our new approach by carrying out a simulation study. Finally, we summarize our work in the conclusion.

Throughout this paper, the following notations are adopted. Let $\langle .,. \rangle$ and $\|.\|$ denote the scalar product and the Euclidean norm, respectively, given by the following:

$$\langle x, y \rangle = x^T y = \sum_{i=1}^{n} x_i y_i, \quad x, y \in \mathbb{R}^n$$

and

$$\|x\| = \sqrt{\langle x, x \rangle} = \sqrt{\sum_{i=1}^{n} x_i^2}$$

2. The Problem

We aim to present an algorithm for solving the following optimization problem:

$$\begin{cases} \min f(x) \\ Ax = b \\ x \geq 0, \end{cases} \tag{P}$$

where $b \in \mathbb{R}^m$ and $A \in \mathbb{R}^{m \times n}$ is a full-rank matrix with $m < n$.

For this purpose, we need the following hypothesis:

Hypothesis 1. *f is nonlinear, twice continuously differentiable, and convex on $\mathcal{L}$, where $\mathcal{L} = \{x \in \mathbb{R}^n : Ax = b;\ x \geq 0\}$ is the set of realizable solutions of (P).*

Hypothesis 2. *(P) satisfies the condition of interior point (IPC), i.e., there exists $x_0 > 0$ such that $Ax_0 = b$.*

Hypothesis 3. *The set of optimal solutions of (P) is nonempty and bounded.*

Notice that these conditions are standard in this context. We refer to [17,20].

If x^* is an optimal solution, there exist two Lagrange multipliers $p^* \in \mathbb{R}^m$ and $q^* \in \mathbb{R}^n$, such that

$$\begin{cases} \nabla f(x^*) + A^T p^* = q^* \geq 0, \\ Ax^* = b, \\ \langle q^*, x^* \rangle = 0. \end{cases} \tag{1}$$

3. Formulation of the Perturbed Problem of (P)

Let us first consider the function ψ defined on $\mathbb{R} \times \mathbb{R}^n$ by the following:

$$\psi(\eta, x) = \begin{cases} f(x) + \sum_{i=1}^{n} \xi(\eta, x_i) & \text{if} \quad x \geq 0,\ Ax = b \\ +\infty & \text{if not,} \end{cases}$$

where $\xi : \mathbb{R}^2 \longrightarrow (-\infty, +\infty]$ is a convex, lower semicontinuous and proper function given by the following:

$$\xi(\eta, \alpha) = \begin{cases} \eta \ln(\eta) - \eta \ln(\alpha) & \text{if} \quad \alpha > 0 \text{ and } \eta > 0, \\ 0 & \text{if} \quad \alpha \geq 0 \text{ and } \eta = 0, \\ +\infty & \text{otherwise.} \end{cases}$$

Thus, ψ is a proper, convex, and lower semicontinuous function.

Furthermore, the function g defined by

$$g(\eta) = \inf_{x \in \mathbb{R}^n} \left[\psi_\eta(x) = f(x) + \sum_{i=1}^{n} \xi(\eta, x_i) \right] \qquad (P\eta)$$

is convex. Notice that for $\eta = 0$, the perturbed problem $(P\eta)$ coincides with the initial problem (P); then, $f^* = g(0)$.

3.1. Existence and Uniqueness of Optimal Solution

To show that the perturbed problem $(P\eta)$ has a unique optimal solution, it is sufficient to demonstrate that the recession cone of ψ_η is reduced to zero.

Proof. For a fixed η, the function ψ_η is proper, convex, and lower semicontinuous. The asymptotic function of ψ_η is defined by the following:

$$(\psi_\eta)_\infty(d) = \lim_{\alpha \to +\infty} \frac{\psi_\eta(x_0 + \alpha d) - \psi_\eta(x_0)}{\alpha},$$

thus, the asymptotic functions of f and ψ_η satisfy the relation:

$$(\psi_\eta)_\infty(d) = \begin{cases} (f)_\infty(x) & \text{if} \quad d \geq 0,\ Ad = 0, \\ +\infty & \text{if not.} \end{cases}$$

Moreover, hypothesis H3 is equivalent to

$$\{d \in \mathbb{R}^n : (f)_\infty(x) \leq 0,\ d \geq 0,\ Ad = 0\} = \{0\}.$$

Then,

$$\{d \in \mathbb{R}^n : (\psi_\eta)_\infty(d) \leq 0\} = \{0\}$$

and from [17], for each non-negative real number η, the strictly convex problem $(P\eta)$ admits a unique optimal solution noted by x^*_η. The solution of the problem (P) is the limit of the solutions sequence of the perturbed problem $(P\eta)$ when η tends to 0. □

3.2. Convergence of the Solution

Now, we are in a position to state the convergence result of $(P\eta)$ to (P), which is proved in Lemma 1 on [18].

Let $\eta > 0$, for all $x \in \mathcal{L}$; we define $\psi(x, \eta) = f_\eta(x)$.

Lemma 1 ([18]). *We consider $\eta > 0$. If the perturbed problem $(P\eta)$ admits an optimal solution x_η, such that $\lim_{\eta \to 0} x_\eta = x^*$, then the problem (P) admits an optimal solution x^*.*

We use the classical prototype of penalty methods. We begin our process with $(x_0, \eta_0) \in \tilde{\mathcal{L}} \times (0, \infty)$, where

$$\tilde{\mathcal{L}} = \{x \in \mathbb{R}^n : x > 0,\ Ax = b\} \tag{2}$$

and the iteration scheme is divided into the following steps:

1. Select $\eta_{k+1} \in (0, \eta_k)$.

2. Establish an approximate solution x_{k+1} for $(P\eta_k)$. It is obvious that $\psi(\eta_k, x_{k+1}) < \psi(\eta_k, x_k)$.

Remark 1. *If the values of the objective functions of the problem (P) and the perturbed problem $(P\eta)$ are equal and finite, then (P) will have an optimal solution if and only if $(P\eta)$ has an optimal solution.*

The iterative process stops when we obtain an acceptable approximation of $g(0)$.

4. Computational Resolution of the Perturbed Problem

Our approach to the numerical solution of the perturbed problem $(P\eta)$, consists of two stages. In the first one, we calculate the descent direction using the Newton approach, and in the second one, we propose an efficient new-minorant-functions approach to compute the displacement step easily and quickly relative to the line search method.

4.1. The Descent Direction

As $(P\eta)$ is strictly convex, the necessary and sufficient optimality conditions state that x_η is an optimal solution of $(P\eta)$ if and only if it satisfies the nonlinear system:

$$\nabla\psi_\eta(x_\eta) = 0.$$

Using the Newton approach, a penalty method is provided to solve the above system, where the vector x_{k+1} in each is given by $x_{k+1} = x_k + \alpha_k d_k$.

The solution of the following quadratic convex optimization problem is necessary to obtain the Newton descent direction d :

$$\min_d \left[\langle \nabla\psi_\eta(x), d\rangle + \frac{1}{2}\left\langle \nabla^2\psi_\eta(x)d, d\right\rangle : Ad = 0 \right] = \min_d [H(\eta, x) : Ad = 0],$$

where $x \in \tilde{\mathcal{L}}$ and

$$\begin{aligned} \psi_\eta(x) &= f(x_\eta) + n\eta\ln\eta - \eta\sum_{i=1}^{n}\ln(x_i) \\ \nabla\psi_\eta(x) &= \nabla f(x) - \eta X^{-1}e \\ \nabla^2\psi_\eta(x) &= \nabla^2 f(x) + \eta X^{-2}e \\ H(\eta, x) &= \langle \nabla\psi_\eta(x), d\rangle + \frac{1}{2}\left\langle \nabla^2\psi_\eta(x)d, d\right\rangle, \end{aligned}$$

with the diagonal matrix $X = \mathbf{diag}(x_i)_{i=\overline{1,n}}$.

The Lagrangian is given by the following:

$$L(x, s) = \left\langle \nabla f(x) - X^{-1}\eta, d\right\rangle + \frac{1}{2}\left\langle \left(\nabla^2 f(x) + X^{-2}\eta\right)d, d\right\rangle + \langle Ad, s\rangle,$$

where $s \in \mathbb{R}^m$ is the Lagrange multiplier. It is sufficient for solving the linear system equations with $n + m$:

$$\begin{cases} \nabla f(x) - \eta X^{-1}e + \langle(\nabla^2 f(x) + X^{-2}\eta)d, d\rangle + A^t s &= 0 \\ Ad &= 0, \end{cases}$$

then,
$$\begin{cases} (\nabla^2 f(x) - \eta X^{-2})d + A^T s &= \eta X^{-1}e - \nabla f(x) \\ Ad &= 0. \end{cases} \tag{3}$$

It is simple to prove that system (3) is non-singular. We obtain
$$\begin{cases} d^T(\nabla^2 f(x) - \eta X^{-2})d + d^T A^T s &= d^T \eta X^{-1}e - d^T \nabla f(x) \\ d^T Ad &= 0, \end{cases}$$

As $d^T A^T s = (Ad)^T s = 0$ and $Ad = 0$, we obtain
$$\left\langle \nabla^2 f(x)d, d \right\rangle + \langle \nabla f(x), d \rangle = \eta \left[\left\langle X^{-1}d, e \right\rangle - \left\| X^{-1}d \right\|^2 \right]. \tag{4}$$

The system can also be written as follows:
$$\begin{cases} (X\nabla^2 f(x)X)(X^{-1}d) + \eta\, I\, (X^{-1}d) + XA^T s &= \eta XX^{-1}e - X\nabla f(x) \\ AX(X^{-1}d) &= 0, \end{cases} . \tag{5}$$

Thus, the Newton descent direction is obtained.
Throughout this paper, we take x instead of x_η.

4.2. Computation of the Displacement Step

This section deals with the numerical solution of the displacement step. We give a brief highlight of the line search methods used in nonlinear optimization problems. Then, we collect some important results of approximate function approaches applied to both semidefinite and linear programming problems. Finally, we propose our new approximate function method for the nonlinear optimization problem (P).

4.2.1. Line Search Methods

The line search methods consists of determining a displacement step α_k, which ensures the sufficient decrease in the objective at each iteration $x_{k+1} = x_k + \alpha_k d_k$, where $\alpha_k > 0$, along the descent direction d_k; in other words, it involves solving the following one-dimensional problem:
$$\varphi(\alpha) = \min_{\alpha > 0} \psi_\eta(x_k + \alpha d_k).$$

The disadvantage of this method is that the solution α is not necessarily optimal, which make the feasibility of x_{k+1} not guaranteed.

The line search techniques of Wolfe, Goldstein-Armijo, and Fibonacci are the most widely used ones. However, generally, their computational volume is costly. This is what made us search for another alternative.

4.2.2. Approximate Functions Techniques

These methods are based on sophisticated techniques introduced by J.P. Crouzeix et al. [15] and A. Leulmi et al. [20] to obtain the solution of a semidefinite optimization problem.

The aim of these techniques is to give a minimized approximation of one real-variable function $\varphi(\alpha)$ defined by
$$\begin{aligned} \varphi(\alpha) &= \frac{1}{\eta}[\psi_\eta(x + \alpha d) - \psi_\eta(x)] \\ &= \frac{1}{\eta}[f(x + \alpha d) - f(x)] - \sum_{i=1}^{n} \ln(1 + \alpha t_i),\ t = X^{-1}d. \end{aligned}$$

The function φ is convex, and we obtain the following:

$$\varphi'(\alpha) = \frac{1}{\eta}\langle \nabla f(x+\alpha d), d\rangle - \sum_{i=1}^{n}\frac{t_i}{1+\alpha t_i},$$
$$\varphi''(\alpha) = \frac{1}{\eta}\left\langle \nabla^2 f(x+\alpha d), d\right\rangle + \sum_{i=1}^{n}\frac{t_i^2}{(1+\alpha t_i)^2}.$$

We find that $\varphi'(0) + \varphi''(0) = 0$, deduced from (4), which is expected since d is the direction of Newton's descent direction.

We aim to avoid the disadvantages of line search methods and accelerate the convergence of the algorithm. For this reason, we have to identify an $\tilde{\alpha}$ that yields a significant decrease in the function $\varphi(\alpha)$. This is the same as solving a polynomial equation of degree $n+1$, where f is a linear function.

Now, we include a few helpful inequalities below, which are used throughout the paper.

H. Wolkowicz et al. [22] see also Crouzeix and Seeger [23] presented the following inequalities:

$$\bar{z} - \sigma_z\sqrt{n-1} \leq \min_i z_i \leq \bar{z} - \frac{\sigma_z}{\sqrt{n-1}}$$
$$\bar{z} + \frac{\sigma_x}{\sqrt{n-1}} \leq \max_i z_i \leq \bar{z} + \sigma_z\sqrt{n-1},$$

where $\bar{z}$ and σ_z represent the mean and the standard deviation, respectively, of a statistical real numbers series $\{z_1, z_2, \ldots, z_n\}$. The later quantities are defined as follows:

$$\bar{z} = \frac{1}{n}\sum_{i=1}^{n} z_i \quad \text{and} \quad \sigma_z^2 = \frac{1}{n}\sum_{i=1}^{n} z_i^2 - \bar{z}^2 = \frac{1}{n}\sum_{i=1}^{n}(z_i - \bar{z})^2.$$

Theorem 1 ([15]). *Let $z_i > 0$, for $i = 1, 2, \ldots, n$. We have the following:*

$$\sum_{i=1}^{n}\ln(z_i) \leq \ln\left(\bar{z} + \sigma_z\sqrt{n-1}\right) + (n-1)\ln\left(\bar{z} - \frac{\sigma_z}{\sqrt{n-1}}\right). \tag{6}$$

where $z_i = 1 + \alpha t_i$, $z = 1 + \alpha t$, and $\sigma_z = \alpha\sigma_t$.

We will proceed to present the paper's principal result.

4.2.3. New Approximate Functions Approach

Let
$$\varphi(\alpha) = \frac{1}{\eta}[f(x+\alpha d) - f(x)] - \sum_{i=1}^{n}\ln(1+\alpha t_i),$$
be defined on $\tilde{\alpha} = \min_{i\in I_-}\left\{\frac{-1}{t_i}\right\}$ such that $I_- = \{i : t_i < 0\}$.

To find the displacement step, it is necessary to solve $\varphi'(\alpha) = 0$. Considering the difficulty of solving a non-algebraic equation, approximate functions are recommended alternatives.

Two novel approximation functions of φ are introduced in the following lemma.

Lemma 2. *For all $\alpha \in [0, \alpha_1^*[$ with $\alpha_1^* = \min(\widehat{\alpha}, \widehat{\alpha}_1)$, we have*

$$\varphi(\alpha) \geq \widehat{\varphi}_1(\alpha),$$

and for all $\alpha \in [0, \alpha_2^*[$ with $\alpha_2^* = \min(\widehat{\alpha}, \widehat{\alpha}_2)$, we obtain

$$\widehat{\varphi}_2(\alpha) \leq \varphi(\alpha),$$

where

$$\widehat{\varphi}_1(\alpha) = \frac{1}{\eta}(f(x+\alpha d) - f(x)) - \ln(1+\delta\alpha) - (n-1)\ln(1+\beta\alpha),$$

and

$$\widehat{\varphi}_2(\alpha) = \frac{1}{\eta}(f(x+\alpha d) - f(x)) - \tau\ln(1+\beta_1\alpha),$$

with

$$\begin{cases} \beta = \bar{t} - \frac{\sigma_t}{\sqrt{n-1}} \\ \delta = \bar{t} + \sigma_t\sqrt{n-1} \\ \beta_1 = \frac{\|t\|^2}{n\bar{t}}. \end{cases} \tag{7}$$

Furthermore, we have

$$\widehat{\varphi}_2(\alpha) \le \widehat{\varphi}_1(\alpha) \le \varphi(\alpha),$$

Proof. We start by proving that

$$\varphi(\alpha) \ge \widehat{\varphi}_1(\alpha),$$

Theorem 1 gives

$$\sum_{i=1}^{n}\ln(z_i) \le \ln\left(\bar{z} + \sigma_z\sqrt{n-1}\right) + (n-1)\ln\left(\bar{z} - \frac{\sigma_z}{\sqrt{n-1}}\right),$$

then,

$$\sum_{i=1}^{n}\ln(1+\alpha t_i) \le \ln(1+\alpha\delta) + (n-1)\ln(1+\alpha\beta),$$

and

$$-\sum_{i=1}^{n}\ln(1+\alpha t_i) \ge -\ln(1+\alpha\delta) - (n-1)\ln(1+\alpha\beta).$$

Hence,

$$\frac{1}{\eta}(f(x+\alpha d) - f(x)) - \sum_{i=1}^{n}\ln(1+\alpha t_i) \ge \frac{1}{\eta}(f(x+\alpha d) - f(x)) - \ln(1+\alpha\delta) - (n-1)\ln(1+\alpha\beta).$$

Therefore,

$$\begin{aligned} \varphi(\alpha) &\ge \widehat{\varphi}_1(\alpha) = \frac{1}{\eta}(f(x+\alpha d) - f(x)) - \ln(1+\alpha\delta) - (n-1)\ln(1+\alpha\beta), \\ \widehat{\varphi}_1'(\alpha) &= \frac{1}{\eta}\langle\nabla f(x+\alpha d) - d\rangle - \frac{\delta}{1+\alpha\delta} - (n-1)\frac{\beta}{1+\alpha\beta}. \end{aligned}$$

Let us consider the following:

$$g(\alpha) = \varphi(\alpha) - \widehat{\varphi}_2(\alpha).$$

We have

$$g''(\alpha) = \sum_{i=1}^{n}\frac{t_i^2}{(1+\alpha t_i)^2} - \tau\frac{\beta_1}{(1+\alpha\beta_1)^2}.$$

Because of the fact that $|t_i| \le \|t\|$ and $n\bar{t} \le \|t\|$, it is easy to see that $\forall\alpha \ge 0,\ g''(\alpha) \ge 0$. Therefore,

$$\frac{1}{\eta}(f(x+\alpha d) - f(x)) - \sum_{i=1}^{n}\ln(1+\alpha t_i) \ge \frac{1}{\eta}(f(x+\alpha d) - f(x)) - \tau\ln(1+\beta_1\alpha),$$

then, $\varphi(\alpha) \le \widehat{\varphi}_2(\alpha)$. □

Hence, the domain of $(\widehat{\varphi}_i)_{i=1,2}$ is included in the domain of φ, which is $(0,\widetilde{\alpha})$, where

$$\widetilde{\alpha} = \max[\alpha : 1+\alpha\delta > 0,\ 1+\alpha\beta > 0].$$

Let us remark that

$$0 = \widehat{\varphi}_i(0) = \varphi(0),\ -\varphi'(0) = -\widehat{\varphi}_i'(0) = \varphi_i''(0) = \widehat{\varphi}_i''(0) > 0,\ i = 1,2.$$

Thus, φ is well approximated by $\widehat{\varphi}_i$ in a neighborhood of 0. Since $\widehat{\varphi}_i$ is strictly convex, it attains its minimum at one unique point $\bar{\alpha}$, which is the unique root of the equation $\widehat{\varphi}_i'(\alpha) = 0$. This point belongs to the domain of $\widehat{\varphi}_i$ $(i = 1,2)$. Therefore, φ is bounded from below by $\widehat{\varphi}_1$:

$$\widehat{\varphi}_1(\bar{\alpha}) \leq \varphi(\bar{\alpha}) < 0$$

And it is also bounded from below by $\widehat{\varphi}_2$:

$$\widehat{\varphi}_2(\bar{\alpha}) \leq \varphi(\bar{\alpha}) < 0.$$

Then, $\bar{\alpha}$ gives an apparent decrease in the function φ.

4.3. Minimize an Auxiliary Function

We now consider the minimization of the function

$$\varphi_1(\alpha) = n\gamma\alpha - \ln(1+\delta\alpha) - (n-1)\ln(1+\beta\alpha),$$

and we also have the following approximate function:

$$\varphi_2(\alpha) = n\gamma\alpha - \tau\ln(1+\beta_1\alpha),$$

where β_1 is defined in (7). Then, we have the following:

$$\begin{aligned} \varphi_1'(\alpha) &= n\gamma - \frac{\delta}{1+\delta\alpha} - (n-1)\frac{\beta}{1+\beta\alpha}, \\ \varphi_1''(\alpha) &= \frac{\delta^2}{(1+\delta\alpha)^2} + (n-1)\frac{\beta^2}{(1+\beta\alpha)^2}. \end{aligned}$$

and

$$\begin{aligned} \varphi_2'(\alpha) &= n\gamma - \tau\tfrac{\beta_1}{(1+\beta_1\alpha)}, \\ \varphi_2''(\alpha) &= \tau\frac{\beta_1^2}{(1+\beta_1\alpha)^2}. \end{aligned}$$

We remark that for $i = 1,2$:

$$\varphi_i(0) = 0,\ \varphi_i'(0) = n(\gamma - \bar{t}),\ \varphi_i''(0) = ||t||^2.$$

We present the conditions $\varphi_i'(0) < 0$ and $\varphi_i''(0) > 0$. The function φ is strictly convex. It attains its minimum at one unique point α such that $\varphi_i'(\alpha) = 0$, which is one of the roots of the equations

$$\gamma\delta\beta\alpha^2 + \alpha(\gamma\delta + \gamma\beta - \delta\beta) + \gamma - \bar{t} = 0, \tag{8}$$

and

$$n\gamma\beta(1+\beta\alpha) - ||t||^2 = 0. \tag{9}$$

For Equation (8), the roots are explicitly calculated, and we distinguish the following cases:

- If $\delta = 0$, we obtain $\bar{\alpha}_1 = \frac{\bar{t}-\gamma}{\gamma\beta}$.

- If $\beta = 0$, we obtain $\bar{\alpha}_1 = \frac{\bar{t}-\gamma}{\gamma\delta}$.
- If $\gamma = 0$, we have $\bar{\alpha}_1 = \frac{-\bar{t}}{\delta\beta}$.
- If $\gamma\delta\beta \neq 0$, $\bar{\alpha}$ is the only root of the second-degree equation that belongs to the domain of definition of φ. We obtain $\triangle = \frac{1}{\gamma^2} + \frac{1}{\beta^2} + \frac{1}{\delta^2} - \frac{2}{\delta\beta} + \left(\frac{2n-4}{n}\right)\left[\frac{1}{\beta\gamma} - \frac{1}{\gamma\delta}\right]$. Both roots are

$$\bar{\alpha}_{1.1} = \frac{1}{2}\left(\frac{1}{\gamma} - \frac{1}{\beta} - \frac{1}{\delta} + \sqrt{\triangle}\right),$$

and

$$\bar{\alpha}_{1.2} = \frac{1}{2}\left(\frac{1}{\gamma} - \frac{1}{\beta} - \frac{1}{\delta} + \sqrt{\triangle}\right).$$

Then, the root of Equation (9) is explicitly calculated, and we have

$$\bar{\alpha}_2 = \left(\frac{\|t\|^2}{\beta(1-\beta)} - \frac{1}{\beta}\right).$$

Consequently, we compute the two values $\bar{\alpha}_i$, $i = 1,2$, explicitly. Then, we take $\bar{\alpha}_1, \bar{\alpha}_2 \in [0, \tilde{\alpha} - \varepsilon[$, where $\varepsilon > 0$ is a fixed precision and $\varphi'(\bar{\alpha}_i) > 0$, $i = 1,2$.

Remark 2. *The computation of $\bar{\alpha}_i$, $i = 1,2$ is performed through a dichotomous procedure in the cases where $\bar{\alpha}_i \notin (0, \tilde{\alpha} - \varepsilon)$, and $\varphi'(\bar{\alpha}_i) > 0$, as follows:*
Put $a = 0$, $b = \tilde{\alpha} - \varepsilon$.
While $|b - a| > \varepsilon$ do
If $\varphi'(\frac{a+b}{2}) < 0$ then, $b = \frac{a+b}{2}$,
else $a = \frac{a+b}{2}$, so $\bar{\alpha}_i = b$.
This computation guarantees a better approximation of the minimum of $\varphi'(\alpha)$ while remaining in the domain of φ.

4.4. *The Objective Function f Is*

4.4.1. Linear

For all x, there exists $c \in \mathbb{R}^n$ such that $f(x) = \langle c, x \rangle$.

The minimum of φ_i is reached at the unique root $\bar{\alpha}$ of the equation $\varphi'(\alpha) = 0$. Then,

$$\widehat{\varphi}_i(\bar{\alpha}) \leq \varphi(\bar{\alpha}) < \widehat{\varphi}_i(0) = \varphi(0) = 0.$$

Take $\gamma = n^{-1}\langle c, d \rangle$ in the auxiliary function φ. The two functions φ and $(\widehat{\varphi}_i)_{i=1,2}$ coincide.

$\bar{\alpha}$ yields a significant decrease in the function ψ_η along the descent direction d. It is interesting to note that the condition $\widehat{\varphi}_i'(0) + \widehat{\varphi}_i''(0) = 0$ $(i = 1,2)$ implies the following:

$$-\widehat{\varphi}_i'(0) = n(\bar{t} - \gamma) = \|t\|^2 = n\left(\bar{t}^2 - \sigma_t^2\right) = \widehat{\varphi}_i''(0) > 0.$$

4.4.2. Convex

$\nabla f(x + \alpha d)$ is no longer constant, and the equation $\widehat{\varphi}_i'(\alpha) = 0$ is not reduced to one equation of a second degree for $i = 1,2$.

We consider another function $\tilde{\varphi}$ less than φ. Given $\widehat{\alpha} \in (0, \tilde{\alpha})$, we have, for all $\alpha \in (0, \widehat{\alpha}]$, the following:

$$\frac{f(x + \alpha d) - f(x)}{\eta} \leq \frac{f(x + \widehat{\alpha} d) - f(x)}{\eta\widehat{\alpha}}\alpha, \tag{10}$$

then,

$$\varphi(\alpha) \geq \tilde{\varphi}_1(\alpha) = \frac{f(x + \widehat{\alpha} d) - f(x)}{\eta\widehat{\alpha}}\alpha - \ln(1 + \alpha\delta) - (n-1)\ln(1 + \alpha\beta)$$

and

$$\varphi(\alpha) \geq \widetilde{\varphi}_2(\alpha) = \frac{f(x+\widehat{\alpha}d) - f(x)}{\eta\widehat{\alpha}}\alpha - \tau\ln(1+\beta_1\alpha),\ \tau \in]0,1[.$$

We choose $\gamma = \frac{f(x+\widehat{\alpha}d)-f(x)}{n\eta\widehat{\alpha}}$ in the auxiliary function φ , and we compute the root $\bar{\alpha}$ of the equation $\varphi_i'(\alpha) = 0$ with $i = 1,2$.

Therefore, we have two cases:

1. Where $\bar{\alpha} \leq \widehat{\alpha}$: We have the following:

$$\varphi(\bar{\alpha}) \geq \widehat{\varphi}_i(\bar{\alpha}) \geq \widetilde{\varphi}_i(\bar{\alpha}),\ \text{for } i = 1,2$$

   and, thus, along the direction d, we obtain a significant decrease in the function ψ_η. The approximation accuracy of φ by $\widetilde{\varphi}_i$ being better for small values of $\widehat{\alpha}$ (for $i = 1,2$), it is recommended to use a new value of $\widehat{\alpha}$, situated between $\widetilde{\alpha}$ and the former $\widehat{\alpha}$, for the next iteration. Moreover, the cost of the supplementary computation is small since it is the cost of one evaluation of f and the resolution of a second-order equation.
2. Where $\bar{\alpha} > \widehat{\alpha}$: The computation of $\widehat{\alpha}$ is performed through a dichotomous procedure (see Remark 3).

5. Description of the Algorithm and Numerical Simulations

5.1. Description of the Algorithm

This section is devoted to introducing our algorithm for obtaining an optimal solution $\bar{x}$ of (P).

Begin

Initialization

$\varepsilon > 0$ is a given precision. $\widehat{\eta} > 0$ and $\sigma \in [0,1]$ are given.

x_0 is a strictly realizable solution from $\tilde{\mathcal{L}}$, $d_0 \in \mathbb{R}^m$.

Iteration

1. Start with $\eta > \widehat{\eta}$.
2. Calculate d and $t = X^{-1}d$.
3. If $\|t\| > \varepsilon$, calculate $\bar{t}, \gamma, \delta, \beta$, and β_1.
4. Determine $\bar{\alpha}$ following (8), (10), or (9) depending on the linear or nonlinear case.
5. Take the new iterate $x = x + \bar{\alpha}d = X(e + \bar{\alpha}t)$ and go back to step 2.
6. If $\|t\| \leq \varepsilon$, a well approximation of $g(\eta)$ has been obtained.
   - **(a)** If $\eta \geq \widehat{\eta}$ and $\eta = \sigma\eta$, return to step 2.
   - **(b)** If $\eta < \widehat{\eta}$, STOP: a well approximate solution of (P) has been obtained.

End algorithm.

The aim of this method is to reduce the number of iterations and the time consumption. In the next section, we provide some examples.

5.2. Numerical Simulations

To assess the superior performance and accuracy of our algorithm, based on our minorant functions, numerical tests are conducted to make comparisons between our new approach and the classical line search method.

For this purpose, in this section, we present comparative numerical tests on different examples taken from the literature [5,24].

We report the results obtained by implementing the algorithm in MATLAB on an Intel Core i7-7700HQ (2.80 GHz) machine with 16.00 Go RAM.

5.2.1. Examples with a Fixed Size

Nonlinear Convex Objective

Example 1. *Let us take the following problem:*

$$\begin{cases} \min \ 2x_1^2 + 2x_2^2 - 2x_1x_2 - 4x_1 - 6x_2 \\ x_1 + x_2 + x_3 = 2 \\ x_1 + 5x_2 + x_4 = 5 \\ x_1, x_2, x_3, x_4 \geq 0. \end{cases}$$

The optimal value is -7.1613, *and the optimal solution is* $x^* = \begin{pmatrix} 1.1290 & 0.7742 & 0.0968 & 0 \end{pmatrix}^t$.

Example 2. *Let us take the following problem:*

$$\begin{cases} \min \ x_1^3 + x_2^3 \\ x_1 - x_2 + x_3 + x_4 = 3 \\ 2x_1 + x_2 - x_3 + x_4 = 2.0086 \\ x_1 + x_3 + 2x_4 = 4.9957 \\ x_1, x_2, x_3, x_4 \geq 0. \end{cases}$$

The optimal value is 0.0390, *and the optimal solution is* $x^* = \begin{pmatrix} 0.3391 & 0 & 0.6652 & 1.9957 \end{pmatrix}^t$.

Example 3. *Let us consider the following problem:*

$$\begin{cases} \min \ x_1^3 + x_2^3 + x_1x_2 \\ 2x_1 - x_2 + x_3 = 8 \\ x_1 + 2x_2 + x_4 = 6 \\ x_1, x_2, x_3, x_4 \geq 0. \end{cases}$$

The optimal value is 1.6157, *and the optimal solution is* $x^* = \begin{pmatrix} 1.1734 & 0 & 5.6532 & 4.8265 \end{pmatrix}^t$.

This table presents the results of the previous examples:

Example	**st1**		**st2**		**LS**	
	iter	**Time (s)**	**iter**	**Time (s)**	**iter**	**Time (s)**
1	12	0.0006	19	0.0015	6	0.0091
2	5	0.0004	9	0.0009	44	0.099
3	3	0.0001	5	0.0006	65	0.89

5.2.2. Example with a Variable Size

The Objective Function f Is

1-Linear: Let us consider the linear programming problem:

$$\zeta = \min[c^T x : x \geq 0, \ Ax = b],$$

where A is an $m \times 2m$ matrix given by the following:

$$\begin{aligned} A[i,j] &= \begin{cases} 1 & \text{if } i = j \quad \text{or } j = i + m \\ 0 & \text{if not,} \end{cases} \\ c[i] &= -1, \ c[i+m] = 0 \text{ and } b[i] = 2, \ \forall i = 1, \ldots m, \end{aligned}$$

where $c, b \in \mathbb{R}^{2m}$.

The results are presented in the table below.

Size	st1		st2		LS	
	iter	Time (s)	iter	Time (s)	iter	Time (s)
5×10	1	0.0021	2	0.0039	9	0.0512
20×40	1	0.0031	3	0.0045	13	0.0821
50×100	2	0.0049	3	0.0032	17	0.3219
100×200	2	0.0053	4	0.0088	19	0.5383
200×400	2	0.0088	4	0.0098	22	0.9220
250×500	3	0.0096	5	0.0125	26	9.2647

2-Nonlinear:

Example 4 (Quadratic case [13]). *Let the quadratic problem be as follows:*

$$\zeta = \min[f(x) : x \geq 0,\ Ax \geq b],$$

with $f(x) = \frac{1}{2}\langle x, Qx\rangle$, *Q is the matrix defined for* $n = 2m$ *by the following:*

$$\begin{aligned} Q[i,j] &= \begin{cases} 2j-1 & \text{if } i > j \\ 2i-1 & \text{if } i < j \\ i(i+1)-1 & \text{if } i = j,\ i,j = 1,..,n \end{cases} \\ A[i,j] &= \begin{cases} 1 & \text{if } i = j \text{ or } j = i+m,\ i = 1,..,m \text{ and } j = 1,..,n \\ 0 & \text{if not} \end{cases} \\ c[i] &= -1,\ c[i+m] = 0 \text{ and } b[i] = 2,\ \forall i = 1,..,m. \end{aligned}$$

This example is tested for many values of n.

The obtained results are given by the following table:

ex(m,n)	st1		st2		LS	
	iter	Time (s)	iter	Time (s)	iter	Time (s)
300×600	5	0.9968	4	0.9699	26	19.5241
400×800	7	18.1448	5	9.6012	35	86.1259
600×1200	12	36.3259	5	19.0099	23	98.2354
1000×2000	21	56.9912	17	41.1012	33	109.2553
1500×3000	28	140.1325	23	95.6903	40	1599.1596

Example 5 (The problem of Erikson [25]). *Let the following be the quadratic problem:*

$$\zeta = \min\left[f(x) = \sum_{i=1}^{n} x_i \ln\left(\frac{x_i}{a_i}\right) : x_i + x_{i+m} = b, x \geq 0\right],$$

where $n = 2m, a_i > 0$ *and* $b \in \mathbb{R}^m$ *are fixed.*

This example is tested for different values of n, a_i, *and* b_i.

The following table resumes the obtained results in the case $(a_i = 2, \forall i = 1,\ldots,n,$ $b_i = 4, \forall i = 1,\ldots,m)$:

ex(m, n)	st1		st2		LS	
	iter	Time (s)	iter	Time (s)	iter	Time (s)
10×20	1	0.0001	2	0.0012	4	0.0236
40×100	2	0.0021	3	0.0033	5	0.7996
100×200	2	0.0043	3	0.0201	5	1.5289
500×1000	2	3.0901	4	5.9619	12	22.1254

In the above tables, we take $\varepsilon = 1.0 \times 10^{-4}$.
We also denote the following:
- (iter) is the number of iterations.
- (time) is the computational time in seconds (s).
- $(\text{st}i)_{i=1,2}$ represents the strategy of approximate functions introduced in this paper.
- (LS) represents the classical line search method.

Commentary: The numerical tests carried out show, without doubt, that our approach leads to a very significant reduction in the cost of calculation and an improvement in the result. When comparing the approximate functions to the line search approach, the number of iterations and computing time are significantly reduced.

6. Conclusions

The contribution of this paper is particular focused on the study of nonlinear optimization problems by using the logarithmic penalty method based on some new approximate functions. We first formulate the problems (P) and $(P\eta)$ with the results of the convergence. Then, we find their solutions by using new approximate functions.

Finally, to lend further support to our theoretical results, a simulation study is conducted to illustrate the good accuracy of the studied approach. More precisely, our new approximate functions approach outperforms the line search one as it significantly reduces the cost and computing time.

Funding: This work has been supported by: The General Directorate of Scientific Research and Technological Development (DGRSDT-MESRS) under the PRFU project number C00L03UN190120220009. Algeria.

Data Availability Statement: Data are contained within the article.

Acknowledgments: The author is very pleased to thank the editor and the reviewers for their helpful suggestions and comments.

Conflicts of Interest: The authors declare no conflicts of interest.

References

1. Frank, M.; Wolfe, B. An algorithm for quadratic programming. *Nav. Res. Logist. Q.* **1956**, *3*, 95–110. [CrossRef]
2. Wolfe, P. A Duality Theorem for Nonlinear Programming. *Q. Appl. Math.* **1961**, *19*, 239–244. [CrossRef]
3. Bracken, J.; M1cCormiek, G.P. *Selected Applications of Nonlinear Programming*; John Wiley & Sons, Inc.: New York, NY, USA, 1968.
4. Fiacco, A.V.; McCormick, G.P. *Nonlinear Programming: Sequential Unconstrained Minimization Techniques*; John Wiley & Sons, Inc.: New York, NY, USA, 1968.
5. Bonnans, J.-F.; Gilbert, J.-C.; Lemaréchal, C.; Sagastizàbal, C. *Numerical Optimization: Theoretical and Practical Aspects*; Mathematics and Applications; Springer: Berlin/Heidelberg, Germany, 2003; Volume 27.
6. Evtushenko, Y.G.; Zhadan, V.G. Stable barrier-projection and barrier-Newton methods in nonlinear programming. In *Optimization Methods and Software*; Taylor & Francis: Abingdon, UK, 1994; Volume 3, pp. 237–256.
7. Nestrov, Y.E.; Nemiroveskii, A. *Interior-Point Polynomial Algorithms in Convex Programming*; SIAM: Philadelphia, PA, USA, 1994.
8. Wright, S.J. *Primal–Dual Interior Point Methods*; SIAM: Philadelphia, PA, USA, 1997.
9. Ye, Y. Interior Point Algorithms: Theory and Analysis. In *Discrete Mathematics Optimization*; Wiley-Interscience Series; John Wiley & Sons: New York, NY, USA, 1997.
10. Powell, M.J.D. *Karmarkar's Algorithm: A View from Nonlinear Programming*; Department of Applied Mathematics and Theoretical Physics, University of Cambridge: Cambridge, UK, 1989; Volume 53.
11. Rosen, J.B. The Gradient Projection Method for Nonlinear Programming. *Soc. Ind. Appl. Math. J. Appl. Math.* **1960**, *8*, 181–217. [CrossRef]

12. Rosen, J.B. The Gradient Projection Method for Nonlinear Programming. *Soc. Ind. Appl. Math. J. Appl. Math.* **1961**, *9*, 514–55 [CrossRef]
13. Ouriemchi, M. Résolution de Problèmes non Linéaires par les Méthodes de Points Intérieurs. Théorie et Algorithmes. Doctor Thesis, Université du Havre, Havre, France, 2006.
14. Forsgren, A.; Gill, P.E.; Wright, M.H. *Interior Methods for Nonlinear Optimization*; SIAM: Philadelphia, PA, USA, 2002; Voluume 4 pp. 525–597.
15. Crouzeix, J.P.; Merikhi, B. A logarithm barrier method for semidefinite programming. *RAIRO-Oper. Res.* **2008**, *42*, 123–13 [CrossRef]
16. Menniche, L.; Benterki, D. A Logarithmic Barrier Approach for Linear Programming. *J. Computat. Appl. Math.* **2017**, *312*, 267–27 [CrossRef]
17. Cherif, L.B.; Merikhi, B. A Penalty Method for Nonlinear Programming. *RAIRO-Oper. Res.* **2019**, *53*, 29–38. [CrossRef]
18. Chaghoub, S.; Benterki, D. A Logarithmic Barrier Method Based On a New Majorant Function for Convex Quadratic Programmin *IAENG Int. J. Appl. Math.* **2021**, *51*, pp 563-568.
19. Leulmi, A. Etude d'une Méthode Barrière Logarithmique via Minorants Functions pour la Programmation Semi-Définie. Doctor Thesis, Université de Biskra, Biskra, Algeria, 2018.
20. Leulmi, A.; Merikhi, B.; Benterki, D. Study of a Logarithmic Barrier Approach for Linear Semidefinite Programming. *J. Sib. Fe Univ. Math. Phys.* **2018**, *11*, 300–312.
21. Leulmi, A.; Leulmi, S. Logarithmic Barrier Method via Minorant Function for Linear Programming. *J. Sib. Fed. Univ. Math. Phy* **2019**, *12*, 191–201. [CrossRef]
22. Wolkowicz, H.; Styan, G.P.H. Bounds for Eigenvalues Using Traces. *Lin. Alg. Appl.* **1980**, *29*, 471–506. [CrossRef]
23. Crouzeix, J.-P.; Seeger, A. New bounds for the extreme values of a finite sample of real numbers. *J. Math. Anal. Appl.* **1996**, *19* 411–426. [CrossRef]
24. Bazraa, M.S.; Sherali, H.D.; Shetty, C.M. *Nonlinear Programming, Willey-Interscience*; John Wiley & Sons, Inc.: Hoboken, NJ, US Toronto, ON, Canada, 2006.
25. Shannon, E. A mathematical theory of communication. *Bell Syst. Tech. J.* **1948**, *27*; 379–423+623–656. [CrossRef]

axioms

MDPI

Article

Strict Vector Equilibrium Problems of Multi-Product Supply–Demand Networks with Capacity Constraints and Uncertain Demands

Ru Li [1,2] **and Guolin Yu** [3,*]

[1] School of Preparatory Education, North Minzu University, Yinchuan 750021, China; liru@nmu.edu.cn
[2] School of Management, Hefei University of Technology, Hefei 230002, China
[3] School of Mathematics and Information Science, North Minzu University, Yinchuan 750021, China
* Correspondence: guolin_yu@126.com or yuguolin@nmu.edu.cn

Abstract: This paper considers a multi-product, multi-criteria supply–demand network equilibrium model with capacity constraints and uncertain demands. Strict network equilibrium principles are proposed both in the case of a single criterion and multi-criteria, respectively. Based on a single criterion, it proves that strict network equilibrium flows are equivalent to vector variational inequalities, and the existence of strict network equilibrium flows is derived by virtue of the Fan–Browder fixed point theorem. Based on multi-criteria, the scalarization of strict network equilibrium flows is given by using Gerstewitz's function without any convexity assumptions. Meanwhile, the necessary and sufficient conditions of strict network equilibrium flows are derived in terms of vector variational inequalities. Finally, an example is given to illustrate the application of the derived theoretical results.

Keywords: strict network equilibrium flows; uncertain demands; vector variational inequalities; Fan–Browder fixed point; Gerstewitz's function

MSC: 90C33; 90B06

1. Introduction

The study of the supply–demand network equilibrium models has been the subject of great interest due to their theoretical challenges and practical application. The fundamental principle is Wardrop's equilibrium principle [1], which states that users in transport networks choose one of the paths among all the paths joining the same origin–destination (OD) pair at minimum cost. After Wardrop, many scholars have proposed various network equilibrium models based on a single criterion. Dong et al. [2] considered a supply chain network equilibrium model with random demands. Meng et al. [3] proposed a note on supply chain network equilibrium models. Nagurney [4] presented a supply chain network equilibrium model and investigated the relationship between transportation and supply chain network equilibria. Nagurney et al. [5] developed an equilibrium model of a competitive supply chain network. Additionally, motivated by practical concerns, network equilibrium models based on multiple criteria cost functions have been studied; for example, Chen and Yen [6] were the first to propose a traffic network equilibrium model based on multiple criteria cost functions without capacity constraints, and present an equivalent relation between vector network equilibrium models and vector variational inequalities. Cheng and Wu [7] presented a multi-product supply–demand network equilibrium model with multiple criteria.

For a supply–demand network, it is well known that when the flows pass through two different paths which contain common arcs at the same time, the capacity constraints of the two paths may interact. So, the capacity constraints are important factors that affect the equilibrium states and the selection of the set of feasible network flows. Based on this cause, a substantial number of works have been devoted to studying the vector equilibrium principle [5,8–14] with capacity constraints of paths. In addition, considering that the data are uncertain in practice and are not known exactly, along with the change of network users' demand preferences and the fluctuation of purchasing power, the demands of network flow should not be fixed, and the network equilibrium with uncertain demands have attracted much attention. Very recently, Cao et al. [15] focused on the traffic network equilibrium problem with uncertain demands, in which the uncertain set consisted of finite discrete scenarios. Subsequently, Wei et al. [16] assumed that the demands belonged to a closed interval and proposed (weak) vector equilibrium principles involving a single product. Proper efficiency is widely applied to solve vector optimization and vector equilibrium problems. It can help one to eliminate some abnormal efficient decisions and provide proper efficient decisions. Several classical proper efficiency measures, such as Benson efficiency [17], super efficiency [18], and Henig efficiency [19], have been applied to solve network equilibrium models. Cheng and Fu [20] introduced a kind of proper efficiency–strict efficiency, and it has been used to solve vector optimization models (for example, see Yu et al. [21]). On the other hand, variational inequality theory is an effective tool to solve equilibrium problems (for example, see Chen and Yen [6]).

In this paper, inspired by the work in [7,10,16,17], we consider strict vector equilibrium principles of a multi-product, multi-criteria supply–demand network with capacity constraints and uncertain demands, where the demands are assumed to belong to a closed interval and are irrelevant to the costs for all OD pairs. The main contribution is to derive the existence results of strict vector equilibrium flows of a multi-product supply–demand network with capacity constraints and uncertain demands by virtue of the Fan–Browder fixed point theorem and obtain the relations between the strict vector equilibrium flows and vector variational inequalities, with both a single criterion and multi-criteria cost functions, which, to the best of our knowledge have not been studied before.

The rest of this article is arranged as follows: in Section 2, some mathematical preliminaries are described. In Section 3, we propose a strict network equilibrium principle for a multi-product supply–demand network problem involving real-valued cost functions with capacity constraints and uncertain demands. The equivalence relation between the strict network equilibrium flow and the strictly efficient solution of variational inequalities is established. The existence of the strict network equilibrium flows is also derived by means of the Fan–Browder fixed point theorem. Section 4 proposes a strict network equilibrium principle for a multi-product supply–demand network problem with capacity constraints and uncertain demands involving vector-valued cost functions, and the similar equivalence relation of strict network equilibrium flows in terms of vector variational inequalities is deduced by using Gerstewitz's scalarization function. Section 5 gives an illustrative example. Section 6 provides a brief summary of the paper.

2. Definition and Preliminaries

In this section, some notations are set and we recall the notions of efficient points of a nonempty set, and the variational inequality and strictly efficient points of a nonempty set. Throughout the paper, we suppose that the vectors are always row vectors unless otherwise stated. Let $\mathbb{R}^n$ be the n-dimensional Euclidean space and $\mathbb{R}^n_+$ be its non-negative orthant. Let $\mathbb{R}^{n\times n}$ be the $n\times n$ matrix space and

$$\mathbb{R}^{n\times n}_+ = \{k = (k_1, \cdots, k_n) \in \mathbb{R}^{n\times n} : k_i = (k_i^1, \cdots, k_i^n)', k_i^j \geq 0, j = 1, \cdots, n\}$$

be its non-negative orthant, where $(k_i^1, \cdots, k_i^n)'$ denotes the transpose of the matrix $(k_i^1, \cdots, k_i^n)$. Given $y, z \in \mathbb{R}^{n\times n}$, let $\langle y, z' \rangle = yz'$ represent the multiplication of matrix y and z. A pointed closed convex cone $\Gamma \subset \mathbb{R}^n$ induces the orderings in $\mathbb{R}^n$: for any $x_1, x_2 \in \mathbb{R}^n$,

$$x_1 \leqslant x_2 \text{ iff } x_2 - x_1 \in \Gamma,$$
$$x_1 < x_2 \text{ iff } x_2 - x_1 \in \text{int}\Gamma,$$

where intΓ denotes the nonempty interior of Γ. For convenience of writing, let $\mathbb{R}^n = X$. Let Ξ_X be a nonempty convex subset of the cone Γ and $\mathrm{cl}(\Xi_X)$ be its closure. $\mathrm{cone}(\Xi_X) = \{\sigma x : \sigma \in R^1_+, x \in \Xi_X\}$ is the conic hull of the set Ξ_X. If $0 \notin \mathrm{cl}(\Xi_X)$, $\Gamma = \mathrm{cone}(\Xi_X)$, then the set Ξ_X is said to be a base of the cone Γ.

Let N be a nonempty subset of X; $H : N \to \mathbb{R}^n$ is a mapping. The notion of efficient points of the set N is as follows.

Definition 1 (see [21]). *A vector $\bar{x} \in N$ is said to be an efficient point of the set N if*

$$(N - \bar{x}) \cap (-\Gamma \backslash \{0\}) = \emptyset.$$

Let EP(N) denote the set of the efficient points of the set N.

The variational inequality is to find a vector $\bar{x} \in N$, such that

$$\langle H(\bar{x}), x - \bar{x} \rangle \geq 0, \ \ \forall x \in N.$$

The concept of strictly efficient points of the set N is as follows.

Definition 2 (see [21]). *Suppose that Ξ_X is a base of Γ. The vector $\bar{x} \in N$ is called a strictly efficient point of the set N with Ξ_X if there is a neighborhood Θ_X of 0, such that*

$$cone(N - \bar{x} + \Gamma) \cap (\Theta_X - \Xi_X) = \emptyset.$$

Let SEP(N) denote the set of strictly efficient points of the set N.

3. Existence of Strict Vector Equilibrium Flows with Single Criterion

For a supply–demand network $\mathcal{G} = [\mathcal{N}, \mathcal{C}, \mathcal{V}, \mathcal{P}, \mathcal{D}]$, let $\mathcal{N}, \mathcal{C}, \mathcal{P}$, and $\mathcal{D}$ denote the set of nodes, the set of arcs, the set of OD pairs, and the uncertain demand vectors, respectively. Let us suppose that there are m different kinds of products passing through the network and that a typical product is denoted by o. For each arc $c \in \mathcal{C}$ and product o, ϱ^o_c represents arc flow of product o between two different nodes. $\mathcal{V} = (\bar{\varrho}^o_c)_{\in C}$ denotes the capacity vector, where $\bar{\varrho}^o_c > 0$ implies the capacity of arc c for the product o. The arc flow ϱ^o_c needs to satisfy the following capacity constraint:

$$0 \leq \varrho^o_c \leq \bar{\varrho}^o_c.$$

Let us assume that there are s OD pairs in the set $\mathcal{P}$. The available paths connecting OD pair $p \in \mathcal{P}$ form the set ω_p, and let $\sum_{p \in \mathcal{P}} |\omega_p| = n$, where n is a positive integer. For each acyclic path $a \in \omega_p$, we denote by $\varrho^o_a \geq 0$ the path flow of the product o on path a. The relation between arc flows and path flows is as follows:

$$\varrho^o_c = \sum_{p \in \mathcal{P}} \sum_{a \in \omega_p} \delta_{ca} \varrho^o_a,$$

where

$$\delta_{ca} = \begin{cases} 1, & if\ c\ belongs\ to\ path\ a, \\ 0, & otherwise. \end{cases}$$

Let us suppose that μ^o_a and λ^o_a are the lower and upper capacity constraints on path a with product o, respectively, i.e.,

$$\mu^o_a \leq \varrho^o_a \leq \lambda^o_a.$$

The matrix $\varrho = (\varrho^o_a)_{m \times n}$ is called a network flow. Thus, each column vector $\varrho_a = (\varrho^1_a, \cdots, \varrho^m_a)'$ of the matrix ϱ is the flow on path a, while the row vector $\varrho^o = (\varrho^o_1, \cdots, \varrho^o_n)$ is the network flow with product o.

We denote demand vectors of the network flow by $\mathcal{D} = (d^o_p(\varepsilon^o_p) : p \in \mathcal{P}, o = 1, \cdots, m)$, where the component $d^o_p(\varepsilon^o_p)$ denotes the uncertain demand for OD pair p and product o.

Let us suppose that $d_p^o(\varepsilon_p^o)$ belongs to a closed interval Δ_p^o, i.e., $d_p^o(\varepsilon_p^o) \in \Delta_p^o = [d_p^o - \varepsilon_p^o, d_p^o + \varepsilon_p^o]$, where d_p^o represents an appropriate fixed demand and $\varepsilon_p^o \geq 0$ denotes a deviation. It is reasonable to assume that the values of d_p^o and ε_p^o that depend on p and o are different for each OD pair and product in practical supply–demand network problems. We would like to point out that the uncertain demand $d_p^o(\varepsilon_p^o)$ that is irrelevant to the costs is significantly different from the one introduced in [12,22].

We say that the network flow ϱ satisfies the uncertain demands constraint if and only if

$$\sum_{a\in\omega_p} \varrho_a^o = d_p^o(\varepsilon_p^o), \ \forall p \in \mathcal{P}, \ o = 1, \cdots, m.$$

A network flow ϱ satisfying both the capacity constraints and the uncertain demands constraints is called a feasible flow. The set of all feasible flows is denoted by

$$Q = \Big\{ \varrho : \mu_a^o \leq \varrho_a^o \leq \lambda_a^o, 0 \leq \sum_{p\in\mathcal{P}} \sum_{a\in\omega_p} \delta_{ca}\varrho_a^o \leq \bar{\varrho}_c^o, \forall c \in \mathcal{C}, \text{and}$$
$$\sum_{a\in\omega_p} \varrho_a^o = d_p^o(\varepsilon_p^o), \forall p \in \mathcal{P}, \forall o = 1, \cdots, m \Big\}.$$

Let $Q \neq \emptyset$. Clearly, Q is closed, convex, and compact.

For each product o, let $h_c^o(\varrho) : \mathbb{R}^{m\times n} \to \mathbb{R}_+$ be the cost function on arc c; the cost function on path $a \in \omega_p$ is computed by

$$h_a^o(\varrho) = \sum_{c\in a} h_c^o(\varrho).$$

The cost on the network is given as a form of matrix $h(\varrho) = (h_a^o(\varrho))_{m\times n}$, where the ath column $h_a(\varrho) = (h_a^1(\varrho), \cdots, h_a^m(\varrho))'$ represents the cost on path a; the oth row $h^o(\varrho) = (h_1^o(\varrho), \cdots, h_n^o(\varrho))$ represents the cost on the network with product o. In this paper, unless otherwise stated, we always assume that for any $p \in \mathcal{P}$ and $a, b \in \omega_p$,

$$h_b(\varrho) - h_a(\varrho) \neq 0, \ \text{ if } \ b \neq a,$$

which has been also used in the literature [7].

Definition 3. *Supposing a flow $\varrho \in Q$,*

(i) *for an arc $c \in \mathcal{C}$ and product $o = 1, \cdots, m$, if $\varrho_c^o = \bar{\varrho}_c^o$, then c is called a saturated arc of product o and flow ϱ, or a nonsaturated arc of product o and flow ϱ.*

(ii) *for a path $a \in \bigcup_{p\in\mathcal{P}} \omega_p$ and product $o = 1, \cdots, m$, if the path a contains a saturated arc c of product o and flow ϱ, then a is called a saturated path of product o and flow ϱ, otherwise, a nonsaturated path of product o and flow ϱ.*

In the following content, we propose the concept of strict network equilibrium flow for a kind of multi-product supply–demand network involving real-valued cost functions with capacity constraints and uncertain demands, which has not been studied in the existing literature. In what follows, we always assume that Ξ is a base of $\mathbb{R}_+^m$, $\tilde{\Xi}$ is a base of $\mathbb{R}_+^{m\times m}$, Θ is a neighborhood of 0 in $\mathbb{R}^m$, and $\tilde{\Theta}$ is a neighborhood of 0 in $\mathbb{R}^{m\times m}$.

Definition 4. *(Strict network equilibrium principle). A feasible network flow $\varrho \in Q$ is a strict network equilibrium flow, if, for each $p \in \mathcal{P}$, $a, b \in \omega_p$, $o = 1, \cdots, m$, there is a neighborhood Θ of 0 in $\mathbb{R}^m$ satisfying $\Theta - \Xi \subset -int\mathbb{R}_+^m$, one has as an implication*

$$\left.\begin{array}{r} cone(h_{\omega_p}(\varrho) + \mathbb{R}_+^m - h_a(\varrho)) \cap (cone(\Theta - \Xi)\backslash\{0\}) = \emptyset \\ h_b(\varrho) - h_a(\varrho) \neq 0 \end{array}\right\} \Rightarrow$$

$\varrho_b^o = \mu_b^o$, $b \neq a$, or $\varrho_a^o = \lambda_a^o$, or path a is a saturated path with product o and flow ϱ.

Now, let us review the concept of the strict efficiency of vector variational inequalities, which will be employed to derive the main conclusions.

Definition 5. *A flow $\varrho \in Q$ is said to be a strictly efficient solution of the vector variational inequality if and only if there exist $\tilde{\Xi}$ and $\tilde{\Theta}$ satisfying $\tilde{\Theta} - \tilde{\Xi} \subset -int\mathbb{R}_+^{m\times m}$,*

$$cone(\langle h(\varrho), (\chi - \varrho)' \rangle + \mathbb{R}_+^{m\times m}) \cap (cone(\tilde{\Theta} - \tilde{\Xi}) \backslash \{0\}) = \emptyset, \ \forall \chi \in Q.$$

It is noteworthy that the vector $\varrho \in Q$ is a strictly efficient solution of the following variational inequality:

$$\text{cone}(\langle h(\varrho), (\chi - \varrho)' \rangle + \mathbb{R}_+^{m\times m}) \cap (\text{cone}(\tilde{\Theta} - \tilde{\Xi}) \backslash \{0\}) = \emptyset, \ \forall \chi \in Q,$$

if the vector $\varrho \in Q$ is a solution of the following variational inequality: find $\varrho \in Q$, satisfying

$$\langle h(\varrho), (\chi - \varrho)' \rangle \notin -\mathbb{R}_+^{m\times m} \backslash \{0\}, \ \forall \chi \in Q,$$

Next, we shall consider the relations between a strictly efficient solution of the vector variational inequality and the strict network equilibrium flow.

Theorem 1. *If the vector $\varrho \in Q$ is a strict network equilibrium flow, then ϱ is a strictly efficient solution of the following variational inequality: find $\varrho \in Q$, satisfying*

$$cone(\langle h(\varrho), (\chi - \varrho)' \rangle + \mathbb{R}_+^{m\times m}) \cap (cone(\tilde{\Theta} - \tilde{\Xi}) \backslash \{0\}) = \emptyset, \ \forall \chi \in Q.$$

Proof. If the vector $\varrho \in Q$ is a strict network equilibrium flow, for each $p \in \mathcal{P}$, $a, b \in \omega_p$, $o = 1, \cdots, m$, it has the following implication:

$$\left.\begin{array}{r} \text{cone}(h_{\omega_p}(\varrho) + \mathbb{R}_+^m - h_a(\varrho)) \cap (\text{cone}(\Theta - \Xi) \backslash \{0\}) = \emptyset \\ h_b(\varrho) - h_a(\varrho) \neq 0 \end{array}\right\} \Rightarrow$$

$\varrho_b^o = \mu_b^o$, $b \neq a$, or $\varrho_a^o = \lambda_a^o$, or path a is a saturated path of product o and flow ϱ.

We first show that

$$\langle h(\varrho), (\chi - \varrho)' \rangle \notin -\mathbb{R}_+^{m\times m}, \ \forall \chi \in Q. \tag{1}$$

For any $\chi \in Q$, it holds

$$\begin{aligned} &\langle h(\varrho), (\chi - \varrho)' \rangle \\ &= \langle (h_1(\varrho), \cdots, h_n(\varrho)), (\chi_1 - \varrho_1, \cdots, \chi_n - \varrho_n)' \rangle \\ &= \sum_{\bar{a}=1}^{n} \langle h_{\bar{a}}(\varrho), (\chi_{\bar{a}} - \varrho_{\bar{a}})' \rangle \\ &= \sum_{p=1}^{s} [\sum_{\bar{a}\in\omega_p} \langle h_{\bar{a}}(\varrho), (\chi_{\bar{a}} - \varrho_{\bar{a}})' \rangle]. \end{aligned}$$

Because $\langle h_{\bar{a}}(\varrho), (\chi_{\bar{a}} - \varrho_{\bar{a}})' \rangle$ is an $m \times m$ matrix, the component is $h_{\bar{a}}^{\rho}(\varrho)(\chi_{\bar{a}}^{\eta} - \varrho_{\bar{a}}^{\eta})$, $\rho, \eta = 1, 2, \cdots, m$; so, $\langle h(\varrho), (\chi - \varrho)' \rangle$ is also an $m \times m$ matrix, the component is $\sum_{p=1}^{s} [\sum_{\bar{a}\in\omega_p} h_{\bar{a}}^{\rho}(\varrho)(\chi_{\bar{a}}^{\eta} - \varrho_{\bar{a}}^{\eta})]$, $\rho, \eta = 1, 2, \cdots, m$. Let

$$\wedge_p(\varrho) = \{\bar{b} \in \omega_p : h_{\bar{b}}(\varrho) \in \text{SEP}\{h_b(\varrho) : b \in \omega_p\}\} \subset \omega_p.$$

Hence, for each $\bar{b} \in \wedge_p(\varrho) \subset \omega_p$,

$$\text{cone}(h_{\omega_p}(\varrho) + \mathbb{R}_+^m - h_{\bar{b}}(\varrho)) \cap (\text{cone}(\Theta - \Xi) \backslash \{0\}) = \emptyset.$$

It follows from Definition 4 that for any $b \in \omega_p$, $o = 1, \cdots, m$ and $b \neq \bar{b}$, $\varrho_b^o = \mu_b^o$, $\varrho_{\bar{b}}^o = \lambda_{\bar{b}}^o$, or path $\bar{b}$ is a saturated path of product o and flow ϱ. Because $\mathrm{SEP}\{h_b(\varrho) : b \in \omega_p\} \subset \mathrm{EP}\{h_b(\varrho) : b \in \omega_p\}$, we obtain

$$h_{\bar{b}}(\varrho) \in \mathrm{EP}\{h_b(\varrho) : b \in \omega_p\},$$

that is,

$$h_b(\varrho) - h_{\bar{b}}(\varrho) \notin -\mathbb{R}_+^m \backslash \{0\}, \forall b \in \omega_p, p \in \mathcal{P} \text{ and } b \neq \bar{b}.$$

Due to $h_b(\varrho) - h_{\bar{b}}(\varrho) \neq 0$, one has

$$h_b(\varrho) - h_{\bar{b}}(\varrho) \notin -\mathbb{R}_+^m, \forall b \in \omega_p, p \in \mathcal{P} \text{ and } b \neq \bar{b}.$$

So there is an $\bar{\rho} = 1, 2, \cdots, m$ such that

$$h_b^{\bar{\rho}}(\varrho) - h_{\bar{b}}^{\bar{\rho}}(\varrho) > 0.$$

Hence, one has

$$\begin{aligned}
&\sum_{p=1}^{s}\left[\sum_{\bar{a}\in\omega_p} h_{\bar{a}}^{\bar{\rho}}(\varrho)(\chi_{\bar{a}}^{\eta} - \varrho_{\bar{a}}^{\eta})\right] \\
&= \sum_{p=1}^{s}\left[\sum_{\bar{a}\in\omega_p\backslash\{\bar{b}\}} h_{\bar{a}}^{\bar{\rho}}(\varrho)(\chi_{\bar{a}}^{\eta} - \varrho_{\bar{a}}^{\eta}) + h_{\bar{b}}^{\bar{\rho}}(\varrho)(\chi_{\bar{b}}^{\eta} - \varrho_{\bar{b}}^{\eta})\right].
\end{aligned}$$

Because $\bar{a} \in \omega_p \backslash \{\bar{b}\}$, we have $\varrho_{\bar{a}}^{\eta} = \mu_{\bar{a}}^{\eta}$, $\varrho_{\bar{b}}^{\eta} = \lambda_{\bar{b}}^{\eta}$ for each $\eta = 1, 2, \cdots, m$,

$$\begin{aligned}
&\sum_{p=1}^{s}\left[\sum_{\bar{a}\in\omega_p} h_{\bar{a}}^{\bar{\rho}}(\varrho)(\chi_{\bar{a}}^{\eta} - \varrho_{\bar{a}}^{\eta})\right] \\
&= \sum_{p=1}^{s}\left[\sum_{\bar{a}\in\omega_p\backslash\{\bar{b}\}} h_{\bar{a}}^{\bar{\rho}}(\varrho)(\chi_{\bar{a}}^{\eta} - \mu_{\bar{a}}^{\eta}) + h_{\bar{b}}^{\bar{\rho}}(\varrho)(\chi_{\bar{b}}^{\eta} - \lambda_{\bar{b}}^{\eta})\right].
\end{aligned}$$

And, because $\bar{a} \in \omega_p \backslash \{\bar{b}\}$, it holds that $h_{\bar{a}}^{\bar{\rho}}(\varrho) > h_{\bar{b}}^{\bar{\rho}}(\varrho)$. Due to $\chi \in Q$, there must exist $\bar{\eta} = 1, 2, \cdots, m$ satisfying $\chi_{\bar{a}}^{\bar{\eta}} - \mu_{\bar{a}}^{\bar{\eta}} > 0$. Hence, we obtain

$$\begin{aligned}
&\sum_{p=1}^{s}\left[\sum_{\bar{a}\in\omega_p\backslash\{\bar{b}\}} h_{\bar{a}}^{\bar{\rho}}(\varrho)(\chi_{\bar{a}}^{\bar{\eta}} - \mu_{\bar{a}}^{\bar{\eta}}) + h_{\bar{b}}^{\bar{\rho}}(\varrho)(\chi_{\bar{b}}^{\bar{\eta}} - \lambda_{\bar{b}}^{\bar{\eta}})\right] \\
&> \sum_{p=1}^{s} h_{\bar{b}}^{\bar{\rho}}(\varrho)\left[\sum_{\bar{a}\in\omega_p} \chi_{\bar{a}}^{\bar{\eta}} - \left(\sum_{\bar{a}\in\omega_p\backslash\{\bar{b}\}} \mu_{\bar{a}}^{\bar{\eta}} + \lambda_{\bar{b}}^{\bar{\eta}}\right)\right] \\
&= \sum_{p=1}^{s} h_{\bar{b}}^{\bar{\rho}}(\varrho)\left[\sum_{\bar{a}\in\omega_p} \chi_{\bar{a}}^{\bar{\eta}} - \left(\sum_{\bar{a}\in\omega_p\backslash\{\bar{b}\}} \varrho_{\bar{a}}^{\bar{\eta}} + \varrho_{\bar{b}}^{\bar{\eta}}\right)\right] \\
&= \sum_{p=1}^{s} h_{\bar{b}}^{\bar{\rho}}(\varrho)\left[\sum_{\bar{a}\in\omega_p} \chi_{\bar{a}}^{\bar{\eta}} - \sum_{\bar{a}\in\omega_p} \varrho_{\bar{a}}^{\bar{\eta}}\right].
\end{aligned}$$

Since $\chi \in Q$ and $\varrho \in Q$, we obtain that

$$\sum_{\bar{a}\in\omega_p} \chi_{\bar{a}}^{\bar{\eta}} = d_p^{\bar{\eta}}(\varepsilon_p^{\bar{\eta}}), \quad \sum_{\bar{a}\in\omega_p} \varrho_{\bar{a}}^{\bar{\eta}} = d_p^{\bar{\eta}}(\varepsilon_p^{\bar{\eta}}).$$

Therefore, there exist $\bar{\rho} = 1, 2, \cdots, m$ and $\bar{\eta} = 1, 2, \cdots, m$, satisfying

$$\begin{aligned}
&\sum_{p=1}^{s}\left[\sum_{\bar{a}\in\omega_p} h_{\bar{a}}^{\bar{\rho}}(\varrho)(\chi_{\bar{a}}^{\bar{\eta}} - \varrho_{\bar{a}}^{\bar{\eta}})\right] \\
&> \sum_{p=1}^{s} h_{\bar{b}}^{\bar{\rho}}(\varrho)\left[d_p^{\bar{\eta}}(\varepsilon_p^{\bar{\eta}}) - d_p^{\bar{\eta}}(\varepsilon_p^{\bar{\eta}})\right] \\
&= 0.
\end{aligned}$$

Thus, inequation (1) holds.

Next, let

$$\mathrm{cone}(\langle h(\varrho), (\chi - \varrho)' \rangle + \mathbb{R}_+^{m\times m}) \cap (\mathrm{cone}(\tilde{\Theta} - \tilde{\Xi})\backslash\{0\}) \neq \emptyset,\ \forall \chi \in Q.$$

Therefore, there must be an $\bar{k} \neq 0$ satisfying

$$\bar{k} \in \mathrm{cone}(\langle h(\varrho), (\chi - \varrho)' \rangle + \mathbb{R}_+^{m\times m}) \cap (\mathrm{cone}(\tilde{\Theta} - \tilde{\Xi})\backslash\{0\}),\ \forall \chi \in Q.$$

We set $\bar{k} = \tilde{\delta}\tilde{k}$, where $\tilde{k} \in \langle h(\varrho), (\chi - \varrho)' \rangle + \mathbb{R}_+^{m\times m}$, $\tilde{\delta} > 0$ because of $\bar{k} \neq 0$. Hence, $\tilde{\delta}\tilde{k} \in \mathrm{cone}(\tilde{\Theta} - \tilde{\Xi})\backslash\{0\}$. Thus there are $\tilde{\sigma} > 0$ and $\tilde{r} \in \tilde{\Theta} - \tilde{\Xi}$ satisfying $\tilde{\delta}\tilde{k} = \tilde{\sigma}\tilde{r}$. Therefore, there are $\tilde{\chi} \in Q$ and $\theta \in \mathbb{R}_+^{m\times m}$ satisfying $\tilde{k} = \frac{\tilde{\sigma}\tilde{r}}{\tilde{\delta}} = \langle h(\varrho), (\tilde{\chi} - \varrho)' \rangle + \theta$, which is equivalent to

$$\langle h(\varrho), (\tilde{\chi} - \varrho)' \rangle = \frac{\tilde{\sigma}\tilde{r}}{\tilde{\delta}} - \theta \in -\mathbb{R}_+^{m\times m},$$

which contradicts (1). Hence, it holds that

$$\mathrm{cone}(\langle h(\varrho), (\chi - \varrho)' \rangle + \mathbb{R}_+^{m\times m}) \cap (\mathrm{cone}(\tilde{\Theta} - \tilde{\Xi})\backslash\{0\}) = \emptyset,\ \forall \chi \in Q.$$

□

Theorem 2. *The vector $\varrho \in Q$ is a strict network equilibrium flow if ϱ is a solution of the following vector variational inequality: find $\varrho \in Q$ satisfying*

$$\langle h(\varrho), (\chi - \varrho)' \rangle \notin -\mathbb{R}_+^{m\times m}\backslash\{0\},\ \forall \chi \in Q. \tag{2}$$

Proof. Assume that $\varrho \in Q$ satisfies inequality (2). For each $p \in \mathcal{P}$ and $a, b \in \omega_p$, $b \neq a$, $o = 1, \cdots, m$, if

$$\mathrm{cone}(h_{\omega_p}(\varrho) + \mathbb{R}_+^m - h_a(\varrho)) \cap (\mathrm{cone}(\Theta - \Xi)\backslash\{0\}) = \emptyset,$$

$h_b(\varrho) - h_a(\varrho) \neq 0$, and a is a nonsaturated path of product o and flow ϱ, we will deduce $\varrho_b^o = \mu_b^o$ or $\varrho_a^o = \lambda_a^o$. Let $\beth_a = \{c \in \mathcal{C} : \text{arc } c \text{ belongs to path } a\}$. We assume that the conclusion is false, i.e., $\varrho_b \neq \mu_b$ or $\varrho_a \neq \lambda_a$. Taking $\nabla^o = \min\{\min_{c\in\beth_a}(\bar{\varrho}_c^o - \varrho_c^o), \varrho_b^o - \mu_b^o, \lambda_a^o - \varrho_a^o\} > 0$ and $\nabla = (\nabla^1, \cdots, \nabla^o, \cdots, \nabla^m)'$, let χ be

$$\chi_{\bar{a}} = \begin{cases} \varrho_{\bar{a}}, & \text{if } \bar{a} \neq b \text{ or } a, \\ \varrho_b - \nabla, & \text{if } \bar{a} = b, \\ \varrho_a + \nabla, & \text{if } \bar{a} = a. \end{cases}$$

Because $\varrho \in Q$, i.e., $\forall p \in \mathcal{P}, o = 1, 2, \cdots, m$, $\sum_{\bar{a}\in\omega_p} \varrho_{\bar{a}}^o = d_p^o(\varepsilon_p^o)$, one has

$$\begin{aligned}
\sum_{\bar{a}\in\omega_p} \chi_{\bar{a}}^o &= \sum_{\bar{a}\in\omega_p\backslash\{b,a\}} \chi_{\bar{a}}^o + \chi_b^o + \chi_a^o \\
&= \sum_{\bar{a}\in\omega_p\backslash\{b,a\}} \varrho_{\bar{a}}^o + \varrho_b^o - \nabla^o + \varrho_a^o + \nabla^o \\
&= \sum_{\bar{a}\in\omega_p} \varrho_{\bar{a}}^o = d_p^o(\varepsilon_p^o).
\end{aligned}$$

So, $\chi \in Q$. Now,

$$\begin{aligned}
&\langle h(\varrho), (\chi - \varrho)' \rangle \\
&= \sum_{\bar{a}=1}^{n} \langle h_{\bar{a}}(\varrho), (\chi_{\bar{a}} - \varrho_{\bar{a}})' \rangle \\
&= \sum_{\bar{a} \neq b,a} \langle h_{\bar{a}}(\varrho), (\varrho_{\bar{a}} - \varrho_{\bar{a}})' \rangle + \langle h_b(\varrho), (\varrho_b - \nabla - \varrho_b)' \rangle + \langle h_a(\varrho), (\varrho_a + \nabla - \varrho_a)' \rangle \\
&= \langle \nabla, (h_a(\varrho) - h_b(\varrho))' \rangle \notin -\mathbb{R}_+^{m \times m} \backslash \{0\}.
\end{aligned}$$

We know that $\langle h(\varrho), (\chi - \varrho)' \rangle$ is an $m \times m$ matrix; the component is $(h_a^\rho(\varrho) - h_b^\rho(\varrho))\varrho_b^\eta$, $\rho, \eta = 1, 2, \cdots, m$. If $\langle \nabla, (h_a(\varrho) - h_b(\varrho))' \rangle \neq 0$, then for each $\rho, \eta = 1, 2, \cdots, m$,

$$(h_a^\rho(\varrho) - h_b^\rho(\varrho))\nabla^\eta \geq 0,$$

with strict inequality holding for some $\rho, \eta = 1, 2, \cdots, m$. By $\nabla^\eta \geq 0$, one has

$$h_a^\rho(\varrho) - h_b^\rho(\varrho) \geq 0,$$

that is,

$$h_a(\varrho) - h_b(\varrho) \in \mathbb{R}_+^m \backslash \{0\},$$

which is equivalent to

$$h_b(\varrho) - h_a(\varrho) \in -\mathbb{R}_+^m \backslash \{0\}.$$

Noticing that

$$-\mathbb{R}_+^m \backslash \{0\} \subset (\text{cone}(\Theta - \Xi) \backslash \{0\}),$$

and

$$h_b(\varrho) - h_a(\varrho) \in \text{cone}(h_{\omega_i}(\varrho) + \mathbb{R}_+^m - h_a(\varrho)), \tag{3}$$

we get

$$h_b(\varrho) - h_a(\varrho) \in \text{cone}(\Theta - \Xi) \backslash \{0\}. \tag{4}$$

By Equations (3) and (4) and $h_b(\varrho) - h_a(\varrho) \neq 0$, we obtain

$$h_b(\varrho) - h_a(\varrho) \in \text{cone}(h_{\omega_p}(\varrho) + \mathbb{R}_+^m - h_a(\varrho)) \cap (\text{cone}(\Theta - \Xi) \backslash \{0\}),$$

a contradiction. Thus, the conclusion $\varrho_b = \mu_b$ or $\varrho_a = \lambda_a$ holds. □

We now propose the existence of strict network equilibrium flow by virtue of an equivalent form of Fan–Browder's fixed point theorem ([23,24]), which is formulated in the following lemma.

Lemma 1 (see [10]). *Let $\mho$ denote a Hausdorff topological vector space; $\mathcal{K}$ is a nonempty compact convex subset of $\mho$. Assume that the set-valued map $g : \mathcal{K} \to 2^{\mathcal{K}} \cup \{\emptyset\}$ has the following conditions:*

(i) for any $\varsigma \in \mathcal{K}$, $g(\varsigma)$ is a convex set;
(ii) for any $\varsigma \in \mathcal{K}$, $\varsigma \notin g(\varsigma)$;
(iii) for any $\iota \in \mathcal{K}$, $g^{-1}(\iota) = \{\varsigma \in \mathcal{K} : \iota \in g(\varsigma)\}$ is an open set in $\mathcal{K}$.

Then, there exists $\tilde{\xi} \in \mathcal{K}$ satisfying $g(\tilde{\xi}) = \emptyset$.

Theorem 3. *Consider a multi-product supply–demand network equilibrium problem with capacity constraints and uncertain demands $\mathcal{G} = [\mathcal{N}, \mathcal{C}, \mathcal{V}, \mathcal{P}, \mathcal{D}]$. Let $\bar{\varrho} \in int\mathbb{R}_+^{m \times m}$ be given. If, for any*

$\chi \in Q$, the function $\langle \bar{\varrho}, \langle h(\varrho), (\chi - \varrho)' \rangle \rangle$ is continuous on Q. Then, the network $\mathcal{G}$ exists as a strict vector equilibrium flow.

Proof. Consider the following variational inequality: find $\varrho \in Q$ satisfying

$$\langle \bar{\varrho}, \langle h(\varrho), (\chi - \varrho)' \rangle \rangle \in \mathbb{R}_+^{m \times m}, \ \forall \chi \in Q. \tag{5}$$

Firstly, we will show that the variational inequality (5) admits a solution. We define a set-valued map $\Omega : Q \to 2^Q \cup \{\emptyset\}$ as $\Omega(\varrho) = \{\chi \in Q : \langle \bar{\varrho}, \langle h(\varrho), (\chi - \varrho)' \rangle \rangle \in \text{int}(-\mathbb{R}_+^{m \times m})\}$. Then, one has the following results:

(i) $\Omega(\varrho)$ is convex;
(ii) for each $\varrho \in Q$, $\varrho \notin \Omega(\varrho)$;
(iii) if $\chi \in \Omega(\varrho)$, one has $\langle \bar{\varrho}, \langle h(\varrho), (\chi - \varrho)' \rangle \rangle \in \text{int}(-\mathbb{R}_+^{m \times m})$, which implies that there exists a $\xi \in \mathbb{R}_+^{m \times m}$ such that $\langle \bar{\varrho}, \langle h(\varrho), (\chi - \varrho)' \rangle \rangle + \xi \in \text{int}(-\mathbb{R}_+^{m \times m})$. Since $\langle \bar{\varrho}, \langle h(\varrho), (\chi - \varrho)' \rangle \rangle$ is continuous on Q by hypothesis, one can reach that there exists an open neighborhood $\Theta(\varrho)$ of ϱ such that

$$\langle \bar{\varrho}, \langle h(\hat{\varrho}), (\chi - \hat{\varrho})' \rangle \rangle < \langle \bar{\varrho}, \langle h(\varrho), (\chi - \varrho)' \rangle \rangle + \xi \in \text{int}(-\mathbb{R}_+^{m \times m}), \ \forall \hat{\varrho} \in \Theta(\varrho)$$

which implies that

$$\Theta(\varrho) \subset \Omega^{-1}(\chi) = \{\varrho \in Q : \langle \varrho, \langle h(\varrho), (\chi - \varrho)' \rangle \rangle \in \text{int}(-\mathbb{R}_+^{m \times m}),$$

i.e., $\Omega^{-1}(\chi)$ is open.

By Lemma 1, we obtain that the variational inequality (5) has a solution $\tilde{\varrho} \in Q$. Next, we prove that $\tilde{\varrho}$ is a strict network equilibrium flow. According to Theorem 2, we needs to prove that $\tilde{\varrho}$ is a solution to the following vector variational inequality:

$$\langle h(\varrho), (\chi - \varrho)' \rangle \notin -\mathbb{R}_+^{m \times m} \backslash \{0\}, \ \forall \chi \in Q.$$

Let us suppose to the contrary that $\tilde{\varrho}$ is not a solution; then, there is $\tilde{\chi} \in Q$, such that $\langle h(\tilde{\varrho}), (\tilde{\chi} - \tilde{\varrho})' \rangle \in -\mathbb{R}_+^{m \times m} \backslash \{0\}$. For $\bar{\varrho} \in \text{int}\mathbb{R}_+^{m \times m}$, we obtain

$$\langle \bar{\varrho}, \langle h(\tilde{\varrho}), (\tilde{\chi} - \tilde{\varrho})' \rangle \rangle \in -\mathbb{R}_+^{m \times m} \backslash \{0\},$$

a contradiction. □

4. Strict Vector Equilibrium Flows with Multi-Criteria via Scalarization

It seems unreasonable for network users to choose a path based on a single criterion. In fact, the network users need to consider time, tariffs, fuel, and other relevant cost factors simultaneously. That is, the cost function is a multi-criteria one. In the following sections, the equilibrium model of the multi-product supply–demand network $\mathcal{G} = [\mathcal{N}, \mathcal{C}, \mathcal{V}, \mathcal{P}, \mathcal{D}]$ based on multi-criteria cost functions is investigated. Let us suppose that the cost on arc $c \in \mathcal{C}$ with product o is: $H_c^o(\varrho) : \mathbb{R}^{m \times n} \to \mathbb{R}_+^e$, where $e > 1$ is a positive integer. The cost on the path $a \in \omega_p$, $p \in P$ with product o is computed by

$$H_a^o(\varrho) = \sum_{c \in a} H_c^o(\varrho).$$

Hence, $H_a^o(\varrho) : \mathbb{R}^{m \times n} \to \mathbb{R}_+^e$ and we set it in the form

$$H_a^o(\varrho) = u_a^o(\varrho)\vartheta_0, \ \forall a \in \omega_p, p \in \mathcal{P} \text{ and } o = 1, \cdots, m, \tag{6}$$

where $u_a^o(\varrho) : \mathbb{R}^{m \times n} \to \mathbb{R}_+$, $\vartheta_0 \in \text{int}\mathbb{R}_+^e$.

The cost on the network concerning product o is denoted by $H^o(\varrho) = (H_1^o(\varrho), \cdots, H_n^o(\varrho))$, the cost on path a is denoted by $H_a(\varrho) = (H_a^1(\varrho), \cdots, H_a^o(\varrho), \cdots, H_a^m(\varrho))$, and the cost of the network is denoted by $H(\varrho) = (H_a(\varrho) : a \in \omega_p, p \in \mathcal{P})$.

In the following, $Y = \mathbb{R}^e$ is a e-dimensional Euclidean space with the ordering cone $\mathbb{R}_+^e$, where $e > 1$ is a positive integer. $\bar{\Xi}$ always denotes a base of $\mathbb{R}_+^{m\times e}$, and $\bar{\Theta}$ denotes a neighborhood of 0 in $\mathbb{R}^{m\times e}$. Firstly, we introduce the concept of strict network equilibrium flow for a multi-product, multi-criteria supply–demand network with capacity constraints and uncertain demands.

Definition 6. *The feasible network flow $\varrho \in Q$ is called a strict network equilibrium flow for a multi-product, multi-criteria supply–demand network with capacity constraints and uncertain demands, if, for any $p \in \mathcal{P}$, $a, b \in \omega_p$, $o = 1, \cdots, m$, there is a neighborhood $\bar{\Theta}$ of 0 in $\mathbb{R}^{m\times e}$, such that $\bar{\Theta} - \bar{\Xi} \subset -int\mathbb{R}_+^{m\times e}$, one has the implication*

$$\left.\begin{array}{r} cone(H_{\omega_p}(\varrho) + \mathbb{R}_+^{m\times e} - H_a(\varrho)) \cap (cone(\bar{\Theta} - \bar{\Xi})\backslash\{0\}) = \emptyset \\ H_b(\varrho) - H_a(\varrho) \neq 0 \end{array}\right\} \Rightarrow$$

$\varrho_b^o = \mu_b^o$, $b \neq a$, or $\varrho_a^o = \lambda_a^o$, or path a is a saturated path of product o and flow ϱ.

As we all know, a viable approach to solve vector problems is to convert them into scalar problems. In this paper, we use the following nonlinear scalarization function (i.e., Gerstewitz's function) to scalarize the vector-valued strict network equilibrium flows without any assumptions about convexity.

Definition 7 (see [25]). *For a given $v \in int\mathbb{R}_+^e$, let $\psi_v : \mathbb{R}^e \to \mathbb{R}$ be defined by*

$$\psi_v(x) = \min\{\delta \in \mathbb{R} : x \in \delta v - \mathbb{R}_+^e\}, \forall x \in \mathbb{R}^e.$$

Lemma 2 and Lemma 3 provide some properties of the above function that we will use in the proof of Theorem 4.

Lemma 2 (see [26]). *Let $v \in int\mathbb{R}_+^e$. For each $\sigma \in \mathbb{R}$ and $x \in \mathbb{R}^e$, one has*

(i) $\psi_v(x) < \sigma \Leftrightarrow x \in \sigma v - int\mathbb{R}_+^e$;
(ii) $\psi_v(x) \leqslant \sigma \Leftrightarrow x \in \sigma v - \mathbb{R}_+^e$;
(iii) $\psi_v(x) \geqslant \sigma \Leftrightarrow x \notin \sigma v - int\mathbb{R}_+^e$;
(iv) $\psi_v(x) > \sigma \Leftrightarrow x \notin \sigma v - \mathbb{R}_+^e$;
(v) $\psi_v(x) = \sigma \Leftrightarrow x \in \sigma v - \partial\mathbb{R}_+^e$, *where $\partial\mathbb{R}_+^e$ is the topological boundary of $\mathbb{R}_+^e$.*

Lemma 3 (see [7]). *Given $v \in int\mathbb{R}_+^e$, $x \in \mathbb{R}^e$, and $\sigma \in \mathbb{R}$, one has*

$$\psi_v(-x) \geqslant -\psi_v(x), \;\; \psi_v(-\sigma x) \geqslant -\psi_v(\sigma x),$$

and

$$\psi_v(-\sigma v) = -\psi_v(\sigma v) = -\sigma.$$

We denote

$$\psi_v \circ H_a^o(\varrho) = \psi_v(H_a^o(\varrho)) = \min\{\delta \in \mathbb{R} : H_a^o(\varrho) \in \delta v - \mathbb{R}_+^e\},$$

for any $\varrho \in Q$, $a \in \omega_p$, $p \in \mathcal{P}$, $o = 1, \cdots, m$;

$$\psi_v \circ H_a(\varrho) = (\psi_v \circ H_a^o(\varrho) : o = 1, \cdots, m)' \in \mathbb{R}^m;$$

and

$$\psi_v(\varrho) = \psi_v \circ H(\varrho) = (\psi_v \circ H_a(\varrho) : a \in \omega_p,\; p \in P) \in \mathbb{R}^{m\times n}.$$

Definition 8. *The feasible network flow $\varrho \in Q$ is called in ψ_v-strict vector equilibrium for a multi-product supply–demand network involving vector-valued cost functions, if, for any $p \in \mathcal{P}$, $a, b \in \omega_p$, $o = 1, \cdots, m$, there exist $v \in int\mathbb{R}^e_+$ and a neighborhood Θ of 0 in $\mathbb{R}^m$ satisfying $\Theta - \Xi \subset -int\mathbb{R}^m_+$, one has the implication*

$$\left.\begin{array}{r} cone(\psi_v \circ H_{\omega_p}(\varrho) + \mathbb{R}^m_+ - \psi_v \circ H_a(\varrho)) \cap (cone(\Theta - \Xi)\backslash\{0\}) = \emptyset \\ \psi_v \circ H_b(\varrho) - \psi_v \circ H_a(\varrho) \neq 0 \end{array}\right\} \Rightarrow$$

$\varrho^o_b = \mu^o_b$, $b \neq a$, or $\varrho^o_a = \lambda^o_a$, or path a is a saturated path of product o and flow ϱ.

Now, we will scalarize strict vector equilibrium problems for a multi-product supply–demand network involving vector-valued cost functions.

Theorem 4. *Let us suppose that $H^o_a(\varrho)$ is defined as in (6) for each $a \in \omega_p$, $p \in \mathcal{P}$, and $o = 1, \cdots, m$. The feasible network flow $\varrho \in Q$ is a strict network equilibrium flow for a multi-product, multi-criteria supply–demand network with capacity constraints and uncertain demands if and only if ϱ is in ψ_{ϑ_0}-strict vector equilibrium.*

Proof. Necessity: suppose that $\varrho \in Q$ is a strict network equilibrium flow for a multi-product, multi-criteria supply–demand network with capacity constraints and uncertain demands. For any $p \in \mathcal{P}$, $a, b \in \omega_p$ and $o = 1, \cdots, m$, it is necessary to verify the following implication:

$$\left.\begin{array}{l} \mathrm{cone}(\psi_{\vartheta_0} \circ H_{\omega_p}(\varrho) + \mathbb{R}^m_+ - \psi_{\vartheta_0} \circ H_a(\varrho)) \cap (\mathrm{cone}(\Theta - \Xi)\backslash\{0\}) = \emptyset \\ \psi_{\vartheta_0} \circ H_b(\varrho) - \psi_{\vartheta_0} \circ H_a(\varrho) \neq 0 \end{array}\right\} \Rightarrow$$

$\varrho^o_b = \mu^o_b$, $b \neq a$, or $\varrho^o_a = \lambda^o_a$, or path a is a saturated path of product o and flow ϱ.
Firstly, it holds that

$$\left\{\begin{array}{l} \mathrm{cone}(\psi_{\vartheta_0} \circ H_{\omega_p}(\varrho) + \mathbb{R}^m_+ - \psi_{\vartheta_0} \circ H_a(\varrho)) \cap (\mathrm{cone}(\Theta - \Xi)\backslash\{0\}) = \emptyset \\ \psi_{\vartheta_0} \circ H_b(\varrho) - \psi_{\vartheta_0} \circ H_a(\varrho) \neq 0 \end{array}\right.$$

implies

$$\left\{\begin{array}{l} \mathrm{cone}(H_{\omega_p}(\varrho) + \mathbb{R}^{m \times e}_+ - H_a(\varrho)) \cap (\mathrm{cone}(\bar{\Theta} - \bar{\Xi})\backslash\{0\}) = \emptyset \\ H_b(\varrho) - H_a(\varrho) \neq 0. \end{array}\right.$$

Indeed, from $\psi_{\vartheta_0} \circ H_b(\varrho) - \psi_{\vartheta_0} \circ H_a(\varrho) \neq 0$, we have

$$H_b(\varrho) - H_a(\varrho) \neq 0,\ \forall\, a, b \in \omega_p\,,\ b \neq a.$$

From (6), one has $H_{\omega_p}(\varrho) = u_{\omega_p}(\varrho) \circ \vartheta_0$, where $u_{\omega_p}(\varrho) = \{u_b(\varrho) : b \in \omega_p\}$, $u_b(\varrho) = (u^1_b(\varrho), \cdots, u^o_b(\varrho), \cdots, u^m_b(\varrho))$. By Lemma 3, it holds that

$$\begin{aligned} \psi_{\vartheta_0} \circ H_{\omega_p}(\varrho) &= \{\psi_{\vartheta_0} \circ H_b(\varrho) : b \in \omega_p\} \\ &= \{(\psi_{\vartheta_0} \circ H^1_b(\varrho), \psi_{\vartheta_0} \circ H^2_b(\varrho), \cdots, \psi_{\vartheta_0} \circ H^m_b(\varrho)) : b \in \omega_p\} \\ &= \{(u^1_b(\varrho), \cdots, u^m_b(\varrho)) : b \in \omega_p\} \\ &= u_{\omega_p}(\varrho). \end{aligned}$$

Therefore, $\mathrm{cone}(\psi_{\vartheta_0} \circ H_{\omega_p}(\varrho) + \mathbb{R}^m_+ - \psi_{\vartheta_0} \circ H_a(\varrho)) \cap (\mathrm{cone}(\Theta - \Xi)\backslash\{0\}) = \emptyset$ turns into

$$\mathrm{cone}(u_{\omega_p}(\varrho) + \mathbb{R}^m_+ - u_a(\varrho)) \cap (\mathrm{cone}(\Theta - \Xi)\backslash\{0\}) = \emptyset.$$

That is, $u_a(\varrho) \in \mathrm{SEP}\{u_b(\varrho) : b \in \omega_p\}$. Due to $\mathrm{SEP}\{u_b(\varrho) : b \in \omega_p\} \subset \mathrm{EP}\{u_b(\varrho) : b \in \omega_p\}$, so $u_a(\varrho) \in \mathrm{EP}\{u_b(\varrho) : b \in \omega_p\}$, that is,

$$u_b(\varrho) - u_a(\varrho) \notin -\mathbb{R}^m_+\backslash\{0\}, \forall b \in \omega_p. \tag{7}$$

Let us suppose that

$$\text{cone}(H_{\omega_p}(\varrho) + \mathbb{R}_+^{m\times e} - H_a(\varrho)) \cap (\text{cone}(\bar{\Theta} - \bar{\Xi})\backslash\{0\}) \neq \emptyset,$$

there is a $\bar{k} \neq 0$ satisfying $\bar{k} \in \text{cone}(H_{\omega_p}(\varrho) + \mathbb{R}_+^{m\times e} - H_a(\varrho)) \cap (\text{cone}(\bar{\Theta} - \bar{\Xi})\backslash\{0\})$. We set $\bar{k} = \tilde{\delta}\tilde{k}$, where $\tilde{k} \in H_{\omega_p}(\varrho) + \mathbb{R}_+^{m\times e} - H_a(\varrho)$, $\tilde{\delta} > 0$. Because $\tilde{\delta}\tilde{k} \in \text{cone}(\bar{\Theta} - \bar{\Xi})\backslash\{0\}$, there exist $\tilde{\sigma} > 0$ and $\tilde{r} \in \bar{\Theta} - \bar{\Xi}$ satisfying $\tilde{\delta}\tilde{k} = \tilde{\sigma}\tilde{r}$. So $\tilde{k} = \frac{\tilde{\sigma}\tilde{r}}{\tilde{\delta}} \in H_{\omega_i}(\varrho) + \mathbb{R}_+^{m\times e} - H_a(\varrho) \cap (\bar{\Theta} - \bar{\Xi})$, $\tilde{k} \neq 0$. Hence, there are $\tilde{b} \in \omega_p, \tilde{\theta} \in \mathbb{R}_+^{m\times e}$ satisfying

$$\tilde{k} = H_{\tilde{b}}(\varrho) + \tilde{\theta} - H_a(\varrho),$$

equivalently,

$$H_{\tilde{b}}(\varrho) - H_a(\varrho) = \tilde{k} - \tilde{\theta} \in -\mathbb{R}_+^{m\times e}.$$

i.e.,

$$H_{\tilde{b}}^o(\varrho) - H_a^o(\varrho) \in -\mathbb{R}_+^e,\ o = 1, \cdots, m.$$

It follows from Lemma 2 that

$$\psi_{\vartheta_0}(H_{\tilde{b}}^o(\varrho) - H_a^o(\varrho)) \leq 0.$$

By (6) and Lemma 3, one has

$$u_{\tilde{b}}^o(\varrho) - u_a^o(\varrho) \leq 0,\ o = 1, \cdots, m,$$

i.e.,

$$u_{\tilde{b}}(\varrho) - u_a(\varrho) \in -\mathbb{R}_+^m.$$

If $u_{\tilde{b}}(\varrho) - u_a(\varrho) = 0$, $H_{\tilde{b}}(\varrho) - H_a(\varrho) = 0$, so $\tilde{k} = \tilde{\theta}$, which contradicts $\tilde{k} \in \bar{\Theta} - \bar{\Xi}$ and $\tilde{\theta} \in \mathbb{R}_+^{m\times e}$. Hence,

$$u_{\tilde{b}}(\varrho) - u_a(\varrho) \in -\mathbb{R}_+^m\backslash\{0\},$$

which leads to a contradiction with (7). Therefore, one has the implication:

$$\begin{cases} \text{cone}(\psi_{\vartheta_0} \circ H_{\omega_p}(\varrho) + \mathbb{R}_+^m - \psi_{\vartheta_0} \circ H_a(\varrho)) \cap (\text{cone}(\Theta - \Xi)\backslash\{0\}) = \emptyset \\ \psi_{\vartheta_0} \circ H_b(\varrho) - \psi_{\vartheta_0} \circ H_a(\varrho) \neq 0 \end{cases}$$

$$\Rightarrow \begin{cases} \text{cone}(H_{\omega_p}(\varrho) + \mathbb{R}_+^{m\times e} - H_a(\varrho)) \cap (\text{cone}(\bar{\Theta} - \bar{\Xi})\backslash\{0\}) = \emptyset \\ H_b(\varrho) - H_a(\varrho) \neq 0. \end{cases}$$

Since $\varrho \in Q$ is a strict network equilibrium flow, for any $p \in \mathcal{P}, a, b \in \omega_p, o = 1, \cdots, m$, one has

$$\left.\begin{array}{r} \text{cone}(H_{\omega_p}(\varrho) + \mathbb{R}_+^{m\times e} - H_a(\varrho)) \cap (\text{cone}(\bar{\Theta} - \bar{\Xi})\backslash\{0\}) = \emptyset \\ H_b(\varrho) - H_a(\varrho) \neq 0 \end{array}\right\} \Rightarrow$$

$\varrho_b^o = \mu_b^o, b \neq a$, or $\varrho_a^o = \lambda_a^o$, or path a is a saturated path of product o and flow ϱ. Hence, we obtain that

$$\left.\begin{array}{l} \text{cone}(\psi_{\vartheta_0} \circ H_{\omega_i}(\varrho) + \mathbb{R}_+^m - \psi_{\vartheta_0} \circ H_a(\varrho)) \cap (\text{cone}(\Theta - \Xi)\backslash\{0\}) = \emptyset \\ \psi_{\vartheta_0} \circ H_b(\varrho) - \psi_{\vartheta_0} \circ H_a(\varrho) \neq 0 \end{array}\right\} \Rightarrow$$

$\varrho_b^o = \mu_b^o, b \neq a$, or $\varrho_a^o = \lambda_a^o$, or path a is a saturated path of product o and flow ϱ, for any $p \in \mathcal{P}, a, b \in \omega_p$ and $o = 1, \cdots, m$.

Sufficiency: assume that $\varrho \in Q$ is in ψ_{ϑ_0}-strict vector equilibrium for a multi-product supply–demand network involving vector-valued cost functions. We first verify the implication

$$\begin{cases} \text{cone}(H_{\omega_p}(\varrho) + \mathbb{R}_+^{m\times e} - H_a(\varrho)) \cap (\text{cone}(\bar{\Theta} - \bar{\Xi})\backslash\{0\}) = \emptyset \\ H_b(\varrho) - H_a(\varrho) \neq 0 \end{cases}$$

$$\Rightarrow \begin{cases} \operatorname{cone}(\psi_{\vartheta_0} \circ H_{\omega_p}(\varrho) + \mathbb{R}^m_+ - \psi_{\vartheta_0} \circ H_a(\varrho)) \cap (\operatorname{cone}(\Theta - \Xi) \backslash \{0\}) = \varnothing \\ \psi_{\vartheta_0} \circ H_b(\varrho) - \psi_{\vartheta_0} \circ H_a(\varrho) \neq 0. \end{cases}$$

If

$$\operatorname{cone}(\psi_{\vartheta_0} \circ H_{\omega_p}(\varrho) + \mathbb{R}^m_+ - \psi_{\vartheta_0} \circ H_a(\varrho)) \cap (\operatorname{cone}(\Theta - \Xi) \backslash \{0\}) \neq \varnothing.$$

The following is similar to the proof of necessity. There is a $\tilde{r} \in (\psi_{\vartheta_0} \circ H_{\omega_p}(\varrho) + \mathbb{R}^m_+ - \psi_{\vartheta_0} \circ H_a(\varrho)) \cap (\Theta - \Xi)$ satisfying $\tilde{r} \neq 0$. Therefore, there are $\tilde{b} \in \omega_p$ and $\hat{\theta} \in \mathbb{R}^m_+$ satisfying

$$\tilde{r} = \psi_{\vartheta_0} \circ H_{\tilde{b}}(\varrho) + \hat{\theta} - \psi_{\vartheta_0} \circ H_a(\varrho).$$

i.e.,

$$\psi_{\vartheta_0} \circ H_{\tilde{b}}(\varrho) - \psi_{\vartheta_0} \circ H_a(\varrho) = \tilde{r} - \hat{\theta} \in -\mathbb{R}^m_+.$$

Together (6) with Lemma 3, one has

$$u_{\tilde{b}}(\varrho) - u_a(\varrho) \in -\mathbb{R}^m_+.$$

Hence, it holds that

$$H_{\tilde{b}}(\varrho) - H_a(\varrho) \in -\mathbb{R}^{m\times e}_+.$$

If $H_{\tilde{b}}(\varrho) - H_a(\varrho) = 0$, $\tilde{r} = \hat{\theta}$, which leads to a contradiction with $\tilde{r} \in \Theta - \Xi$ and $\hat{\theta} \in \mathbb{R}^m_+$. Therefore,

$$H_{\tilde{b}}(\varrho) - H_a(\varrho) \in -\mathbb{R}^{m\times e}_+ \backslash \{0\}. \tag{8}$$

Because $\operatorname{cone}(H_{\omega_p}(\varrho) + \mathbb{R}^{m\times e}_+ - H_a(\varrho)) \cap (\operatorname{cone}(\bar{\Theta} - \bar{\Xi}) \backslash \{0\}) = \varnothing$, then $H_a(\varrho) \in \mathrm{SEP}\{H_b(\varrho) : b \in \omega_p\}$. Therefore, $H_a(\varrho) \in \mathrm{EP}\{H_b(\varrho) : b \in \omega_p\}$, i.e.,

$$H_b(\varrho) - H_a(\varrho) \notin -\mathbb{R}^{m\times e}_+ \backslash \{0\}, \forall b \in \omega_p,$$

which leads to a contradiction with (8). Hence, it holds that

$$\operatorname{cone}(\psi_{\vartheta_0} \circ H_{\omega_p}(\varrho) + \mathbb{R}^m_+ - \psi_{\vartheta_0} \circ H_a(\varrho)) \cap (\operatorname{cone}(\Theta - \Xi) \backslash \{0\}) = \varnothing.$$

Additionally, due to $H_b(\varrho) - H_a(\varrho) \neq 0$, one has $\psi_{\vartheta_0} \circ H_b(\varrho) - \psi_{\vartheta_0} \circ H_a(\varrho) \neq 0$. It follows from Definition 8 that $\varrho^o_b = \mu^o_b, b \neq a$, or $\varrho^o_a = \lambda^o_a$, or path a is a saturated path of product o and flow ϱ, for any $p \in \mathcal{P}, a, b \in \omega_p$ and $o = 1, \cdots, m$. Therefore, $\varrho \in Q$ is a strict network equilibrium flow for a multi-product, multi-criteria supply–demand network with capacity constraints and uncertain demands. This completes the proof. □

It should be noted that the relations among strict network equilibrium flows involving real-valued cost functions, ψ_{ϑ_0}-strict vector equilibrium flows, and vector variational inequalities have been investigated in Theorems 1, 2, and 4. Then, strict network equilibrium flows for a multi-product supply–demand network involving vector-valued cost functions can be replaced by the following corresponding vector variational inequality: find $\varrho \in Q$ satisfying

$$\langle \psi_{\vartheta_0}(\varrho), (\chi - \varrho)' \rangle \notin -\mathbb{R}^{m\times m}_+ \backslash \{0\}, \forall \chi \in Q. \tag{9}$$

Additionally, it was shown in [7] (see Theorem 3.2 and Theorem 3.3) that the variational inequality (9) is equivalent to the following variational inequality: find $\varrho \in Q$ satisfying

$$\langle H(\varrho), (\chi - \varrho)' \rangle \notin -(\mathbb{R}^e_+)^{m\times m} \backslash \{0\}, \forall \chi \in Q.$$

These approaches allow us to obtain strict network equilibrium flows for a multi-product supply–demand network involving vector-valued cost functions.

5. An Illustrative Example

In this section, an example is provided to demonstrate the application of the obtained theoretical results. The example has the network topology depicted in Figure 1. Table 1 summarizes the constituent paths of each OD pair.

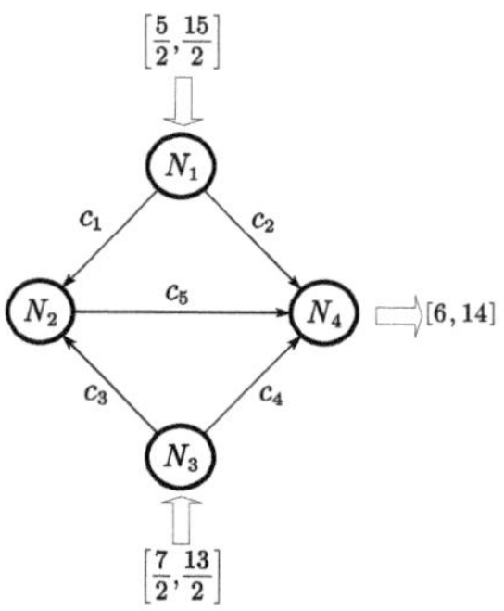

Figure 1. Network topology of the example.

Table 1. OD pairs and paths.

p	OD_p		ω_p
1	$\mathcal{N}_1 \to \mathcal{N}_4$	a_1	(c_1, c_5)
		a_2	(c_2)
2	$\mathcal{N}_3 \to \mathcal{N}_4$	a_3	(c_3, c_5)
		a_4	(c_4)

The network consists of four nodes: $\mathcal{N} = \{\mathcal{N}_1, \mathcal{N}_2, \mathcal{N}_3, \mathcal{N}_4\}$ and five arcs: $\mathcal{C} = \{c_1, c_2, c_3, c_4, c_5\}$. We assume that $\mathcal{V} = \{\bar{\varrho}^1_{c_1}, \bar{\varrho}^1_{c_2}, \bar{\varrho}^1_{c_3}, \bar{\varrho}^1_{c_4}, \bar{\varrho}^1_{c_5}\} = \{5, 4, 3, 6, 4\}$, $\mathcal{P} = \{\{\mathcal{N}_1, \mathcal{N}_4\}, \{\mathcal{N}_3, \mathcal{N}_4\}\}$, $m = 1$, $e = 2$, and $\mathcal{D} = \{d^1_1(\varepsilon^1_1), d^1_2(\varepsilon^1_2)\}$, where $d^1_1 = 5$, $d^1_2 = 5$, $\varepsilon^1_1 = \frac{5}{2}$, $\varepsilon^1_2 = \frac{3}{2}$, then $d^1_1(\varepsilon^1_1) \in [\frac{5}{2}, \frac{15}{2}]$, $d^1_2(\varepsilon^1_2) \in [\frac{7}{2}, \frac{13}{2}]$. Let $(\mu^1_1, \mu^1_2, \mu^1_3, \mu^1_4) = (2, \frac{3}{2}, \frac{1}{2}, 1)$ and $(\lambda^1_1, \lambda^1_2, \lambda^1_3, \lambda^1_4) = (5, 4, 3, 6)$. The costs on each arc are chosen as follows:

$$H^1_{c_1}(\varrho^1_1) = (\varrho^1_1, \varrho^1_1), \quad H^1_{c_2}(\varrho^1_2) = (4\varrho^1_2, 5\varrho^1_2), \quad H^1_{c_3}(\varrho^1_3) = (2\varrho^1_3, 3\varrho^1_3),$$
$$H^1_{c_4}(\varrho^1_4) = (5\varrho^1_4, 6\varrho^1_4), \quad H^1_{c_5}(\varrho^1_1) = (\varrho^1_1, 2\varrho^1_1), \quad H^1_{c_5}(\varrho^1_3) = (\varrho^1_3, 2\varrho^1_3).$$

By a direct calculation, we derive the costs on four different paths:

$$H^1_1(\varrho^1_1) = H^1_{a_1}(\varrho^1_1) + H^1_{a_5}(\varrho^1_1) = (2\varrho^1_1, 3\varrho^1_1), \quad H^1_2(\varrho^1_2) = H^1_{a_2}(\varrho^1_2) = (4\varrho^1_2, 5\varrho^1_2),$$
$$H^1_3(\varrho^1_3) = H^1_{a_3}(\varrho^1_3) + H^1_{a_5}(\varrho^1_3) = (3\varrho^1_3, 5\varrho^1_3), \quad H^1_4(\varrho^1_4) = H^1_{a_4}(\varrho^1_4) = (5\varrho^1_4, 6\varrho^1_4).$$

Setting $\varrho = (\varrho^1_1, \varrho^1_2, \varrho^1_3, \varrho^1_4) = (3, 2, 1, 4)$. Obviously, $\varrho \in Q$ is a feasible network flow. Thus,

$$H^1_1(\varrho^1_1) = (6, 9), \quad H^1_2(\varrho^1_2) = (8, 10), \quad H^1_3(\varrho^1_3) = (3, 5), \quad H^1_4(\varrho^1_4) = (20, 24).$$

Now, we verify that the feasible flow ϱ is a strict vector equilibrium flow. For OD pairs $\{\mathcal{N}_1, \mathcal{N}_4\}$, $\{\mathcal{N}_3, \mathcal{N}_4\}$, we choose $\bar{\Theta} = (0, 1)$ and $\bar{\Xi} = (1, 1)$; it holds that

$$\begin{cases} \text{cone}(H^1_2(\varrho^1_2) + \mathbb{R}^2_+ - H^1_1(\varrho^1_1)) \cap (\text{cone}(\bar{\Theta} - \bar{\Xi}) \backslash \{0\}) = \emptyset \\ H_2(\varrho) - H_1(\varrho) \neq 0 \end{cases}$$

and

$$\begin{cases} \text{cone}(H_4^1(\varrho_4^1) + \mathbb{R}_+^2 - H_3^1(\varrho_3^1)) \cap (\text{cone}(\bar{\Theta} - \bar{\Xi}) \backslash \{0\}) = \emptyset \\ H_4(\varrho) - H_3(\varrho) \neq 0 \end{cases}$$

Since the arc flow $\varrho_{c_5}^1$ is

$$\varrho_{c_5}^1 = \sum_{i \in \mathcal{I}} \sum_{k \in \omega_i} \delta_{ck} \varrho_k^j = \varrho_1^1 + \varrho_3^1 = 4 = \bar{\varrho}_{c_5}^1,$$

it follows from Definition 3 that arc c_5 is a saturated arc of flow ϱ, paths 3 and 5 are saturated paths of flow ϱ. Hence, by Definition 6, we obtain that ϱ is a strict vector equilibrium flow.

Next, we show that $\varrho = (\varrho_1^1, \varrho_2^1, \varrho_3^1, \varrho_4^1) = (3, 2, 1, 4)$ is a solution of the following variational inequality:

$$\langle H(\varrho), (\chi - \varrho)' \rangle \notin -\mathbb{R}_+^2 \backslash \{0\}, \forall \chi \in Q. \tag{10}$$

We take $\chi = (\chi_1^1, \chi_2^1, \chi_3^1, \chi_4^1) = (3, 3, 1, 4)$; it is obvious that $\chi \in Q$. Direct computation shows that

$$\begin{aligned}
&\langle H(\varrho), (\chi - \varrho)' \rangle \\
&= \langle (H_1^1(\varrho_1^1), H_2^1(\varrho_2^1), H_3^1(\varrho_3^1), H_4^1(\varrho_4^1)), (\chi_1^1 - \varrho_1^1, \chi_2^1 - \varrho_2^1, \chi_3^1 - \varrho_3^1, \chi_4^1 - \varrho_4^1)' \rangle \\
&= \left\langle \begin{pmatrix} 2\varrho_1^1 & 4\varrho_2^1 & 3\varrho_3^1 & 5\varrho_4^1 \\ 3\varrho_1^1 & 5\varrho_2^1 & 5\varrho_3^1 & 6\varrho_4^1 \end{pmatrix}, \begin{pmatrix} 3 - \varrho_1^1, & 3 - \varrho_2^1, & 1 - \varrho_3^1, & 4 - \varrho_4^1 \end{pmatrix}' \right\rangle \\
&= \begin{pmatrix} 2\varrho_1^1(3 - \varrho_1^1) + 4\varrho_2^1(3 - \varrho_2^1) + 3\varrho_3^1(1 - \varrho_3^1) + 5\varrho_4^1(4 - \varrho_4^1) \\ 3\varrho_1^1(3 - \varrho_1^1) + 5\varrho_2^1(3 - \varrho_2^1) + 5\varrho_3^1(1 - \varrho_3^1) + 6\varrho_4^1(4 - \varrho_4^1) \end{pmatrix}' \\
&= \begin{pmatrix} 8, 10 \end{pmatrix} \notin -\mathbb{R}_+^2 \backslash \{0\}.
\end{aligned}$$

Therefore, the strict vector equilibrium flow $\varrho = (3, 2, 1, 4)$ is a solution of variational inequality (10).

6. Conclusions

This paper considered the strict network equilibrium flows for a multi-product supply–demand network with capacity constraints and uncertain demands, where the uncertain demands were assumed to be in a closed interval. The main contribution is theoretical in nature, in that we derived the existence results of strict network equilibrium flows by virtue of the Fan–Browder fixed point theorem based on a single criterion cost function and showed that such a strict network equilibrium flow for a multi-product supply–demand network with capacity constraints and uncertain demands is equivalent to a vector variational inequality when considering both real value and vector value cost function, and we developed a scalarization method for strict vector equilibrium flows based on vector-valued cost functions by using Gerstewitz's function. The results obtained in this paper provide a viable approach to solving the multi-product, multi-criteria supply–demand network equilibrium model with capacity constraints and uncertain demands.

In this paper, we presented an analytical framework based on the concept of network equilibrium to attain optimal performance for a multi-product supply–demand network with capacity constraints and uncertain demands. In future research, designing concrete simulation experiments and developing substantial areas of applications of the theory presented in our paper should be considered as a potential research project.

Author Contributions: Conceptualization, R.L. and G.Y.; methodology, R.L. and G.Y.; writing—original draft preparation, R.L.; writing—review and editing, R.L. and G.Y. All authors have read and agreed to the published version of the manuscript.

Funding: This research was supported by the National Natural Science Foundation of China (No.12361062;No.62366001) and the Natural Science Foundation of the Ningxia Province of China (No.2023AAC02053).

Data Availability Statement: No new data were created or analyzed in this study. Data sharing is not applicable to this article.

Conflicts of Interest: The authors declare no conflicts of interest.

References

1. Wardrop, J.G. Some theoretical aspects of road traffic research. *Proc. Inst. Civ. Eng.* **1952**, *1*, 325–378. [CrossRef]
2. Dong, J.; Zhang, D.; Nagurney, A. A supply chain network equilibrium model with random demands. *Eur. J. Oper. Res.* **2004**, *15* 194–212. [CrossRef]
3. Meng, Q.; Huang, Y.K.; Chen, R.L. A note on supply chain network equilibrium models. *Transport. Res. E* **2008**, *184*, 13–2 [CrossRef]
4. Nagurney, A. On the relationship between supply chain and transportation network equilibria: A supernetwork equivalenc with computations. *Transport. Res. E* **2006**, *42*, 293–316. [CrossRef]
5. Nagurney, A.; Dong, J.; Zhang, D. A supply chain network equilibrium model. *Transport. Res. E* **2002**, *38*, 281–303. [CrossRef]
6. Chen, G.Y.; Yen, N.D. *On the Variational Inequality Model for Network Equilibrium*; Internal Report 196; Department of Mathematic University of Pisa: Pisa, Italy, 1993; pp. 724–735.
7. Cheng, T.C.E.; Wu, Y.N. A multi-product, multi-criterion supply-demand network equilibrium model. *Oper. Res.* **2006**, *5* 544–554. [CrossRef]
8. Khanh, P.O.; Luu, L.M. On the existence of solutions to vector quasivariational inequalities and quasicomplementarity problem with applications to traffic network equilibria. *J. Optimiz. Theory Appl.* **2004**, *123*, 533–548. [CrossRef]
9. Khanh, P.O.; Luu, L.M. Some existence results for quasi-variational inequalities involving multifunctions and applications t traffic equilibrium problems. *J. Global Optim.* **2005**, *32*, 551–568. [CrossRef]
10. Lin, Z. The study of traffic equilibrium problems with capacity constraints of arcs. *Nonlinear Anal. Real World Appl.* **2010**, *1* 2280–2284. [CrossRef]
11. Lin, Z. On existence of vector equilibrium flows with capacity constraints of arcs. *Nonlinear Anal. Theory Methods Appl.* **2010**, *7* 2076–2079. [CrossRef]
12. Li, S.J.; Teo, K.L.; Yang, X.Q. Vector equilibrium problems with elastic demands and capacity constraints. *J. Global Optim.* **2007**, *3* 647–660. [CrossRef]
13. Li, S.J.; Teo, K.L.; Yang, X.Q. A remark on a standard and linear vector network equilibriium problem with capacity constraint *Eur. J. Oper. Res.* **2008**, *184*, 13–23. [CrossRef]
14. Li, S.J.; Yang, X.Q.; Chen, G.Y. A note on vector network equilibrium principles. *Math. Methods Oper. Res.* **2008**, *184*, 13–2 [CrossRef]
15. Cao, J.D.; Li, R.X.; Huang, W.; Guo, J.H.; Wei, Y. Traffic network equilibrium problems with demands uncertainty and capacit constraints of arcs by scalarization approaches. *Sci. China Technol. Sci.* **2018**, *61*, 1642–1653. [CrossRef]
16. Wei, H.Z.; Chen, C.R.; Wu, B.W. Vector network equilibrium problems with uncertain demands and capacity constraints of arc *Optim. Lett.* **2021**, *15*, 1113–1131. [CrossRef]
17. Wu, Y.N.; Cheng, T.C.E. Benson efficiency of a multi-criterion network equilibrium model. *Pac. J. Optim.* **2009**, *5*, 443–458.
18. Wu, Y.N.; Peng, Y.C.; Peng, L.; Xu, L. Super efficiency of multicriterion network equilibrium model and vector variationa inequality. *J. Optim. Theory App.* **2012**, *153*, 485–496. [CrossRef]
19. Gong, X.H. Efficiency and Hening efficiency for vector equilibrium problems. *J. Optimiz. Theory App.* **2001**, *108*, 139–15 [CrossRef]
20. Cheng, Y.H.; Fu, W.T. Strong efficiency in a locally convex space. *Math. Methods Oper. Res.* **1999**, *50*, 373–384. [CrossRef]
21. Yu, G.L.; Zhang, Y.; Liu, S.Y. Strong duality with strict efficiency in vector optimization involving nonconvex set-valued maps. *Math.* **2017**, *37*, 223–230.
22. Konnov, I.V. Vector network equilibrium problems with elastic demands. *J. Global Optim.* **2013**, *57*, 521–531. [CrossRef]
23. Browder, F.E. The fixed point theory of multi-valued mappings in topological vector spaces. *Math. Ann.* **1968**, *177*, 283–30 [CrossRef]
24. Fan, K. A generalization of Tychonoffs fixed point theorem. *Math. Ann.* **1961**, *142*, 305–310. [CrossRef]
25. Chen, G.Y.; Goh, C.J.; Yang, X.Q. Vector network equilibrium problems and nonlinear scalarization methods. *Math. Methods Ope Res.* **1999**, *49*, 239–253.
26. Chen, G.Y.; Yang, X.Q. Characterizations of variable domination structures via nonlinear scalarization. *J. Optim. Theory App.* **200** *112*, 97–110. [CrossRef]

axioms

MDPI

Article

Packing Spheres into a Minimum-Height Parabolic Container

Yuriy Stoyan [1], Georgiy Yaskov [1], Tetyana Romanova [1,2], Igor Litvinchev [3], José Manuel Velarde Cantú [4,*] and Mauricio López Acosta [4]

1 Pidhornyi Institute of Mechanical Engineering Problems, vul. Komunalnykiv, 2/10, 61046 Kharkiv, Ukraine; stoyan@ipmach.kharkov.ua (Y.S.); yaskov@ipmach.kharkov.ua (G.Y.); t.romanova@leeds.ac.uk (T.R.)
2 Leeds University Business School, University of Leeds, Leeds LS2 9JT, UK
3 Graduate Program in Systems Engineering, Nuevo Leon State University (UANL), Av. Universidad s/n, Col. Ciudad Universitaria, San Nicolas de los Garza 66455, Mexico; igorlitvinchev@gmail.com
4 Technological Institute of Sonora (ITSON), Navojoa-City 85870, Mexico; mlopeza@itson.edu.mx
* Correspondence: jose.velarde@itson.edu.mx

Abstract: Sphere packing consists of placing several spheres in a container without mutual overlapping. While packing into regular-shape containers is well explored, less attention is focused on containers with nonlinear boundaries, such as ellipsoids or paraboloids. Packing n-dimensional spheres into a minimum-height container bounded by a parabolic surface is formulated. The minimum allowable distances between spheres as well as between spheres and the container boundary are considered. A normalized Φ-function is used for analytical description of the containment constraints. A nonlinear programming model for the packing problem is provided. A solution algorithm based on the feasible directions approach and a decomposition technique is proposed. The computational results for problem instances with various space dimensions, different numbers of spheres and their radii, the minimal allowable distances and the parameters of the parabolic container are presented to demonstrate the efficiency of the proposed approach.

Keywords: packing; multidimensional spheres; paraboloid; Φ-function; nonlinear optimization

MSC: 05B40; 52C15; 52C17; 90C26

1. Introduction

Sphere packing is a well-studied area of research that involves arranging identical or non-identical spherical items within a given volume (container), subject to certain constraints. This problem has a wide range of applications, making it a versatile and important topic in both theoretical and practical contexts [1]. According to the typology of packing and cutting problems introduced in [2], packing problems are considered in two main formulations: open dimension problems (ODP) and knapsack problems. The ODP is aimed at optimizing the dimension(s) of a container, while packing the maximum number of identical objects or maximizing the total volume of packed objects is a knapsack problem. Typically, continuous nonlinear programming (NLP) models are used to formulate an ODP, while for the knapsack problem, mixed integer NLP models are implemented.

Our interest in irregular containers is motivated by the following considerations. Packing problems for regular-shaped containers (rectangles, circles) are well studied for 2D objects, such as circles [3], ovals [4,5] and ellipses [6–8]. Rich theoretical and empirical results are presented in these papers, where various NLP models and exact/heuristic/metaheuristic solution techniques are accompanied by extensive computational experiments to demonstrate the efficiency of the proposed approaches. Different NLP models and solution algorithms for packing 3D objects into regular 3D containers (cuboids, spheres, and cylinders) can be found, e.g., in [9,10] for spherical and in [11] for ellipsoidal shapes, together with corresponding empirical results obtained for different numbers of objects and various container shapes. In all these works, geometric tools for modeling non-overlapping and containment conditions in Euclidean and non-Euclidean [4,5,9] metrics are provided. Algorithms based on combinations of smart heuristics and nonlinear optimization techniques are designed. The proposed solution approaches allow us to find the optimal solutions for small and medium-sized instances, while reasonably good feasible solutions are obtained for larger instances. However, as was highlighted in review papers [12–15], challenging packing problems in irregular containers are much less investigated. Several publications consider ellipsoidal containers [16,17], while there are only a few works focusing on packing for multiply connected domains and cardioids [18] and paraboloids [19]. Sphere packing into irregular containers arises in, e.g., material science [20,21] and nanotechnology [22]. A simple application of sphere packing into a parabolic container can be found in the food industry [23], where a parabolic dish container must be designed to store candies. To the best of our knowledge, in the n-dimensional case, the problem of packing spheres into an optimized parabolic container has not been considered before.

A brief review of the papers related to packing in irregular containers is provided below. An approach to constructing analytical non-intersection and containment conditions for non-oriented convex two-dimensional objects, defined by second-order curves, is proposed in [16]. This approach was applied to a problem of packing circles into an ellipse and minimizing the ellipse size. Packing algorithms applied to different-shaped two-dimensional domains are studied in [18], including rectangles, ellipses, crosses, multiply connected domains and even cardioid shapes. The authors introduce a novel approach centered around the concept of "image" disks, enabling the study of packing within fixed containers. Paper [19] focuses on Apollonian circle packing. The method has been used in various models, including geological sheer bands. Mathematical equations utilizing hyperbolas and ellipses are applied. This approach is applicable to a generic, closed, convex contour given the parametrization of its boundary. In the aerospace industry, packing into parabolic or other non-traditional containers is a significant challenge due to the specific shapes and delicate nature of many components [19]. The container is divided by horizontal racks into sub-containers. The proposed mathematical model considers the minimal and maximal allowable distances between objects subject to the behavior constraints of the mechanical system (equilibrium, moments of inertia and stability constraints). The paper describes a solution approach based on the multistart strategy, Shor's r-algorithm and accelerated search for the terminal nodes of the solution tree.

The objective of this paper is to develop a modeling and solutions approach to an ODP that consists of packing n-dimensional spheres into a minimum-height parabolic container. For analytical description of the placement constraints, the Φ-function technique [24] is used. This approach allows us to present mathematical models of optimized packing problems in the form of continuous NLP problems. To describe the containment of spheres in the parabolic container, a new Φ-function for the nD case is introduced. Using a section of the nD paraboloid and spheres by hyperplanes, it is iteratively reduced to consideration of the Φ-function in the 2D case. The Φ-function involves an additional variable parameter that is dynamically adjusted by solving a one-dimensional optimization problem. An approach based on the feasible directions method (FDM) [25] is developed considering the special properties of the Φ-function.

The contributions of the paper are as follows:

- A new problem of packing spheres into a minimum-height parabolic container in n-dimensional space;
- A new Φ-function for analytical description of the containment of a sphere into a parabolic container in n-dimensional space;
- An approach based on the feasible directions scheme considering the specific characteristics of the Φ-function.
- New benchmarks for various sphere radii and the parameters of the parabolic container in n-dimensional space for $n = 2, 3, 4, 5$.

The remainder of this paper is organized as follows. Section 2 describes the problem statement. Section 3 introduces geometrical tools for constructing a mathematical model of the packing problem. A mathematical model is formulated in Section 4. Section 5 presents a modification of the FDM. Section 6 provides the computational results for problem instances in several dimensions, with different numbers of spheres and their radii and various values of the minimal allowable distances and the parameters of the parabolic container. Section 7 concludes.

2. Problem Statement

Let a convex domain bounded by a parabolic surface and a hyperplane be defined in n-dimensional Euclidean space $\mathbb{R}^n$ as follows: $P_n(h) = P_n \cap H_n$ where $P_n = \{X = (x_1, x_2, \ldots, x_n) \in \mathbb{R}^n : \sum\limits_{i=1}^{n-1} x_i^2 - 2px_n \leq 0\}$ and $H_n = \{X \in \mathbb{R}^n : x_n - h \leq 0\}$, i.e.,

$$P_n(h) = \{X \in \mathbb{R}^n : \sum_{i=1}^{n-1} x_i^2 - 2px_n \leq 0,\ x_n - h \leq 0\}. \tag{1}$$

Further, we refer the domain $P_n(h)$ to a container of variable height $h > 0$, with the predefined parameter $p > 0$.

And let a collection of nD spheres $S_j, j \in J = \{1, 2, \ldots, m\}$ with variable centers $y_j = (y_{j1}, y_{j2}, \ldots, y_{jn}) \in \mathbb{R}^n, j \in J$, be given and denoted by

$$S_j(y_j) = \{X \in \mathbb{R}^n : \|X - y_j\| - r_j \leq 0\}, j \in J. \tag{2}$$

In addition, the minimal allowable distances between each pair of spheres $S_t(y_t)$ and $S_j(y_j)$, as well as between a sphere $S_j(y_j)$ and the boundary of the container $P_n(h)$, are given, respectively, as δ_{tj} and δ_j.

Packing problem. Pack spheres $S_j(y_j), j \in J$, into the minimum-height container $P_n(h)$, considering the minimal allowable distances $\delta_{tj}, t < j \in J$, and $\delta_j, j \in J$.

To describe the placement constraints of the packing problem analytically, the Φ-function technique is used. For the reader's convenience, the main definitions of the phi-function are provided in Appendix A. More details can be found in, e.g., Chapter 15 of [26].

The distance constraint for two spheres can be defined using the adjusted Φ-function in the form

$$\Phi_{tj}(y_t, y_j) = \|y_t - y_j\|^2 - (r_t + r_j + \delta_{tj})^2.$$

Therefore,

$$\Phi_{tj}(y_t, y_j) \geq 0 \Leftrightarrow dist(S_t(y_t), S_j(y_j)) \geq \delta_{tj},$$

$$dist(S_t(y_t), S_j(y_j)) = \min_{a \in S_t(y_t), b \in S_j(y_j)} \|a - b\|,\ a = (a_1, a_2, \ldots, a_n), b = (b_1, b_2, \ldots, b_n).$$

In Section 3, we introduce a continuous and everywhere defined function that allows us to describe the containment of each sphere into a parabolic container.

3. The Φ-Function for Containment Constraints

To describe analytically the containment constraint, $S_j(y_j) \subset P_n(h) \Leftrightarrow \text{int}S_j(y_j) \cap P_n^*(h) = \varnothing$, let us define a phi-function for an nD sphere $S_j(y_j)$ (2) and the object $P_n^*(h) = \mathbb{R}^n \setminus \text{int}P_n(h)$ (the compliment of the container $P_n(h)$ interior to the whole space $\mathbb{R}^n$).

Note that $P_n^*(h) = P_n^* \cup H_n^*$, where $H_n = \{X \in \mathbb{R}^n : x_n - h \geq 0\}$ and

$$P_n^* = \{X \in \mathbb{R}^n : \sum_{i=1}^{n-1} x_i^2 - 2px_n \geq 0\}. \tag{3}$$

A Φ-function for a sphere $S_j(y_j)$ and the object $P_n^*(h)$ can be stated in the following form:

$$\Phi_j^*(y_j, y_{jn}, h) = \min\{ \Phi_j(y_j) - \delta_j, \Theta_j(y_{jn}, h)\}, \tag{4}$$

where $\Phi_j(y_j)$ is a Φ-function for a sphere $S_j(y_j)$ and the object P_n^*, and $\Theta_j(y_{jn}, h) = h - y_{jn} - r_j$ is a Φ-function for a sphere $S_j(y_j)$ and a half-space H_n^*.

Let us define a Φ-function for a sphere $S_j(y_j)$ and the object P_n^*. We state that $S_j(y_j) \subset P_n$ if $P_n^* \cap \text{int}S_j(y_j) = \varnothing$.

Firstly, construct an $(n-1)$D hyperplane K_1 passing through axis Ox_n of P_n and the center $y_j = (y_{j1}, y_{j2}, \ldots, y_{jn})$ of the nD sphere $S_j(y_j)$. Then, the section $K_1 \cap P_n$ yields the parabolic domain

$$P_{n-1} = \{X \in \mathbb{R}^{n-1} : -z_1^2 - \sum_{i=3}^{n-1} x_i^2 + 2px_n = 0\},$$

where $z_1 = \pm\sqrt{x_1^2 + x_2^2}$, while the section $K_1 \cap S_j(y_j)$ yields the $(n-1)$D-sphere $S_{j(n-1)}$ of radius r_j and the center $y_{j(n-1)} = (z_{j1}, y_{j3}, \ldots, y_{jn}), z_{j1} = \text{sign}(y_{j1})\sqrt{y_{j1}^2 + y_{j2}^2}$.

By analogy, an $(n-2)$D-hyperplane K_2 passing through axis Ox_n of P_{n-1} and the center $y_{j(n-1)}$ of $S_{j(n-1)}$ is constructed. Then, the section $K_2 \cap P_{n-1}$ yields the parabolic domain

$$P_{n-2} = \{X \in \mathbb{R}^{n-2} : - z_2^2 - \sum_{i=4}^{n-1} x_i^2 + 2px_n = 0\},$$

where $z_2 = \pm\sqrt{\sum_{i=1}^{3} x_i^2}$, while the section $K_2 \cap S_{j(n-1)}$ yields the $(n-2)$D-sphere $S_{j(n-2)}$ of radius r_j and the center $y_{j(n-2)} = (z_{j2}, y_{j4}, \ldots, y_{jn}), z_{j2} = \text{sign}(z_{j1})\sqrt{\sum_{i=1}^{3} y_{ji}^2}$.

The iterative procedure continues until the 2D parabolic domain $P_2 = \left\{X \in \mathbb{R}^2 : -z_{(n-1)}^2 + 2px_n = 0\right\}$ with $z_{n-1} = \text{sign}(z_{j(n-2)})\sqrt{\sum_{i=1}^{n-1} x_i^2}$ and the 2D sphere S_{j2} of radius r_j and the center $(z_{j(n-1)}, y_{jn})$ are obtained.

Note that $\text{sign}(z_{j(n-2)}) = \text{sign}(z_{j(n-3)}) = \ldots = \text{sign}(z_{j1}) = \text{sign}(y_{j1})$. This means that the construction of the Φ-function for the object P_n^* (3) and the nD sphere $S_j(y_j)$ (2) is reduced to deriving the Φ-function for the object P_2^* and the 2D sphere S_{j2}.

Let an equation of the tangent 03D2$_j$ to the boundary of P_2 be given

$$f(z_{n-1}, x_n, t_j) = -z_{n-1}\sqrt{2p}t_j + p(x_n + t_j^2) = 0$$

for any $t_j \in \mathbb{R}^1$. Note that different tangents 03D2$_j(t_j)$ can be generated for different values of t_j.

Let a point $(z_{n-1}, x_n) = (t_j\sqrt{2p}, t_j^2)$ be a tangency point of 03D2$_j(t_j)$ and the boundary of P_2. Then, the normal equation of 03D2$_j(t_j)$ takes the form

$$f_j(z_{n-1}, x_n, t_j) = -\frac{z_{n-1}\sqrt{2p}t_j - p(x_n + t_j^2)}{\sqrt{2pt_j^2 + p^2}} = 0. \tag{5}$$

Thus, the normalized Φ-function for the 2D sphere S_{j2} and the half-plane specified by the inequality $f_j(z_{n-1}, x_n, t_j) \leq 0$ can be defined as follows:

$$\Phi_{j0}(z_{j(n-1)}, y_{jn}, t_j) = f_j(z_{j(n-1)}, y_{jn}, t_j) - r_j. \tag{6}$$

Substituting $f_j(z_{n-1}, x_n, t_j)$ (5) into (6), the function $\omega_j(t_j) = (-z_{j,(n-1)}\sqrt{2p}t_j - p(y_{jn} + t_j^2))/\sqrt{2pt_j^2 + p^2}$ can be defined.

Then, we search for t_j^* at which the function $\omega_j(t_j^*)$ reaches the minimum corresponding to the distance between the center of S_{j2} and the boundary of P_2. Consequently, bearing in mind $z_{n-1} = \pm\sqrt{\sum_{i=1}^{n-1} x_i^2}$, the normalized Φ-function for $S_j(y_j)$ and P_2^* (3) takes the form

$$\Phi_j(y_j) = \min_{t_j \in [\beta_{j1}, \beta_{j2}]} \Phi_{j0}(z_{j(n-1)}, y_{jn}, t_j). \tag{7}$$

To find the optimal value of $t_j \in [\beta_{j1}, \beta_{j2}]$, a bisection technique [25] is applied.

Let us consider two cases for the locations of the center of S_{j2} with respect to P_2: case 1 corresponds to $(z_{j(n-1)}, y_{jn}) \in P_2$; case 2 corresponds to $(z_{j(n-1)}, y_{jn}) \notin P_2$.

Assume $(\widehat{z}_{j(n-1)}, \widehat{y}_{jn}) \in P_2$ and $\widehat{y}_{jn} \geq 0$. Here, $(\widehat{z}_{j(n-1)}, \widehat{y}_{jn})$ is the center point of the sphere S_{j2}. Let us consider two tangents 03D2$_j(t_{j1})$ and 03D2$_j(t_{j2})$ to frP_2 at points $A(\sqrt{2p\widehat{y}_{jn}}, \widehat{y}_{jn})$ and $B(\widehat{z}_{j(n-1)}, \widehat{z}^{\,2}_{j(n-1)}/(2p))$ for corresponding $t_{j1} = \sqrt{\widehat{y}_{jn}}$ and $t_{j2} = \widehat{z}_{j(n-1)}/\sqrt{2p}$ (Figure 1). Therefore, $[\beta_{j1}, \beta_{j2}] = [\widehat{z}_{j(n-1)}/\sqrt{2p}, \sqrt{\widehat{y}_{jn}}]$.

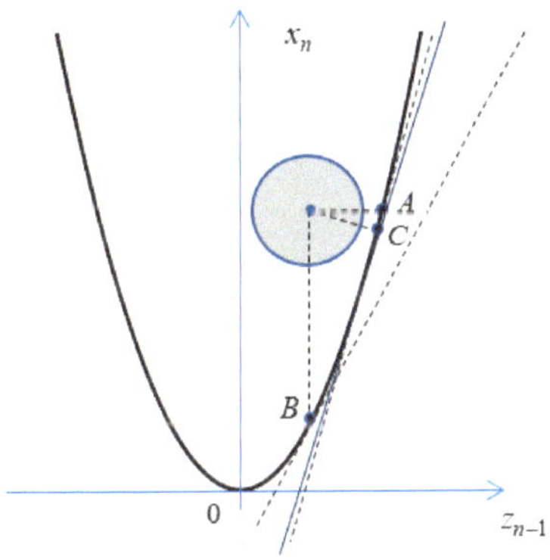

Figure 1. Illustration of interaction of S_{j2} and the boundary of P_2 in 2D.

In Figure 1, the segment AB of the parabola that corresponds to $t_j \in [\beta_{j1}, \beta_{j2}]$ is shown. The tangent 03D2$_j(t_j^*)$ at the point $C(\sqrt{2p\widehat{y}_{jn}}, \widehat{y}_{jn}, t_j^*)$ corresponds to $t_j^* = \underset{t_j \in [\beta_{j1}, \beta_{j2}]}{\operatorname{argmin}} \Phi_{j0}(\widehat{z}_{j(n-1)}, \widehat{y}_{jn}, t_j)$.

Let $(z_{j(n-1)}, y_{jn}) \in P_2$ (case 1); then,

$$[\beta_{j1}, \beta_{j2}] = \begin{cases} [\frac{z_{j(n-1)}}{\sqrt{2p}}, \sqrt{y_{jn}}] \text{ if } z_{j(n-1)} \geq 0 \text{ (case 1.1)} \\ [-\sqrt{y_{jn}}, \frac{z_{j(n-1)}}{\sqrt{2p}}] \text{ if } z_{j(n-1)} < 0 \text{ (case 1.2)} \end{cases} . \tag{8}$$

Let $(z_{j(n-1)}, y_{jn}) \notin P_2$(case 2); then,

$$[\beta_{j1}, \beta_{j2}] = \begin{cases} [\sqrt{y_{jn}}, \frac{z_{j(n-1)}}{\sqrt{2p}}] \text{ if } z_{j(n-1)} \geq 0,\ y_{jn} \geq 0 \text{ (case 2.1)} \\ [-\frac{|z_{j(n-1)}|}{\sqrt{2p}}, \frac{|z_{j(n-1)}|}{\sqrt{2p}}] \text{ if } y_{jn} < 0 \text{ (case 2.2)} \\ [-\frac{z_{j(n-1)}}{\sqrt{2p}}, \sqrt{y_{jn}}] \text{ if } z_{j(n-1)} < 0,\ y_{jn} \geq 0 \text{ (case 2.3)} \end{cases} . \tag{9}$$

Figure 2 illustrates two cases: a sphere is arranged inside the parabolic domain P_2 $\Phi_j(y_j) \geq 0$(Figure 2a), and a sphere is arranged outside the parabolic domain P_2, $\Phi_j(y_j) < 0$ (Figure 2b).

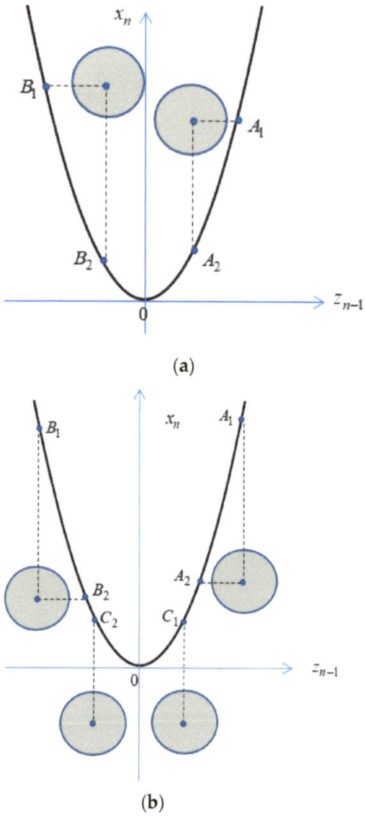

Figure 2. Arrangements of S_{j2} with respect to P_2 for different $t_j \in [\beta_{j1}, \beta_{j2}]$: (**a**) $(z_{j(n-1)}, y_{jn}) \in P_2$; (**b**) $(z_{j(n-1)}, y_{jn}) \notin P_2$.

In particular, to calculate $t \in [\beta_{j1}, \beta_{j2}]$, case 1.1 (8) is used for the parabolic segment A_1, A_2, while case 1.2 (8) is used for the parabolic segment B_1, B_2 (Figure 2a); case 2.1 (9) is used for the parabolic segment A_1, A_2, case 2.2 (9) is used for the parabolic segment C_1, C_2, and case 2.3 in (9) is used for the parabolic segment B_1, B_2 (Figure 2b).

4. Mathematical Model

A mathematical model of the packing problem can be formulated as follows:

$$\min_{Y,h} h \tag{10}$$

subject to

$$\begin{aligned} \Phi_{tj}(y_t, y_j) &= \|y_t - y_j\|^2 - (r_t + r_j + \delta_{tj})^2 \geq 0,\ t < j \in J \\ \Phi_j^*(y_j, y_{jn}, h) &= \min\{\ \Phi_j(y_j) - \delta_j, \Theta_j(y_{jn}, h)\} \geq 0,\ j \in J \end{aligned} \tag{11}$$

where $Y = (y_1, y_2, \ldots, y_m) \in \mathbb{R}^{mn}$.

Note that the inequality $\Phi_j^*(y_j, y_{jn}, h) \geq 0$ in (11) is equivalent to the system of inequalities $\Phi_j(y_j) - \delta_j \geq 0$ and $\Theta_j(y_{jn}, h) \geq 0$ and ensures the arrangement of the nD sphere $S_j(y_j)$ fully inside the parabolic container $P_n(h)$.

The number of inequalities specifying the feasible region (11) is equal to $\chi = 0.5m(m-1) + 2m$. The dimensions of a solution matrix for W are $(mn+1) \times \chi$.

Thus, the number of inequalities/variables in the inequality system (11) is increased drastically by enlarging m. The solution matrix is strongly sparse. The problem is NP-hard [27].

Since we cannot define t_j explicitly, then we need to solve the optimization problems of the form (7) for each sphere $S_j(y_j)$ on each iteration of the solution process of the problem (10), (11). We do not use the solvers BARON [28] or IPOPT [29] for the original problem because of the dynamic nature of the Φ-function. Instead, a modification of the feasible directions method is developed.

The following solution strategy scheme for the problem (10), (11) is proposed:

1. Take a sufficiently large height h^0 of the container that guarantees a placement of spheres $S_j(y_j)$, $j \in J$, fully inside $P(h^0)$;
2. Generate the sphere centers $y_j^0, j \in J$, randomly so that $S_j(y_j^0) \subset P(h^0), j \in J, \Phi_{tj}(y_t^0, y_j^0) \geq 0$, $t < j \in J$;
3. Apply the modification of the FDM to solve the problem (10), (11) for a set of feasible starting points.
4. Select the best solution.

5. Solution Algorithm

In contrast to the problem considered in [30], in this study, the spheres are of different radii, and the Φ-function describing the containment of a sphere into the container involves an additional parameter, which is dynamically changed during the optimization process.

The FDM for the problem (10), (11) is implemented using the iterative formula

$$Y^{k+1} = Y^k + \lambda^k Z^k, \; k = 0,1,2,\ldots, \tag{12}$$

where $Y^0 \in W$ (for $k = 0$) is a starting feasible point, Z^k is a search direction vector, and $\lambda^k > 0$ is a parameter that controls the step size.

Let $\varphi(Y) = h$ denote the objective function. A vector Z^k in (12) should provide $Y^k \in W$. To search for a vector Z^k, the following linear programming problem is solved:

$$(Z^k, \alpha^k) = \text{argmax}\alpha \text{ s.t. } 03D2 = (Z, \alpha) \in G^k, \tag{13}$$

$$G^k = \Big\{(Z,\alpha) \in \mathbb{R}^{\chi+1} : \nabla\Phi_{tj}(y_t^k, y_j^k) \cdot Z \geq \alpha, \; t < j \in J, \; \nabla\Phi_j(y_j^k) \cdot Z \geq \alpha,$$
$$\nabla\Theta_j(y_{jn}^k, h^k) \cdot Z \geq \alpha, -\nabla\varphi(h^k) \cdot Z \geq \alpha, \; |z_i| \leq 1, \; i \in \Xi = \{1,2,\ldots,\chi\}\Big\}, \tag{14}$$

where $Z = (z_1, z_2, \ldots, z_\chi) \in \mathbb{R}^\chi$, $\alpha \in \mathbb{R}^1$, $\Phi_j(y_j^k)$ is constructed according to (7).

Note that in (11), each $\Phi_{tj}(y_t, y_j)$ is an inverse convex function, and each $\Theta_j(y_{jn}, h)$ is a linear function. The vector of feasible directions may be orthogonal to the gradients of these constraints, so the inequalities $\nabla\Phi_{tj}(y_t^k, y_j^k) \cdot Z \geq \alpha$ and $\nabla\Theta_j(y_{jn}^k, h^k) \cdot Z \geq \alpha$ in (14) are replaced with $\nabla\Phi_{tj}(y_t^k, y_j^k) \cdot Z \geq 0$ and $\nabla\Theta_j(y_{jn}^k, h^k) \cdot Z \geq 0$, respectively.

To reduce the dimension of the problem (10), (11) and consequently of the problem (13), (14), a decomposition strategy [31] based on the degree of feasibility is employed.

When considering all the placed spheres, the majority of them are positioned at a significant distance from each other. The inequalities in the system (11) are satisfied with a considerable margin, and they can be disregarded when forming the optimization vector. At each step, only a subset of inequalities from the system (11) is considered, specifically those with a low degree of feasibility. During the optimization process, a parameter $\varepsilon^k > 0$ determining the degree of feasibility is adjusted dynamically, regulating the system constraints at each step. If an inequality is not considered in the optimization process at a certain step but is violated during the step's execution, the admissibility is controlled using the parameter λ^k in iterative Formula (12).

Let us denote the inverse convex and linear inequalities in the system (11) as $g_s(Y) \geq 0$, $s \in \Lambda \subset \Xi$ and the rest of the inequalities as $q_s(Y) \geq 0$, $s \in \Gamma \subset \Xi$ $(\Lambda \cup \Gamma = \Xi, \Lambda \cap$

$\Gamma = \varnothing$), and let $E^k = \left\{s \in \Lambda : 0 \le g_s(Y^k) \le \varepsilon^k\right\}$ and $B^k = \left\{s \in \Gamma : 0 \le q_s(Y^k) \le \varepsilon^k\right\}$. Here, $\varepsilon^k > 0$ is a threshold value. Then, the problem (13), (14) takes the form

$$(Z^k, \alpha^k) = \text{argmax}\alpha \text{ s.t. } (Z, \alpha) \in G_k, \tag{15}$$

$$G_k = \Big\{(Z, \alpha) \in \mathbb{R}^{\chi+1} : \nabla g_i(Y^k) \cdot Z \ge 0,\ i \in E^k,\ \nabla q_i(Y^k) \cdot Z \ge \alpha,\ i \in B^k, \\ -\nabla \varphi(h^k) \cdot Z \ge \alpha,\ |z_i| \le 1,\ i \in \Xi\Big\}. \tag{16}$$

Taking into account the problem (15), (16), the following step-by-step algorithm is employed to solve problem (10), (11).

Step 1. Take a sufficiently large height h^0 of the container that guarantees a placement of spheres $S_j(y_j), j \in J$, fully inside $P_n(h^0)$.

Step 2. Generate the sphere centers $y_j^0, j \in J$, randomly so that $S_j\left(y_j^0\right) \subset P_n(h^0)$, $j \in J, \Phi_{tj}(y_t^0, y_j^0) \ge 0,\ t < j \in J$.

Step 3. Set $k := 0, \varepsilon^0 := \varepsilon > 0$.

Step 4. Define the functions $\Phi_j(y_j^k)$ (7).

Step 5. Form the sets E^k, B^k.

Step 6. Set $\lambda^k := 1$.

Step 7. Calculate (Z^k, α^k) (Problem (15), (16)).

Step 8. If $\alpha^k \le 0$ (there is no a feasible direction decreasing the objective $\varphi(Y) = h$), then set $\varepsilon^k := \varepsilon^k/2$ and go to Step 5; otherwise ($\alpha^k > 0$), go to Step 9.

Step 9. Set $Y^{k+1} := Y^k + \lambda^k Z^k$ (12).

Step 10. If $Y^{k+1} \notin W$, then set $\lambda^k := \lambda^k/2$ and go to Step 9; otherwise, go to Step 11.

Step 11. If $\|Y^{k+1} - Y^k\| < \tau$, then stop algorithm; otherwise, set $\varepsilon^{k+1} := \varepsilon^k, k := k+1$ and go to Step 4.

A schematic illustration of the proposed approach is shown in Figure 3. Three consecutive iterations of the FDM in 2D are illustrated in Figure 3a–c. An arrangement of 2D spheres corresponding to the stop criterion, $\|Y^{k+1} - Y^k\| < \tau$, at Step 11 is shown in Figure 3d.

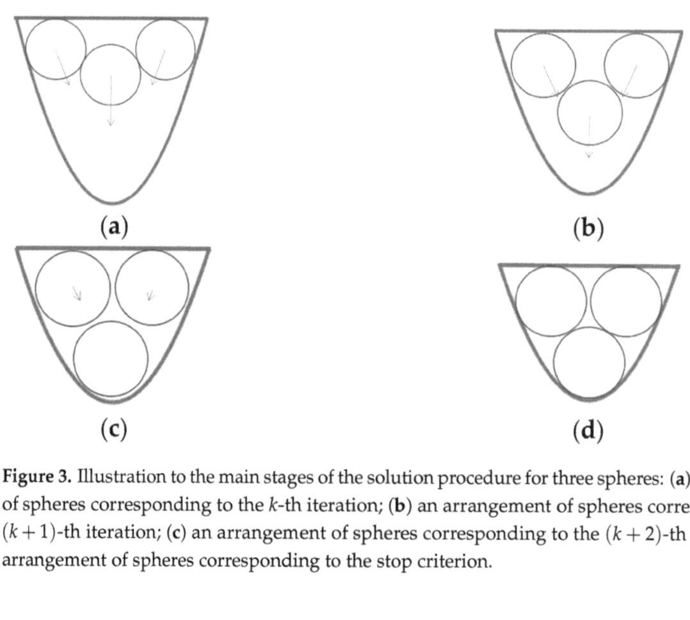

Figure 3. Illustration to the main stages of the solution procedure for three spheres: (**a**) an arrangement of spheres corresponding to the k-th iteration; (**b**) an arrangement of spheres corresponding to the $(k+1)$-th iteration; (**c**) an arrangement of spheres corresponding to the $(k+2)$-th iteration; (**d**) an arrangement of spheres corresponding to the stop criterion.

A flowchart corresponding to the solution strategy is presented in Figure 4.

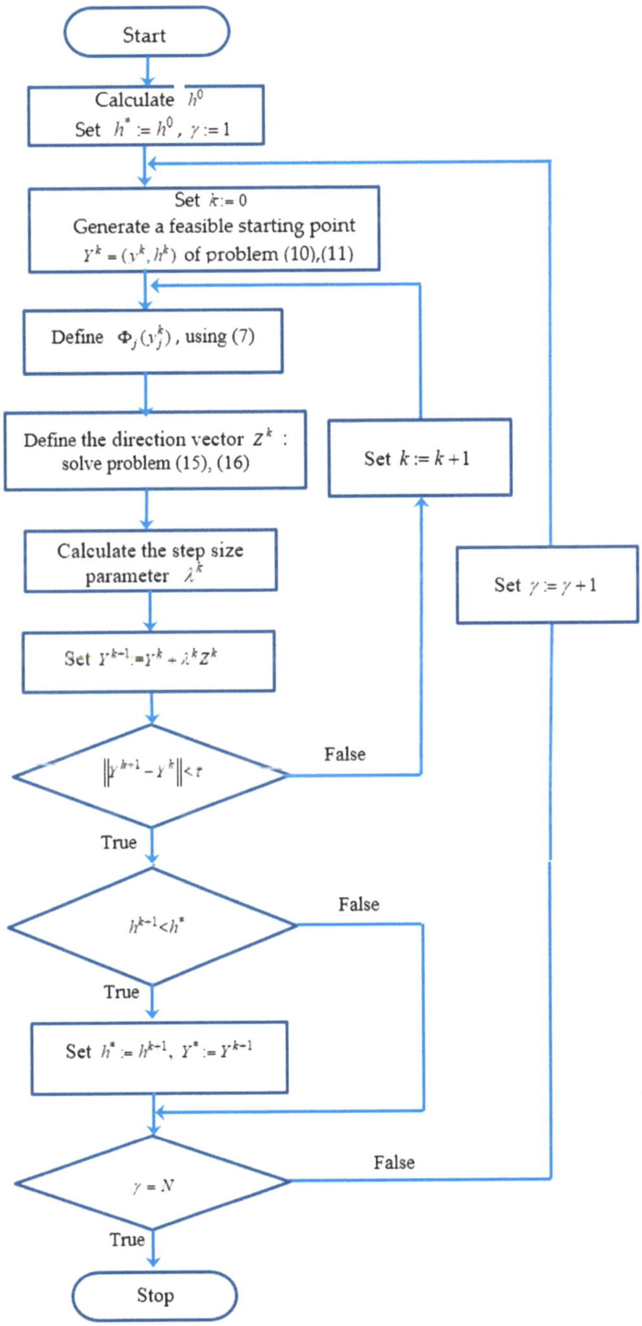

Figure 4. The flowchart of the main algorithm.

6. Computational Results

The proposed approach was numerically tested for eleven instances of the problem (9), (10) with different (a) dimensions, n = 2, 3, 4, 5; (b) numbers of spheres, m = 50, 100, 200; b) radii, $r_j, j = 1, \ldots, m$; (c) minimal allowable distances, δ_{tj}, δ_j, $t < j \in J, j \in J$; (d) parameters p of the parabolic container, $p = 1, 2, 5, 10$. For all the examples, we set $\varepsilon^0 = \varepsilon = 1, \tau = 10^{-6}$. For each problem instance, 10 starting points were generated. The computations were performed using an Intel® Core™ i3-6100T, 3.20 GHz, 8.00 GB of RAM.

Example 1. $n = 2$, $m = 100$, $r_j = 1.177$, $j = 1, \ldots, 24$, $r_j = 1.117$, $i = 25, \ldots, 48$, $r_j = 0.97$, $j = 49, \ldots, 72$, $r_j = 0.927$, $j = 73, \ldots, 96$, $r_j = 0.86$, $j = 97, \ldots, 100$; $p = 1$, $\delta_{tj} = \delta_j = 0$. The best solution found by our algorithm for 5 min is $h* = 37.518079$.

Example 2. $n = 2$, $m = 200$, $r_j = 1.177$, $j = 1, \ldots, 24$, $r_j = 1.117$, $j = 25, \ldots, 48$, $r_j = 0.97$, $j = 49, \ldots, 72$, $r_j = 0.927$, $j = 73, \ldots, 96$, $r_j = 0.86$, $j = 97, \ldots, 120$, $r_j = 0.812$, $j = 121, \ldots, 144$, $r_j = 0.762$, $j = 145, \ldots, 168$, $r_j = 0.726$, $j = 169, \ldots, 192$, $r_j = 0.664$, $j = 193, \ldots, 200$; $p = 1$, $\delta_{tj} = \delta_j = 0$. The best solution found by our algorithm for 20 min is $h* = 49.511450$.

Example 3. $n = 2$, $m = 100$, the radii are as in Example 1; $p = 5$, $\delta_{tj} = \delta_j = 0$, $h^0 = 30$. The best solution found by our algorithm for 5 min is $h* = 21.695951$.

Example 4. $n = 2$, $m = 50$, $\{r_j, j = 1, \ldots, 50\}$ = {1.177, 1.177, 1.177, 1.177, 1.117, 1.117, 1.117, 1.117, 1.117, 0.970, 0.970, 0.970, 0.970, 0.970, 0.927, 0.927, 0.927, 0.927, 0.927, 0.860, 0.860, 0.860, 0.860, 0.860, 0.812, 0.812, 0.812, 0.812, 0.812, 0.762, 0.762, 0.762, 0.762, 0.762, 0.726, 0.726, 0.726, 0.726, 0.726, 0.664, 0.664, 0.664, 0.664, 0.664, 0.627, 0.627, 0.627, 0.627, 0.627}, $p = 5$, $\delta_{tj} \in [0.1, 0.5]$, $\delta_j \in [0.1, 1]$. The best solution found by our algorithm for 2 min is $h* = 11.577099$.

The corresponding placements of the spheres in Examples 1–4 are shown in Figure 5a–d.

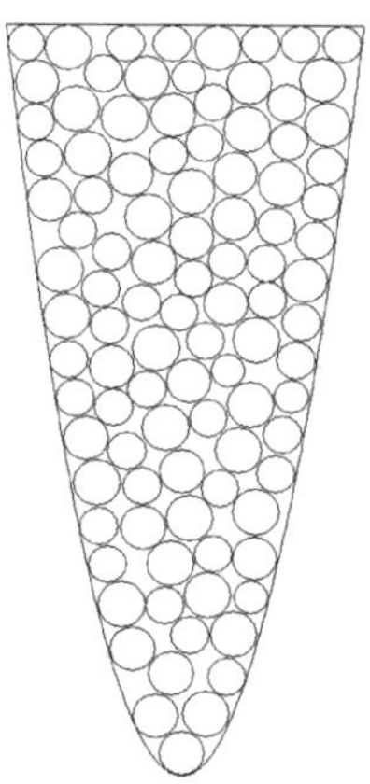

(a)

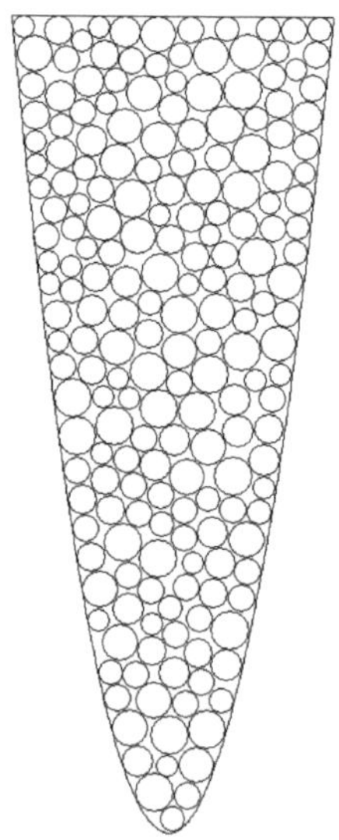

(b)

Figure 5. *Cont.*

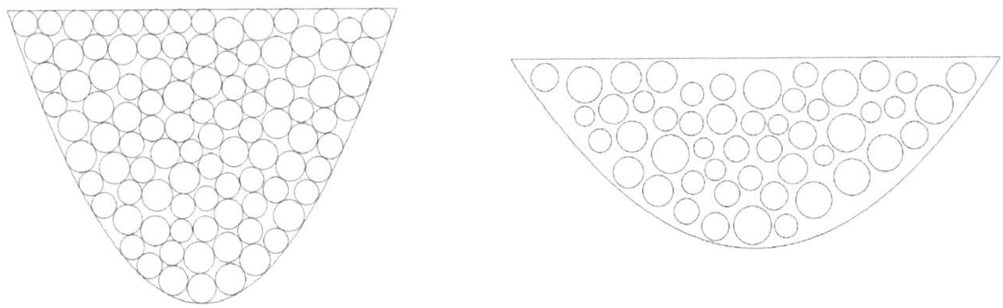

(c) (d)

Figure 5. Optimized arrangement of 2D spheres: (**a**) Example 1; (**b**) Example 2; (**c**) Example 3; (**d**) Example 4.

Example 5. $n = 3, m = 50, \{r_j, j = 1, \ldots, 50\} = \{0.527, 0.564, 0.566, 0.592, 0.612,$ $0.680, 0.747, 0.760, 0.807, 0.845, 0.850, 0.853, 0.855, 0.868, 0.887, 0.891, 0.934, 0.947, 0.955,$ $0.961, 1.044, 1.085, 1.180, 1.189, 1.210, 1.229, 1.237, 1.274, 1.275, 1.281, 1.292, 1.309, 1.325,$ $1.374, 1.399, 1.404, 1.430, 1.484, 1.491, 1.493, 1.525, 1.551, 1.551, 1.636, 1.670, 1.739, 1.819,$ $2.050, 2.171\}$, $p = 2, \delta_{tj} = \delta_j = 0$. The best solution found by our algorithm for 3 min is $h* = 11.927860$.

Example 6. $n = 3, m = 200, \{r_j, j = 1, \ldots, 200\} = \{2.171, 2.171, 2.171, 2.171, 2.050,$ $2.050, 2.050, 2.050, 1.819, 1.819, 1.819, 1.819, 1.739, 1.739, 1.739, 1.739, 1.670, 1.670, 1.670,$ $1.670, 1.636, 1.636, 1.636, 1.636, 1.551, 1.551, 1.551, 1.551, 1.551, 1.551, 1.551, 1.551, 1.525,$ $1.525, 1.525, 1.525, 1.493, 1.493, 1.493, 1.493, 1.491, 1.491, 1.491, 1.491, 1.484, 1.484, 1.484,$ $1.484, 1.484, 1.484, 1.484, 1.484, 1.430, 1.430, 1.430, 1.430, 1.404, 1.404, 1.404, 1.404, 1.399,$ $1.399, 1.399, 1.399, 1.374, 1.374, 1.374, 1.374, 1.325, 1.325, 1.325, 1.325, 1.309, 1.309, 1.309,$ $1.309, 1.292, 1.292, 1.292, 1.292, 1.281, 1.281, 1.281, 1.281, 1.275, 1.275, 1.275, 1.275, 1.274,$ $1.274, 1.274, 1.274, 1.237, 1.237, 1.237, 1.237, 1.229, 1.229, 1.229, 1.229, 1.210, 1.210, 1.210,$ $1.210, 1.189, 1.189, 1.189, 1.189, 1.180, 1.180, 1.180, 1.180, 1.085, 1.085, 1.085, 1.085, 1.044,$ $1.044, 1.044, 1.044, 0.961, 0.961, 0.961, 0.961, 0.955, 0.955, 0.955, 0.955, 0.947, 0.947, 0.947,$ $0.947, 0.934, 0.934, 0.934, 0.934, 0.891, 0.891, 0.891, 0.891, 0.887, 0.887, 0.887, 0.887, 0.868,$ $0.868, 0.868, 0.868, 0.855, 0.855, 0.855, 0.855, 0.853, 0.853, 0.853, 0.853, 0.850, 0.850, 0.850,$ $0.850, 0.845, 0.845, 0.845, 0.845, 0.807, 0.807, 0.807, 0.807, 0.760, 0.760, 0.760, 0.760, 0.747,$ $0.747, 0.747, 0.747, 0.680, 0.680, 0.680, 0.680, 0.612, 0.612, 0.612, 0.612, 0.592, 0.592, 0.592,$ $0.592, 0.566, 0.566, 0.566, 0.566, 0.564, 0.564, 0.564, 0.564, 0.527, 0.527, 0.527, 0.527\}$, $p = 2$, $\delta_{tj} = \delta_j = 0$. The best solution found by our algorithm for 35 min is $h* = 22.612047$.

Example 7. $n = 3, m = 100, \{r_j, j = 1, \ldots, 100\} = \{2.171, 2.171, 2.050, 2.050, 1.819,$ $1.819, 1.739, 1.739, 1.670, 1.670, 1.636, 1.636, 1.551, 1.551, 1.551, 1.551, 1.525, 1.525, 1.493,$ $1.493, 1.491, 1.491, 1.484, 1.484, 1.484, 1.484, 1.430, 1.430, 1.404, 1.404, 1.399, 1.399, 1.374,$ $1.374, 1.325, 1.325, 1.309, 1.309, 1.292, 1.292, 1.281, 1.281, 1.275, 1.275, 1.274, 1.274, 1.237,$ $1.237, 1.229, 1.229, 1.210, 1.210, 1.189, 1.189, 1.180, 1.180, 1.085, 1.085, 1.044, 1.044, 0.961,$ $0.961, 0.955, 0.955, 0.947, 0.947, 0.934, 0.934, 0.891, 0.891, 0.887, 0.887, 0.868, 0.868, 0.855,$ $0.855, 0.853, 0.853, 0.850, 0.850, 0.845, 0.845, 0.807, 0.807, 0.760, 0.760, 0.747, 0.747, 0.680,$ $0.680, 0.612, 0.612, 0.592, 0.592, 0.566, 0.566, 0.564, 0.564, 0.527, 0.527\}$, $p = 10, \delta_{tj} = \delta_j = 0$, $h^0 = 40$. The best solution found by our algorithm for 10 min is $h* = 7.577422$.

Example 8. $n = 3, m = 100$, the radii are as in Example 7; $p = 10, \delta_{tj} \in [0.1, 0.5]$, $\delta_j \in [0.1, 1]$. The best solution found by our algorithm for 10 min is $h* = 9.727001$.

The corresponding placements of the 3D spheres in Examples 5–8 are shown in Figure 6a–d.

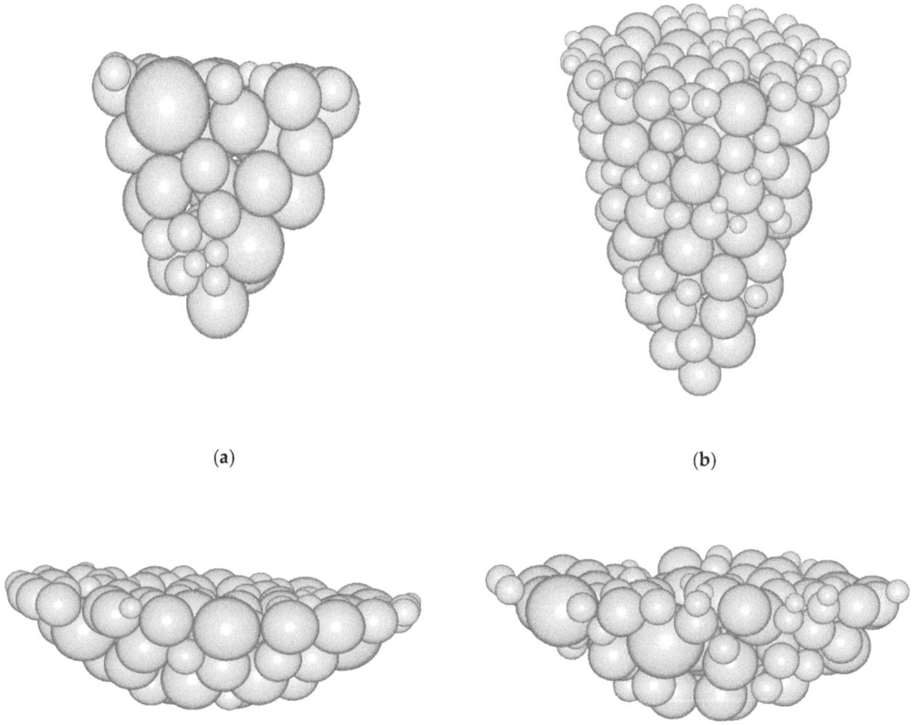

(a) (b) (c) (d)

Figure 6. Optimized arrangement of 3D spheres: (**a**) Example 5; (**b**) Example 6; (**c**) Example 7; (**d**) Example 8.

Example 9. $n = 4, m = 100$, the radii are as in Example 7; $p = 2, \delta_{tj} = \delta_j = 0$. The best solution found by our algorithm for 15 min is $h* = 22.612047$.

Example 10. $n = 4, m = 200$, the radii are as in Example 6; $p = 2, \delta_{tj} = \delta_j = 0$. The best solution found by our algorithm for 45 min is $h* = 14.628068$.

Example 11. $n = 4, m = 200$, the radii are as in Example 6; $p = 2, \delta_{tj} = \delta_j = 0$. The best solution found by our algorithm for 55 min is $h* = 11.791466$.

7. Conclusions

Employing mathematical models offers a structured and systematic approach to problem-solving, facilitating precise analysis and prediction of outcomes [32]. In this paper, a mathematical model for packing different spheres into a minimal-height parabolic container is proposed. Non-overlapping and containment conditions are formulated using the phi-function approach. The minimal allowed distance between the spheres and the boundary of the container is considered. The problem belongs to a class of irregular packing problems due to the nonstandard container shape.

To solve the corresponding nonlinear optimization problem, a feasible directions approach combined with the hot start technique is proposed. A decomposition scheme is applied to reduce the number of constraints in the subproblem used to find the search direction. Numerical experiments are provided to demonstrate the efficiency of the proposed solution scheme. A detailed description of the problem instances and corresponding solutions are reported to form a benchmark for future research.

Our future research is focused on the following issues. The number of non-overlapping constraints grows quadratically with an increase in the number of spheres, resulting in a large-scale optimization problem. These constraints have a specific structure which can be used either for direct solution of the original problem or to construct tight bounds for the optimal objective [33,34]. The proposed approach is based on modeling the interactions between the spheres and the boundary of the parabolic container. It also can be applied to a broader class of containers, e.g., circular hyperboloids (single- and double-sheeted), spheroids or ellipsoids. Packing problems on surfaces [35] can also be considered, as well as various applications of spherical systems [36] and logistics [37]. Some results in these directions are forthcoming.

Author Contributions: Conceptualization, G.Y., Y.S., T.R., I.L. and J.M.V.C.; methodology, G.Y., Y.S., T.R. and I.L.; software, Y.S. and M.L.A.; validation, G.Y. and J.M.V.C.; formal analysis, G.Y., Y.S., T.R. and I.L.; investigation, G.Y., Y.S., T.R., I.L., J.M.V.C. and M.L.A.; resources, G.Y. and Y.S.; data curation, G.Y. and Y.S.; writing—original draft preparation, G.Y., Y.S., T.R., I.L., J.M.V.C. and M.L.A.; writing, review and editing, G.Y., Y.S., T.R., I.L., J.M.V.C. and M.L.A.; visualization, G.Y. and Y.S.; supervision, G.Y., Y.S., T.R., I.L. and J.M.V.C.; project administration, J.M.V.C., M.L.A. and Y.S.; funding acquisition, J.M.V.C., M.L.A. and G.Y. All authors have read and agreed to the published version of the manuscript.

Funding: The second and the third authors were partially supported by the Volkswagen Foundation (grant #97775), and the third author was supported by the British Academy (grant #100072), while the last two authors were partially supported by the Technological Institute of Sonora (ITSON), Mexico, through the Research Promotion and Support Program (PROFAPI 2024).

Data Availability Statement: The data presented in this study are available on request from the corresponding authors.

Acknowledgments: The authors would like to thank anonymous referees for constructive and positive comments.

Conflicts of Interest: The authors declare no conflicts of interest.

Appendix A

For the reader's convenience, the main definitions and properties of the Φ-functions are provided. More details can be found, e.g., in [23,25], Chapter 15.

Let A be a geometric object. The position of the object A is defined by a motion vector $u_A = (v_A, \theta_A)$, where v_A is a translation vector and θ_A is a vector of the rotation parameters. The object A, rotated by θ_A and translated by v_A, is denoted by $A(u_A)$.

For two objects $A(u_A)$ and $B(u_B)$, a Φ-function allows us to distinguish the following three cases: (a) $A(u_A)$ and $B(u_B)$ do not overlap, i.e., $A(u_A)$ and $B(u_B)$ do not have any common points; (b) $A(u_A)$ and $B(u_B)$ are in contact, i.e., $A(u_A)$ and $B(u_B)$ have only common frontier points; (c) $A(u_A)$ and $B(u_B)$ are overlapping so that $A(u_A)$ and $B(u_B)$ have common interior points.

Following the definition [26], a continuous and everywhere defined function, denoted by $\Phi^{AB}(u_A, u_B)$, is called a Φ-function of the objects $A(u_A)$ and $B(u_B)$ if the following conditions are fulfilled:

$$\Phi^{AB}(u_A, u_B) > 0, \text{ for } A(u_A) \cap B(u_B) = \varnothing$$

$$\Phi^{AB}(u_A, u_B) = 0, \text{ for } \mathrm{int}A(u_A) \cap \mathrm{int}B(u_B) = \varnothing \text{ and } frA(u_A) \cap frB(u_B) \neq \varnothing;$$

$$\Phi^{AB}(u_A, u_B) < 0, \text{ for } \mathrm{int}A(u_A) \cap \mathrm{int}B(u_B) \neq \varnothing.$$

Here, frA denotes the boundary of the object A, while $\mathrm{int}A$ stands for its interior. Thus,

$$\Phi^{AB}(u_A, u_B) \geq 0 \Leftrightarrow \mathrm{int}A(u_A) \cap \mathrm{int}B(u_B) = \varnothing$$

To describe a containment constraint $A(u_A) \subset B(u_B)$, a phi-function for the objects A and $B^* = R^n \backslash \mathrm{int}B$ is used.

In the case, $\Phi^{AB^*}(u_A, u_B) \geq 0 \Leftrightarrow \mathrm{int}A(u_A) \cap \mathrm{int}B^*(u_B) = \varnothing \Leftrightarrow A(u_A) \subset B(u_B)$.

To model the distance constraints for two objects, the normalized Φ-function is applied.

A Φ-function of the objects $A(u_A)$ and $B(u_B)$ is called a normalized phi-function $\widetilde{\Phi}^{AB}(u_A, u_B)$ if the values of the function coincide with the Euclidean distance between the objects $A(u_A)$ and $B(u_B)$ when $\mathrm{int}A(u_A) \cap \mathrm{int}B(u_B) = \varnothing$.

Therefore,

$$\widetilde{\Phi}^{AB}(u_A, u_B) \geq \rho \Leftrightarrow dist\{A(u_A), B(u_B)\} \geq \rho.$$

References

1. Scheithauer, G. Introduction to Cutting and Packing Optimization. In *International Series in Operations Research & Management Science*; Springer: Cham, Switzerland, 2018; Volume 263, pp. 385–405. [CrossRef]
2. Wäscher, G.; Haußner, H.; Schumann, H. An improved typology of cutting and packing problems. *Eur. J. Oper. Res.* **2007**, *183* 1109–1130. [CrossRef]
3. Castillo, I.; Kampas, F.J.; Pinter, J.D. Solving circle packing problems by global optimization: Numerical results and industrial applications. *Eur. J. Oper. Res.* **2008**, *191*, 786–802. [CrossRef]
4. Kampas, F.J.; Castillo, I.; Pinter, J.D. Optimized ellipse packings in regular polygons. *Optim. Lett.* **2019**, *13*, 1583–1613. [CrossRef]
5. Kallrath, J.; Rebennack, S. Cutting ellipses from area-minimizing rectangles. *J. Glob. Optim.* **2014**, *59*, 405–437. [CrossRef]
6. Pankratov, A.; Romanova, T.; Litvinchev, I. Packing ellipses in an optimized rectangular container. *Wirel. Netw.* **2020**, *26* 4869–4879. [CrossRef]
7. Kampas, F.J.; Pintér, J.D.; Castillo, I. Packing ovals in optimized regular polygons. *J. Glob. Optim.* **2020**, *77*, 175–196. [CrossRef]
8. Castillo, I.; Pintér, J.D.; Kampas, F.J. The boundary-to-boundary p-dispersion configuration problem with oval objects. *J. Oper Res. Soc.* **2024**, 1–11. [CrossRef]
9. Elser, V. Packing spheres in high dimensions with moderate computational effort. *Phys. Rev. E* **2023**, *108*, 034117. [CrossRef] [PubMed]
10. Litvinchev, I.; Fischer, A.; Romanova, T.; Stetsyuk, P. A new class of irregular packing problems reducible to sphere packing in arbitrary norms. *Mathematics* **2024**, *12*, 935. [CrossRef]
11. Kallrath, J. Packing ellipsoids into volume-minimizing rectangular boxes. *J. Glob. Optim.* **2017**, *67*, 151–185. [CrossRef]
12. Leao, A.A.S.; Toledo, F.M.B.; Oliveira, J.F.; Carravilla, M.A.; Alvarez-Valdes, R. Irregular packing problems: A review of mathematical models. *Eur. J. Oper. Res.* **2020**, *282*, 803–822. [CrossRef]
13. Guo, B.; Zhang, Y.; Hu, J.; Li, J.; Wu, F.; Peng, Q.; Zhang, Q. Two-dimensional irregular packing problems: A review. *Front. Mech. Eng.* **2022**, *8*, 966691.
14. Rao, Y.; Luo, Q. Intelligent algorithms for irregular packing problem. In *Intelligent Algorithms for Packing and Cutting Problem*, Engineering Applications of Computational Methods; Springer: Singapore, 2022; Volume 10. [CrossRef]
15. Lamas-Fernandez, C.; Bennell, J.A.; Martinez-Sykora, A. Voxel-based solution Aapproaches to the three-dimensional irregular packing problem. *Oper. Res.* **2023**, *71*, 1298–1317. [CrossRef]
16. Gil, M.; Patsuk, V. Phi-functions for objects bounded by the second-order curves and their application to packing problems. In *Smart Technologies in Urban Engineering*; Arsenyeva, O., Romanova, T., Sukhonos, M., Tsegelnyk, Y., Eds.; STUE 2022, Lecture Notes in Networks and Systems; Springer: Cham, Switzerland, 2023; Volume 536. [CrossRef]
17. Santini, C.; Mangini, F.; Frezza, F. Apollonian Packing of Circles within Ellipses. *Algorithms* **2023**, *16*, 129. [CrossRef]
18. Amore, P.; De la Cruz, D.; Hernandez, V.; Rincon, I.; Zarate, U. Circle packing in arbitrary domains featured. *Phys. Fluids* **2023**, *35*, 127112. [CrossRef]
19. Kovalenko, A.A.; Romanova, T.E.; Stetsyuk, P.I. Balance Layout Problem for 3D-Objects: Mathematical Model and Solution Methods. *Cybern. Syst. Anal.* **2015**, *51*, 556–565. [CrossRef]
20. Burtseva, L.; Pestryakov, A.; Romero, R.; Valdez, B. Petranovskii. Some aspects of computer approaches to simulation of bimodal sphere packing in material engineering. *Adv. Mater. Res.* **2014**, *1040*, 585–591. [CrossRef]
21. Ungson, Y.; Burtseva, L.; Garcia-Curiel, E.R.; Valdez Salas, B.; Flores-Rios, B.L.; Werner, F.; Petranovskii, V. Filling of Irregular Channels with Round Cross-Section: Modeling Aspects to Study the Properties of Porous Materials. *Materials* **2018**, *11*, 1901. [CrossRef] [PubMed]
22. Burtseva, L.; Valdez Salas, B.; Romero, R.; Werner, F. Recent advances on modelling of structures of multi-component mixtures using a sphere packing approach. *Int. J. Nanotechnol.* **2016**, *13*, 44–59. [CrossRef]
23. Available online: https://olofly.com/product/huni-badger-parabolic-dish-container/ (accessed on 7 April 2023).
24. Chernov, N.; Stoyan, Y.; Romanova, T. Mathematical model and efficient algorithms for object packing problem. *Comput. Geom. Theory Appl.* **2010**, *43*, 535–553. [CrossRef]
25. Nocedal, J.; Wright, S.J. *Numerical Optimization*; Springer Series in Operations Research and Financial Engineering; Springer: New York, NY, USA, 2006.
26. Kallrath, J. *Business Optimization Using Mathematical Programming*; Springer: London, UK, 2021; ISBN 978-3-030-73237-0.

7. Chen, D. Sphere Packing Problem. In *Encyclopedia of Algorithms*; Kao, M.Y., Ed.; Springer: Boston, MA, USA, 2008. [CrossRef]
8. Sahinidis, N. BARON User Manual v. 2024.5.8. Available online: https://minlp.com/downloads/docs/baron%20manual.pdf (accessed on 8 May 2024).
9. IPOPT: Documentation. Available online: https://coin-or.github.io/Ipopt/ (accessed on 14 January 2023).
0. Stoyan, Y.; Yaskov, G. Packing congruent hyperspheres into a hypersphere. *J. Glob. Optim.* **2012**, *52*, 855–868. [CrossRef]
1. Romanova, T.; Stoyan, Y.; Pankratov, A.; Litvinchev, I.; Marmolejo, J.A. Decomposition algorithm for irregular placement problems. In *Intelligent Computing and Optimization, Proceedings of the 2nd International Conference on Intelligent Computing and Optimization 2019 (ICO 2019), Koh Samui, Thailand, 3–4 October 2019*; Intelligent Systems and Computing; Springer: Cham, Switzerland, 2019; Volume 1072, pp. 214–221.
2. Animasaun, I.L.; Shah, N.A.; Wakif, A.; Mahanthesh, B.; Sivaraj, R.; Koriko, O.K. *Ratio of Momentum Diffusivity to Thermal Diffusivity: Introduction, Meta-Analysis, and Scrutinization*; Chapman and Hall/CRC: New York, NY, USA, 2022. [CrossRef]
3. Litvinchev, I.S. Refinement of Lagrangian bounds in optimization problems. *Comput. Math. Math. Phys.* **2007**, *47*, 1101–1108. [CrossRef]
4. Litvinchev, I.; Rangel, S.; Saucedo, J. A Lagrangian bound for many-to-many assignment problems. *J. Comb. Optim.* **2010**, *19*, 241–257. [CrossRef]
5. Lai, X.; Yue, D.; Hao, J.K.; Glover, F.; Lü, Z. Iterated dynamic neighborhood search for packing equal circles on a sphere. *Comput. Oper. Res.* **2023**, *151*, 106121. [CrossRef]
6. Asadi Jafari, M.H.; Zarastvand, M.; Zhou, J. Doubly curved truss core composite shell system for broadband diffuse acoustic insulation. *J. Vib. Control* **2023**. [CrossRef]
7. Bulat, A.; Kiseleva, E.; Hart, L.; Prytomanova, O. Generalized Models of Logistics Problems and Approaches to Their Solution Based on the Synthesis of the Theory of Optimal Partitioning and Neuro-Fuzzy Technologies. In *System Analysis and Artificial Intelligence*; Studies in Computational Intelligence; Zgurovsky, M., Pankratova, N., Eds.; Springer: Cham, Switzerland, 2023; Volume 1107, pp. 355–376. [CrossRef]

axioms

MDPI

Article

Simultaneous Method for Solving Certain Systems of Matrix Equations with Two Unknowns

Predrag S. Stanimirović [1,2], Miroslav Ćirić [1], Spyridon D. Mourtas [2,3], Gradimir V. Milovanović [1,4] and Milena J. Petrović [5,*]

[1] Faculty of Sciences and Mathematics, University of Niš, Višegradska 33, 18108 Niš, Serbia; pecko@pmf.ni.ac.rs (P.S.S.); miroslav.ciric@pmf.edu.rs (M.Ć.); gvm@mi.sanu.ac.rs (G.V.M.)
[2] Laboratory "Hybrid Methods of Modelling and Optimization in Complex Systems", Siberian Federal University, Prosp. Svobodny 79, Krasnoyarsk 660041, Russia
[3] Department of Economics, Division of Mathematics-Informatics and Statistics-Econometrics, National and Kapodistrian University of Athens, Sofokleous 1 Street, 10559 Athens, Greece; spirmour@econ.uoa.gr
[4] Serbian Academy of Sciences and Arts, Kneza Mihaila 35, 11000 Belgrade, Serbia
[5] Faculty of Sciences and Mathematics, University of Priština in Kosovska Mitrovica, Lole Ribara 29, 38220 Kosovska Mitrovica, Serbia
* Correspondence: milena.petrovic@pr.ac.rs

Abstract: Quantitative bisimulations between weighted finite automata are defined as solutions of certain systems of matrix-vector inequalities and equations. In the context of fuzzy automata and max-plus automata, testing the existence of bisimulations and their computing are performed through a sequence of matrices that is built member by member, whereby the next member of the sequence is obtained by solving a particular system of linear matrix-vector inequalities and equations in which the previously computed member appears. By modifying the systems that define bisimulations, systems of matrix-vector inequalities and equations with k unknowns are obtained. Solutions of such systems, in the case of existence, witness to the existence of a certain type of partial equivalence, where it is not required that the word functions computed by two WFAs match on all input words, but only on all input words whose lengths do not exceed k. Solutions of these new systems represent finite sequences of matrices which, in the context of fuzzy automata and max-plus automata, are also computed sequentially, member by member. Here we deal with those systems in the context of WFAs over the field of real numbers and propose a different approach, where all members of the sequence are computed simultaneously. More precisely, we apply a simultaneous approach in solving the corresponding systems of matrix-vector equations with two unknowns. Zeroing neural network (ZNN) neuro-dynamical systems for approximating solutions of heterotypic bisimulations are proposed. Numerical simulations are performed for various random initial states and comparison with the *Matlab*, linear programming solver `linprog`, and the pseudoinverse solution generated by the standard function `pinv` is given.

Keywords: weighted finite automata; zhang neural network; bisimulation; pseudoinverse

MSC: 15A24; 65F20; 68T05

1. Introduction, Motivation and Methodology

One of the main issues in the theory of weighted automata is the *equivalence problem*, which determines whether two weighted automata are equivalent, that is, whether they compute the same word function. In the case of the most general class of weighted automata over a semiring, as well as in the case of most of its subclasses, that problem is undecidable or computationally hard (cf. [1,2]). Only in rare cases it is solvable in polynomial time. This fact has created the need to find methods of determining equivalence that may not work in all cases, but in cases where they are applicable, they can be efficiently realized. The most powerful tools used for these purposes are *bisimulations*. This notion was introduced by Milner [3] and Park [4], in the context of classical non-deterministic automata, as binary relations that can recognize and relate the states of two automata with similar roles, and thus testify the equivalence between them. Around the same time, bisimulations also appeared in mathematics, in modal logic and set theory (cf. [5–11]). It is worth noting that propositional modal logic is the fragment of first-order logic invariant under bisimulation (cf. [5,7]). Bisimulations are employed today in many areas of computer science, such as functional or object-oriented languages, types, data types, domains, databases, compilers optimizations, program analysis, and verification tools. For more information about bisimulations and their applications we refer to [7–16].

With the transition from traditional Boolean-valued systems to quantitative ones, which are more suitable for modeling numerous properties of real-world systems, there was a need for bisimulations to be quantitative as well. Quantitative bisimulations would be modeled by matrices whose entries would measure the similarity of the roles played by the states of considered systems. Such bisimulations were first introduced and studied in [17,18], in the framework of fuzzy finite automata. The approach to bisimulations initiated in this research consists in defining bisimulations as solutions of certain systems of mixed matrix-vector inequalities and equations. That way, the proposed approach reduces the issues of the existence of bisimulations and their computing to the problems of solving the aforementioned matrix-vector inequalities and equations. Subsequently, fundamentally equal approach was used in the contexts of weighted finite automata (WFAs) over additively idempotent semirings [19], max-plus automata [20], and WFAs over the field of real numbers $\mathbb{R}$ [21], as well as in the most general context of WFAs over a semiring [22]. A similar approach to bisimulations was used in [23–27] (see also [28,29]), while various extensions of quantitative bisimulations were introduced in [30–35].

Procedures for testing existence and computing bisimulations developed for fuzzy finite automata in [18], max-plus automata in [20], and WFAs over additively idempotent semirings in [19], consist of building non-increasing sequences of matrices whose infima, if they satisfy certain conditions, represent the greatest bisimulations. The sequences are built member by member, where each member is derived from the previous one, as a solution of a certain system of matrix inequalities in which the previously computed member also appears. On the other hand, the methodology used in computing bisimulations for WFAs over $\mathbb{R}$ is different from the methodology used in computing bisimulations for fuzzy automata, max-plus automata or WFAs over an additively idempotent semiring.

In practical applications of WFAs, it is often not important whether the word functions of two automata have the same values on all input words, but it is enough to test equality on all input words whose length does not exceed a given natural number k. Such kind of partial equivalence, known as k-equivalence, is often more expedient than the classical equivalence. As shown in [20] (see also [35]), systems of matrix-vector inequalities and equations defining bisimulations can be transformed into simpler systems of matrix-vector inequalities and equations with k unknown matrices whose solutions witness to the existence of k-equivalence between two WFAs. In the mentioned papers, an approach similar to the one used in the calculation of bisimulations was used, where a finite sequence of matrices which represents a solution of a new system with k unknowns, is derived by constructing the next member in the sequence from the previous one. However, such a sequential approach has certain drawbacks. Namely, the next member of a sequence depends on the previous one, which does not have to be unique. Inappropriate choices among candidates for previous members can lead to unwanted situation in which the sequence cannot be continued, while for a different choice the sequence can be continued. This means that although our system has a solution, it may happen that this approach fails to give a solution. For this reason, we propose a different, simultaneous approach, where all members of the sequence of the solution are built simultaneously. Particularly, further on in this paper we deal with solving systems with two unknowns, while systems with more unknowns will be the subject of study in our further research.

Systems of matrix-vector equations required in heterotypic bisimulations in this paper are considered over $\mathbb{R}$, and their solutions are obtained as numerical approximations of solutions to systems of linear matrix-vector equations. A special difficulty is the fact that the required matrix-vector equations are not consistent in the general case. In this way, solving those systems is considered as numerical linear algebra problem.

The proposed algorithm for solving the problem is based on the zeroing neural network (ZNN) dynamic models. It should be noted that ZNN dynamic models were originally created for tracking the time-varying matrix inverse [36]. Later iterations of these models were dynamic models for figuring out the time-varying Moore–Penrose [37]. These days, they are also used to solve generalized inversion problems, such as time-varying outer inverse [38], time-varying Drazin inverse [39], and time-varying ML-weighted pseudoinverse [40]. Additionally, real-world ZNN dynamic model applications include image restoration [41], mobile manipulator control [42,43], chaotic systems synchronization [44], and solving time-variant quadratic programming [45]. A comprehensive survey regarding the application of the ZNN model is available at [46].

Designing a ZNN model is the algorithm consisting of two generic stages. In the initial step, it is necessary to declare a proper matrix or vector ZEF, denoted by $E(t)$. The ZEF $E(t)$ is properly defined if its zero point $E(t) = 0$ coincides with the theoretical solution (TSOL) of the problem. Zhang and Guo in the monograph [47] presented an extensive overview of diverse Zhang functions on different domains. Secondly, the dynamic system based on the time-derivative of $E(t)$

$$\dot{E}(t) = -\lambda E(t) \tag{1}$$

needs to be applied. The convergence speed of the dynamics (1) is controlled by the quantity $\lambda \in \mathbb{R}^+$. It is known that (1) converges faster proportionally with increasing values of λ [47]. The principal outcome of the continuous learning principle in (1) is to force the convergence $E(t) \to 0$ as $t \to \infty$ at an exponential rate λ [47,48]. A feasible ZEF is therefore considered as a tracking indicator during the development of ZNN learning in (1). The essence in defining the ZNN dynamical evolution is an efficient control over the underlying system through appropriate ZEF $E(t)$ and the error dynamics (1).

The models developed in [21] for bisimulations between WFAs over $\mathbb{R}$ are established using a ZNN dynamics in resolving systems of vector-matrix inequalities. Our goal in current research is to solve the system consisting of two vector equations and a variable number of linear matrix equations required in heterotypic bisimulations between WFAs. A mixed system of vector-matrix equations is obtained as a particular k-equivalence problem between two WFAs, resulting in a system with two unknown matrices U_1 and U_2. Such system is inconsistent in the vast majority of cases. Starting from the useful property of the ZNN model in generating approximate solutions to matrix-vector inequalities, confirmed in [21], it was a logical decision to define and implement ZNN neuro-dynamical systems for approximating matrix-vector systems arising from the 2-equivalence between WFAs. Since the considered linear matrix-vector system is not inconsistent in general, the ZNN dynamical system is defined utilizing the induced normal system and its best approximate solution generated in terms of the Moore–Penrose inverse. Numerical simulations are performed to verify effectiveness of the proposed ZNN models and comparison with the *Matlab* linear programming solver `linprog` and the pseudoinverse solution generated by the standard function `pinv`.

In this work, given that underlying linear vector-matrix systems are not solvable in the general case, our proposed action is to use the normal system that generates the best approximate solution, based on the utilization of the Moore–Penrose inverse. Finally, ZNN dynamics is applied as the tool for finding the best approximate solution.

Main results derived in this paper are emphasized as follows.

- A specific approach, based on the k-equivalence of two WFAs and simultaneous approach with two unknown matrices, is applied for solving matrix-vector equations required in heterotypic bisimulations between WFAs.

- ZNN neuro-dynamical systems for approximating the k-equivalence problem based on heterotypic bisimulations are proposed.
- Numerical simulation is presented for various random initial states and comparison with the *Matlab* linear programming solver `linprog` and the pseudoinverse solution generated by the standard function `pinv` is given.

Overall structure of our presentation is as follows. After the introduction section, the problem statement, motivation as well as justification of proposed methodology are presented in Section 2. ZNN design for solving matrix-vector systems corresponding to heterotypic bisimulations based on the k-equivalence of two WFAs and simultaneous approach with two unknown matrices is presented in Section 3. Numerical experiments on the k-equivalence problem arising from heterotypic bisimulations with two unknowns are presented in Section 4. The closing section extracts some terminate comments and describes possibilities for further research on this topic.

2. Preliminaries and Problem Formulation

In the sequel, $\mathbb{N}$ will denote the set of natural numbers (without zero), and $\mathbb{N}_0 = \mathbb{N} \cup \{0\}$. For any pair $i, j \in \mathbb{N}_0$ satisfying $i < j$, it will be denoted $[i..j] = \{t \in \mathbb{N}_0 \mid i \leqslant t \leqslant j\}$. Moreover, $\mathfrak{X}$ will be a non-empty and finite set with $r \in \mathbb{N}$ elements, known as *alphabet*, while $\mathfrak{X}^+ = \{x_1 \cdots x_t \mid t \in \mathbb{N},\, x_1, \ldots, x_t \in \mathfrak{X}\}$ will denote all finite sequences of entries from $\mathfrak{X}$, which are termed as *words* over $\mathfrak{X}$, and $\mathfrak{X}^* = \mathfrak{X}^+ \cup \{\varepsilon\}$, such that $\varepsilon \notin \mathfrak{X}^+$ is a symbol standing for the empty word.

A *weighted finite automaton* (WFA) over $\mathbb{R}$ and an input alphabet $\mathfrak{X}$ is defined as a tuple $\mathcal{A} = (m, \sigma^A, \{M_x^A\}_{x \in \mathfrak{X}}, \tau^A)$, in which

- m is a natural number, called the *dimension* of $\mathcal{A}$,
- $\sigma^A \in \mathbb{R}^{1 \times m}$ is the *initial weights vector,*
- $\{M_x^A\}_{x \in \mathfrak{X}} \subset \mathbb{R}^{m \times m}$ is the family of *transition matrices*, each of which corresponds to one input letter $x \in \mathfrak{X}$, and
- $\tau^A \in \mathbb{R}^{m \times 1}$ is the *terminal weights vector.*

The numbers from the set $\{1, \ldots, m\}$ can be interpreted as *states* of the automaton $\mathcal{A}$, and for any state i, the i-th entries of the vectors σ^A and τ^A can be understood as measures of certainty that the automaton will start working from that state or finish working in that state, respectively, while for the states i and j, the (i, j)-th entry of the matrix M_x^A can be understood as a measure of certainty that the automaton will move from the state i to state j under the influence of the input signal represented by the letter x. Inputs of the vector σ^A are called *initial weights*, the entries of τ^A are called *terminal weights*, while the entries of the matrix M_x^A are called *transition weights*.

The *behavior* of the WFA $\mathcal{A}$ is defined as the *word function* $[\![\mathcal{A}]\!] : \mathfrak{X}^* \to \mathbb{R}$ which to any word $u = x_1 \ldots x_s \in \mathfrak{X}^+, x_1, \ldots, x_s \in \mathfrak{X}$ assigns the weight $[\![\mathcal{A}]\!](u)$ which is computed as

$$[\![\mathcal{A}]\!](u) = \sigma^A M_{x_1}^A \cdots M_{x_s}^A \tau^A = \sigma^A M_u^A \tau^A, \tag{2}$$

where $M_u^A = M_{x_1}^A \cdots M_{x_s}^A$, and

$$[\![\mathcal{A}]\!](\varepsilon) = \sigma^A \tau^A. \tag{3}$$

It is said that the automaton $\mathcal{A}$ computes the function $[\![\mathcal{A}]\!]$.

Consider two WFAs $\mathcal{A} = (m, \sigma^A, \{M_x^A\}_{x \in \mathfrak{X}}, \tau^A)$ and $\mathcal{B} = (n, \sigma^B, \{M_x^B\}_{x \in \mathfrak{X}}, \tau^B)$ over $\mathbb{R}$ and an alphabet $\mathfrak{X} = \{x_1, \ldots, x_r\}$. Here, we are interested in systems of matrix and vector equations that define the so-called heterotypic bisimulations between $\mathcal{A}$ and $\mathcal{B}$, as proposed in [22]. These are the following two systems:

$$\begin{aligned}
&\text{(hfbb-1)} \quad \sigma^A = \sigma^B\, U^{\mathrm{T}} \\
&\text{(hfbb-2)} \quad U^{\mathrm{T}} M_x^A = M_x^B\, U^{\mathrm{T}} \quad (x \in \mathfrak{X} = \{x_1, \ldots, x_r\}) \\
&\text{(hfbb-3)} \quad U^{\mathrm{T}} \tau^A = \tau^B
\end{aligned} \tag{4}$$

and

$$
\begin{array}{ll}
\text{(hbfb-1)} & \tau^A = U\,\tau^B \\
\text{(hbfb-2)} & M_x^A\,U = U\,M_x^B \quad (x \in \mathfrak{X} = \{x_1,\dots,x_r\}) \\
\text{(hbfb-3)} & \sigma^A\,U = \sigma^B
\end{array}
\tag{5}
$$

where U is an unknown matrix of dimension $m \times n$. Matrices which are solutions of (4) are called *forward-backward heterotypic bisimulations* (*fbb* for short) between $\mathcal{A}$ and $\mathcal{B}$, and those which are solutions of (5) are *backward-forward heterotypic bisimulations* (*bfb* for short) between $\mathcal{A}$ and $\mathcal{B}$ [22].

Recall that the automata $\mathcal{A}$ and $\mathcal{B}$ are equivalent if $[\![\mathcal{A}]\!](u) = [\![\mathcal{B}]\!](u)$, for every word $u \in \mathfrak{X}^*$. However, in real-word applications it is not always necessary that this equality holds for all words $u \in \mathfrak{X}^*$; it is often enough that it holds for all words of length $|u| \leqslant k$, for a given natural number k. If this relaxed condition holds, then we say that the automata $\mathcal{A}$ and $\mathcal{B}$ are *k-equivalent*, and the equivalence problem can be transformed into the *k-equivalence problem*, which decides whether the automata $\mathcal{A}$ and $\mathcal{B}$ are k-equivalent.

The problem of k-equivalence will be the subject of a separate study, and here we will only present without proofs the way in which the existence of k-equivalence between automata can be witnessed, similar to the way bisimulations testify to the existence of equivalence.

Consider WFAs $\mathcal{A} = (m, \sigma^A, \{M_x^A\}_{x\in\mathfrak{X}}, \tau^A)$ and $\mathcal{B} = (n, \sigma^B, \{M_x^B\}_{x\in\mathfrak{X}}, \tau^B)$ and a sequence of matrices $\{U_i\}_{i\in[0..k]} \subset \mathbb{R}^{m\times n}$ that satisfies the following conditions obtained from the system (4):

$$
\begin{array}{lll}
(\text{fbb-}1^k) & \sigma^A = \sigma^B U_0^{\mathrm{T}}, & \\
(\text{fbb-}2^k) & U_{i-1}^{\mathrm{T}} M_x^A = M_x^B U_i^{\mathrm{T}}, & \text{for all } x \in \mathfrak{X} \text{ and } i \in [1\dots k], \\
(\text{fbb-}3^k) & U_i^{\mathrm{T}} \tau^A = \tau^B, & \text{for each } i \in [0\dots k].
\end{array}
\tag{6}
$$

If such a sequence exists, then the automata $\mathcal{A}$ and $\mathcal{B}$ are k-equivalent. Therefore, our task is to determine existence of matrices $U_0, U_1, \dots, U_k$ satisfying (6). Note that (6) can be understood as a system of equations with $k+1$ unknown matrices $U_0, U_1, \dots, U_k$, so our task is to find a solution to that system.

Sequences of matrices (possibly infinite), defined in a similar way as in (6), were studied in [35], in the circumstances of fuzzy finite automata, and in [20], in the circumstances of max-plus automata. Sequences defined in [35] were called *depth-bounded bisimulations*. The *sequential approach* used in [20], applied to solving the system (6), consists of building a sequence $U_0, U_1, \dots, U_k$ member by member, starting from the zero member U_0, which is computed by solving the equation (fbb-1^k), while the i-th member is computed after the $(i-1)$st member, by solving the system of equations $U_{i-1}^{\mathrm{T}} M_x^A = M_x^B U_i^{\mathrm{T}}$ and $U_i^{\mathrm{T}} \tau^A = \tau^B$, with one unknown U_i.

Since U_{i-1} is not unique in the general case, the disadvantage of the sequential approach is that finding a solution for the unknown U_i depends on the choice of the particular solution for the unknown U_{i-1}. Therefore, it may happen that for some choice of a solution for U_{i-1} there is no solution for the unknown U_i, in which case formation of the sequence interrupts and we cannot find solutions for all the unknowns, although such solutions may exist.

Consequently, the question arises whether it is possible to apply the *simultaneous approach*, where solutions for all unknowns are sought at the same time. Here, we will consider the application of the simultaneous approach for the instance of the system (6) with two unknowns. For the sake of simplicity, we will denote those unknowns by U_1 and U_2, instead of U_0 and U_1, as was done in (6). In other words, we will deal with the following system of matrix-vector equations:

$$\begin{cases} \sigma^B U_1^{\mathrm{T}} = \sigma^A, \\ U_2^{\mathrm{T}} \tau^A = \tau^B, \\ U_1^{\mathrm{T}} M_{x_i}^A = M_{x_i}^B U_2^{\mathrm{T}}, \qquad \text{for each } i \in [1 \ldots r], \end{cases} \tag{7}$$

where U_1 and U_2 are unknown matrices of dimension $m \times n$. In the dual case, we deal with the following system of matrix-vector equations based on (5):

$$\begin{cases} \sigma^A U_2 = \sigma^B, \\ U_1 \tau^B = \tau^A, \\ U_1 M_{x_i}^B = M_{x_i}^A U_2, \qquad \text{for each } i \in [1 \ldots r], \end{cases} \tag{8}$$

where U_1 and U_2 stand for $m \times n$ unknown matrices.

The ZNN evolution is a validated matrix equations solver, confirmed in survey papers [48–50] and in a number of research papers [51–54]. Based on the initial step in the construction of ZNN dynamics, it is necessary to define a proper error function for each matrix and vector equation that is included in the system which is being resolved. The development strategy of ZNN dynamics arising from multiple Zhang error functions (ZEFs) has been utilized in several research articles, of which the most important are [38,55,56]. The ZNN models studied so far with common error functions enabled the convergence of each error function to approximation of its zero. The main idea is to generate an appropriate composite error block matrix which involves individual error functions.

The problem considered in current research is more complex, since systems of matrix and vector equations required in (7) and (8) are not solvable in the general case. The ZNN design is known as a confirmed tool for forcing the underlying error function to zero with global exponential convergence. So, it is expectable that the error functions corresponding to (7) and (8) can be forced to zero, which will lead to approximate solutions of these matrix-vector system.

Global convergence of ZNN design for arbitrary initial state can be used as a confirmation of its efficiency in solving (7) and (8). Details are described in subsequent section.

3. ZNN for Solving the Proposed Systems

This section develops, investigates, and tests two novel ZNN models aimed to solving the matrix-vector systems (4) and (5). Let $\mathcal{A} = \left(m, \sigma^A, \{M_{x_i}^A\}_{x_i \in \mathfrak{X}}, \tau^A\right)$ and $\mathcal{B} = \left(n, \sigma^B, \{M_{x_i}^B\}_{x_i \in \mathfrak{X}}, \tau^B\right)$ be WFAs over $\mathbb{R}$ and the alphabet $\mathfrak{X} = \{x_1, \ldots, x_r\}$, defined by $M_{x_i}^A \in \mathbb{R}^{m \times m}, \sigma^A \in \mathbb{R}^{1 \times m}, \tau^A \in \mathbb{R}^{m \times 1}$ and $M_{x_i}^B \in \mathbb{R}^{n \times n}, \sigma^B \in \mathbb{R}^{1 \times n}, \tau^B \in \mathbb{R}^{n \times 1}, i \in [1..r]$.

The $p \times 1$ vectors with all inputs equal 1 (resp. 0) will be termed as $\mathbf{1}_p$ (resp. $\mathbf{0}_p$), whereas the $p \times r$ matrix with all entries equal to 1 (resp. 0) will be termed as $\mathbf{1}_{p,r}$ and $\mathbf{0}_{p,r}$. Following the conventional notation, the $q \times q$ identity matrix will be marked by I_q, whereas $\mathrm{vec}(), \otimes, ()^{\dagger}$ and $\|\,\|_{\mathrm{F}}$ will mean the vectorization, the Kronecker product product, pseudoinversion, and the Frobenius norm, in that order.

3.1. The ZNNL-hfbb Model

Following the priority (hfbb-3) and (hfbb-1) and then (hfbb-2), let us consider the system (7) as a model for solving (4). In line with the adopted order in solving (4), the next equations must be satisfied:

$$\begin{cases} \sigma^B U_1^{\mathrm{T}}(t) - \sigma^A = \mathbf{0}_m^{\mathrm{T}}, \\ U_2^{\mathrm{T}}(t) \tau^A - \tau^B = \mathbf{0}_n, \\ U_1^{\mathrm{T}}(t) M_{x_i}^A - M_{x_i}^B U_2^{\mathrm{T}}(t) = \mathbf{0}_{n,m}, \end{cases} \tag{9}$$

where $U_1(t), U_2(t) \in \mathbb{R}^{m\times n}$ denote unknown matrices. Exploiting vectorization and the Kronecker product, (9) is reformulated in the equivalent form

$$\begin{cases} (I_m \otimes \sigma^B)\mathrm{vec}(U_1^{\mathrm{T}}(t)) - (\sigma^A)^{\mathrm{T}} = \mathbf{0}_m, \\ ((\tau^A)^{\mathrm{T}} \otimes I_n)\mathrm{vec}(U_2^{\mathrm{T}}(t)) - \tau^B = \mathbf{0}_n, \\ ((M_{x_i}^A)^{\mathrm{T}} \otimes I_n)\mathrm{vec}(U_1^{\mathrm{T}}(t)) - (I_m \otimes M_{x_i}^B)\mathrm{vec}(U_2^{\mathrm{T}}(t)) = \mathbf{0}_{mn}. \end{cases} \tag{10}$$

To calculate solutions $U_1(t), U_2(t)$ in a more efficient manner, (10) must be made simpler. Lemma 1 is restated from [57].

Lemma 1. *For $W \in \mathbb{R}^{m\times n}$, let $\mathrm{vec}(W) \in \mathbb{R}^{mn}$ denote the matrix W vectorization. What is stated below is true:*

$$\mathrm{vec}(W^{\mathrm{T}}) = P\,\mathrm{vec}(W), \tag{11}$$

where $P \in \mathbb{R}^{mn\times mn}$ is an appropriate permutation matrix depended from the number of columns n and rows m of matrix W.

The procedure for generating the permutation matrix P used in (11) is demonstrated in Algorithm 1 from [21]. Using P in generating $\mathrm{vec}(U^{\mathrm{T}}(t))$, (10) can be rewritten as

$$\begin{cases} (I_m \otimes \sigma^B)P\,\mathrm{vec}(U_1(t)) - (\sigma^A)^{\mathrm{T}} = \mathbf{0}_m, \\ ((\tau^A)^{\mathrm{T}} \otimes I_n)P\,\mathrm{vec}(U_2(t)) - \tau^B = \mathbf{0}_n, \\ ((M_{x_i}^A)^{\mathrm{T}} \otimes I_n)P\,\mathrm{vec}(U_1(t)) - (I_m \otimes M_{x_i}^B)P\,\mathrm{vec}(U_2(t)) = \mathbf{0}_{mn}, \end{cases} \tag{12}$$

while its corresponding matrix form is

$$L_{fbb}\begin{bmatrix}\mathrm{vec}(U_1(t))\\ \mathrm{vec}(U_2(t))\end{bmatrix} - \begin{bmatrix}(\sigma^A)^{\mathrm{T}}\\ \tau^B \\ \mathbf{0}_{rmn}\end{bmatrix} = \mathbf{0}_z, \tag{13}$$

in which $z = rmn + m + n$ and

$$L_{fbb} = \begin{bmatrix}(I_m \otimes \sigma^B)P & \mathbf{0}_{m,mn} \\ \mathbf{0}_{n,mn} & ((\tau^A)^{\mathrm{T}} \otimes I_n)P \\ W_1 & W_2\end{bmatrix} \in \mathbb{R}^{z\times 2mn},$$
$$W_1 = \begin{bmatrix}((M_{x_1}^A)^{\mathrm{T}} \otimes I_n)P \\ ((M_{x_2}^A)^{\mathrm{T}} \otimes I_n)P \\ \vdots \\ ((M_{x_r}^A)^{\mathrm{T}} \otimes I_n)P\end{bmatrix} \in \mathbb{R}^{rmn\times mn}, \quad W_2 = \begin{bmatrix}(-I_m \otimes M_{x_1}^B)P \\ (-I_m \otimes M_{x_2}^B)P \\ \vdots \\ (-I_m \otimes M_{x_r}^B)P\end{bmatrix} \in \mathbb{R}^{rmn\times mn}. \tag{14}$$

Based on considered transformations, the ZNN learning exploits the following ZEF, which is based on (13), for satisfying simultaneously all the equations in (9):

$$E_{fbb}(t) = L_{fbb}\begin{bmatrix}\mathrm{vec}(U_1(t))\\ \mathrm{vec}(U_2(t))\end{bmatrix} - \begin{bmatrix}(\sigma^A)^{\mathrm{T}}\\ \tau^B \\ \mathbf{0}_{rmn}\end{bmatrix}, \tag{15}$$

where $U_1(t)$ and $U_2(t)$ are unknown matrices. The time-derivative of (15) is the following:

$$\dot{E}_{fbb}(t) = L_{fbb}\begin{bmatrix}\mathrm{vec}(\dot{U}_1(t))\\ \mathrm{vec}(\dot{U}_2(t))\end{bmatrix}. \tag{16}$$

Then, combining Equations (15) and (16) with the ZNN design (1), the following can be obtained:

$$L_{fbb}\begin{bmatrix}\mathrm{vec}(\dot{U}_1(t))\\ \mathrm{vec}(\dot{U}_2(t))\end{bmatrix} = -\lambda E_{fbb}(t). \tag{17}$$

As a result, setting

$$\mathbf{x}(t)=\begin{bmatrix}\mathrm{vec}(U_1(t))\\ \mathrm{vec}(U_2(t))\end{bmatrix}\in\mathbb{R}^{2mn}, \qquad \dot{\mathbf{x}}(t)=\begin{bmatrix}\mathrm{vec}(\dot{U}_1(t))\\ \mathrm{vec}(\dot{U}_2(t))\end{bmatrix}\in\mathbb{R}^{2mn}, \tag{18}$$

the following dynamics are developed

$$L_{fbb}\,\dot{\mathbf{x}} = -\lambda E_{fbb}(t). \tag{19}$$

The normal equation corresponding to (19) is given in the form

$$\left(L_{fbb}\right)^{\mathrm{T}} L_{fbb}\,\dot{\mathbf{x}} = -\lambda\left(L_{fbb}\right)^{\mathrm{T}} E_{fbb}(t),$$

which leads to the Moore–Penrose best approximate solution

$$\dot{\mathbf{x}} = L_{fbb}^{\dagger}\left(-\lambda E_{fbb}(t)\right). \tag{20}$$

Appropriately defined *Matlab*'s `ode` solver is utilized to solve the ZNN design based on (20), and marked as ZNNL-hfbb. The ZNNL-hfbb's convergence and stability is considered in Theorem 1.

Theorem 1. *Let $\mathcal{A} = \left(m,\sigma^A,\{M^A_{x_i}\}_{x_i\in\mathfrak{X}},\tau^A\right)$ and $\mathcal{B} = \left(n,\sigma^B,\{M^B_{x_i}\}_{x_i\in\mathfrak{X}},\tau^B\right)$ be WFAs over $\mathbb{R}$, such that $M^A_{x_i}\in\mathbb{R}^{m\times m}$, $\sigma^A\in\mathbb{R}^{1\times m}$, $\tau^A\in\mathbb{R}^{m\times 1}$ and $M^B_{x_i}\in\mathbb{R}^{n\times n}$, $\sigma^B\in\mathbb{R}^{1\times n}$, $\tau^B\in\mathbb{R}^{n\times 1}$, $i\in[1..r]$. The dynamical system* (17) *inline with the ZNN* (1) *generate the TSOL*

$$\mathbf{x}_{\mathcal{S}}(t) = \left[\mathrm{vec}(U_{1,\mathcal{S}}(t))^{\mathrm{T}} \quad \mathrm{vec}(U_{2,\mathcal{S}}(t))^{\mathrm{T}}\right]^{\mathrm{T}},$$

which is stable in view of the theory of Lyapunov.

Proof. Let

$$\begin{cases}\sigma^B U^{\mathrm{T}}_{1,\mathcal{S}}(t)-\sigma^A = \mathbf{0}^{\mathrm{T}}_m,\\ U^{\mathrm{T}}_{2,\mathcal{S}}(t)\tau^A-\tau^B = \mathbf{0}_n,\\ U^{\mathrm{T}}_{1,\mathcal{S}}(t)M^A_{x_i}-M^B_{x_i}U^{\mathrm{T}}_{2,\mathcal{S}}(t) = \mathbf{0}_{n,m}.\end{cases} \tag{21}$$

Using vectorization, the Kronecker product, and the permutation matrix P for generating $\mathrm{vec}(U^{\mathrm{T}}_{1,\mathcal{S}}(t)(t))$ and $\mathrm{vec}(U^{\mathrm{T}}_{2,\mathcal{S}}(t)(t))$, the aforementioned system is reformulated as follows:

$$\begin{cases}(I_m\otimes\sigma^B)P\,\mathrm{vec}(U_{1,\mathcal{S}}(t))-(\sigma^A)^{\mathrm{T}} = \mathbf{0}_m,\\ ((\tau^A)^{\mathrm{T}}\otimes I_n)P\,\mathrm{vec}(U_{2,\mathcal{S}}(t))-\tau^B = \mathbf{0}_n,\\ ((M^A_{x_i})^{\mathrm{T}}\otimes I_n)P\,\mathrm{vec}(U_{1,\mathcal{S}}(t))-(I_m\otimes M^B_{x_i})P\mathrm{vec}(U_{2,\mathcal{S}}(t)) = \mathbf{0}_{mn},\end{cases} \tag{22}$$

or in equivalent form

$$L_{fbb}\begin{bmatrix}\mathrm{vec}(U_{1,\mathcal{S}}(t))\\ \mathrm{vec}(U_{2,\mathcal{S}}(t))\end{bmatrix} - \begin{bmatrix}(\sigma^A)^{\mathrm{T}}\\ \tau^B\\ \mathbf{0}_{rmn}\end{bmatrix} = \mathbf{0}_z \tag{23}$$

where L_{fbb} is declared in (14).

Further, the substitution

$$\mathbf{x}_{\mathcal{O}}(t) := -\mathbf{x}(t) + \mathbf{x}_{\mathcal{S}}(t) = \begin{bmatrix} -\text{vec}(U_1(t)) + \text{vec}(U_{1,\mathcal{S}}(t)) \\ -\text{vec}(U_2(t)) + \text{vec}(U_{2,\mathcal{S}}(t)) \end{bmatrix}$$

gives

$$\mathbf{x}(t) = \mathbf{x}_{\mathcal{S}}(t) - \mathbf{x}_{\mathcal{O}}(t) = \begin{bmatrix} \text{vec}(U_{1,\mathcal{S}}(t)) - \text{vec}(U_{1,\mathcal{O}}(t)) \\ \text{vec}(U_{2,\mathcal{S}}(t)) - \text{vec}(U_{2,\mathcal{O}}(t)) \end{bmatrix},$$

which leads to the first derivative of $\mathbf{x}(t)$

$$\dot{\mathbf{x}}(t) = \dot{\mathbf{x}}_{\mathcal{S}}(t) - \dot{\mathbf{x}}_{\mathcal{O}}(t) = \begin{bmatrix} \text{vec}(\dot{U}_{1,\mathcal{S}}(t)) - \text{vec}(\dot{U}_{1,\mathcal{O}}(t)) \\ \text{vec}(\dot{U}_{2,\mathcal{S}}(t)) - \text{vec}(\dot{U}_{2,\mathcal{O}}(t)) \end{bmatrix}.$$

As a consequence, the substitution $\mathbf{x}(t) = \mathbf{x}_{\mathcal{S}}(t) - \mathbf{x}_{\mathcal{O}}(t)$ in (13) for leads to

$$E_{\mathcal{S}}(t) = L_{fbb} \begin{bmatrix} \text{vec}(U_{1,\mathcal{S}}(t)) - \text{vec}(U_{1,\mathcal{O}}(t)) \\ \text{vec}(U_{2,\mathcal{S}}(t)) - \text{vec}(U_{2,\mathcal{O}}(t)) \end{bmatrix} - \begin{bmatrix} (\sigma^A)^{\mathrm{T}} \\ \tau^B \\ \mathbf{0}_{rmn} \end{bmatrix}, \tag{24}$$

or equivalently

$$E_{\mathcal{S}}(t) = L_{fbb}(\mathbf{x}_{\mathcal{S}}(t) - \mathbf{x}_{\mathcal{O}}(t)) - \begin{bmatrix} (\sigma^A)^{\mathrm{T}} \\ \tau^B \\ \mathbf{0}_{rmn} \end{bmatrix}. \tag{25}$$

The subsequent dynamics arise from (1):

$$\dot{E}_{\mathcal{S}}(t) = L_{fbb} \begin{bmatrix} \text{vec}(\dot{U}_{1,\mathcal{S}}(t)) - \text{vec}(\dot{U}_{1,\mathcal{O}}(t)) \\ \text{vec}(\dot{U}_{2,\mathcal{S}}(t)) - \text{vec}(\dot{U}_{2,\mathcal{O}}(t)) \end{bmatrix} = -\lambda E_{\mathcal{S}}(t), \tag{26}$$

with equivalent form

$$\dot{E}_{\mathcal{S}}(t) = L_{fbb}(\dot{\mathbf{x}}_{\mathcal{S}}(t) - \dot{\mathbf{x}}_{\mathcal{O}}(t)) = -\lambda E_{\mathcal{S}}(t). \tag{27}$$

The Lyapunov function chosen to confirm the convergence is defined by

$$\mathcal{Z}(t) = \frac{1}{2}\|E_{\mathcal{S}}(t)\|_{\mathrm{F}}^2 = \frac{1}{2}\mathrm{tr}\Big(E_{\mathcal{S}}(t)(E_{\mathcal{S}}(t))^{\mathrm{T}}\Big). \tag{28}$$

The following could be concluded in this case:

$$\dot{\mathcal{Z}}(t) = \frac{2\mathrm{tr}\Big((E_{\mathcal{S}}(t))^{\mathrm{T}}\dot{E}_{\mathcal{S}}(t)\Big)}{2} = \mathrm{tr}\Big((E_{\mathcal{S}}(t))^{\mathrm{T}}\dot{E}_{\mathcal{S}}(t)\Big) = -\lambda\mathrm{tr}\Big((E_{\mathcal{S}}(t))^{\mathrm{T}}E_{\mathcal{S}}(t)\Big). \tag{29}$$

Based on (29), it can be concluded

$$
\begin{aligned}
&\dot{\mathcal{Z}}(t)\begin{cases} <0, E_{\mathcal{S}}(t)\neq 0,\\ =0, E_{\mathcal{S}}(t)=0,\end{cases}\\
&\Leftrightarrow \dot{\mathcal{Z}}(t)\begin{cases} <0, L_{fbb}(\mathbf{x}_{\mathcal{S}}(t)-\mathbf{x}_{\mathcal{O}}(t))-\mathbf{b}_{fbb}\neq 0,\\ =0, L_{fbb}(\mathbf{x}_{\mathcal{S}}(t)-\mathbf{x}_{\mathcal{O}}(t))-\mathbf{b}_{fbb}=0,\end{cases}\\
&\Leftrightarrow \dot{\mathcal{Z}}(t)\begin{cases} <0, L_{fbb}\begin{bmatrix}\mathrm{vec}(U_{1,\mathcal{S}}(t))-\mathrm{vec}(U_{1,\mathcal{O}}(t))\\ \mathrm{vec}(U_{2,\mathcal{S}}(t))-\mathrm{vec}(U_{2,\mathcal{O}}(t))\end{bmatrix}-\begin{bmatrix}(\sigma^A)^{\mathrm{T}}\\ \tau^B\\ \mathbf{0}_{rmn}\end{bmatrix}\neq 0,\\ =0, L_{fbb}\begin{bmatrix}\mathrm{vec}(U_{1,\mathcal{S}}(t))-\mathrm{vec}(U_{1,\mathcal{O}}(t))\\ \mathrm{vec}(U_{2,\mathcal{S}}(t))-\mathrm{vec}(U_{2,\mathcal{O}}(t))\end{bmatrix}-\begin{bmatrix}(\sigma^A)^{\mathrm{T}}\\ \tau^B\\ \mathbf{0}_{rmn}\end{bmatrix}=0,\end{cases}\\
&\Leftrightarrow \dot{\mathcal{Z}}(t)\begin{cases} <0, & \begin{bmatrix}\mathrm{vec}(U_{1,\mathcal{O}}(t))\\ \mathrm{vec}(U_{2,\mathcal{O}}(t))\end{bmatrix}\neq 0,\\ =0, & \begin{bmatrix}\mathrm{vec}(U_{1,\mathcal{O}}(t))\\ \mathrm{vec}(U_{2,\mathcal{O}}(t))\end{bmatrix}=0.\end{cases}\\
&\Leftrightarrow \dot{\mathcal{Z}}(t)\begin{cases} <0, & \mathbf{x}_{\mathcal{O}}(t)\neq 0,\\ =0, & \mathbf{x}_{\mathcal{O}}(t)=0.\end{cases}
\end{aligned}
\tag{30}
$$

Furthermore, because $E_{\mathcal{S}}(0)=0$ and $\mathbf{x}_{\mathcal{O}}(t)$ are the equilibrium points of (27), the following holds:

$$\forall\, \mathbf{x}_{\mathcal{O}}(t)\neq 0, \quad \dot{\mathcal{Z}}(t)\leq 0. \tag{31}$$

It becomes visible that the equilibrium state

$$\mathbf{x}_{\mathcal{O}}(t)=-\mathbf{x}(t)+\mathbf{x}_{\mathcal{S}}(t)=\begin{bmatrix}-\mathrm{vec}(U_1(t))+\mathrm{vec}(U_{1,\mathcal{S}}(t))\\ -\mathrm{vec}(U_2(t))+\mathrm{vec}(U_{2,\mathcal{S}}(t))\end{bmatrix}=0$$

is stable in the sense of Lyapunov. After all is considered, as $t\to\infty$, the following holds

$$\mathbf{x}(t)=\begin{bmatrix}\mathrm{vec}(U_1(t))\\ \mathrm{vec}(U_2(t))\end{bmatrix}\to\mathbf{x}_{\mathcal{S}}(t)=\begin{bmatrix}\mathrm{vec}(U_{1,\mathcal{S}}(t))\\ \mathrm{vec}(U_{2,\mathcal{S}}(t))\end{bmatrix},$$

which was our original intention. □

Theorem 2. *Let* $\mathcal{A}=\left(m,\sigma^A,\{M^A_{x_i}\}_{x_i\in\mathfrak{X}},\tau^A\right)$ *and* $\mathcal{B}=\left(n,\sigma^B,\{M^B_{x_i}\}_{x_i\in\mathfrak{X}},\tau^B\right)$ *be WFAs defined by* $M^A_{x_i}\in\mathbb{R}^{m\times m}$, $\sigma^A\in\mathbb{R}^{1\times m}$, $\tau^A\in\mathbb{R}^{m\times 1}$ *and* $M^B_{x_i}\in\mathbb{R}^{n\times n}$, $\sigma^B\in\mathbb{R}^{1\times n}$, $\tau^B\in\mathbb{R}^{n\times 1}$, $i\in[1..r]$. *Starting from an arbitrary initialization* $\mathbf{x}(0)$, *the ZNNL-hfbb design* (20) *converges exponentially to* $\mathbf{x}^*(t)$, *which coincides with the TSOL of* (4).

Proof. The system (9) defines the solution $\mathbf{x}(t)=[\mathrm{vec}(U_1(t))^{\mathrm{T}},\mathrm{vec}(U_2(t))^{\mathrm{T}}]^{\mathrm{T}}$, which affiliates to the backward–forward bisimulation between $\mathcal{A}$ and $\mathcal{B}$. Next, the system (9) is rewritten into (10) and then into (13) for generating $\mathrm{vec}(U^{\mathrm{T}}_{1,\mathcal{S}}(t)(t))$ and $\mathrm{vec}(U^{\mathrm{T}}_{2,\mathcal{S}}(t)(t))$. Thirdly, the ZEF (15) is established to solve the system (13) and the ZNN evolution is exploited to generate the solution $\mathbf{x}(t)$ of (4). Later, (17) is generated by the ZNN design (1) aimed to zeroing (15). In accordance with Theorem 1, the $E_{fbb}(t)\to 0$ as $t\to\infty$. In consequence, the solution of the dynamical system (20) tends to $\mathbf{x}^*(t)=[\mathrm{vec}(U^*_1(t))^{\mathrm{T}},\mathrm{vec}(U^*_2(t))^{\mathrm{T}}]^{\mathrm{T}}$ as $t\to\infty$. Moreover, it is evident that (20) is another form of (17). □

3.2. The ZNNL-hbfb Model

According to the system (8) arising from (5), the subsequent matrix-vector equations must be fulfilled:

$$\begin{cases} \tau^A - U_1(t)\tau^B = \mathbf{0}_m, \\ \sigma^A U_2(t) - \sigma^B = \mathbf{0}_n^{\mathrm{T}}, \\ M_{x_i}^A U_2(t) - U_1(t) M_{x_i}^B = \mathbf{0}_{m,n}, \end{cases} \tag{32}$$

where $U_1(t), U_2(t) \in \mathbb{R}^{m\times n}$ imply unknown matrices. Applying vectorization and the Kronecker product, the system (32) is rewritten into

$$\begin{cases} -((\tau^B)^{\mathrm{T}} \otimes I_m)\mathrm{vec}(U_1(t)) + \tau^A = \mathbf{0}_m, \\ (I_n \otimes \sigma^A)\mathrm{vec}(U_2(t)) - (\sigma^B)^{\mathrm{T}} = \mathbf{0}_n, \\ (I_n \otimes M_{x_i}^A)\mathrm{vec}(U_2(t)) - ((M_{x_i}^B)^{\mathrm{T}} \otimes I_m)\mathrm{vec}(U_1(t)) = \mathbf{0}_{mn}. \end{cases} \tag{33}$$

Then, the corresponding matrix form of (33) is the following:

$$L_{bfb}\begin{bmatrix}\mathrm{vec}(U_1(t))\\ \mathrm{vec}(U_2(t))\end{bmatrix} - \begin{bmatrix}-\tau^A\\ (\sigma^B)^{\mathrm{T}}\\ \mathbf{0}_{rmn}\end{bmatrix} = \mathbf{0}_z, \tag{34}$$

where

$$L_{bfb}=\begin{bmatrix}-(\tau^B)^{\mathrm{T}}\otimes I_m & \mathbf{0}_{m,mn}\\ \mathbf{0}_{n,mn} & I_n\otimes\sigma^A\\ W_1 & W_2\end{bmatrix}\in\mathbb{R}^{z\times 2mn},$$
$$W_1=\begin{bmatrix}-(M_{x_1}^B)^{\mathrm{T}}\otimes I_m\\ -(M_{x_2}^B)^{\mathrm{T}}\otimes I_m\\ \vdots\\ -(M_{x_r}^B)^{\mathrm{T}}\otimes I_m\end{bmatrix}\in\mathbb{R}^{rmn\times mn},\quad W_2=\begin{bmatrix}I_n\otimes M_{x_1}^A\\ I_n\otimes M_{x_2}^A\\ \vdots\\ I_n\otimes M_{x_r}^A\end{bmatrix}\in\mathbb{R}^{rmn\times mn}. \tag{35}$$

Following that, the ZNN develops on the following ZEF based on (34), for simultaneous solving of the equations in (32):

$$E_{bfb}(t) = L_{bfb}\begin{bmatrix}\mathrm{vec}(U_1(t))\\ \mathrm{vec}(U_2(t))\end{bmatrix} - \begin{bmatrix}-\tau^A\\ (\sigma^B)^{\mathrm{T}}\\ \mathbf{0}_{2mn}\end{bmatrix}, \tag{36}$$

in which $U_1(t)$ and $U_2(t)$ are unknowns. The derivative of (36) is equal to

$$\dot{E}_{bfb}(t) = L_{bfb}\begin{bmatrix}\mathrm{vec}(\dot{U}_1(t))\\ \mathrm{vec}(\dot{U}_2(t))\end{bmatrix}. \tag{37}$$

Combining (36) and (37) with the ZNN (1), the following can be obtained:

$$L_{bfb}\begin{bmatrix}\mathrm{vec}(\dot{U}_1(t))\\ \mathrm{vec}(\dot{U}_2(t))\end{bmatrix} = -\lambda E_{bfb}(t). \tag{38}$$

As a result, setting

$$\dot{\mathbf{x}}(t)=\begin{bmatrix}\mathrm{vec}(\dot{U}_1(t))\\ \mathrm{vec}(\dot{U}_2(t))\end{bmatrix}\in\mathbb{R}^{2mn},\quad \mathbf{x}(t)=\begin{bmatrix}\mathrm{vec}(U_1(t))\\ \mathrm{vec}(U_2(t))\end{bmatrix}\in\mathbb{R}^{2mn}, \tag{39}$$

the next model is obtained

$$L_{bfb}\dot{\mathbf{x}} = -\lambda E_{bfb}(t), \tag{40}$$

whose best approximate solution is

$$\dot{\mathbf{x}} = L_{bfb}^{\dagger}\left(-\lambda E_{bfb}(t)\right). \tag{41}$$

A suitable *Matlab*'s ode solver can be used in the implementation of the ZNN design (41), termed as the ZNNL-hbfb. The ZNNL-hbfb convergence and stability are investigated in the Theorem 3.

Theorem 3. *Let* $\mathcal{A} = \left(m, \sigma^A, \{M^A_{x_i}\}_{x_i \in \mathfrak{X}}, \tau^A\right)$ *and* $\mathcal{B} = \left(n, \sigma^B, \{M^B_{x_i}\}_{x_i \in \mathfrak{X}}, \tau^B\right)$ *be WFAs over* $\mathbb{R}$*, determined by* $M^A_{x_i} \in \mathbb{R}^{m\times m}$, $\sigma^A \in \mathbb{R}^{1\times m}$, $\tau^A \in \mathbb{R}^{m\times 1}$ *and* $M^B_{x_i} \in \mathbb{R}^{n\times n}$, $\sigma^B \in \mathbb{R}^{1\times n}$, $\tau^B \in \mathbb{R}^{n\times 1}$, $i \in [1..r]$. *The dynamical system* (38) *inline with the ZNN* (1) *generates the TSOL* $\mathbf{x}_S(t)$*, which is stable in the Lyapunov sense.*

Proof. The verification is analogous to the proof of Theorem 1. □

Theorem 4. *Let* $\mathcal{A} = \left(m, \sigma^A, \{M^A_{x_i}\}_{x_i \in \mathfrak{X}}, \tau^A\right)$ *and* $\mathcal{B} = \left(n, \sigma^B, \{M^B_{x_i}\}_{x_i \in \mathfrak{X}}, \tau^B\right)$ *be WFA over* $\mathbb{R}$ *defined upon* $M^A_{x_i} \in \mathbb{R}^{m\times m}$, $\sigma^A \in \mathbb{R}^{1\times m}$, $\tau^A \in \mathbb{R}^{m\times 1}$ *and* $M^B_{x_i} \in \mathbb{R}^{n\times n}$, $\sigma^B \in \mathbb{R}^{1\times n}$, $\tau^B \in \mathbb{R}^{n\times 1}$, $i \in [1..r]$. *Starting from an arbitrary initialization* $\mathbf{x}(0)$*, the ZNNL-hbfb design* (41) *converges exponentially to* $\mathbf{x}^*(t)$*, which coincides with the TSOL of* (5).

Proof. The verification is analogous to the proof of Theorem 2. □

4. Numerical Experiments on the Proposed Models

The behavior of the ZNNL-hfbb (20) and the ZNNL-hbfb (41) are examined in each of the four numerical examinations. During the computation, the *Matlab* ode45 solver was selected inside the time span $[0, 10]$ under both relative and absolute tolerances equal to 10^{-15}. In addition, the output produced by the ZNN is compared against the results of the *Matlab* functions linsolve and pinv (with the default settings) in solving (13) in Examples 1 and 2, and solving (34) in Examples 3 and 4. All numerical experiments are performed using the *Matlab* R2022a environment.

Example 1. *Let* $m = 4$, $n = 2$, $r = 2$, $\mathfrak{X} = \{x_1, x_2\}$*, and consider WFAs*

$$\mathcal{A} = \left(4, \sigma^A, \{M^A_{x_i}\}_{x_i \in \mathfrak{X}}, \tau^A\right) \quad \text{and} \quad \mathcal{B} = \left(2, \sigma^B, \{M^B_{x_i}\}_{x_i \in \mathfrak{X}}, \tau^B\right).$$

Accordingly, $M^A_{x_i} \in \mathbb{R}^{4\times 4}$, $\sigma^A \in \mathbb{R}^{1\times 4}$, $\tau^A \in \mathbb{R}^{4\times 1}$ *and* $M^B_{x_i} \in \mathbb{R}^{2\times 2}$, $\sigma^B \in \mathbb{R}^{1\times 2}$, $\tau^B \in \mathbb{R}^{2\times 1}$. *Consider*

$$\sigma^A = \begin{bmatrix} -918/29 & -228/29 & -228/29 & 222/29 \end{bmatrix}, \quad \tau^A = \begin{bmatrix} -1 & -1 & 1 & 1 \end{bmatrix}^{\mathrm{T}},$$

$$M^A_{x_1} = \begin{bmatrix} 3 & 6 & 9 & 12 \\ 3 & 3 & 3 & 3 \\ 3 & 3 & 3 & 3 \\ -12 & -9 & -6 & -3 \end{bmatrix}, \quad M^A_{x_2} = \begin{bmatrix} -2 & -4 & -6 & -8 \\ -2 & -2 & -2 & -2 \\ -2 & -2 & -2 & -2 \\ 8 & 6 & 4 & 2 \end{bmatrix}$$

and

$$\sigma^B = \begin{bmatrix} -2 & -4 \end{bmatrix}, \quad \tau^B = \begin{bmatrix} 8 & 8 \end{bmatrix}^{\mathrm{T}}, \quad M^B_{x_1} = \begin{bmatrix} 3 & 3 \\ 3 & 3 \end{bmatrix}, \quad M^B_{x_2} = \begin{bmatrix} -2 & -2 \\ -2 & -2 \end{bmatrix}.$$

The gain parameter has been chosen as $\lambda = 10$ *and the initialization conditions (ICs) are equal to:* $IC_1 : \mathbf{x}(0) = \mathbf{1}_{16}$, $IC_2 : \mathbf{x}(0) = -\mathbf{1}_{16}$. *It is important to mention that the initialization condition refers to the value of* $\mathbf{x}(t)$ *at* $t = 0$.

The results generated by the ZNNL-hfbb are arranged in Figure 1.

Example 2. *Let $m = 4$, $n = 2$, $r = 3$, $\mathfrak{X} = \{x_1, x_2, x_3\}$, and examine WFAs over $\mathbb{R}$ defined by $\mathcal{A} = \left(4, \sigma^A, \{M^A_{x_i}\}_{x_i \in \mathfrak{X}}, \tau^A\right)$ and $\mathcal{B} = \left(2, \sigma^B, \{M^B_{x_i}\}_{x_i \in \mathfrak{X}}, \tau^B\right)$ satisfying $M^A_{x_i} \in \mathbb{R}^{4\times 4}$, $\sigma^A \in \mathbb{R}^{1\times 4}$, $\tau^A \in \mathbb{R}^{4\times 1}$ and $M^B_{x_i} \in \mathbb{R}^{2\times 2}$, $\sigma^B \in \mathbb{R}^{1\times 2}$, $\tau^B \in \mathbb{R}^{2\times 1}$. Let us choose*

$$\sigma^A = \begin{bmatrix} 0 & 57/2 & 57/2 & 12 \end{bmatrix}, \quad \tau^A = \begin{bmatrix} 2 & 2 & 2 & 2 \end{bmatrix}^{\mathrm{T}}, \quad M^A_{x_1} = \begin{bmatrix} 3 & 9 & 6 & 12 \\ 3 & 3 & 3 & 3 \\ 3 & 3 & 3 & 3 \\ -12 & -9 & -6 & -3 \end{bmatrix},$$

$$M^A_{x_2} = \begin{bmatrix} -2 & -6 & -4 & -8 \\ -2 & -2 & -2 & -2 \\ -2 & -2 & -2 & -2 \\ 8 & 6 & 4 & 2 \end{bmatrix}, \quad M^A_{x_3} = \begin{bmatrix} -5 & -15 & -10 & -20 \\ -5 & -5 & -5 & -5 \\ -5 & -5 & -5 & -5 \\ 20 & 15 & 10 & 5 \end{bmatrix}$$

and

$$\sigma^B = \begin{bmatrix} 1 & 2 \end{bmatrix}, \ \tau^B = \begin{bmatrix} 32 & 40 \end{bmatrix}^{\mathrm{T}}, \ M^B_{x_1} = \begin{bmatrix} 3 & 3 \\ 3 & 3 \end{bmatrix}, \ M^B_{x_2} = \begin{bmatrix} -2 & -2 \\ -2 & -2 \end{bmatrix}, \ M^B_{x_3} = \begin{bmatrix} -5 & -5 \\ -5 & -5 \end{bmatrix}.$$

The ZNN gain parameters are chosen as $\lambda = 10$ and $\lambda = 100$, while the IC has been chosen as $\mathbf{x}(0) = \mathbf{1}_{16}$. The outputs of ZNNL-hfbb are shown in Figure 1.

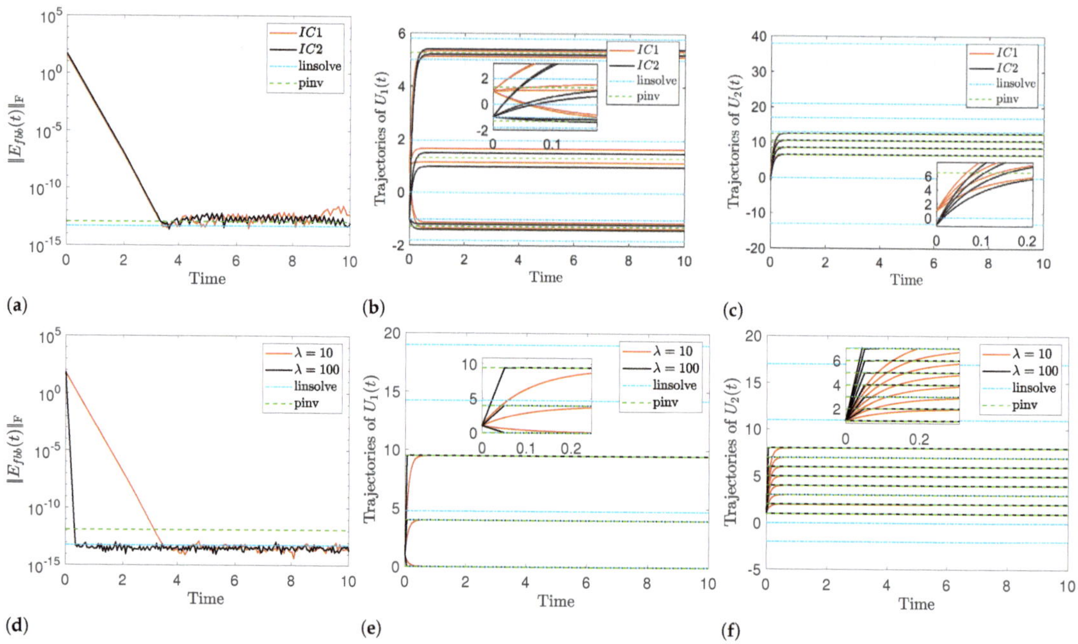

Figure 1. Errors and trajectories generated by ZNNL-hfbb in Examples 1 and 2. (**a**) Example 1: ZEF errors. (**b**) Example 1: Trajectories of $U_1(t)$. (**c**) Example 1: Trajectories of $U_2(t)$. (**d**) Example 2: ZEF errors. (**e**) Example 2: Trajectories of $U_1(t)$. (**f**) Example 2: Trajectories of $U_2(t)$.

Example 3. *Let $m = 3$, $n = 2$, $r = 2$, $\mathfrak{X} = \{x_1, x_2\}$, and consider WFAs*

$$\mathcal{A} = \left(3, \sigma^A, \{M^A_{x_i}\}_{x_i \in \mathfrak{X}}, \tau^A\right) \quad \textit{and} \quad \mathcal{B} = \left(2, \sigma^B, \{M^B_{x_i}\}_{x_i \in \mathfrak{X}}, \tau^B\right)$$

satisfying $M^A_{x_i} \in \mathbb{R}^{3\times 3}, \sigma^A \in \mathbb{R}^{1\times 3}, \tau^A \in \mathbb{R}^{3\times 1}$ *and* $M^B_{x_i} \in \mathbb{R}^{2\times n}, \sigma^B \in \mathbb{R}^{1\times 2}, \tau^B \in \mathbb{R}^{2\times 1}$. *Let us choose*

$$\sigma^A = \begin{bmatrix} 2 & 2 & 2 \end{bmatrix}, \quad \tau^A = \begin{bmatrix} -1/2 & -1/2 & -1/2 \end{bmatrix}^{\mathrm{T}},$$

$$M^A_{x_1} = \begin{bmatrix} -3 & -1 & 1 \\ -1 & -1 & 1 \\ -1 & -1 & 1 \end{bmatrix}, \quad M^A_{x_2} = \begin{bmatrix} -3/2 & -1/2 & 1/2 \\ -1/2 & -1/2 & 1/2 \\ -1/2 & -1/2 & 1/2 \end{bmatrix}$$

and

$$\sigma^B = \begin{bmatrix} 2 & 8 \end{bmatrix}, \quad \tau^B = \begin{bmatrix} -1/2 & -2 \end{bmatrix}^{\mathrm{T}}, \quad M^B_{x_1} = \begin{bmatrix} -1 & -3 \\ -1 & -2 \end{bmatrix}, \quad M^B_{x_2} = \begin{bmatrix} -1/2 & -3/2 \\ -1/2 & -1 \end{bmatrix}.$$

The design parameter has been selected as $\lambda = 10$ *and two ICs have been used:* $IC_1 : \mathbf{x}(0) = \mathbf{1}_{12}$, $IC_2 : \mathbf{x}(0) = -\mathbf{1}_{12}$.

The outputs of the ZNNL-hbfb are arranged in Figure 2.

Example 4. *Let* $m = 3$, $n = 2$, $r = 3$ *and* $\mathfrak{X} = \{x_1, x_2, x_3\}$, *and consider WFAs* $\mathcal{A} = \left(3, \sigma^A, \{M^A_{x_i}\}_{x_i \in \mathfrak{X}}, \tau^A\right)$ *and* $\mathcal{B} = \left(2, \sigma^B, \{M^B_{x_i}\}_{x_i \in \mathfrak{X}}, \tau^B\right)$. *Clearly* $M^A_{x_i} \in \mathbb{R}^{3\times 3}, \sigma^A \in \mathbb{R}^{1\times 3}, \tau^A \in \mathbb{R}^{3\times 1}$ *and* $M^B_{x_i} \in \mathbb{R}^{2\times 2}, \sigma^B \in \mathbb{R}^{1\times 2}, \tau^B \in \mathbb{R}^{2\times 1}$. *Consider*

$$\sigma^A = \begin{bmatrix} 2 & 2 & 2 \end{bmatrix}, \quad \tau^A = \begin{bmatrix} -1/2 & -1/2 & -1/2 \end{bmatrix}^{\mathrm{T}},$$

$$M^A_{x_1} = \begin{bmatrix} -3 & -1 & 1 \\ -1 & -1 & 1 \\ -2 & -1 & 1 \end{bmatrix}, \quad M^A_{x_2} = \begin{bmatrix} -3/2 & -1/2 & 1/2 \\ -1/2 & -1/2 & 1/2 \\ -1 & -1/2 & 1/2 \end{bmatrix}, \quad M^A_{x_3} = \begin{bmatrix} -3/4 & 1/4 & 1/4 \\ -1/4 & -1/4 & 1/4 \\ -1/2 & -1/4 & 1/4 \end{bmatrix}$$

as well as

$$\sigma^B = \begin{bmatrix} 2 & 4 \end{bmatrix}, \quad \tau^B = \begin{bmatrix} -1/2 & -1 \end{bmatrix}^{\mathrm{T}},$$

$$M^B_{x_1} = \begin{bmatrix} -1 & -3 \\ -1 & -2 \end{bmatrix}, \quad M^B_{x_2} = \begin{bmatrix} -1/2 & -3/2 \\ -1/2 & -1 \end{bmatrix}, \quad M^B_{x_3} = \begin{bmatrix} -1/4 & -3/4 \\ -1/4 & -1/2 \end{bmatrix}.$$

Gain parameters of ZNN are $\lambda = 10$ *and* $\lambda = 100$, *while the IC is* $\mathbf{x}(0) = \mathbf{1}_{12}$.

The outcomes generated by ZNNL-hbfb are arranged in Figure 2.

Results Analysis

This part presents the results from the four numerical examples that examine the performance of the ZNN models, which are shown in Figures 1 and 2. Particularly, Figures 1a,d and 2a,d show the ZEF errors in Examples 1–4, respectively, while Figures 1b,e and 2b,e show the trajectories of $U_1(t)$, and Figures 1c,f and 2c,f show the trajectories of $U_2(t)$.

According to results generated in Example 1, the next outcomes are observable for the ZNNL-hfbb initiated by IC_1 and IC_2 and forced by $\lambda = 10$. Figure 1a shows the ZNNL-hfbb model's ZEF norms. Both ZNNs are initiated by a large error cost at $t = 0$ and both ZEFs converge in the time span $[10^{-15}, 10^{-13}]$, with an insignificant error at $t = 3.5$. In this way, the ZNNL-hfbb behavior confirms Theorem 2 by the convergence to a result near to zero for two random ICs. Figure 1b,c displays the trajectories generated by $U_1(t)$ and $U_2(t)$, respectively. Included graphs indicate that $U_1(t)$ and $U_2(t)$ do not generate close trajectories initiated by IC_1 and IC_2 , but the convergence speed is similar in both cases. Therefore, the ZNNL-hfbb appears to give dissimilar solutions for a series of ICs, but the convergence behavior of its solutions is proven to match the convergence behavior of the linked ZEFs.

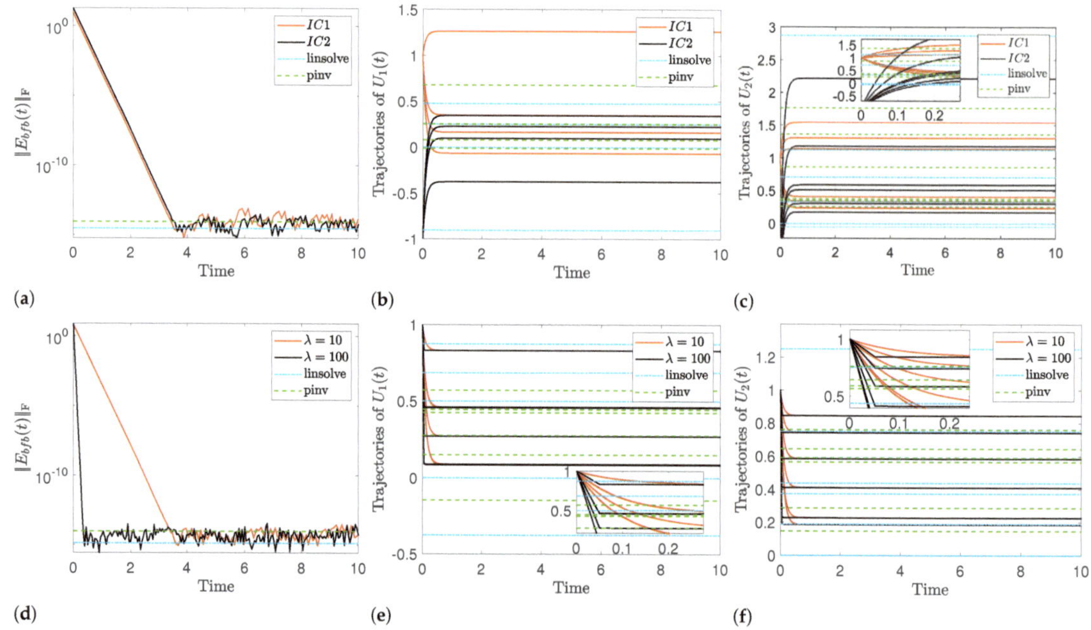

Figure 2. Errors and trajectories generated by ZNNL-hbfb in Examples 3 and 4. (**a**) Example 3: ZEF errors. (**b**) Example 3: Trajectories of $U_1(t)$. (**c**) Example 3: Trajectories of $U_2(t)$. (**d**) Example 4: ZEF errors. (**e**) Example 4: Trajectories of $U_1(t)$. (**f**) Example 4: Trajectories of $U_2(t)$.

In Example 2, under $\lambda = 10$ and $\lambda = 100$, the next observations for the ZNN-hfbb are concluded. Figure 1d shows the norm of ZNN-hfbb's ZEFs. Both evaluations in this figure start with a large error cost at $t = 0$ and converge in $[10^{-15}, 10^{-13}]$ at $t = 0.3$ for $\lambda = 100$, and at $t = 3.5$ for $\lambda = 10$, with a negligible error. Accordingly, the ZNN's convergence features are confirmed by the norm of the ZNN-hfbb's ZEF, which depends on λ. So, the results generated in ZNN-hfbb confirms Theorem 2 by the convergence to a quantity near to zero. Figure 1e and 1f, respectively, show the trajectories of the model's solutions $U_1(t)$ and $U_2(t)$. Obtained results point out that the trajectories of $U_1(t)$ and $U_2(t)$ converge much faster in the environment $\lambda = 100$ than in $\lambda = 10$. Besides that, $U_1(t)$ compared to $U_2(t)$ generates close trajectories in environments $\lambda = 10$ and $\lambda = 100$, individually. So, the ZNN-hfbb produces the same $U_1(t)$ and $U_2(t)$ solutions for different λ, and their convergence behavior coincides with the convergence of the related ZEFs.

In Example 3, the next conclusions for ZNNL-hbfb, beginning with IC_1 and IC_2 for $\lambda = 10$, are observable. Figure 2a shows the ZNNL-hbfb's ZEFs. Both evolutions are started from a large error at $t = 0$ and both ZEFs converge inside the time span $[10^{-16}, 10^{-13}]$ with an insignificant error at $t = 3.5$. Accordingly, the ZNNL-hbfb model confirms Theorem 4 by the convergence to a value near to zero for two distinctive ICs. Figure 2b and 2c, respectively, present the trajectories of $U_1(t)$ and $U_2(t)$. Generated results point out that the trajectories of $U_1(t)$ and $U_2(t)$ are not close in both instances IC_1 and IC_2 , but their convergence behavior is similar. Consequently, the ZNNL-hbfb generates diverse solutions related to different ICs, and its convergence behavior matches with the convergence behavior of the associated ZEFs.

Example 4 initiates the subsequent conclusions regarding ZNN-hbfb under the accelerations $\lambda = 10$ and $\lambda = 100$. Figure 2d exhibits the ZNN-hbfb's ZEFs. Both instances of the ZNN-hbfb evaluation in this figure start with a large error cost at $t = 0$ and converge in $[10^{-16}, 10^{-13}]$ at $t = 0.3$ for $\lambda = 100$, and at $t = 3.5$ for $\lambda = 10$, with a negligible error. In other words, the ZNN's convergence is certified by the ZNN-hbfb's ZEF, which depends on λ, and the ZNN-hbfb certifies Theorem 4 with its own convergence to a quantity near to zero. Figure 2e and 2f display the trajectories of $U_1(t)$ and $U_2(t)$, respectively. Involved graphs indicate that the trajectories of $U_1(t)$ and $U_2(t)$ converge faster via $\lambda = 100$ compared to $\lambda = 10$. Also, $U_1(t)$ and $U_2(t)$ generated close trajectories via $\lambda = 10$ and $\lambda = 100$ individually. So, the ZNN-hbfb generates the same $U_1(t)$ and $U_2(t)$ for different λ, and its convergence coincides with the convergence pattern of the associated ZEFs.

The following outcomes are obtained when the ZNN-hbfb and ZNN-hbfb models are compared to the *Matlab*'s functions `linsolve` and `pinv`. Particularly, Figures 1a,d and 2a,d demonstrate that for the ZNN-hfbb and ZNN-hbfb models, the `linsolve` and the `pinv` yield similar low error prices in all examples when compared. Additionally, Figure 1b,c demonstrates that the trajectories generated by $U_1(t)$ and $U_2(t)$ are different between the ZNN, the `linsolve`, and `pinv`. Figure 1e,f shows that the ZNN and the `linsolve` create distinct trajectories for $U_1(t)$ and $U_2(t)$, while the ZNN and the `pinv` create identical trajectories. Figure 2b,c demonstrates that the trajectories generated by $U_1(t)$ and $U_2(t)$ are different between the ZNN, compared to `linsolve` and `pinv`. Figure 2e,f shows that the ZNN, the `linsolve`, and `pinv` all create distinct trajectories for $U_1(t)$ and $U_2(t)$. Therefore, in all examples, the ZNN-hfbb and ZNN-hbfb models perform similarly with `linsolve` and `pinv`.

The following conclusions can be drawn from the previously indicated analysis of the numerical examples:

- The ZNNL-hfbb and ZNNL-hbfb models can efficiently solve the systems (4) and (5), respectively.
- All models' behaviors are conditioned by values λ and their solutions are conditioned by ICs.
- Comparing considered ZNNs against the `linsolve` and `pinv`, it is discovered that both the ZNN-hfbb and ZNN-hbfb models exhibit comparable performance to the `linsolve` and `pinv`.
- The approximation of the TSOL $\mathbf{x}^*(t)$ in the ZNNL-hfbb and ZNNL-hbfb models is achieved faster via $\lambda = 100$ than via $\lambda = 10$.

When everything is considered, the ZNNL-hfbb and ZNNL-hbfb models perform in an appropriate and efficient manner in finding the solution of (4) and (5), respectively.

In conclusion, as the ZNN design parameter λ increases, the TSOL $\mathbf{x}^*(t)$ is approximated more quickly. Therefore, it is suggested to set the parameter λ as high as the hardware will allow.

5. Concluding Remarks

Current investigation is aimed at investigating and solving the equivalence and partial k-equivalence problem between WFAs, i.e., determining whether two WFAs generate the same word function or word functions that coincide on all input words whose lengths do not exceed positive integer value k. Our approach is based on the unification of two principal scientific areas, namely the ZNN dynamical systems and the existence of (approximate) heterotypic bisimulations between WFAs over $\mathbb{R}$. Two types of quantitative heterotypic bisimulations are proposed as solutions to particular systems of matrix-vector equations over $\mathbb{R}$. As a result, presented research is aimed to the development and analysis of two original ZNN models, called as ZNNL-hbfb and ZNNL-hfbb, for finding approximate solutions of matrix-vector equations involved in considered heterotypic bisimulations. A convergence analysis is given. Simulation examples are executed under various initialization states. Comparison with the *Matlab* linear programming solver `linprog` and the pseudoinverse solution generated by the standard function `pinv` is shown and superior achievements of the ZNN dynamics are recorded. The simulation examples also revealed another significant finding for the suggested ZNN models: the TSOL is approximated faster as the ZNN design parameter λ increases. The models solved in actual research utilize the ZNN dynamics established upon a larger number of equations and initiated ZEFs and continue research from [38,55,56].

Further research can be developed in the direction of solving minimization problems aimed to finding a WFA with the minimal number of states equivalent to the given WFA. Another optimization problem could be based on finding solutions of the corresponding systems of matrix-vector inequalities and equations of minimal matrix rank. Further research could be aimed at the topic of solving the k-equivalence problems with more than two unknown matrices. Additionally, since all kinds of noise significantly affect the accuracy of the suggested ZNN techniques, it is important to note that the suggested ZNN models have the drawback of being noise intolerant. Future work might therefore concentrate on modifying these models for ZNN dynamical systems that handle noise and improve integration. Finally, the ZNN models developed in this paper give a universal principle for solving arbitrary systems of matrix-vector equations and for solving arbitrary problems arising from such systems.

Author Contributions: Conceptualization, M.Ć., P.S.S. and S.D.M.; methodology, P.S.S. and S.D.M.; software, S.D.M.; validation, M.Ć., P.S.S. and S.D.M.; formal analysis, P.S.S., M.Ć., S.D.M. and G.V.M.; investigation, P.S.S., S.D.M. and G.V.M.; resources, S.D.M.; data curation, S.D.M. and M.J.P.; writing—original draft preparation, M.Ć. and P.S.S.; writing—review and editing, P.S.S., S.D.M., M.Ć. and G.V.M.; visualization, S.D.M.; supervision, M.Ć., P.S.S. and G.V.M.; project administration, M.J.P., P.S.S. and G.V.M. funding acquisition, M.J.P. All authors have read and agreed to the published version of the manuscript.

Funding: This work was supported by the Ministry of Science and Higher Education of the Russian Federation (Grant No. 075-15-2022-1121).

Data Availability Statement: The data supporting this study will be available on request to the authors.

Acknowledgments: Predrag Stanimirović and Miroslav Ćirić acknowledge the support by the Science Fund of the Republic of Serbia, Grant No. 7750185, Quantitative Automata Models: Fundamental Problems and Applications - QUAM. Predrag Stanimirović and Miroslav Ćirić are also supported by the Ministry of Science, Technological Development and Innovation, Republic of Serbia, Contract No. 451-03-65/2024-03/200124. Research of G.V.M. was partly supported by the Serbian Academy of Sciences and Arts (Project Φ-96). The author Milena J. Petrović gratefully acknowledges support from the Project supported by Ministry of Education, Science and Technological Development of the Republic of Serbia project no. 451-03-65/2024-03/200123.

Conflicts of Interest: The authors declare no conflicts of interest.

References

1. Daviaud, L. Containment and Equivalence of Weighted Automata: Probabilistic and Max-Plus Cases. In *Language and Automat Theory and Applications. LATA 2020*; Lect. Notes Comput. Sci; Leporati, A., Martín-Vide, C., Shapira, D., Zandron, C., Eds Springer: Cham, Switzerland, 2020; Volume 12038, pp. 17–32.
2. Almagor, S.; Boker, U.; Kupferman, O. What's decidable about weighted automata? *Inf. Comput.* **2022**, *282*, 104651. [CrossRef]
3. Milner, R. *A Calculus of Communicating Systems*; Lect. Notes Comput. Sci; Springer: Berlin/Heidelberg, Germany, 1980; Volum 92.
4. Park, D. Concurrency and automata on infinite sequences. In *Theoretical Computer Science*; Deussen, P., Ed.; Lecture Notes i Computer Science; Springer: Berlin/Heidelberg, Germany, 1981; Volume 104, pp. 167–183.
5. van Benthem, J. Modal Correspondence Theory. Ph.D. Thesis, Universiteit van Amsterdam, Amsterdam, The Netherland, 197
6. van Benthem, J. Correspondence Theory. In *Handbook of Philosophical Logic*; Gabbay, D., Guenthner, F., Eds.; Springe Berlin/Heidelberg, Germany, 200; Volume 3, pp. 325–408.
7. Blackburn, P.; de Rijke, M.; Venema, Y. *Modal Logic*; Cambridge University Press: Cambridge, UK, 2001.
8. Sangiorgi, D. On the origins of bisimulation and coinduction. *ACM Trans. Program. Lang. Syst.* **2009**, *31*, 111–151. [CrossRef]
9. Sangiorgi, D. Origins of bisimulation and coinduction. In *Advanced Topics in Bisimulation and Coinduction*; Sangiorgi, D., Rutten, J Eds.; Cambridge University Press: Cambridge, UK, 2012; pp. 1–37.
10. Sangiorgi, D.; Rutten, J., Eds. *Advanced Topics in Bisimulation and Coinduction*; Cambridge University Press: Cambridge, UK, 201
11. Pous, D.; Sangiorgi, D. Bisimulation and coinduction enhancements: A historical perspective. *Form. Asp. Comput.* **2019**, *3* 733–749. [CrossRef]
12. Milner, R. *Communication and Concurrency*; Prentice-Hall: Upper Saddle River, NJ, USA, 1989.
13. Milner, R. *Communicating and Mobile Systems: The p-Calculus*; Cambridge University Press: Cambridge, UK, 1999.
14. Roggenbach, M.; Majster-Cederbaum, M. Towards a unified view of bisimulation: A comparative study. *Theor. Comput. Sci.* **200** *238*, 81–130. [CrossRef]

15. Aceto, L.; Ingolfsdottir, A.; Larsen, K.G.; Srba, J. *Reactive Systems: Modelling, Specification and Verification*; Cambridge University Press: Cambridge, UK, 2007.
16. Cassandras, C.G.; Lafortune, S. *Introduction to Discrete Event Systems*; Springer: New York, NY, USA, 2008.
17. Ćirić, M.; Ignjatović, J.; Damljanović, N.; Bašić, M. Bisimulations for fuzzy automata. *Fuzzy Sets Syst.* **2012**, *186*, 100–139. [CrossRef]
18. Ćirić, M.; Ignjatović, J.; Jančić, I.; Damljanović, N. Computation of the greatest simulations and bisimulations between fuzzy automata. *Fuzzy Sets Syst.* **2012**, *208*, 22–42. [CrossRef]
19. Damljanović, N.; Ćirić, M.; Ignjatović, J. Bisimulations for weighted automata over an additively idempotent semiring. *Theor. Comput. Sci.* **2014**, *534*, 86–100. [CrossRef]
20. Ćirić, M.; Micić, I.; Matejić, J.; Stamenković, A. Simulations and bisimulations for max-plus automata. *Discret. Event Dyn. Syst.* **2024**, *34*, 269–295. [CrossRef]
21. Stanimirović, P.S.; Ćiri; M.; Mourtas, S.D.; Brzaković, P.; Karabašević, D. Simulations and bisimulations between weighted finite automata based on time-varying models over real numbers. *Mathematics* **2024**, *12*, 2110. [CrossRef]
22. Ćirić, M.; Ignjatović, J.; Stanimirović, P.S. Bisimulations for weighted finite automata over semirings. *Res. Sq.* 2022, *submitted to Soft Computing*. [CrossRef]
23. Ésik, Z.; Kuich, W. A generalization of Kozen's axiomatization of the equational theory of the regular sets. In *Words, Semigroups, and Transductions*; Ito, M., Paun, G., Yu, S., Eds.; World Scientific: River Edge, NJ, USA, 2001; pp. 99–114.
24. Beal, M.P.; Lombardy, S.; Sakarovitch, J. On the equivalence of Z-automata, In *Automata, Languages and Programming, 32nd International Colloquium, ICALP 2005*; Caires, L., Italiano, G.F., Monteiro, L., Palamidessi, C., Yung, M., Eds.; Lecture Notes in Computer Science; Springer: Berlin/Heidelberg, Germany, 2005; Volume 3580, pp. 397–409.
25. Beal, M.P.; Lombardy, S.; Sakarovitch, J. Conjugacy and equivalence of weighted automata and functional transducers. In *Computer Science—Theory and Applications, First International Symposium on Computer Science in Russia, CSR 2006*; Grigoriev, D., Harrison, J., Hirsch, E.A., Eds.; Lect. Notes Comput. Sci; Springer: Berlin/Heidelberg, Germany, 2006; Volume 3967, pp. 58–69.
26. Buchholz, P. Bisimulation relations for weighted automata. *Theor. Comput. Sci.* **2008**, *393*, 109–123. [CrossRef]
27. Ésik, Z.; Maletti, A. Simulation vs. equivalence. *arXiv* **2010**, arXiv:1004.2426. [CrossRef]
28. Sakarovitch, J. *Elements of Automata Theory*; Cambridge University Press: Cambridge, UK, 2009.
29. Sakarovitch, J. Automata and rational expressions. In *Handbook of Automata Theory*; Pin, J.É., Ed.; European Mathematical Society Publishing House: Berlin/Heidelberg, Germany, 2021; Volume 1, pp. 39–78.
30. Jančić, I., Weak bisimulations for fuzzy automata. *Fuzzy Sets Syst.* **2014**, *249*, 49–72. [CrossRef]
31. Stanimirović, S.; Micić, I. On the solvability of weakly linear systems of fuzzy relation equations. *Inf. Sci.* **2022**, *607*, 670–687. [CrossRef]
32. Micić, I.; Nguyen, L.A.; Stanimirović, S. Characterization and computation of approximate bisimulations for fuzzy automata. *Fuzzy Sets Syst.* **2022**, *442*, 331–350. [CrossRef]
33. Nguyen, L.A. Fuzzy simulations and bisimulations between fuzzy automata. *Int. J. Approx. Reason.* **2023**, *155*, 113–131. [CrossRef]
34. Nguyen, L.A.; Micić, I.; Stanimirović, S. Fuzzy minimax nets. *IEEE Trans. Fuzzy Syst.* **2023**, *31*, 2799–2808. [CrossRef]
35. Nguyen, L.A.; Micić, I.; Stanimirović, S. Depth-bounded fuzzy simulations and bisimulations between fuzzy automata. *Fuzzy Sets Syst.* **2023**, *473*, 108729. [CrossRef]
36. Zhang, Y.; Ge, S.S. Design and analysis of a general recurrent neural network model for time-varying matrix inversion. *IEEE Trans. Neural Netw.* **2005**, *16*, 1477–1490. [CrossRef]
37. Chai, Y.; Li, H.; Qiao, D.; Qin, S.; Feng, J. A neural network for Moore-Penrose inverse of time-varying complex-valued matrices. *Int. J. Comput. Intell. Syst.* **2020**, *13*, 663–671. [CrossRef]
38. Stanimirović, P.S.; Mourtas, S.D.; Mosić, D.; Katsikis, V.N.; Cao, X.; Li, S. Zeroing Neural Network approaches for computing time-varying minimal rank outer inverse. *Appl. Math. Comput.* **2024**, *465*, 128412. [CrossRef]
39. Qiao, S.; Wang, X.Z.; Wei, Y. Two finite-time convergent Zhang neural network models for time-varying complex matrix Drazin inverse. *Linear Algebra Appl.* **2018**, *542*, 101–117. [CrossRef]
40. Qiao, S.; Wei, Y.; Zhang, X. Computing time-varying ML-weighted pseudoinverse by the Zhang neural networks. *Numer. Funct. Anal. Optim.* **2020**, *41*, 1672–1693. [CrossRef]
41. Kovalnogov, V.N.; Fedorov, R.V.; Demidov, D.A.; Malyoshina, M.A.; Simos, T.E.; Katsikis, V.N.; Mourtas, S.D.; Sahas, R.D. Zeroing neural networks for computing quaternion linear matrix equation with application to color restoration of images. *AIMS Math.* **2023**, *8*, 14321–14339. [CrossRef]
42. Abbassi, R.; Jerbi, H.; Kchaou, M.; Simos, T.E.; Mourtas, S.D.; Katsikis, V.N. Towards higher-order zeroing neural networks for calculating quaternion matrix inverse with application to robotic motion tracking. *Mathematics* **2023**, *11*, 2756. [CrossRef]
43. Cao, M.; Xiao, L.; Zuo, Q.; Tan, P.; He, Y.; Gao, X. A fixed-time robust ZNN model with adaptive parameters for redundancy resolution of manipulators. *IEEE Trans. Emerg. Top. Comput. Intell.* **2024**, *8*, 3886–3898. [CrossRef]
44. Xiao, L.; Cao, P.; Song, W.; Luo, L.; Tang, W. A fixed-time noise-tolerance ZNN model for time-variant inequality-constrained quaternion matrix least-squares problem. *IEEE Trans. Neural Netw. Learn. Syst.* **2024**, *35*, 10503–10512. [CrossRef]
45. Jin, L.; Zhang, Y.; Li, S.; Zhang, Y. Modified ZNN for time-varying quadratic programming with inherent tolerance to noises and its application to kinematic redundancy resolution of robot manipulators. *IEEE Trans. Ind. Electron.* **2016**, *63*, 6978–6988. [CrossRef]

46. Wang, T.; Zhang, Z.; Huang, Y.; Liao, B.; Li, S. Applications of Zeroing Neural Networks: A Survey. *IEEE Access* **2024**, *12*, 51346–51363. [CrossRef]
47. Zhang, Y.; Guo, D. *Zhang Functions and Various Models;* Springer: Berlin/Heidelberg, Germany, 2015.
48. Li, L.; Xiao, L.; Wang, Z.; Zuo, Q. A survey on zeroing neural dynamics: Models, theories, and applications. *Int. J. Syst. Sci.* **2024**, 1–34. [CrossRef]
49. Jin, L.; Li, S.; Liao, B.; Zhang, Z. Zeroing neural networks: A survey. *Neurocomputing* **2017**, *267*, 597–604. [CrossRef]
50. Hua, C.; Cao, X.; Xu, Q.; Liao, B.; Li, S. Dynamic Neural Network Models for Time-Varying Problem Solving: A Survey on Model Structures. *IEEE Access* **2023**, *11*, 65991–66008. [CrossRef]
51. Guo, D.; Yi, C.; Zhang, Y. Zhang neural network versus gradient-based neural network for time-varying linear matrix equation solving. *Neurocomputing* **2011**, *74*, 3708–3712. [CrossRef]
52. Li, Z.; Zhang, Y. Improved Zhang neural network model and its solution of time-varying generalized linear matrix equations. *Expert Syst. Appl.* **2010**, *37*, 7213–7218. [CrossRef]
53. Zhang, Y.; Chen, K. Comparison on Zhang neural network and gradient neural network for time-varying linear matrix equation $AXB = C$ solving. In Proceedings of the 2008 IEEE International Conference on Industrial Technology—ICIT, Chengdu, China, 21–24 April 2008; pp. 1–6. [CrossRef]
54. Xiao, L.; Liao, B.; Li, S.; Chen, K. Nonlinear recurrent neural networks for finite-time solution of general time-varying linear matrix equations. *Neural Netw.* **2018**, *98*, 102–113. [CrossRef]
55. Katsikis, V.N.; Mourtas, S.D.; Stanimirović, P.S.; Zhang, Y. Solving complex-valued time-varying linear matrix equations via QR decomposition with applications to robotic motion tracking and on angle-of-arrival localization. *IEEE Trans. Neural Netw. Learn. Syst.* **2021**, *33*, 3415–3424. [CrossRef]
56. Simos, T.E.; Katsikis, V.N.; Mourtas, S.D.; Stanimirović, P.S. Unique non-negative definite solution of the time-varying algebraic Riccati equations with applications to stabilization of LTV system. *Math. Comput. Simul.* **2022**, *202*, 164–180. [CrossRef]
57. Graham, A. *Kronecker Products and Matrix Calculus with Applications;* Courier Dover Publications: Mineola, NY, USA, 2018.

axioms

rticle

Convergence Analysis for Cayley Variational Inclusion Problem Involving XOR and XNOR Operations

rifuzzaman [1], Syed Shakaib Irfan [1] and Iqbal Ahmad [2,*]

[1] Department of Mathematics, Aligarh Muslim University, Aligarh 202002, India; gn9848@myamu.ac.in (A.); ssirfan.mm@amu.ac.in (S.S.I.)
[2] Department of Mechanical Engineering, College of Engineering, Qassim University, Buraydah 52571, Saudi Arabia
* Correspondence: i.ahmad@qu.edu.sa

Abstract: In this article, we introduce and study a generalized Cayley variational inclusion problem incorporating XOR and XNOR operations. We establish an equivalent fixed-point formulation and demonstrate the Lipschitz continuity of the generalized Cayley approximation operator. Furthermore, we analyze the existence and convergence of the proposed problem using an implicit iterative algorithm. The iterative algorithm and numerical results presented in this study significantly enhance previously known findings in this domain. Finally, a numerical result is provided to support our main result and validate the proposed algorithm using MATLAB programming.

Keywords: algorithms; numerical result; resolvent operator; XOR and XNOR operations; Cayley approximation operator

MSC: 47H05; 49H10; 47J25

1. Introduction

In 1994, Hassouni and Moudafi [1] introduced the concept of variational inclusion, a generalized form of variational inequalities. Since then, variational inclusions have been extensively studied by researchers to address challenges in diverse fields such as finance, economics, transportation, network analysis, engineering and technology.

A further generalization of Wiener–Hopf equations, known as resolvent equations, were introduced by Noor [2]. Various generalized resolvent operators associated with different monotone operators can be found in the literature. Among these, Cayley approximation operators play a significant role in variational analysis, as they are closely related to resolvent operators. These operators have been effectively applied to study wave equations, heat equations, heat flow and coupled linear sound equations.

Additionally, when dealing with two Boolean operands, the XOR operation determines whether they can pass one another or obstruct each other. A practical demonstration of XOR logic can be observed using polarizing filters, such as those found in polarizing sunglasses. If we hold a polarizing filter up to the lenses of these sunglasses and look through both filters in series, light will pass through when the filters are aligned. However, if one filter is rotated by 90 degrees, the combination blocks the light. This process visually demonstrates XOR logic behavior.

The XOR logical operation is a binary operation that takes two Boolean operands and returns true only if the operands differ, yielding a false result when both operands are identical. XOR is commonly employed to test for the simultaneous falsehood of two conditions and is extensively used in cryptography, error detection (producing parity bits) and fault tolerance. Similarly, the XNOR operation compares two input bits and produces one output bit. If the input bits are identical, the result is one; otherwise, it is zero. Like XOR, XNOR is both commutative and associative. These operations are utilized in hardware for generating pseudo-random numbers and are fundamental in digital computing and linear separability applications. For further details on the XOR operation, refer to the resources listed [3–9].

In this article, we explore a generalized Cayley inclusion problem involving multi-valued operators and the XOR operation, owing to the significance and applications of the previously mentioned concepts. An iterative algorithm is developed based on the fixed-point equation, and we derive results on existence and convergence. This has applications in solving heat, wave and heat flow problems. A numerical result is presented using MATLAB2024b, accompanied by computational tables and convergence graphs for illustration.

2. Elementary Tools

In this paper, we assume that $\check{E}$ is a real-ordered Hilbert space equipped with norm $||.||$ and inner product $\langle .,. \rangle$. Again, $C \subseteq \check{E}$ is a closed convex cone, $C(\check{E})$ is the family of nonempty compact subsets of $\check{E}$, and $2^{\check{E}}$ represents the set of all nonempty subsets of $C(\check{E})$.

Definition 1 ([10]). *Let r and t be two elements in the real-ordered Hilbert space $\check{E}$. Consider lub $\{r,t\}$ and glb $\{r,t\}$ for the set $\{r,t\}$ to exist, where lub means least upper bound and glb means greatest lower bound for the set $\{r,t\}$. Then, some binary operations are defined as follows:*

(i) $r \vee t = inf\{r,t\}$;
(ii) $r \wedge t = sup\{r,t\}$;
(iii) $r \oplus t = (r-t) \vee (r-t)$;
(iv) $r \odot t = (r-t) \wedge (t-r)$.

Here, $\vee$ is the least upper bound or inf for the set $\{r,t\}$, $\wedge$ is the greatest lower bound or sup for the set $\{r,t\}$, $\oplus$ is called an XOR operation and $\odot$ is called an XNOR operation.

Definition 2 ([10]). *Let r be any element of the set $C_{\check{E}}$; then, $C_{\check{E}}$ is said to be a cone which implies $\lambda r \in C_{\check{E}}$ for every positive scalar λ.*

Definition 3 ([11,12]). *A cone $C_{\check{E}}$ is said to be a normal cone if and only if there exists a constant $\lambda_{\Pi_{\check{E}}} > 0$ such that $0 \leq r \leq t$ implies $||r|| \leq \lambda_{\Pi_{\check{E}}} \leq ||t||$.*

Definition 4 ([11,12]). *Let r and t be two elements in $\check{E}$; then, $C_{\check{E}}$ is called a cone, provided $r \leq t$ holds if and only if $r - t \in C_{\check{E}}$, where r and t are said to be comparable if either $r \leq t$ or $t \leq r$. The comparable elements are represented by $r \propto t$.*

Proposition 1 ([12]). *Let $\oplus$ and $\odot$ be the XOR operation and XNOR operation, respectively. Then, the following conditions hold:*

(i) $r \odot t = 0, (r \odot t) = (t \odot r), (r \oplus t) = 0, (r \oplus t) = (t \oplus r), (r \odot t) = -(r \oplus t)$;
(ii) *if* $r \propto 0$ *then* $-r \oplus 0 \leq r \leq r \oplus 0$;
(iii) $(\lambda r) \oplus (\lambda t) = |\lambda|(r \oplus t)$;
(iv) $0 \leq r \oplus t$, *if* $r \propto t$;
(v) *if* $r \propto t$ *then* $r \oplus t = 0$ *if and only if* $r = t$.

Proposition 2 ([11]). *Let $C_{\check{E}}$ be a normal cone in $\check{E}$ with normal constant $\lambda_{\Pi_{\check{E}}} > 0$,; then, for each $r,t \in \check{E}$ the following postulate are holds:*

(i) $||0 \oplus 0|| = ||0|| = 0$;
(ii) $||r \vee t|| = ||r|| \vee ||t|| \leq ||r|| + ||t||$;
(iii) $||r \oplus t|| \leq ||r - t|| \leq \lambda_{\Pi}||r \oplus t||$;
(iv) if $r \propto t$, then $||r \oplus t|| \leq ||r - t||$.

Definition 5. *A single-valued mapping $\breve{A} : \breve{E} \to \breve{E}$ is called Lipchitz-continuous if there exists a constant $\lambda_{\breve{A}} > 0$ such that*

$$||\breve{A}(r) - \breve{A}(t)|| \leq \lambda_{\breve{A}}||r - t||, \forall\ r, t \in \breve{E}.$$

Definition 6. *Let us consider $\Upsilon : \breve{E} \times \breve{E} \times \breve{E} \to \breve{E}$ as a single-valued mapping and $D : \breve{E} \to 2^{\breve{E}}$ as the multi-valued mapping. Then,*

(i) *Υ is called Lipschitz continuous in the first argument if there exists a constant $\lambda_{\Upsilon_1} > 0$ and for any $\mu_1 \in D(r), \mu_2 \in D(t)$ such that*

$$||\Upsilon(\mu_1, ., .) - \Upsilon(\mu_2, ., .)|| \leq \lambda_{\Upsilon_1}||\mu_1 - \mu_2||, \forall\, r, t \in C(\breve{E}).$$

(ii) *Υ is called Lipschitz continuous in the second argument if there exists a constant $\lambda_{\Upsilon_2} > 0$ and for any $\mu_1 \in D(r), \mu_2 \in D(t)$ such that*

$$||\Upsilon(., \mu_1, .) - \Upsilon(., \mu_2, .)|| \leq \lambda_{\Upsilon_2}||\mu_1 - \mu_2||, \forall\, r, t \in C(\breve{E}).$$

(iii) *Υ is called Lipschitz continuous in the third argument if there exists a constant $\lambda_{\Upsilon_3} > 0$ and for any $\mu_1 \in D(r), \mu_2 \in D(t)$ such that*

$$||\Upsilon(., ., \mu_1) - \Upsilon(., ., \mu_2)|| \leq \lambda_{\Upsilon_3}||\mu_1 - \mu_2||, \forall\, r, t \in C(\breve{E}).$$

Definition 7. *Consider a multi-valued mapping $\psi : \breve{E} \to C(\breve{E})$ that is said to be $\mathcal{D}$-Lipschitz continuous. Then, there exists a constant $\lambda_{\mathcal{D}_\psi} > 0$ such that*

$$\mathcal{D}(\psi(r), \psi(t)) \leq \lambda_{\mathcal{D}_\psi}||r - t||, \forall\, r, t \subset C(\breve{E}).$$

Definition 8. *Suppose $D : \breve{E} \to 2^{\breve{E}}$ is a multi-valued mapping and $\breve{A} : \breve{E} \to \breve{E}$ is a single-valued mapping. The resolvent operator $R^D_{\breve{A},\rho} : \breve{E} \to \breve{E}$ is defined as*

$$R^D_{\breve{A},\rho}(t) = [\breve{A} + \rho D]^{-1}(t), \forall\, r, t \in \breve{E}.$$

τ is an identity mapping and $\rho > 0$ is a constant.

Definition 9. *Suppose $D : \breve{E} \to 2^{\breve{E}}$ is a multi-valued mapping and $\breve{A} : \breve{E} \to \breve{E}$ is a single-valued mapping. The Cayley approximation operator $C^D_{\breve{A},\rho} : \breve{E} \to \breve{E}$ is defined as*

$$C^D_{\breve{A},\rho}(t) = \left[2R^D_{\breve{A},\rho} - \breve{A}\right](t), \forall\, r, t \in \breve{E}.$$

τ is an identity mapping and $\rho > 0$ is a constant.

Definition 10. *Let $\breve{A} : \breve{E} \to \breve{E}$ be a single-valued mapping and $D : \breve{E} \to 2^{\breve{E}}$ be a multi-valued mapping. Then,*

(i) *$\breve{A}$ is called strong comparison mapping if $\breve{A}$ is comparison mapping and $\breve{A}(r) \propto \breve{A}(t)$ if and only if $r \propto t, \forall\, r, t \in \breve{E}$.*

(ii) $\check{A}$ is called ρ-order non-extended mapping if there exists a constant $\rho > 0$ such that

$$\rho(r \oplus t) \leq (\check{A}(r) \oplus \check{A}(t)), \forall\, r, t \in \check{E}.$$

(iii) $\check{A}$ is called a comparison mapping if $r \propto t, r \propto \check{A}(r)$ and $t \propto \check{A}(t)$, such that

$$\check{A}(r) \propto \check{A}(t), \forall\, r, t \in \check{E}.$$

(iv) D is called a comparison mapping if any $\vartheta_r \in D(r), r \propto \vartheta_r$ and if $r \propto t$, as well as for any $\vartheta_r \in D(r)$ and $\vartheta_t \in D(t)$, such that

$$\vartheta_r \propto \vartheta_t, \forall\, r, t \in \check{E}.$$

(v) The comparison mapping D is called an $\alpha-$ non-ordinary difference mapping if $\vartheta_r \in D(r)$ and $\vartheta_t \in D(t)$ such that

$$(\vartheta_r \oplus \vartheta_t) \oplus \alpha_{\check{A}}(r \oplus t) = 0,\ \forall\, r, t \in \check{E}.$$

(vi) The comparison mapping D is called ρ-ordered rectangular mapping. If there exists a constant $\rho > 0$, then there exists $\vartheta_r \in D(r)$ and $\vartheta_t \in D(t)$ such that

$$\langle(\vartheta_r \odot \vartheta_t) - (r \oplus t)\rangle \geq \rho||r \oplus t||^2,\ \forall\, r, t \in \check{E}.$$

(vii) D is called a weak comparison mapping if any $r, t \in \check{E}$ or $r \propto t$ and there exists $\vartheta_r \in D(r), \vartheta_t \in D(t), r \propto \vartheta_r$, and $t \propto \vartheta_t$ such that

$$\vartheta_r \propto \vartheta_t, \forall\, r, t \in \check{E}.$$

(viii) D is called $\rho-$ weak-ordered different mapping if there exists a constant $\rho > 0$, and there exists $\vartheta_r \in D(r)$ and $\vartheta_t \in D(t)$ such that

$$\rho(\vartheta_r - \vartheta_t) \propto (r - t), \forall\, r, t \in \check{E}.$$

(ix) A weak comparison mapping D is called $(\alpha_{\check{A}}, \rho)-$ weak ANODD if it is an $\alpha_{\check{A}}$ weak non-ordinary difference mapping and ρ-order different weak-comparison mapping with respect to $\check{A}$ and

$$(\check{A} + \rho D)\check{E} = \check{E}, \forall\, \rho > 0.$$

Lemma 1. *Suppose a multi-valued mapping $D : \check{E} \to 2^{\check{E}}$ is an ordered $(\alpha_{\check{A}}, \rho)$-weak ANODD mapping and $\check{A} : \check{E} \to \check{E}$ is called ξ-order non-extended mapping with respect to $\check{A}$ such that*

$$\left|\left|R^D_{\check{A},\rho}(r) \oplus R^D_{\check{A},\rho}(t)\right|\right| \leq R_\theta||r \oplus t||, \forall\, r, t \in \check{E}.$$

where $R_\theta = \frac{1}{\xi(\alpha_{\check{A}}\rho - 1)}, \rho > \frac{1}{\xi}$, and $\alpha_{\check{A}} > \frac{1}{\rho}$.

Thus, the resolvent operator $R^D_{\check{A},\rho}$ is Lipschitz-type-continuous.

Proposition 3. *Suppose $D : \check{E} \to 2^{\check{E}}$ is a multi-valued mapping and a single-valued mapping $\check{A} : \check{E} \to \check{E}$ is $\lambda_{\check{A}}$-Lipschitz continuous. Then, the generalized Cayley approximation operator*

$C^D_{\breve{A},\rho}$ is λ_C- Lipschitz continuous, which provides $r \propto t, \breve{A}(r) \propto \breve{A}(t), R^D_{\breve{A},\rho}(r) \propto R^D_{\breve{A},\rho}(t)$ and $C^D_{\breve{A},\rho}(r) \propto C^D_{\breve{A},\rho}(t)$ such that

$$\left|\left|C^D_{\breve{A},\rho}(r) \oplus C^D_{\breve{A},\rho}(t)\right|\right| \leq \lambda_C ||r \oplus t||, \; \forall \, r, t \in \breve{E}.$$

where $\lambda_C = \frac{\xi\lambda_{\breve{A}}(\alpha_{\breve{A}}\rho - 1) + 2}{\xi(\alpha_{\breve{A}}\rho - 1)}$.

Proof. Using the Lipschitz continuity of $\breve{A}$ and $R^D_{\breve{A},\rho}$, we evaluate

$$\begin{aligned}
\left|\left|C^D_{\breve{A},\rho}(r) \oplus C^D_{\breve{A},\rho}(t)\right|\right| &= \left|\left|[2R^D_{\breve{A},\rho} - \breve{A}](r) \oplus [2R^D_{\breve{A},\rho} - \breve{A}](t)\right|\right| \\
&\leq ||\breve{A}(r) \oplus \breve{A}(t)|| + 2\left|\left|R^D_{\breve{A},\rho}(r) \oplus R^D_{\breve{A},\rho}(t)\right|\right| \\
&\leq \lambda_{\breve{A}} ||r \oplus t|| + \frac{2}{\xi(\alpha_{\breve{A}}\rho - 1)} ||r \oplus t|| \\
&\leq \frac{\xi\lambda_{\breve{A}}(\alpha_{\breve{A}}\rho - 1) + 2}{\xi(\alpha_{\breve{A}}\rho - 1)} ||r \oplus t|| \\
&= \lambda_C ||r \oplus t||
\end{aligned}$$

where $\lambda_C = \frac{\xi\lambda_{\breve{A}}(\alpha_{\breve{A}}\rho - 1) + 2}{\xi(\alpha_{\breve{A}}\rho - 1)}$. □

3. Statement of the Cayley Inclusion Problem

Suppose $g, \breve{A}, \breve{B} : \breve{E} \to \breve{E}$ are the single-valued mappings and also $D : \breve{E} \to 2^{\breve{E}}$ are the multi-valued mapping; again, let us consider $\Upsilon : \breve{E} \times \breve{E} \times \breve{E} \to \breve{E}$ to be another mapping and $\psi, \phi, \varphi : \breve{E} \to C(\breve{E})$ to be the multi-valued mappings. Let $C^D_{\breve{A},\rho}$ be the generalized Cayley approximation operators for any $\rho > 0$.

Find $r \in \breve{E}, \breve{u} \in \psi(r), \breve{v} \in \phi(r)$ and $\breve{w} \in \varphi(r)$ such that

$$0 \in C^D_{\breve{A},\rho}(\breve{B}(r)) + \Upsilon(\breve{u}, \breve{v}, \breve{w}) \oplus D(g(r)). \tag{1}$$

If $C^D_{\breve{A},\rho}(\breve{B}(r)) = 0, \Upsilon(\breve{u}, \breve{v}, \breve{w}) = 0$ and $D(g(r)) = D(r)$, then problem (1) reduces to the problem of finding $r \in \breve{E}$ such that

$$0 \in D(r)$$

which is the fundamental issue involving the XOR operation and the Cayley approximation operator, represented by Rockafellar [13].

4. Fixed-Point Formulation and Iterative Algorithm

In this section, we demonstrate that problem (1) is equivalent to a fixed-point equation.

Lemma 2. *Let us consider $r \in \breve{E}, \breve{u} \in \psi(r), \breve{v} \in \phi(r)$ and $\breve{w} \in \varphi(r)$ to be the solutions of Cayley variational inclusion problem (1) involving an XOR operation and an XNOR operation if and only if the following equation is satisfied:*

$$g(r) = R^D_{\breve{A},\rho}\left[\breve{A}(g(r)) + \rho\left\{\Upsilon(\breve{u}, \breve{v}, \breve{w}) \odot C^D_{\breve{A},\rho}(\breve{B}(r))\right\}\right]. \tag{2}$$

Proof. Suppose $r \in \breve{E}, \breve{u} \in \psi(r), \breve{v} \in \phi(r)$ and $\breve{w} \in \varphi(r)$ satisfy Equation (2). Then, we have

$$\begin{aligned} g(r) &= R^D_{\breve{A},\rho}\Big[\breve{A}(g(r)) + \rho\Big\{\Upsilon(\breve{u},\breve{v},\breve{w}) \odot C^D_{\breve{A},\rho}(\breve{B}(r))\Big\}\Big] \\ &= (\breve{A}+\rho D)^{-1}\Big[\breve{A}(g(r)) + \rho\Big\{\Upsilon(\breve{u},\breve{v},\breve{w}) \odot C^D_{\breve{A},\rho}(\breve{B}(r))\Big\}\Big] \\ (\breve{A}+\rho D)g(r) &= \breve{A}(g(r)) + \rho\Big\{(\Upsilon(\breve{u},\breve{v},\breve{w}) \odot C^D_{\breve{A},\rho}(\breve{B}(r))\Big\} \\ &= \breve{A}(g(r)) + \rho\Big\{\Upsilon(\breve{u},\breve{v},\breve{w}) \odot C^D_{\breve{A},\rho}(\breve{B}(r))\Big\} \end{aligned}$$

$$\begin{aligned} D(g(r)) &= \Upsilon(\breve{u},\breve{v},\breve{w}) \odot C^D_{\breve{A},\rho}(\breve{B}(r)) \\ \Upsilon(\breve{u},\breve{v},\breve{w}) \odot D(g(r)) &= \Upsilon(\breve{u},\breve{v},\breve{w}) \odot \Upsilon(\breve{u},\breve{v},\breve{w}) \odot C^D_{\breve{A},\rho}(\breve{B}(r)) \\ &= C^D_{\breve{A},\rho}(\breve{B}(r)) \\ 0 &\in C^D_{\breve{A},\rho}(\breve{B}(r)) + \Upsilon(\breve{u},\breve{v},\breve{w}) \oplus D(g(r)), \end{aligned}$$

which is the required Cayley variational inclusion problem (1). Now, we establish the subsequent algorithm utilizing Lemma 2 to solve the Cayley variational inclusion problem (1). □

5. Main Result

In this section, we establish an existence and convergence result via Algorithm 1 for the generalized Cayley variational inclusion problem, which incorporates XOR and XNOR operations (1).

Algorithm 1 For every $r_0 \in \breve{E}, \breve{u} \in \psi(r_0), \breve{v} \in \phi(r_0)$ and $\breve{w} \in \varphi(r_0)$, enumerate the sequence$\{r_n\}, \{\breve{u}_n\}, \{\breve{v}_n\}$ and $\{\breve{w}_n\}$ by taking after the iterative algorithm.

$$g(r_{n+1}) = (1-\alpha)g(r_n) + \alpha R^D_{\breve{A},\rho}\Big[\breve{A}(g(r_n)) + \rho\Big\{\Upsilon(\breve{u}_n,\breve{v}_n,\breve{w}_n) \odot C^D_{\breve{A},\rho}(\breve{B}(r_n))\Big\}\Big]. \tag{3}$$

Let us consider $\breve{u}_{n+1} \in \psi(r_{n+1}), \breve{v}_{n+1} \in \phi(r_{n+1})$ and $\breve{w}_{n+1} \in \varphi(r_{n+1})$ such that

$$||\breve{u}_n - \breve{u}_{n+1}|| \le \mathcal{D}(\psi(r_n), \psi(r_{n-1})), \tag{4}$$
$$||\breve{v}_n - \breve{v}_{n+1}|| \le \mathcal{D}(\phi(r_n), \phi(r_{n-1})), \tag{5}$$
$$||\breve{w}_n - \breve{w}_{n+1}|| \le \mathcal{D}(\varphi(r_n), \varphi(r_{n-1})), \tag{6}$$

where $0 \le \alpha \le 1$ and $\rho > 0$ are constants and $n = 0, 1, 2, 3, \cdots$

Theorem 1. *Let $\breve{E}$ be a real-ordered Hilbert space and $C_{\breve{E}}$ be a normal cone in $\breve{E}$. Let us consider $g, \breve{A}, \breve{B} : \breve{E} \to \breve{E}$ as Lipschitz continuous mappings with constants $\lambda_g > 0, \lambda_{\breve{A}} > 0$, and $\lambda_{\breve{B}} > 0$, respectively. Also, we consider $\Upsilon : \breve{E} \times \breve{E} \times \breve{E} \to \breve{E}$ to be a Lipschitz continuous mapping with constants $\lambda_{\Upsilon_1} > 0, \lambda_{\Upsilon_2} > 0$ and $\lambda_{\Upsilon_3} > 0$, respectively, and $D : \breve{E} \to 2^{\breve{E}}$ to be the multi-valued mapping. Let $C^D_{\breve{A},\rho}$ be the generalized Cayley approximation operator with Lipschitz continuous λ_C, let the generalized resolvent operator $R^D_{\breve{A},\rho}$ be R_θ Lipschitz continuous and let $\psi, \phi, \varphi : \breve{E} \to C(\breve{E})$ be the multi-valued mappings with constants $\lambda_{\mathcal{D}_\psi} > 0, \lambda_{\mathcal{D}_\phi} > 0$ and $\lambda_{\mathcal{D}_\varphi} > 0$, respectively. $r \propto t, R^D_{\breve{A},\rho}(r) \propto R^D_{\breve{A},\rho}(t), C^D_{\breve{A},\rho}(\breve{A}(r)) \propto C^D_{\breve{A},\rho}(\breve{A}(t)), g(r_{n+1}) \propto g(r_n), \Upsilon(\breve{u}_n,\breve{v}_n,\breve{w}_n) \propto \Upsilon(\breve{u}_{n-1},\breve{v}_{n-1},\breve{w}_{n-1})$ and $\breve{A}(r) \propto \breve{A}(t)$ for all $r, t \in \breve{E}$, where $\rho > 0$ is a constant. Suppose that the following conditions are satisfied:*

$$0 < \frac{\lambda_{\Pi_{\breve{E}}}}{\delta_g}\Big\{(1-\alpha)\lambda_g + \alpha R_\theta \lambda_{\breve{A}}\lambda_g + \alpha\rho R_\theta \lambda_C \lambda_{\breve{B}} + \alpha\rho R_\theta \lambda_{\Upsilon_1}\lambda_{\mathcal{D}_\psi} + \alpha\rho R_\theta \lambda_{\Upsilon_2}\lambda_{\mathcal{D}_\phi}$$
$$+\alpha\rho R_\theta \lambda_{\Upsilon_3}\lambda_{\mathcal{D}_\varphi}\Big\} < 1 \tag{7}$$

where $R_\theta = \frac{1}{\xi(\alpha_{\breve{A}}\rho - 1)}, \rho > \frac{1}{\xi}, \alpha_{\breve{A}} > \frac{1}{\rho}, \lambda_C = \frac{\xi\lambda_{\breve{A}}(\alpha_{\breve{A}}\rho-1)+2}{\xi(\alpha_{\breve{A}}\rho-1)}, 0 \le \alpha \le 1, \rho > 0, n = 0,1,2,3,\cdots$ *Then,* $(r, \breve{u}, \breve{v}, \breve{w})$ *is the solution of the Cayley variational inclusions problem (1) involving an XOR operation and an XNOR operation, and the sequences* $\{r_n\}, \{\breve{u}_n\}, \{\breve{v}_n\}$ *and* $\{\breve{w}_n\}$*, generated by Algorithm 1, strongly convergence at* $r, \breve{u}, \breve{v}$ *and* $\breve{w}$*, respectively.*

Proof. We have

$$\begin{aligned}
0 \le g(r_{n+1}) \oplus g(r_n) &= \Big\{(1-\alpha)g(r_n) + \alpha R^D_{\breve{A},\rho}\Big[\breve{A}(g(r_n)) + \rho\Big\{\Upsilon(\breve{u}_n, \breve{v}_n, \breve{w}_n) \\
&\quad \odot C^D_{\breve{A},\rho}(\breve{B}(r_n))\Big\}\Big]\Big\} \oplus \Big\{(1-\alpha)g(r_{n-1}) + \alpha R^D_{\breve{A},\rho}\Big[\breve{A}(g(r_{n-1})) \\
&\quad + \rho\Big\{\Upsilon(\breve{u}_{n-1}, \breve{v}_{n-1}, \breve{w}_{n-1}) \odot C^D_{\breve{A},\rho}(\breve{B}(r_{n-1}))\Big\}\Big]\Big\} \\
&\le (1-\alpha)(g(r_n) \oplus g(r_{n-1})) + \alpha\Big\{R^D_{\breve{A},\rho}\Big[\breve{A}(g(r_n)) \\
&\quad + \rho\Big\{\Upsilon(\breve{u}_n, \breve{v}_n, \breve{w}_n) \odot C^D_{\breve{A},\rho}(\breve{B}(r_n))\}\Big] \oplus R^D_{\breve{A},\rho}\Big[\breve{A}(g(r_{n-1})) \\
&\quad + \rho\Big\{\Upsilon(\breve{u}_{n-1}, \breve{v}_{n-1}, \breve{w}_{n-1}) \odot C^D_{\breve{A},\rho}(\breve{B}(r_{n-1}))\Big\}\Big]\Big\}.
\end{aligned} \tag{8}$$

Using (4), (5), (6), (iii) of Proposition 2, and (8), we obtain,

$$\begin{aligned}
||g(r_{n+1}) \oplus g(r_n)|| \le\; & (1-\alpha)\lambda_{\Pi_{\breve{E}}}||g(r_n) \oplus g(r_{n-1})|| + \alpha\lambda_{\Pi_{\breve{E}}}||R^D_{\breve{A},\rho}[\breve{A}(g(r_n)) \\
& +\rho\{\Upsilon(\breve{u}_n, \breve{v}_n, \breve{w}_n) \odot C^D_{\breve{A},\rho}(\breve{B}(r_n))\}] \oplus R^D_{\breve{A},\rho}[\breve{A}(g(r_{n-1})) \\
& +\rho\{\Upsilon(\breve{u}_{n-1}, \breve{v}_{n-1}, \breve{w}_{n-1}) \odot C^D_{\breve{A},\rho}(\breve{B}(r_{n-1}))\}]|| \\
\le\; & (1-\alpha)\lambda_{\Pi_{\breve{E}}}||g(r_n) \oplus g(r_{n-1})|| + \alpha\lambda_{\Pi_{\breve{E}}}R_\theta||[\breve{A}(g(r_n)) \\
& +\rho\{\Upsilon(\breve{u}_n, \breve{v}_n, \breve{w}_n) \odot C^D_{\breve{A},\rho}(\breve{B}(r_n))\}] \oplus [\breve{A}(g(r_{n-1})) \\
& +\rho\{\Upsilon(\breve{u}_{n-1}, \breve{v}_{n-1}, \breve{w}_{n-1}) \odot C^D_{\breve{A},\rho}(\breve{B}(r_{n-1}))\}]|| \\
\le\; & (1-\alpha)\lambda_{\Pi_{\breve{E}}}||g(r_n) \oplus g(r_{n-1})|| + \alpha\lambda_{\Pi_{\breve{E}}}R_\theta||\breve{A}(g(r_n)) \\
& \oplus\breve{A}(g(r_{n-1}))|| + \alpha\rho R_\theta\lambda_{\Pi_{\breve{E}}}||\Upsilon(\breve{u}_n, \breve{v}_n, \breve{w}_n) \\
& \oplus\Upsilon(\breve{u}_{n-1}, \breve{v}_{n-1}, \breve{w}_{n-1})|| + \alpha\rho R_\theta\lambda_{\Pi_{\breve{E}}}||C^D_{\breve{A},\rho}(\breve{B}(r_n)) \\
& \oplus C^D_{\breve{A},\rho}(\breve{B}(r_{n-1}))|| \\
\le\; & (1-\alpha)\lambda_{\Pi_{\breve{E}}}\lambda_g||r_n \oplus r_{n-1}|| + \alpha\lambda_{\Pi_{\breve{E}}}R_\theta\lambda_{\breve{A}}||g(r_n) \\
& \oplus g(r_{n-1})|| + \alpha\rho R_\theta\lambda_{\Pi_{\breve{E}}}||\Upsilon(\breve{u}_n, \breve{v}_n, \breve{w}_n) \\
& \oplus\Upsilon(\breve{u}_{n-1}, \breve{v}_{n-1}, \breve{w}_{n-1})|| + \alpha\rho R_\theta\lambda_{\Pi_{\breve{E}}}\lambda_C||\breve{B}(r_n) \oplus \breve{B}(r_{n-1})|| \\
\le\; & (1-\alpha)\lambda_{\Pi_{\breve{E}}}\lambda_g||r_n \oplus r_{n-1}|| + \alpha\lambda_{\Pi_{\breve{E}}}R_\theta\lambda_{\breve{A}}\lambda_g||r_n \\
& \oplus r_{n-1}|| + \alpha\rho R_\theta\lambda_{\Pi_{\breve{E}}}\lambda_C\lambda_{\breve{B}}||r_n \oplus r_{n-1}|| \\
& +\alpha\rho R_\theta\lambda_{\Pi_{\breve{E}}}||\Upsilon(\breve{u}_n, \breve{v}_n, \breve{w}_n) \oplus \Upsilon(\breve{u}_{n-1}, \breve{v}_{n-1}, \breve{w}_{n-1})||.
\end{aligned} \tag{9}$$

Now, we have the following from the definition of $\mathcal{D}$-Lipschitz continuity and (i) of Proposition 1.

$$\begin{aligned}
& ||\Upsilon(\breve{u}_n, \breve{v}_n, \breve{w}_n) \oplus \Upsilon(\breve{u}_{n-1}, \breve{v}_{n-1}, \breve{w}_{n-1})|| \\
= \; & ||\Upsilon(\breve{u}_n, \breve{v}_n, \breve{w}_n) \oplus \Upsilon(\breve{u}_{n-1}, \breve{v}_n, \breve{w}_n) \oplus \Upsilon(\breve{u}_{n-1}, \breve{v}_n, \breve{w}_n) \\
& \oplus \Upsilon(\breve{u}_{n-1}, \breve{v}_{n-1}, \breve{w}_n) \oplus \Upsilon(\breve{u}_{n-1}, \breve{v}_{n-1}, \breve{w}_n) \oplus \Upsilon(\breve{u}_{n-1}, \breve{v}_{n-1}, \breve{w}_{n-1})|| \\
= \; & ||\Upsilon(\breve{u}_n, \breve{v}_n, \breve{w}_n) \oplus \Upsilon(\breve{u}_{n-1}, \breve{v}_n, \breve{w}_n)|| + ||\Upsilon(\breve{u}_{n-1}, \breve{v}_n, \breve{w}_n) \oplus \Upsilon(\breve{u}_{n-1}, \breve{v}_{n-1}, \breve{w}_n)|| \\
& + ||\Upsilon(\breve{u}_{n-1}, \breve{v}_{n-1}, \breve{w}_n) \oplus \Upsilon(\breve{u}_{n-1}, \breve{v}_{n-1}, \breve{w}_{n-1})|| \\
\leq \; & \lambda_{\Upsilon_1} ||\breve{u}_n \oplus \breve{u}_{n-1}|| + \lambda_{\Upsilon_2} ||\breve{v}_n \oplus \breve{v}_{n-1}|| + \lambda_{\Upsilon_3} ||\breve{w}_n \oplus \breve{w}_{n-1}|| \\
\leq \; & \lambda_{\Upsilon_1} \mathcal{D}(\psi(r_n), \psi(r_{n-1})) + \lambda_{\Upsilon_2} \mathcal{D}(\phi(r_n), \phi(r_{n-1})) + \lambda_{\Upsilon_3} \mathcal{D}(\varphi(r_n), \varphi(r_{n-1})) \\
\leq \; & \lambda_{\Upsilon_1} \lambda_{\mathcal{D}_\psi} ||r_n \oplus r_{n-1}|| + \lambda_{\Upsilon_2} \lambda_{\mathcal{D}_\phi} ||r_n \oplus r_{n-1}|| + \lambda_{\Upsilon_3} \lambda_{\mathcal{D}_\varphi} ||r_n \oplus r_{n-1}||.
\end{aligned} \tag{10}$$

Combining (9) and (10), we obtain

$$\begin{aligned}
||g(r_{n+1}) \oplus g(r_n)|| \leq \; & (1-\alpha)\lambda_{\Pi_{\breve{E}}} \lambda_g ||r_n \oplus r_{n-1}|| + \alpha \lambda_{\Pi_{\breve{E}}} R_\theta \lambda_{\breve{A}} \lambda_g ||r_n \oplus r_{n-1}|| \\
& + \alpha\rho R_\theta \lambda_{\Pi_{\breve{E}}} \lambda_C \lambda_{\breve{B}} ||r_n \oplus r_{n-1}|| + \alpha\rho R_\theta \lambda_{\Pi_{\breve{E}}} \lambda_{\Upsilon_1} \lambda_{\mathcal{D}_\psi} ||r_n \\
& \oplus r_{n-1}|| + \alpha\rho R_\theta \lambda_{\Pi_{\breve{E}}} \lambda_{\Upsilon_2} \lambda_{\mathcal{D}_\phi} ||r_n \oplus r_{n-1}|| \\
& + \alpha\rho R_\theta \lambda_{\Pi_{\breve{E}}} \lambda_{\Upsilon_3} \lambda_{\mathcal{D}_\varphi} ||r_n \oplus r_{n-1}|| \\
\leq \; & \{(1-\alpha)\lambda_{\Pi_{\breve{E}}} \lambda_g + \alpha \lambda_{\Pi_{\breve{E}}} R_\theta \lambda_{\breve{A}} \lambda_g + \alpha\rho R_\theta \lambda_{\Pi_{\breve{E}}} \lambda_C \lambda_{\breve{B}} \\
& + \alpha\rho R_\theta \lambda_{\Pi_{\breve{E}}} \lambda_{\Upsilon_1} \lambda_{\mathcal{D}_\psi} + \alpha\rho R_\theta \lambda_{\Pi_{\breve{E}}} \lambda_{\Upsilon_2} \lambda_{\mathcal{D}_\phi} \\
& + \alpha\rho R_\theta \lambda_{\Pi_{\breve{E}}} \lambda_{\Upsilon_3} \lambda_{\mathcal{D}_\varphi}\} ||r_n \oplus r_{n-1}||.
\end{aligned} \tag{11}$$

Using (iv) of Proposition 2 in (11), we have

$$\begin{aligned}
||g(r_{n+1}) - g(r_n)|| \leq \; & \{(1-\alpha)\lambda_{\Pi_{\breve{E}}} \lambda_g + \alpha \lambda_{\Pi_{\breve{E}}} R_\theta \lambda_{\breve{A}} \lambda_g + \alpha\rho R_\theta \lambda_{\Pi_{\breve{E}}} \lambda_C \lambda_{\breve{B}} \\
& + \alpha\rho R_\theta \lambda_{\Pi_{\breve{E}}} \lambda_{\Upsilon_1} \lambda_{\mathcal{D}_\psi} + \alpha\rho R_\theta \lambda_{\Pi_{\breve{E}}} \lambda_{\Upsilon_2} \lambda_{\mathcal{D}_\phi} \\
& + \alpha\rho R_\theta \lambda_{\Pi_{\breve{E}}} \lambda_{\Upsilon_3} \lambda_{\mathcal{D}_\varphi}\} ||r_n - r_{n-1}||.
\end{aligned} \tag{12}$$

Since g is strongly monotone , we have

$$||g(r_{n+1}) - g(r_n)|| \geq \delta_g ||r_{n+1} - r_n||$$

which implies that

$$||r_{n+1} - r_n|| \leq \frac{1}{\delta_g} ||g(r_{n+1}) - g(r_n)||. \tag{13}$$

Now, combining (12) and (13), we obtain

$$\begin{aligned}
||r_{n+1} - r_n|| \leq \; & \frac{1}{\delta_g} \Big\{(1-\alpha)\lambda_{\Pi_{\breve{E}}} \lambda_g + \alpha \lambda_{\Pi_{\breve{E}}} R_\theta \lambda_{\breve{A}} \lambda_g + \alpha\rho R_\theta \lambda_{\Pi_{\breve{E}}} \lambda_C \lambda_{\breve{B}} + \alpha\rho R_\theta \lambda_{\Pi_{\breve{E}}} \lambda_{\Upsilon_1} \lambda_{\mathcal{D}_\psi} \\
& + \alpha\rho R_\theta \lambda_{\Pi_{\breve{E}}} \lambda_{\Upsilon_2} \lambda_{\mathcal{D}_\phi} + \alpha\rho R_\theta \lambda_{\Pi_{\breve{E}}} \lambda_{\Upsilon_3} \lambda_{\mathcal{D}_\varphi}\Big\} ||r_n - r_{n-1}|| \\
\leq \; & \frac{\lambda_{\Pi_{\breve{E}}}}{\delta_g} \Big\{(1-\alpha)\lambda_g + \alpha R_\theta \lambda_{\breve{A}} \lambda_g + \alpha\rho R_\theta \lambda_C \lambda_{\breve{B}} + \alpha\rho R_\theta \lambda_{\Upsilon_1} \lambda_{\mathcal{D}_\psi} \\
& + \alpha\rho R_\theta \lambda_{\Upsilon_2} \lambda_{\mathcal{D}_\phi} + \alpha\rho R_\theta \lambda_{\Upsilon_3} \lambda_{\mathcal{D}_\varphi}\Big\} ||r_n - r_{n-1}|| \\
\leq \; & \Omega(\theta) ||r_n - r_{n-1}||,
\end{aligned} \tag{14}$$

where

$$\Omega(\theta) = \frac{\lambda_{\Pi_{\check{E}}}}{\delta_g}\Big\{(1-\alpha)\lambda_g + \alpha R_\theta \lambda_{\check{A}}\lambda_g + \alpha\rho R_\theta \lambda_C \lambda_{\check{B}} + \alpha\rho R_\theta \lambda_{Y_1}\lambda_{\mathcal{D}_\psi} + \alpha\rho R_\theta \lambda_{Y_2}\lambda_{\mathcal{D}_\phi} + \alpha\rho R_\theta \lambda_{Y_3}\lambda_{\mathcal{D}_\varphi}\Big\}$$

From condition (7), it is clear that $\Omega(\theta) < 1$, where $\Omega(\theta) = \frac{\lambda_{\Pi_{\check{E}}}}{\delta_g}\{(1-\alpha)\lambda_g + \alpha R_\theta \lambda_{\check{A}}\lambda_g + \alpha\rho R_\theta \lambda_C \lambda_{\check{B}} + \alpha\rho R_\theta \lambda_{Y_1}\lambda_{\mathcal{D}_\psi} + \alpha\rho R_\theta \lambda_{Y_2}\lambda_{\mathcal{D}_\phi} + \alpha\rho R_\theta \lambda_{Y_3}\lambda_{\mathcal{D}_\varphi}\}$. Consequently, (14) implies that $\{r_n\}$ is a Cauchy sequence in $\check{E}$. Thus, there exists $r \in \check{E}$ such that $r_n \to r$ as $n \to \infty$.

From (4), (5) and (6), we have

$$||\breve{u}_n - \breve{u}_{n-1}|| \le \mathcal{D}(\psi(r_n), \psi(r_{n-1})) \le \lambda_{\mathcal{D}_\psi}||r_n \oplus r|| \le \lambda_{\mathcal{D}_\psi}||r_n - r||, \tag{15}$$

$$||\breve{v}_n - \breve{v}_{n-1}|| \le \mathcal{D}(\phi(r_n), \phi(r_{n-1})) \le \lambda_{\mathcal{D}_\phi}||r_n \oplus r|| \le \lambda_{\mathcal{D}_\phi}||r_n - r||, \tag{16}$$

$$||\breve{w}_n - \breve{w}_{n-1}|| \le \mathcal{D}(\varphi(r_n), \varphi(r_{n-1})) \le \lambda_{\mathcal{D}_\varphi}||r_n \oplus r|| \le \lambda_{\mathcal{D}_\varphi}||r_n - r||. \tag{17}$$

Thus $\{\breve{u}_n\}, \{\breve{v}_n\}$ and $\{\breve{w}_n\}$, are also Cauchy sequences in $\check{E}$. Therefore, there exists $r \in \check{E}, \breve{u} \in \psi(r), \breve{v} \in \phi(r)$ and $\breve{w} \in \varphi(r)$ such that $\breve{u}_n \to \breve{u}$, $\breve{v}_n \to \breve{v}$ and $\breve{w}_n \to \breve{w}$ as $n \to \infty$. Next, we show that $\breve{u}_n \to \breve{u} \in \psi(r), \breve{v}_n \to \breve{v} \in \phi(r)$ and $\breve{w}_n \to \breve{w} \in \varphi(r)$ as $n \to \infty$.

Furthermore,

$$\begin{aligned} d(\breve{u}, \psi(r)) &\le inf\{||\breve{u} \quad t||, t \subset \psi(r)\} \\ &\le ||\breve{u} - \breve{u}_n|| + d(\breve{u}_n, \psi(r)) \\ &\le ||\breve{u} - \breve{u}_n|| + d(\psi(r_n), \psi(r)) \\ &\le ||\breve{u} - \breve{u}_n|| + \lambda_{\mathcal{D}_\psi}||r_n \oplus r|| \\ &\le ||\breve{u} - \breve{u}_n|| + \lambda_{\mathcal{D}_\psi}||r_n \oplus r|| \quad \to 0, \text{as } n \to \infty. \end{aligned}$$

Since $\psi(r)$ is closed, we have $\breve{u} \in \psi(r)$. Similarly, we can show that $\breve{v} \in \phi(r)$ and $\breve{w} \in \varphi(r)$. Finally, we apply the continuity of $g, \check{A}, \check{B}, Y, R^D_{\check{A},\rho}$, and $C^D_{\check{A},\rho}$, which implies that

$$g(r) = R^D_{\check{A},\rho}\Big[\check{A}(g(r)) + \rho\Big\{Y(\breve{u}, \breve{v}, \breve{w}) \odot C^D_{\check{A},\rho}(\check{B}(r))\Big\}\Big].$$

By Lemma 2, $r \in \check{E}$ is the solution of the Cayley variational inclusion problem (1), where $\breve{u} \in \psi(r), \breve{v} \in \phi(r)$ and $\breve{w} \in \varphi(r)$. □

6. Numerical Result

To illustrate Theorem 1, we present the following numerical example, implemented using MATLAB 2024b, accompanied by three computation tables and three convergence graphs.

Example 1. *Suppose $\check{E} = R$ involving inner product $\langle .,. \rangle$ and norm $||.||$, and $D : \check{E} \to 2^{\check{E}}$ is a multi-valued mapping.*

(i) Again, let us consider $g, \check{A}, \check{B} : \check{E} \to \check{E}$ to be the single-valued mappings, $Y : \check{E} \times \check{E} \times \check{E} \to \check{E}$ to be another single-valued mapping, and $\psi, \phi, \varphi : \check{E} \to C(\check{E})$ to be another multi-valued mapping such that

$$D(r) = \{4r\} \text{ and } g(r) = \frac{5r}{3}.$$

Then, for any $r_1, r_2 \in \check{E}$, *we have*

$$\begin{aligned} \|\, g(r_1) - g(r_2)\| &= \left\|\frac{5r_1}{3} - \frac{5r_2}{3}\right\| \\ &= \frac{5}{3}\|\, r_1 - r_2\| \\ &\leq 2\|\, r_1 - r_2\|\,. \end{aligned}$$

Thus, g is Lipschitz continuous with constant $\lambda_g = 2$ *and*

$$\begin{aligned} \|g(r_1) - g(r_2)\| &= \left\|\frac{5}{3}r_1 - \frac{5}{3}r_2\right\| \\ &= \frac{5}{3}\|r_1 - r_2\| \\ &\geq \frac{4}{3}\|r_1 - r_2\|. \end{aligned}$$

Similarly, g is strongly monotone with constant $\delta_g = \frac{4}{3}$.

(ii) *Suppose* $\Upsilon : \check{E} \times \check{E} \times \check{E} \to \check{E}$ *is the single-valued mapping and* $\psi, \phi, \varphi : \check{E} \to C(\check{E})$ *is the multi-valued mappings such that*

$$\psi(r) = \left\{\frac{r}{6}\right\},\ \phi(r) = \left\{\frac{r}{5}\right\},\ \varphi(r) = \left\{\frac{r}{4}\right\},\ \text{and } \Upsilon(\breve{u}, \breve{v}, \breve{w}) = \left\{\frac{\breve{u}}{2} + \frac{\breve{v}}{2} + \frac{\breve{w}}{2}\right\}.$$

Now, we have

$$\begin{aligned} \mathcal{D}(\psi(r), \psi(t)) &= \max\left\{\sup_{r\in S(r)} d(r, F(t)),\ \sup_{t\in S(t)} d(F(r), t)\right\} \\ &\leq \max\left\{\left\|\frac{r}{6} - \frac{t}{6}\right\|, \left\|\frac{t}{6} - \frac{r}{6}\right\|\right\} \\ &\leq \frac{1}{6}\max\{\|r - t\|, \|t - r\|\} \\ &\leq \frac{1}{5}\max\|r - t\|. \end{aligned}$$

So, ψ *is* $\mathcal{D}$*-Lipschitz continuous with constant* $\lambda_{\mathcal{D}_\psi} = \frac{1}{5}$. *Similarly, we have to show that* $\lambda_{\mathcal{D}_\phi} = \frac{1}{4}$, *and* $\lambda_{\mathcal{D}_\varphi} = \frac{1}{3}$.
Hence, Υ *is Lipschitz continuous in three arguments with constant* $\lambda_{\Upsilon_1} = \lambda_{\Upsilon_2} = \lambda_{\Upsilon_3} = 1$.
Thus, we obtain

$$\begin{aligned} \Upsilon(\breve{u}, \breve{v}, \breve{w}) &= \left(\frac{r}{12} + \frac{r}{10} + \frac{r}{8}\right) \\ &= \frac{37}{120}r. \end{aligned}$$

(iii) *Suppose* $\breve{A}, \breve{B} : \check{E} \to \check{E}$ *is the single-valued mappings;* $D : \check{E} \to 2^{\check{E}}$ *is a multi-valued mapping such that*

$$\breve{A}(r) = \frac{r}{3} \text{ and } \breve{B}(r) = \frac{r}{2}.$$

Now, we have

$$\begin{aligned} \|\breve{A}(r_1) - \breve{A}(r_2)\| &= \left\|\frac{r_1}{3} - \frac{r_2}{3}\right\| \\ &= \frac{1}{3}\|r_1 - r_2\| \\ &\leq \frac{1}{2}\|r_1 - r_2\|. \end{aligned}$$

Thus, $\breve{A}$ is Lipschitz continuous with constant $\lambda_{\breve{A}} = \frac{1}{2}$. Similarly, we have to show that $\breve{B}$ is Lipschitz continuous with constant $\lambda_{\breve{B}} = \frac{2}{3}$. In addition, $\breve{A}$ and $\breve{B}$ are ξ-ordered non-extended mappings with constant $\xi = 1$.

(iv) Suppose $D : \breve{E} \to 2^{\breve{E}}$ is the multi-valued mappings and for every constant $\rho > 0$ such that

$$D(r) = \{4r\}.$$

Now, letting $\rho = 1$, it is clear that D is $(\alpha_{\breve{A}}, \rho)$-weak ANODD mapping with $\alpha_{\breve{A}} = 3$.

(v) Now, we calculate the obtained resolvent operators $R^{D}_{\breve{A},\rho}$ such that

$$\begin{aligned} R^{D}_{\breve{A},\rho}(r) &= (\breve{A} + \rho D)^{-1}(r) \\ &= \frac{3r}{13}. \end{aligned}$$

Also, we have

$$\begin{aligned} \left|\left|R^{D}_{\breve{A},\rho}(r_1) \oplus R^{D}_{\breve{A},\rho}(r_2)\right|\right| &= \left|\left|\frac{3r_1}{13} \oplus \frac{3r_2}{13}\right|\right| \\ &= \frac{3}{13}||r_1 \oplus r_2|| \\ &\leq \frac{1}{2}||r_1 \oplus r_2||. \end{aligned}$$

Thus, $R^{D}_{\breve{A},\rho}$ is Lipschitz continuous with constant $R_\theta = \frac{1}{2}$, where $R_\theta = \frac{1}{\xi(\alpha_{\breve{A}}\rho - 1)}, \rho > \frac{1}{\alpha_{\breve{A}}}$.

(vi) Using the values of $R^{D}_{\breve{A},\rho}$, we obtain the generalized Cayley approximation operator as

$$\begin{aligned} C^{D}_{\breve{A},\rho}(r) &= \left[2R^{D}_{\breve{A},\rho} - \breve{A}\right](r) \\ &= \frac{6r}{13} - \frac{r}{3} \\ &= \frac{5r}{39}. \end{aligned}$$

Now, we have

$$\begin{aligned} ||C^{D}_{\breve{A},\rho}(r_1) \oplus C^{D}_{\breve{A},\rho}(r_2)|| &= \left|\left|\frac{5r_1}{39} \oplus \frac{5r_2}{39}\right|\right| \\ &= \frac{5}{39}||r_1 \oplus r_2|| \\ &\leq \frac{3}{2}||r_1 \oplus r_2||. \end{aligned}$$

Thus, $C^{D}_{\breve{A},\rho}$ is Lipschitz continuous with constant $\lambda_C = \frac{3}{2}$ where $\lambda_C = \frac{\xi\lambda_{\breve{A}}(\alpha_{\breve{A}}\rho - 1) + 2}{\xi(\alpha_{\breve{A}}\rho - 1)}$.

(vii) Now, we consider the interval $0 \leq \frac{1}{10} \leq r \leq t \leq 1$ and $\lambda_{\Pi_{\breve{E}}} = \frac{1}{2}$.

(viii) Considering the constants calculated above, condition (7) of Theorem 1 is satisfied.

(ix) Now putting all values in Equation (3), we obtain

$$\begin{aligned} g(r_{n+1}) &= (1-\alpha)g(r_n) + \alpha R^{D}_{\breve{A},\rho}\left[\breve{A}(g(r_n)) + \rho\left\{\Upsilon(\breve{u}_n, \breve{v}_n, \breve{w}_n) \odot C^{D}_{\breve{A},\rho}(\breve{B}(r_n))\right\}\right] \\ r_{n+1} &= (1-\alpha)r_n + \frac{78174}{608400}\alpha r_n = (1 - 0.87\alpha)r_n. \end{aligned}$$

In this numerical result, we consider three cases for the composition of the computation table and convergence graph we use the tools of MATLAB-R2024b with some different initial values *of r_0 and the value of constant α, where $0 \leq \alpha \leq 1$.*

In the first case, Consider $\alpha = \frac{1}{5}$, and various initial values $r_0 = -2, -1.5, -1, 1, 1.5, 2$. We obtain an excellent graph of the convergence sequence $\{r_{n+1}\}$ which converges at $r = 0$ (after fifty-one iterations), which is the solution of the Cayley variational inclusion problem (1). It is shown through a computation table (Table 1) and convergence graph (Figure 1).

Table 1. The values of the convergent sequence $\{r_n\}$ with initial values $r_0 = -2, -1.5, -1, 1, 1.5, 2$.

No. of Iterations	$r_0 = -2$	$r_0 = -1.5$	$r_0 = -1$	$r_0 = 1$	$r_0 = 1.5$	$r_0 = 2$
n = 1	−1.65200	−1.23900	−0.82600	0.82600	1.23900	1.65200
n = 2	−1.36460	−1.02340	−0.68220	0.68220	1.02340	1.36460
n = 3	−1.12710	−0.84534	−0.56356	0.56356	0.84534	1.12710
n = 4	−0.93100	−0.69825	−0.46550	0.46550	0.69825	0.93100
n = 5	−0.76901	−0.57676	−0.38450	0.38450	0.57676	0.76901
n = 6	−0.63520	−0.47640	−0.31760	0.31760	0.47640	0.63520
n = 15	−0.11369	−0.08526	−0.05684	0.05684	0.08526	0.11369
n = 20	−0.04371	−0.03278	−0.02185	0.02185	0.03278	0.04371
n = 25	−0.01680	−0.01260	−0.00840	0.00840	0.01260	0.01680
n = 35	−0.00248	−0.00186	−0.00124	0.00124	0.00186	0.00248
n = 51	−0.00011	−0.00000	−0.00000	0.00000	0.00000	0.00011
n = 55	−0.00000	−0.00000	−0.00000	0.00000	0.00000	0.00000

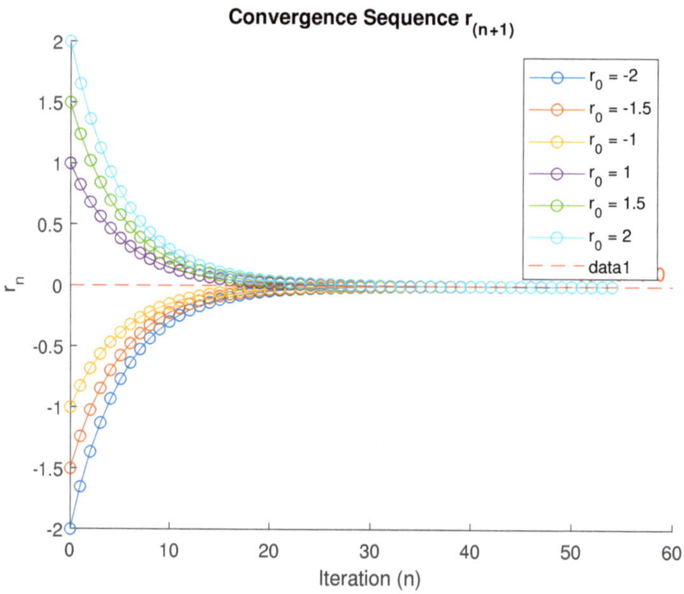

Figure 1. Graphical representation of a convergence sequence of $\{r_{n+1}\}$ with different initial values. when $\alpha = \frac{1}{5}$.

In the second case, Suppose $\alpha = \frac{1}{2}$, and the same initial values. We get a computation table (Table 2) and a graph (Figure 2) of the convergence sequence $\{r_{n+1}\}$ which converges at $r = 0$ (after eighteen iterations), which is the solution of the Cayley variational inclusion problem (1).

Table 2. The values of the convergent sequence $\{r_n\}$ with initial values $r_0 = -2, -1.5, -1, 1, 1.5, 2$.

No. of Iterations	$r_0 = -2$	$r_0 = -1.5$	$r_0 = -1$	$r_0 = 1$	$r_0 = 1.5$	$r_0 = 2$
n = 1	−1.13000	−0.84750	−0.56500	0.56500	0.84750	1.13000
n = 2	−0.63845	−0.47884	−0.31922	0.31922	0.47884	0.63845
n = 3	−0.36072	−0.27054	−0.18036	0.18036	0.27054	0.36072
n = 4	−0.20381	−0.15286	−0.10190	0.10190	0.15286	0.20381
n = 5	−0.11515	−0.08636	−0.05757	0.05757	0.08636	0.11515
n = 6	−0.06506	−0.04879	−0.03253	0.03253	0.04879	0.06506
n = 7	−0.03675	−0.02757	−0.01838	0.01838	0.02757	0.03675
n = 11	−0.00663	−0.00497	−0.00331	0.00331	0.00497	0.00663
n = 14	−0.00119	−0.00089	−0.00059	0.00059	0.00089	0.00119
n = 17	−0.00021	−0.00016	−0.00010	0.00010	0.00016	0.00021
n = 18	−0.00012	−0.00000	−0.00000	0.00000	0.00000	0.00012
n = 19	−0.00000	−0.00000	−0.00000	0.00000	0.00000	0.00000
n = 30	−0.00000	−0.00000	−0.00000	0.00000	0.00000	0.00000

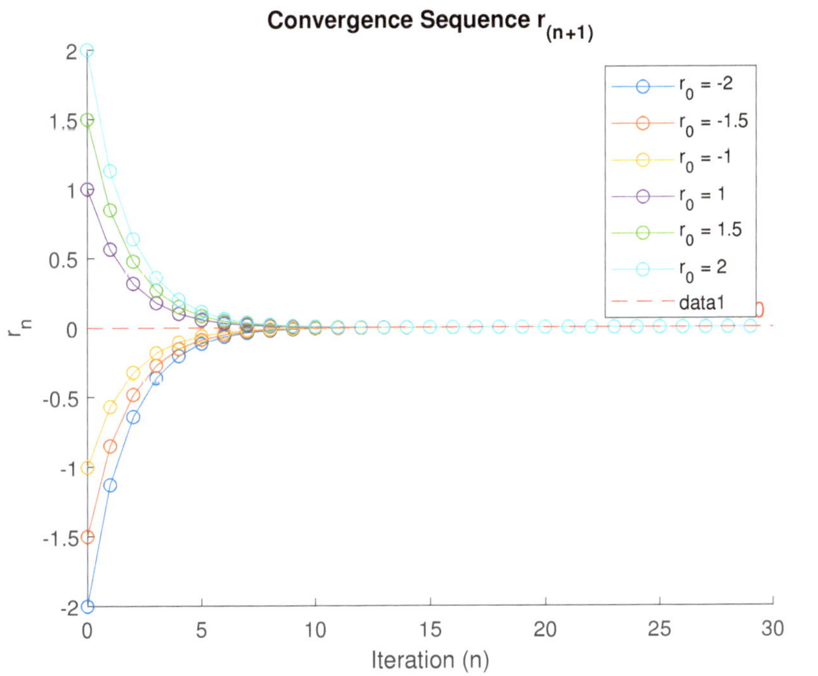

Figure 2. Graphical representation of a convergence sequence of $\{r_{n+1}\}$ with different initial values. when $\alpha = \frac{1}{2}$.

In the third case, Suppose $\alpha = \frac{4}{5}$, and the same initial values. We get a another computation table (Table 3) and a graph (Figure 3) of the convergence sequence $\{r_{n+1}\}$ which converges at $r = 0$ (after eight iterations), which is the solution of the Cayley variational inclusion problem (1).

Table 3. The values of the convergent sequence $\{r_n\}$ with initial values $r_0 = -2, -1.5, -1, 1, 1.5, 2$.

No. of Iterations	$r_0 = -2$	$r_0 = -1.5$	$r_0 = -1$	$r_0 = 1$	$r_0 = 1.5$	$r_0 = 2$
n = 1	−0.60800	−0.45600	−0.30400	0.30400	0.45600	0.60800
n = 2	−0.18483	−0.13862	−0.09241	0.09241	0.13862	0.18483
n = 3	−0.05618	−0.04214	−0.02809	0.02809	0.04214	0.05618
n = 4	−0.01708	−0.01281	−0.00854	0.00854	0.01281	0.01708
n = 5	−0.00519	−0.00389	−0.00259	0.00259	0.00389	0.00519
n = 6	−0.00157	−0.00118	−0.00078	0.00078	0.00118	0.00157
n = 7	−0.00047	−0.00035	−0.00023	0.00023	0.00035	0.00047
n = 8	−0.00014	−0.00010	−0.00000	0.00000	0.00010	0.00014
n = 9	−0.00000	−0.00000	−0.00000	0.00000	0.00000	0.00000
n = 10	−0.00000	−0.00000	−0.00000	0.00000	0.00000	0.00000
n = 15	−0.00000	−0.00000	−0.00000	0.00000	0.00000	0.00000
n = 20	−0.00000	−0.00000	−0.00000	0.00000	0.00000	0.00000
n = 30	−0.00000	−0.00000	−0.00000	0.00000	0.00000	0.00000

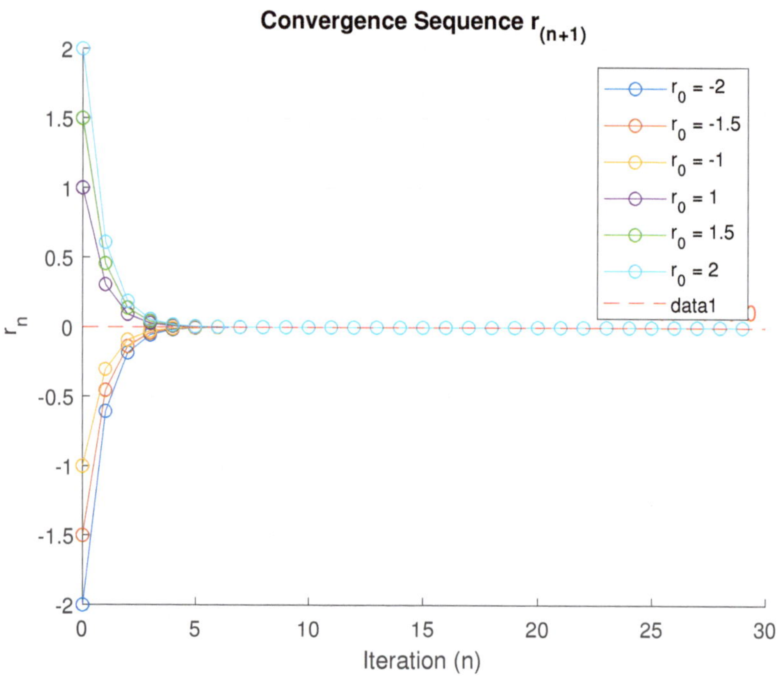

Figure 3. Graphical representation of a convergence sequence $\{r_{n+1}\}$ with different initial values when $\alpha = \frac{4}{5}$.

7. Conclusions

In the draft, we explored a generalized Cayley variational inclusion problem incorporating XOR and XNOR operations in a real-ordered Hilbert space. We analyzed the existence of solutions for the proposed problem using a fixed-point formulation. The proposed algorithms efficiently address generalized Cayley inclusions and solve equations involving XOR and XNOR operations. Furthermore, a numerical result is provided to support our main result and validate the proposed algorithm using MATLAB programming, demonstrating the rapid convergence of the mathematical model and its effectiveness in achieving optimal solutions. From the above Figures 1–3, we notice that the sequence r_{n+1}

converges to $r = 0$. In Figure 1, this occurs within fifty-one iterations, when $\alpha = \frac{1}{5}$; in Figure 2, within eighteen iterations, when $\alpha = \frac{1}{2}$; and in Figure 3, in eight iterations, when $\alpha = \frac{4}{5}$. This pattern indicates that as the value of α increases within the range $0 \leq \alpha \leq 1$, the convergence rate accelerates.

Author Contributions: Conceptualization: A. and S.S.I.; Methodology: A. and S.S.I.; Software: A. and S.S.I.; Validation: A. and I.A.; Formal Analysis: A. and S.S.I.; Writing—original draft preparation: A. and I.A.; Writing—review and editing: I.A. and S.S.I.; Funding: I.A. All authors have read and agreed to the published version of the manuscript.

Funding: The Researchers would like to thank the Deanship of Graduate Studies and Scientific Research at Qassim University for financial support (QU-APC-2025).

Institutional Review Board Statement: Not applicable.

Data Availability Statement: Data are contained within the article.

Conflicts of Interest: The authors declare no conflicts of interest.

References

1. Hassouni, A.; Moudafi, A. A perturbed algorithm for variational inclusions. *J. Math. Anal. Appl.* **1994**, *185*, 706–712. [CrossRef]
2. Noor, M.A. Generalized set-valued variational inclusions and resolvent equations. *J. Math. Anal. Appl.* **1998**, *228*, 206–220. [CrossRef]
3. Ahmad, I.; Irfan, S.S.; Farid, M.; Shukla, P. Nonlinear ordered variational inclusion problem involving XOR operation with fuzzy mappings. *J. Inequal. Appl.* **2020**, *2020*, 36. [CrossRef]
4. Ahmad, I.; Pang, C.T.; Ahmad, R.; Ishtyak, M. System of Yosida inclusions involving XOR-operation. *J. Nonlinear Convex Anal.* **2017**, *18*, 831–845.
5. Ayaka, M.; Tomomi, Y. Applications of the Hille—Yosida theorem to the linearized equations of coupled sound and heat flow. *AIMS Math.* **2016**, *1*, 165–177. [CrossRef]
6. Chang, S.S. Set-valued variational inclusions in Banach spaces. *J. Math. Anal. Appl.* **2000**, *248*, 438–454. [CrossRef]
7. Chang, S.; Yao, J.C.; Wang, L.; Liu, M.; Zhao, L. On the inertial forward-backward splitting technique for solving a system of inclusion problems in Hilbert spaces. *Optimization* **2021**, *70*, 2511–2525. [CrossRef]
8. Yosida, K. *Functional Analysis, Grundlehren der Mathematischen Wissenschaften*; Springer: New York, NY, USA, 1971.
9. Iqbal, J.; Rajpoot, A.K.; Islam, M.; Ahmad, R.; Wang, Y. System of Generalized Variational Inclusions Involving Cayley Operators and XOR-Operation in q-Uniformly Smooth Banach Spaces. *Mathematics* **2022**, *10*, 2837. [CrossRef]
10. Khan, A.A.; Tammer, M.; Zalinescu, C. *Set-Valued Optimization: An Introduction with Applications*; Springer: New York, NY, USA, 2015.
11. Iqbal, J.; Wang, Y.; Rajpoot, A.K.; Ahmad, R. Generalized Yosida inclusion problem involving multi-valued operator with XOR operation. *Demonstr. Math.* **2024**, *57*, 20240011. [CrossRef]
12. Ali, I.; Ahmad, R.; Wen, C.F. Cayley Inclusion Problem Involving XOR-Operation. *Mathematics* **2019**, *7*, 302. [CrossRef]
13. Rockafellar, R. Monotone Operators and the Proximal Point Algorithm. *Siam J. Cont. Optim.* **1976**, *14*, 877–898. [CrossRef]

MDPI AG
Grosspeteranlage 5
4052 Basel
Switzerland
Tel.: +41 61 683 77 34

Axioms Editorial Office
E-mail: axioms@mdpi.com
www.mdpi.com/journal/axioms

www.ingramcontent.com/pod-product-compliance
Lightning Source LLC
Chambersburg PA
CBHW041352210926
51850CB00013B/3053
9783725841714